The Private Side of American History

READINGS IN EVERYDAY LIFE

The Private Side
of American History

READINGS IN EVERYDAY LIFE

II
SINCE
1865

EDITED BY Thomas R. Frazier

THE BERNARD M. BARUCH COLLEGE
OF THE CITY UNIVERSITY OF NEW YORK

UNDER THE GENERAL EDITORSHIP OF
John Morton Blum
YALE UNIVERSITY

Harcourt Brace Jovanovich, Inc.

NEW YORK   CHICAGO   SAN FRANCISCO   ATLANTA

In memory of

Thomas F. O'Dea, a humane scholar

ISBN: 0-15-571963-7

Library of Congress Catalog Card Number: 74-25578

Printed in the United States of America

PICTURE CREDITS

COVER Clockwise from left: Library of Congress; courtesy of Herbert Gans; Harbrace; Culver Pictures; Cities Service Co. photo by Fritz Henle; (foreground) Library of Congress; (background) International Museum of Photography at George Eastman House, photo by Lewis Hine.

7 Historical Pictures Service, Chicago. **32** Culver Pictures. **47** Culver Pictures. **70** The Bettmann Archive. **101** Courtesy Planned Parenthood of New York. **126** International Museum of Photography at George Eastman House (Lewis Hine photo). **140** Culver Pictures. **160** Courtesy Bambi Shefelton. **197** F.S.A. photo by Dorothea Lange, collection Library of Congress. **225** Culver Pictures. **237** *Los Angeles Times*. **253** Cities Service Co. photo by Fritz Henle. **277** Courtesy Herbert Gans. **308** Bonnie Freer. **336** Irene Fertik. **348** A.T. & T.

Preface

Most studies of history concentrate on public figures and public affairs, the events and people that most historians consider important or influential. What is left out in these traditional presentations is the ordinary, day-to-day life of most of the members of the given society—that is, the "private side" of history. This phrase is not meant to suggest events hidden from public view, but rather personal incidents and the attitudes of ordinary people—especially their responses to the policies of the dominant power in their society.

This collection of essays presents a sampling of the varied attitudes, life styles, living arrangements, and cultural conflicts that have affected the American people. The selections deal both with the mainstream culture and with cultural groups considered deviant by the mainstream. Portrayed here are people—rich and poor, black and white, male and female, young and not so young—as they go about their daily tasks, trying to provide for themselves a satisfactory way of life. This portrayal is necessarily incomplete, for only an encyclopedic work could encompass the complexity of everyday life in American history. But it is hoped that the essays presented here will give the reader a taste of the manifold cultures found within American society today and in the past.

The sixteen selections, arranged in roughly chronological order, are grouped into four sections, each of which concludes with an annotated bibliography. The headnotes provided for each selection attempt to place the subject of the selection in its historical context. A brief introduction to the volume describes the major areas that should be considered in a historical study of everyday life.

For assistance in preparing this volume I would like to thank most of all Thomas A. Williamson and William J. Wisneski, my editors at Harcourt Brace Jovanovich, who suggested the theme of this work and provided encouragement. For scholarly assistance I would like to express my appreciation to the following colleagues: Carol Berkin and Stanley Buder, The Bernard M. Baruch College of the City University of New York; John Harper, The College of New Rochelle; Gary Nash, University of California, Los Angeles; John Morton Blum, Yale University; Robert Bannister, Swarthmore College; Daniel J. Walkowitz, Rutgers University; Laurence Veysey, University of California, Santa Cruz; Paula S. Fass, University of California, Berkeley; Stephan Thernstrom, Harvard University; and Robert Sklar, The University of Michigan.

THOMAS R. FRAZIER

Contents

PREFACE   *v*

Introduction   *1*

1865–1900
The Gilded Age

Morality on the Middle Border   7
   LEWIS ATHERTON

A Little Milk, A Little Honey: Jewish Immigration in America   *32*
   DAVID BOROFF

Patent Medicine Advertising in the Late Nineteenth Century   *47*
   JAMES HARVEY YOUNG

The Social Insulation of the Traditional Elite   *70*
   E. DIGBY BALTZELL

Suggestions for Further Reading   *96*

1900–1930
The Early Twentieth Century

The Family, Feminism, and Sex at the Turn of the Century   *101*
   DAVID M. KENNEDY

Slavic Immigrants in the Steel Mills   *126*
   DAVID BRODY

Konklave in Kokomo   *140*
   ROBERT COUGHLAN

Training the Young   *160*
   ROBERT S. LYND AND HELEN MERRELL LYND

Suggestions for Further Reading   *191*

1930–1952
Depression and War

What the Depression Did to People   *197*
EDWARD ROBB ELLIS

Race Relations in a Southern Town   *225*
HORTENSE POWDERMAKER

Repression of Mexican-Americans in Los Angeles   *237*
CAREY McWILLIAMS

An American Sacred Ceremony   *253*
W. LLOYD WARNER

Suggestions for Further Reading   *271*

1952–1975
Contemporary Society

The Quality of Suburban Life   277
HERBERT J. GANS

The Counter-Culture   *308*
WILLIAM L. O'NEILL

The Meaning of "Soul"   *336*
ULF HANNERZ

Inside the New York Telephone Company   *348*
ELINOR LANGER

Suggestions for Further Reading   *372*

Topical Table of Contents

WORK: CONDITIONS AND ATTITUDES

A Little Milk, A Little Honey:
  Jewish Immigration in America   DAVID BOROFF   *32*
Slavic Immigrants in the Steel Mills   DAVID BRODY   *126*
What the Depression Did to People   EDWARD ROBB ELLIS   *197*
Inside the New York Telephone Company   ELINOR LANGER   *348*

EDUCATION AND RECREATION

Morality on the Middle Border   LEWIS ATHERTON   7
A Little Milk, A Little Honey:
  Jewish Immigration in America   DAVID BOROFF   *32*
The Social Insulation of the Traditional Elite   E. DIGBY BALTZELL   *70*
Training the Young   ROBERT S. LYND AND HELEN MERRELL LYND   *160*
The Quality of Suburban Life   HERBERT J. GANS   277
The Counter-Culture   WILLIAM L. O'NEILL   *308*
The Meaning of "Soul"   ULF HANNERZ   *336*

SEX, THE HOME, AND THE FAMILY

A Little Milk, A Little Honey:
  Jewish Immigration in America   DAVID BOROFF   *32*
The Social Insulation of the Traditional Elite   E. DIGBY BALTZELL   *70*
The Family, Feminism, and Sex at the
  Turn of the Century   DAVID M. KENNEDY   *101*
Slavic Immigrants in the Steel Mills   DAVID BRODY   *126*
What the Depression Did to People   EDWARD ROBB ELLIS   *197*
The Quality of Suburban Life   HERBERT J. GANS   277
The Counter-Culture   WILLIAM L. O'NEILL   *308*
The Meaning of "Soul"   ULF HANNERZ   *336*

RELIGION, THOUGHT, AND VALUES

Morality on the Middle Border   LEWIS ATHERTON   7
A Little Milk, A Little Honey:
  Jewish Immigration in America   DAVID BOROFF   *32*
The Family, Feminism, and Sex at the
  Turn of the Century   DAVID M. KENNEDY   *101*
Konklave in Kokomo   ROBERT COUGHLAN   *140*
An American Sacred Ceremony   W. LLOYD WARNER   *253*
The Counter-Culture   WILLIAM L. O'NEILL   *308*
The Meaning of "Soul"   ULF HANNERZ   *336*

HEALTH, DISEASE, AND DEATH

A Little Milk, A Little Honey:
  Jewish Immigration in America   DAVID BOROFF   *32*
Patent Medicine Advertising in the
  Late Nineteenth Century   JAMES HARVEY YOUNG   *47*
Slavic Immigrants in the Steel Mills   DAVID BRODY   *126*
What the Depression Did to People   EDWARD ROBB ELLIS   *197*
Race Relations in a Southern Town   HORTENSE POWDERMAKER   *225*

VIOLENCE AND WAR

Slavic Immigrants in the Steel Mills   DAVID BRODY   *126*
Konklave in Kokomo   ROBERT COUGHLAN   *140*
Race Relations in a Southern Town   HORTENSE POWDERMAKER   *225*
Repression of Mexican-Americans in Los Angeles   CAREY MC WILLIAMS   *237*
An American Sacred Ceremony   W. LLOYD WARNER   *253*

SOCIAL CONTROL

Morality on the Middle Border   LEWIS ATHERTON   *7*
The Social Insulation of the Traditional Elite   E. DIGBY BALTZELL   *70*
Slavic Immigrants in the Steel Mills   DAVID BRODY   *126*
Konklave in Kokomo   ROBERT COUGHLAN   *140*
Training the Young   ROBERT S. LYND AND HELEN MERRELL LYND   *160*
Race Relations in a Southern Town   HORTENSE POWDERMAKER   *225*
Repression of Mexican-Americans in Los Angeles   CAREY MC WILLIAMS   *237*
The Meaning of "Soul"   ULF HANNERZ   *336*

Introduction

In recent years the traditional presentation of American history in schools and colleges has come under criticism. The growth of various liberation movements in the 1960s has led to a rewriting of many history texts to include material on blacks, American Indians, white ethnic groups, and women, among others. New Left historiography has brought about a reconsideration of economic and class interests both domestically and in foreign policy. A third area in which the historical record has been remiss is the one represented by the essays reprinted in this volume—the realm of the everyday life of the American people, the private side of American history. The traditional emphasis on public events has resulted in an historical record that fails to provide sufficient insight into the role of ordinary people in the development of our culture and society. Their feelings, the ways in which they responded or reacted to public events, the hopes, desires, and needs that have been the basis of their response are now recognized by many American historians as a legitimate and important area of historical concern.

In attempting to understand and write about the everyday life of ordinary people, it has been necessary for historians to draw on the theoretical and methodological approaches of the social sciences. Several of the selections in this volume, in fact, have been written by professional sociologists and anthropologists. Historians are only just beginning to apply to recent American history the new historiographical approach so well represented in Volume I of *The Private Side of American History*, which treats America's early growth.

This second volume is concerned not so much with a growing America as with the attempts to build a national culture based on "traditional American values" in the face of serious challenges by different groups who have little desire to participate in such a value system at the expense of their own culture and perceived past. The consensus on the national culture so sought has proved to be extremely fragile and ultimately incapable of being sustained. When history is viewed from the perspective of the "movers and shakers" of the nation, as it has been in the traditional textbooks, the consensus appears to have been established. When the everyday life of the American people is examined, however, the fragility of the consensus is clear. While the people may appear quietly to acquiesce in the dominant culture of the society, they go right on living their lives, often outside its stated values.

In this volume we will examine the attempts to establish a cultural consensus and will look at those who try to pattern their lives after its perceived values. We will look more often, however, at those who live by a different set of norms, those whose continued existence challenges the dominant culture and who, ultimately, refuse to abide by the rules of what has been called "the American way of life." The groups dealt with in this volume fall, for the most part, then, into the category of those left out of, or briefly mentioned in, the traditional texts: women, poor people, ethnic minorities, and the young, among others. But the focus here is not on the causes of their oppression or the conflicts in which they engage in their attempts to come to grips with the dominant power in our society. We concentrate, rather, on the effects of their oppression and the adaptations and adjustments they have made in their attempts to live as fully as possible under often difficult circumstances. Throughout the nation's history, the majority of the people in the United States have lived outside the dominant culture; so we are, in fact, exploring here the private lives of most Americans.

What we are concerned with, then, are the things that most Americans do most of the time—the day-to-day activities and experiences that concern and shape the individual and, thus, are factors in shaping American society. This "private side" of American history is revealed by studying those areas of concern common to the majority of people throughout history.

The quality of individual life to a large extent is determined by such basic factors as work, education, and family relationships. By examining what work people do, how they feel about what they do, what its effect is on them, and whether or not it does what they expect it to—provides them with a living—we can see the effect employment, or lack of it, has on society as a whole. We need also to understand the impact that the various sources of education in our society—schools, mass media, advertising, family and peer group interaction, and religious institutions, among others—have on the total development of the individual. Because, traditionally, the family has been one of the major forces shaping an individual's life, we must look at the family structure in the United States and see how changes in the structure affect the lives of all of its members. We should also note the impact of changes in the society on the various members of the family in their relationships with each other.

Religion is another important part of American life. The religious institutions have been a major force in the establishing of societal norms, and religious ideas have often been influential in forming counter-norms and in providing emotional support for those outside the mainstream of American culture. So, an understanding of the roles religion has played in the cultural development of America is necessary to our study.

Also important are those areas of concern that, for the most part, are even less directly governed by the individual. Included here are such factors as health, disease, and death; violence and war; and social control. We can examine how the people of the United States have dealt with these crucial and, in some cases, ultimate questions. We will consider their responses to the improved quality of medical care over the past century; the myths and realities of medicine and how the people have perceived these issues; how death is handled; and the value placed on human life in general and on particular lives. We will explore both personal and institutional violence as well as the social function of war—war as an example of foreign policy is not considered; we are more concerned here with war as an integrative factor in society. And we will examine the means society uses to shape the individual's behavior to the desired norm. Here we will consider how the dominant society attempts to assimilate or govern the groups it considers deviant; the actions "deviant" groups take to maintain their distinctiveness—and the price they pay for their efforts; and, of particular importance, the way certain institutions such as schools and churches operate directly or indirectly as agents of social control. The areas of concern considered here by no means exhaust the possible categories for the study of everyday life, but they are at least suggestive of the kinds of experiences that must be covered in exploring the private side of American history.

In this volume, each section contains at least one selection that attempts to delineate the norms or activities of one segment of the dominant culture. The other selections describe behavior or attitudes that deviate from the traditional norms. The volume begins with an essay that thoroughly explores the values of small-town Midwestern society. The norms described there still operate, under the rubric "traditional American values," and serve as an appropriate place to begin our consideration of everyday life in America since the middle of the last century. Other essays in this section describe the urban culture of immigrant Jews in New York City, the continued reliance of many Americans on unscientific patent medicines even in the face of significantly improved medical practice, and the attempt by the traditional elite to escape from a changing society by withdrawing into restrictive enclaves where they need associate only with their own numbers.

In the next section, the way the American high school socializes its pupils and indoctrinates them with the point of view of the dominant culture is presented. In contrast to this socialization, we see changes that are taking place in family life and sexual relations; the development of an urban, ethnic, industrial class made up increasingly in this period of immigrants from Central and Southern Europe; and the rather desperate and pathetic attempt by the Ku Klux Klan to perpetuate in a rapidly changing society the "traditional values" delineated in the opening section.

The first essay in the third section shows how the Great Depression brought into question many of the widely held attitudes about the promise of American life. In this section also, we see the way dominant society has dealt with two of its prominent nonwhite minorities, blacks and chicanos. The concluding essay in this section describes how civil religion can serve as an integrative force in American life, especially when the symbols being dealt with are national rather than particularistic.

The last section opens with an analysis of the quality of suburban life, a mode of existence chosen by a majority of the American people at the present time. Also considered here is the powerful and persistent counterculture movement that affected so many Americans, particularly the young, in the 1960s. Standing in sharp contrast to suburban life is the culture of the urban black ghetto, explored here by a social anthropologist.

The concluding selection describes the conditions of work and the level of consciousness of women in a traditionally sex-typed, white-collar occupation.

This volume provides but a sampling of the enormous variety of life-styles and life experiences of the groups and individuals who make up what we call the American nation. The editor has attempted to acquaint the student with the possibility of better understanding the history of the United States through a study of the many different ways in which people have shaped their lives in order that they might live with as much of their essential humanity intact as possible. For many this has been an extremely difficult task because of the structural disorders in American society. Only if these disorders are seen for what they are, however, and seriously challenged, will the private lives of the American people improve in significant ways.

1865–1900
The Gilded Age

Morality on the Middle Border

LEWIS ATHERTON

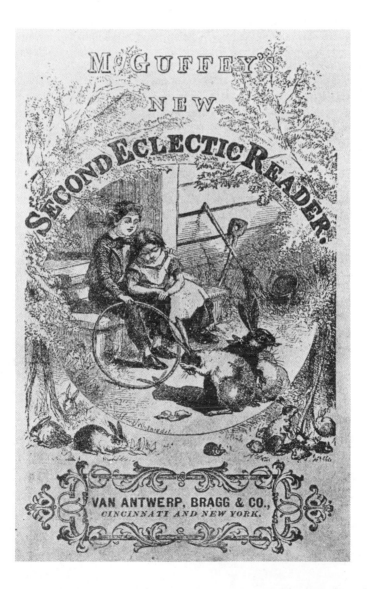

In a recent attempt to find a term that could be used to describe the "traditional" American value system, politicians and their intellectual supporters have devised the phrase "middle America." Although it is recognized that the belief system expressed in the phrase may have Midwestern roots, "middle America" is not a geographical term. Middle Americans live in Suffolk County, New York, and Orange County, California, as well as in Peoria, Illinois.

It is important to point out that there really is a "middle America" that proclaims the values attributed to it. And, although the appellation is modern, the belief system is not. One finds in the values of "middle America" a restatement of a basic conflict of American life—the antagonism between the urban and rural (or small town) ways of life. This conflict is at least as old as the agrarian philosophy expressed by Thomas Jefferson in the late eighteenth century.

The phrase "middle America" is particularly apt because much of the intellectual and spiritual content of traditional American morality found its strongest advocates and clearest statements in the Midwest, or, as the area was called in the late nineteenth century, the Middle Border. Some of America's greatest creative writers of the late nineteenth and early twentieth centuries—Mark Twain, Hamlin Garland, and Sherwood Anderson among others—grew up on the Middle Border and have immortalized its culture in their works. These writers, whose works both celebrate and derogate Midwestern life, provide insight into the ethics and morality that pervaded the Midwestern culture.

Certainly one of the primary sources of Midwestern morality was Protestant Christianity. The East may have contained the intellectual giants of WASP (White Anglo-Saxon Protestant) culture, but the Midwest provided the substance both of revivalistic piety and popular ethical teaching. The Sunday school, not the academy, provided Midwestern Protestants with much of their understanding of religion and morals. The famous **McGuffey's Readers** used in the public schools and in home instruction became another major source of religious and ethical teaching, since most of those who learned to read on the Middle Border did so with the aid of McGuffey's books.

Lewis Atherton of the University of Missouri, a son of the Middle Border himself, describes in the selection reprinted below the substance of Midwestern morality as portrayed and propagandized by the **Readers.** He properly stresses the religious underpinnings of the moral world portrayed by McGuffey. Belief in the existence of God and belief in his ultimate judgment act as moral levers whereby the powerful urges of mankind can be turned from sinful pursuits and moved in a heavenward direction. Although it was true that less than half of the

Midwestern population were affiliated with churches, religious institutions had widespread influence in the community because most of the leaders in any town or village were active members. Protestant morality was also espoused in newspapers and the vast number of popular magazines whose existence was as ephemeral as their presence was ubiquitous.

Atherton deals here not only with the public and official morality but also with elements of actual practice that were often in conflict with it. He points out that the upper classes in the towns often operated on a different ethical wave length than did the mainstream. Rarely, however, did they publically challenge the official morality. There were, of course, others who defied the norms; most communities had their share of drunkards, village atheists, and other ne'er-do-wells, as well as those deviants by definition—Roman Catholics.

The structure of morality built up on the Middle Border still stands as a conservative judgment on the looser, more flexible morality developed in the cities. Its continued appeal has led to a recent attempt by groups of concerned citizens to restore the **McGuffey's Readers** as a learning tool in Midwestern schools in order to combat the godless, materialistic teaching they find there today.

CHURCH, SCHOOL, AND HOME

Between 1850 and 1900 Americans bought one hundred million copies of William Holmes McGuffey's school readers.[1] Though well re-

"Ethics, Folklore, and Morality on the Middle Border" (Editor's title: "Morality on the Middle Border"). Reprinted from *Main Street on the Middle Border* by Lewis Atherton, pp. 65–88, 95–100, copyright © 1954 by Indiana University Press, Bloomington. Reprinted by permission of the publisher.

[1] Richard D. Mosier, *Making the American Mind: Social and Moral Ideas in the McGuffey Readers* (New York, 1947), 168. I am indebted to this study and to Harvey C. Minnich, *William Holmes McGuffey and IIis Readers* (New York, 1936) for biographical detail concerning McGuffey and for suggestive leads. The material cited in this study comes from the 1857 edition of McGuffey Readers, the titles of which follow: *McGuffey's New First Eclectic Reader: For Young Learners* (Cincinnati, 1857); *McGuffey's New Second Eclectic Reader: For Young Learners* (Cincinnati, 1857); *McGuffey's New Third Eclectic Reader: For Young Learners* (Cincinnati, 1857); *McGuffey's New Fourth Eclectic Reader: Instructive Lessons for the Young* (Cincinnati, 1857); *McGuffey's New Fifth Eclectic Reader: Selected and Original Exercises for Schools* (Cincinnati, 1857); and *McGuffey's New Sixth Eclectic Reader: Exercises in Rhetorical Reading, with Introductory Rules and Examples* (Cincinnati, 1857). In the absence of graded schools the titles lacked the same significance that they would bear today. For instance, many pupils got no further than the third reader. Material in the sixth reader was very advanced in nature and would be read today not earlier than junior high school.

ceived virtually everywhere, they appealed particularly to the Middle Border. As an apostle of religion, morality, and education, McGuffey wanted to bolster midwestern civilization against the dangers inherent in pioneering new frontiers. Since his Readers were directed to a supposedly classless society, they were all-inclusive in their appeal, and from them came a set of principles which remained unchallenged in the minds of common people until the turn of the century.

McGuffey worried so much about frontier dangers that he overlooked the revolutionary changes in transportation, manufacturing, and management which were then taking place. The 1857 revision of his Readers, which most Midwesterners studied, barely mentioned steamboats, and railroads received no attention at all. Pupils learned about horse-drawn transportation, about merchant rather than manufacturer, about artisan in place of factory laborer, of the outdoors, of birds and farm animals, of gossipy barbers, of Longfellow's "Village Blacksmith," and of town pumps, watering troughs, and village greens:

> Then contented with my State,
> Let me envy not the great;
> Since true pleasures may be seen,
> On a cheerful village green.[2]

Moreover, children learned that village and country life surpassed that in cities. As a rule, McGuffey simply ignored urban ways or used them as examples of corruption. The story, "Mysterious Stranger," described the unhappiness of a man from another planet when he learned that city pleasures in our world were accompanied with the penalty of death. Still another story told of "Old Tom Smith," the drunkard, whose downfall came from city life. Through a clerkship in a city store, he became acquainted with bad company. Instead of spending his evenings reading, he went to theatres, balls, and suppers. Drinking and card playing followed next, and soon thereafter his saintly mother had to pay large gambling debts for him. Although his mother and wife grieved themselves to death over his city vices, nothing could stop his drinking. The story ended with reception of the news that he had received a ten-year prison sentence for stealing.[3] Village boys often misbehaved in McGuffey's stories but they seldom fell prey to major vices.

McGuffey's emphasis on rural and village life pleased an agrarian age. His environmental picture squared with physical facts, and people knew just enough of the outside world to share his doubts about cities. His Readers thus gained strength by applying the eternal verities to a simple culture, uncomplicated by urban and industrial problems. This very strength, however, became a source of weakness as village and farm gave way to city and factory.

McGuffey ideals retreated slowly. Rural America believed in a classless society, which helped enforce still other pressures toward con-

---

[2] *Third Reader*, 201–202.
[3] See *Sixth Reader*, 206–211, 398–400, and *Third Reader*, 118–120.

formity. In the 1830's Tocqueville commented on the tyranny of the majority in making Americans conform to a common pattern. Although disagreeing with Tocqueville's analysis, James Bryce said much the same in the 1880's. According to him, American public opinion was not stated along class lines; it applied to all. In Bryce's estimation, Americans believed that common sense resided in the minds of the majority, with a consequent "fatalism of the multitude" evident in much of American life. Ed Howe commented that city people would behave better if they knew one another as well as did villagers who heard gossip about their sins on the way home from committing them,[4] thus implying that conformity was even greater in small towns.

Perhaps also an emphasis on the immediately useful and the practical contributed to the survival of current moral values. An Iowa lawyer who spent his youth in a small town commented that most pioneers were of the earth, earthy. They knew practical things—weather, rains, common plants and animals, good livestock. But they were not philosophers.[5] Whatever the explanation, small-town beliefs changed slowly, and this characteristic gave village life an impression of stability and permanence.

The God-centered, small-town code emphasized man's immortality. School and home both paid obeisance to God's plan and God's laws, for everything fell within His master plan. From McGuffey's Readers the pupil learned that Jesus was above Plato, Socrates, and all the philosophers, for He was a God.[6] Evidences of His power and wisdom existed on every hand. McGuffey proved this with simple stories. Washington's father, for instance, secretly planted seeds in a design which spelled out George's name when they sprouted. Although George was surprised, he refused to accept his father's suggestion that chance explained the phenomenon. His father now admitted that he had planted the seeds to teach George a lesson, and urged the boy to look around him at God's planning on every hand. And thus, said McGuffey, driving home his point as usual, from that day George never doubted the existence of a God who was the creator and owner of all things.[7]

Even the problem of evil in a universe governed by divine law was explained to school boys through simple stories. Everything happened for the best and every object had a purpose in the great plan of things. When one of two boys caught in a thunderstorm remarked that he hated the evil lightning, the other explained that lightning was necessary to purify the air of bad vapors, a greater good thus offsetting a lesser evil.[8] Understanding would always clarify the appearance of evil. An observant boy asked his father to help him cut down thorn bushes and thistles which were snagging wool from the sides of passing sheep. Since parents in McGuffey's Readers were always wiser than children, the boy profited by taking his father's advice to wait until morning. In doing so, he discovered that birds

---

[4] Edgar W. Howe, *Plain People* (New York, 1929), 305.
[5] Roger S. Galer, "Recollections of Busy Years," *Iowa Journal of History and Politics*, XLII (January, 1944), 3–72.
[6] *Fifth Reader*, 280–282.
[7] *Fourth Reader*, 82–83.
[8] *Ibid.*, 180–183.

used the wool to build their nests, and that God indeed was wise and good and had made everything for the best.[9]

A former resident of Hillsboro, Iowa, described the operation of this philosophy in his childhood days. Belief in God was universal. People wondered why certain things occurred, chiefly the deaths of children and very good people, but no one doubted God's existence and His fatherly care. If a death occurred, the Lord willed it. The Lord sent afflictions to punish sin and disbelief. The Lord could be prevailed upon to help His people out of difficulties. If the corn needed rain, the churches set a day of prayer. If success accompanied this, it had been the proper thing to do; if intercession failed, the people had not prayed with sufficient faith. The heavenly books were balanced daily by an omniscient bookkeeper who recorded every act. The idea of universal and impersonal law was displeasing. These people wisely turned to something warmer, something more directly personal in which man played the central part. He participated in a drama which included sky and earth, which began with Adam, and which would end only when the heavens were rolled up as a scroll.[10]

McGuffey taught that society depended on religion. Christianity was conducive to national prosperity. It raised the poor from want, brought rich and poor together on a common level for an hour of prayer, and promoted good order and harmony. Self-respect and elevation of character, softness and civility of manners came from religious teaching. Christianity strengthened the family circle as a source of instruction, comfort, and happiness.[11] Moreover,

> If you can induce a community to doubt the genuineness and authenticity of the Scriptures; to question the reality and obligations of religion; to hesitate, undeciding, whether there be any such thing as virtue or vice; whether there be an eternal state of retribution beyond the grave; or whether there exists any such being as God, you have broken down the barriers of moral virtue, and hoisted the floodgates of immorality and crime.[12]

Insofar as school books are concerned, small-town Mid-America now reads of miracles of science. God, church, and even human death are generally ignored. Separation of church and state and a desire to shield children from morbid thoughts help explain this marked change. Perhaps, however, it would not have occurred had science not become the god of so many people, for gods are too important to be omitted in formal education of the young.

In the second half of the nineteenth century grade schools commonly opened the day with brief devotional exercises. Lessons also had a religious

---

[9] *Third Reader*, 139–142.
[10] Galer, "Recollections of Busy Years."
[11] *Fifth Reader*, 306–307.
[12] *Sixth Reader*, 421–423.

slant. McGuffey's *First Reader* pictured a little girl kneeling in prayer and asking God to protect her from sin.[13] A poem in the *Second Reader* stressed the blessings of immortality:

> A little child who loves to pray,
> And read his Bible too,
> Shall rise above the sky one day,
> And sing as angels do;
> Shall live in Heaven, that world above,
> Where all is joy, and peace, and love.[14]

These simple stories and poems in public-school readers document the tremendous shift in faith between the nineteenth and twentieth centuries, from a man-centered and God-centered universe on the one hand to an impersonal and science-centered universe on the other.

McGuffey also stressed the need for public schools. "We must educate!" Literary as well as religious institutions must keep pace with the headlong rush of western settlement. If the Middle Border expected to preserve republican institutions and universal suffrage, both *head* and *heart* must be trained.[15] McGuffey thus urged pupils to feverish activity:

> Haste thee, school boy, haste away,
> While thy youth is bright and gay;
> Seek the place with knowledge blest;
> It will guide to endless rest;
> Haste thee, school boy, haste away,
> While thy youth is bright and gay.[16]

Newspapers expressed the same ideas.[17] Parents supposedly could do nothing finer for their children than to educate them.[18] Although children often attended school only irregularly and quit at an early age, and less than half the adult population were formal church members,[19] citizens generally believed that churches and schools made communities "decent

---

13 *First Reader*, 26.

14 *Second Reader*, 81.

15 *Fifth Reader*, 150–153.

16 *Third Reader*, 21–22.

17 See, for example, article on value of schools in Algona, Iowa, *The Upper Des Moines*, March 7, 1867, and a similar article in Gallatin, Missouri, *North Missourian*, March 10, 1893.

18 Comment on removal of H. C. Callison from Jamesport to Gallatin, in Gallatin, Missouri, *North Missourian*, September 1, 1893.

19 For the state of Illinois as a whole in 1900, for instance, only 46.6 per cent of adults were church members. United States Bureau of the Census, *Religious Bodies, 1906* (Washington, 1910), I, 305–308.

places" in which to live.[20] Even real-estate promotion—the most absorbing interest of all—stressed the presence of churches and schools as selling points.

McGuffey ranked family life with church and school as a third major conservator of ideals. Families were like a bundle of twigs; the strength of all far surpassed that of the individual:

> We are all here!
> Father, Mother,
> Sister, Brother,
> All who hold each other dear.[21]

McGuffey stressed love of brother and sister in a nature poem which Theodore Roosevelt later was to criticize for its ignorance of birds:

> Birds in their little nests agree;
> And 'tis a shameful sight,
> When children of one family
> Fall out, and chide, and fight.[22]

Idealization of motherhood and the mother's central position in family life was a frequent theme. One poem referred to the mother's voice:

> It always makes me happy, too,
> To hear its gentle tone;
> I know it is the voice of love
> From a heart that is my own.[23]

Mutual interdependence was illustrated in simple stories. In one, grandfather sat in his easy chair before the fire, smoking his pipe. The family dog reclined nearby, and grandmother was busy at her spinning wheel. A granddaughter sat on the man's knee. As he thought about the death of the child's mother, tears rolled down his cheeks. Although the innocent child had not yet realized her loss, she was already repaying her grandparents for their care by catching the flies which buzzed around grandpa's head.[24]

McGuffey stressed complete obedience to parental direction and parental ideals in return for the love and care lavished on younger members of the family. The poem "Casabianca" told of a boy burning to death on the deck of a naval vessel in obedience to his father's order to await his return, which was prevented by the father's death during the

---

[20] Edward O. Moe and Carl C. Taylor, *Culture of a Contemporary Rural Community: Irwin, Iowa, Rural Life Studies* No. 5 (Washington, 1942), 61.

[21] *Sixth Reader*, 167–168.

[22] *Second Reader*, 151–152.

[23] *Ibid.*, 101–103.

[24] *Fifth Reader*, 51–52.

naval battle then under way. While such Spartan obedience may seem unduly severe to modern-day parents, it obviously was better to die than to suffer the intense remorse of a daughter who returned to her mother's grave in the village cemetery thirteen years after the funeral. Grief overwhelmed her at the memory of how unwillingly she had brought a glass of water at her mother's request the night of the latter's death. True, she had planned to ask forgiveness the following morning, but her mother was then cold in death.[25] "Meddlesome Matty" received her just deserts in McGuffey's stories, as did a group of curious boys who applied to a rich old squire's advertisement for a youth to wait on him at table. To test the applicants, he filled his reception room with appealing items. The first boy could not resist eating a luscious-appearing cherry, only to find it filled with cayenne pepper, and others received equally just rewards for their curiosity. The one applicant who sat in the room for twenty minutes without yielding to temptation got the job, and ultimately a legacy from the rich old squire.[26] Obedience paid off in many ways in McGuffey's stories, as the disobedient little fish learned after being pulled from the water on a hook:

> And as he faint and fainter grew,
> With hollow voice he cried,
> Dear mother, had I minded you,
> I need not thus have died.[27]

At company dinners, McGuffey-trained parents made children eat at the second table and also expected them to be seen and not heard. Elders were always addressed as "Mr." and "Mrs." by properly reared children. At the same time, parents wanted their offspring to have every advantage of religion and education, if they really had taken the McGuffey lessons to heart.

CULTURAL PATTERNS

Church, school, and home thus furnished education for *heart* and *mind*, a process which involved the teaching of an extensive code of morality. Without doubt, this fitted best the needs and desires of a pious, church-going, middle-class society. For such people, the McGuffey code was both adequate and right. In their estimation, it underlay decent society in this world and salvation in the next. Midwestern ideals did not come solely from this one middle-class group, however. Although it dominated education and fought hard to enforce its convictions, it was never able to establish conformity on the part of all citizens.

At least four additional sources competed with and modified the dominant middle-class code. The first can be loosely identified as upper

[25] *Fourth Reader*, 172–174, 239–241.
[26] *Fifth Reader*, 65–69.
[27] *Second Reader*, 84–85.

class in nature, although its ramifications were broader than simple class structure. Virtually everywhere on the Middle Border were families which held substantial or respectable places in society without bowing to the McGuffey code. Episcopalians like Benjamin F. Mackall of Moorhead, Minnesota, and Daniel M. Storer of Shakopee, Minnesota, danced and played cards and ignored the gloomy restrictions which dominated so many of their contemporaries. Even good Presbyterians and Methodists who read more than church and secular newspapers often slighted McGuffey's code. In 1865 Helen Clift Shroyer of New Castle, Indiana, and her friends played euchre and seven-up without the slightest sense of guilt; and she and her fiancé accompanied others to a dance in a neighboring town which lasted so late that they reached home at five in the morning. Her wedding trip included visits to the Chicago theatre. Oyster suppers, cards, dances, popcorn parties, visits to ice cream parlors, and Sunday afternoon buggy rides appealed to her. She dodged funerals if at all possible and ignored many of the common commercial entertainments. The "Mysterious Man," a sleight-of-hand performer, was passed by on the grounds that she was too tired to attend, a lame excuse for one of her energy. She was critical of a temperance lecture which she made herself attend, and was bored in Brother Norris' Sunday School class because she thought he could not teach "worth a cent." The Sunday reading of the *Atlantic Monthly*, which she and her husband enjoyed, may have taken the bloom from Brother Norris' penetrating remarks on the scriptures.[28] The families of Edgar Lee Masters and Thomas Hart Benton were neither pious nor active church members, and both taught their children a set of standards which deviated from McGuffey's code. Zona Gale's father, a self-educated railroad engineer, taught her that the spirit of man is God, and that no other God exists. From him she obtained other convictions, like pacifism, which ran counter to dominant middle-class beliefs.[29] Such families generally dared not flaunt their heresies in the face of local society, especially since they relied on local people for their livelihood, but they did maintain a measure of individuality.

Catholics represented still another departure from the dominant code. In their views on education, Sabbath recreation, and intoxicants, they clashed with middle-class Protestant sentiments. Although McGuffey opposed religious intolerance, anti-Catholic feeling existed in midwestern country towns. Don Marquis, himself the product of a small Illinois town, pictures this in his novel, *Sons of the Puritans*. Aunt Matilda, guardian of the dominant small-town code, becomes alarmed when she learns that a Catholic has been entertaining village youngsters with stories. She suspects him of showing them beads, speaking in Latin, and even of exhibiting idols, with an invitation to fall down and worship them. Aunt Matilda

[28] Kate Milner Rabb, "A Hoosier Listening Post," feature section of Indianapolis *Star*, March 14 to May 24, 1935. During this period the column carried the Shroyer diary which may also be found in a folder of clippings from the column, Indiana State Library, Indianapolis.

[29] August Derleth, *Still Small Voice: The Biography of Zona Gale* (New York, 1940), 27–28.

belongs to the group that circulates rumors about collections of firearms in Catholic churches.[30] Bromfield's novel, *The Farm*, in large measure the story of his family's life in Ohio, recounts the anti-Catholic sentiment which a youngster in his family heard in livery stables, police stations, and other gathering places. Copies of a paper, *The Menace*, containing vivid accounts of rapes committed by Catholic priests and of illegitimate children born to Catholic nuns, passed from hand to hand. Secret passages supposedly connected homes of priests with neighboring convents so they could visit nuns at their convenience.[31] An occasional minister condemned Catholicism from the pulpit. In a Thanksgiving Day sermon in 1869 at Centreville, Michigan, a Methodist preacher boasted that infidel France and Catholic Mexico had been incapable of reaching the same high civilization then prevalent in Protestant America. Three generations locally, he said, had been sufficient to stamp out Romanism in family life.[32] Similarly, a Baptist preacher preparing for a revival meeting at Gallatin, Missouri, in 1893, claimed that Protestants modelled themselves on Christ while Catholics worshipped lesser figures.[33]

Although many immigrants were Catholics, it is well to note that still another cultural influence in small towns came from foreign immigration. Immigrants could not know all the shadings of the dominant, moralistic code followed by middle-class Protestants. A considerable number of German Lutherans and Catholics at Monroe, Wisconsin, in the late 1860's and early 1870's, organized a local Turnverein and carried on an active social program in Turner's Hall. Masked balls, beer drinking, and uniformed acrobatic groups of young Germans performing on the bars and trapeze conflicted with local ideas of proper behavior. People got along, to the credit of all groups, but "Christians" sniffed nonetheless. In December, 1869, the Monroe editor reported that the Turners had decided to close their bar on Sunday nights in favor of a "Lyceum Concert." Older and wiser heads had persuaded the younger people to make the change. Perhaps a Turner's idea of God was different from that of a "genuine" Christian, said the editor. If the Turners thought God liked conviviality, a good glass of lager beer, or even a comic song, the community might indulge them so long as they closed their bar on Sunday.[34]

Lastly, every community had a group of inhabitants who simply ignored the middle-class code of respectability and religious observance. They drank and fought and caroused and "cussed," or they hunted on Sunday, shunned the churches, and pursued their simple pleasures without yielding to community pressure to lead a "better" life. Here, then, was the cultural pattern—a dominant middle-class Protestant group given to religion and stern morality; an upper-class group of "respectable" peo-

30 Don Marquis, *Sons of the Puritans* (New York, 1939), 30–33.

31 Louis Bromfield, *The Farm* (New York, 1935), 157–162.

32 Centreville, Michigan, *St. Joseph County Republican*, November 27, 1869.

33 Gallatin, Missouri, *North Missourian*, April 14, 1893.

34 See accounts in Monroe, Wisconsin, *Monroe Sentinel*, January 13, 27, February 3, March 3, April 7, May 5, and December 8, 29, 1869, for activities of the group and comments by the editor of the local paper.

ple who failed to see any necessary connection between pleasure and sin; Catholics; foreigners; and a "lower" class, which ignored the dominant code except perhaps for temporary allegiance following revival meetings. In spite of latent antagonisms, villagers lived close together and could not avoid influencing one another. It was a rare boy indeed who grew to manhood solely as the product of one cultural layer.

Outstanding interpreters of small-town culture have recognized this diversity of beliefs. Americans chuckle at the exploits of Huckleberry Finn, son of the town drunkard, who was free to swear, smoke, swim and go barefooted, and who ran away from riches when they came his way simply because he refused to conform to local standards of respectability. Mark Twain grew up in small midwestern towns and he knew from experience the conflicting cultural patterns within such communities. When Van Wyck Brooks later wrote *The Ordeal of Mark Twain*,[35] in which he presented Mark as wanting to rebel against a sex-warped and barren culture, he ignored the many cultural differences illustrated in Twain's own small-town characters. Bernard De Voto has pointed out the dangerous oversimplification in Brooks' thesis and the many strands running through midwestern culture.[36] In the so-called "battle of the village" which novelists fought in the early twentieth century, some, like Zona Gale, emphasized sweetness and light, and others, like Sinclair Lewis, concentrated on the drab and monotonous aspects of town life. In such novels, emphasis became distortion instead of insight, and they inevitably fell below the level of realism which Twain achieved.

MIDDLE-CLASS IDEALS

The dominant, middle-class code of McGuffey and his followers held that life was a serious business. In selections like Longfellow's "Psalm of Life" readers were urged to make the most of their opportunities:

> Tell me not in mournful numbers,
> Life is but an empty dream!
>
> .   .   .   .   .
>
> Life is real! Life is earnest!
>
> .   .   .   .   .
>
> Footprints on the sands of time.
>
> .   .   .   .   .
>
> Let us, then, be up and doing,
>   With a heart for any fate;
> Still achieving, still pursuing,
>   Learn to labor and to wait.[37]

---

[35] Van Wyck Brooks, *The Ordeal of Mark Twain* (New York, 1920).
[36] Bernard De Voto, *Mark Twain's America* (Boston, 1932).
[37] *Sixth Reader*, 212.

Even the ancients were cited to the same effect. Hercules turned away from the siren called "Pleasure" to follow a maiden whose path to happiness involved both pain and labor.[38] In this selection, and others like "Hugh Idle and Mr. Toil," [39] McGuffey stressed the virtues of labor. Youngsters who took him seriously could not indulge in leisurely enjoyment of wealth later on without a sense of guilt. Moreover, perseverance was highly recommended:

> Once or twice though you should fail,
> Try, Try, Again;
> If you would at last prevail,
> Try, Try, Again;
> If we strive, 'tis no disgrace,
> Though we may not win the race;
> What should you do in that case?
> Try, Try, Again.[40]

Truth, honesty, and courage belonged to the cluster of desirable traits. Washington's father so loved truth that nailing George in a coffin and following him to the grave would have been less painful than hearing a lie from the boy's lips. When George cut down the cherry tree, he manfully told his father "I can't tell a *lie*, father. You know I can't tell a *lie*." And his father in turn joyfully cried, "Come to my arms, my dearest boy. . . ." Common people could be equally noble. Susan's widowed mother made the family living by taking in washing, and Susan helped by making deliveries. On one occasion, Farmer Thompson gave her two bills in payment by mistake. She was severely tempted. The additional money would mean a new coat for mother, and little sister could have the old one to wear to Sunday School. Little brother could have a new pair of shoes. In spite of such desperate need, Susan corrected the mistake, and, sobbing with anguish, refused a shilling's reward on the grounds that she did not want to be paid for honesty. In this case, she received only a lightened heart, but McGuffey's heroines usually gained financially as well. McGuffey also stressed courage, even at the risk of ridicule. A boy who snowballed the schoolhouse to avoid the taunts of others, when he knew the act was wrong, was pictured as lacking in true courage.[41]

Contentment, modesty, and kindness were praised. One story told of Jupiter permitting unhappy people to exchange burdens with others. One man discarded his modesty instead of his ignorance; another his memory rather than his crimes. An old man threw off his gout in favor of a male heir, only to obtain an undutiful son discarded by an angry father. All begged Jupiter to restore their old afflictions. Patience stood by as they resumed their old troubles and automatically reduced their loads by a

[38] *Ibid.,* 215–217.
[39] *Fourth Reader,* 231–236.
[40] *Ibid.,* 95–96.
[41] See *Third Reader,* 233–236, 110–113, 144–148.

third. The moral was plain, according to McGuffey. One should never repine over his own problems or envy another, since no man could rightly judge his neighbor's misfortune.[42] A beauty who tossed her glove into a ring with lions to prove her lover's devotion, only to have him throw it in her face after regaining it, showed the silliness of vanity.[43] A poem about Mary's lamb demonstrated the rewards for kindness to animals. When it followed her to school one day, and the children marvelled at its affection, the teacher commented:

> And you each gentle animal
> To you, for life may bind,
> And make it follow at your call,
> If you are always *kind.*[44]

Greed, revenge, and selfishness toward others were castigated in stories which made plain the moral involved. "The Tricky Boy," for instance, was mean and given to teasing others. When a tired little girl asked help in shifting a jug of milk to her head in order to rest her weary arms, he purposely let it fall to the ground and break. He thought it was fun to see her cry until he slipped on the ground, made slick by the spilled milk, and was laid up for three months with a broken leg.[45]

While McGuffey's code has been ridiculed for its emphasis on material rewards for virtue and unremitting labor—and a hasty reading of his stories may seem to bear this out—he offered a nicely balanced philosophy in which life's purpose and rewards transcended material gains. In his own life and in his Readers, McGuffey preached against the foolishness of material ambition alone, to which so many of his pupils turned:

> Praise—when the ear has grown too dull to hear;
> Gold—when the senses it should please are dead;
> Wreaths—when the hair they cover has grown gray,
> Fame—when the heart it should have thrill'd is numb.[46]

Newspapers and preachers supported McGuffey's scheme of values. In 1870, the Centreville, Michigan, paper published a letter addressed to "My Dear Obadiah," urging young men to attend church, to act and dress modestly, to be ambitious, and to abhor drinking, smoking, and chewing. A companion letter to "My Dear Dorinda" encouraged girls to be sober and thoughtful in preparation for marriage and motherhood. Many were interested only in clothes, and their vocabulary was studded with vapid expressions like, "I thought I should die," "O my," "What are you going

---

42 *Ibid.,* 215–217.
43 *Ibid.,* 335–336.
44 *Second Reader,* 99–101.
45 *Third Reader,* 80–81.
46 *Sixth Reader,* 217–218.

to wear," "O ain't that pretty," "Now you're real mean," "You think you're smart, don't you," and "Well I don't care, there now." The writer asked what such girls could do in the kitchen or sick room.[47] A Chatfield, Minnesota, sermon on the "Fast Young Man" in 1896 pictured various types—"the Dude," "the Softie," "the Lazy," "the Dissipate." Young men, said the preacher, should adopt habits of personal cleanliness, avoid bad company, retire early at night, and practice modesty.[48]

Protestant pulpit and press also generally supported McGuffey's views on Sabbath observance. At Monroe, Wisconsin, in 1896, the local Presbyterian preacher asked bicycle riders to discontinue the practice of visiting neighboring towns in groups on Sunday. Another local preacher used the bicycle problem as a springboard for discussing the relation of Sabbath observance to morals as a whole. Granting that times had changed and that the Sabbath was made for man, he insisted that people still must square their actions with their consciences. In developing this theme, he offered a number of observations paralleling McGuffey's ideals. Gambling at church affairs was as evil as gambling in saloons. Card playing wasted time that could be better employed. A man should feel just as free to encircle the waist of his neighbor's wife in a round dance as he would on the way home from prayer meeting. And there was no more harm in a bicycle "spin" on Sunday than in a drive with horse and carriage; less, as a matter of fact, if the horse was tired. People winked at bigger sins on weekdays, liquor drinking for example.[49]

McGuffey firmly believed in private property and in its blessings to society. He quoted Blackstone to prove that necessity begat property and recourse was had to civil society to insure it. Private property had enabled a part of society to provide subsistence for all. It had insured leisure to cultivate the mind, invent useful arts, and to promote science. Simple stories again drove home the lesson. Although a little chimney sweep wanted more than anything else a beautiful, tune-playing watch which he saw in a lady's boudoir, he did not touch it because of his aversion to stealing. Fortunately for him, the lady saw him resist the temptation and took him as her ward. Education and success naturally followed. If he had stolen the watch, said McGuffey, he would have gone to jail. One could not steal the smallest thing without sin, and children should remember that God's eye saw all that transpired.[50]

McGuffey also recognized an obligation of the rich to aid the unfortunate. "Grateful Julian" set the standard. Beyond old rags for clothing and a straw pallet, he possessed nothing but a rabbit which he dearly loved. When he fell ill, a rich and good man took him in and cured his sickness. In return, Julian wished to present the rabbit to his benefactor, an act which so touched the latter that he sent the boy to school. Julian naturally grew up into a bright and honest lad.[51] Moreover, people were

[47] Centreville, Michigan, *St. Joseph County Republican*, January 15 and 22, 1870.
[48] Chatfield, Minnesota, *Chatfield Democrat*, September 17, 1896.
[49] Monroe, Wisconsin, *Monroe Sentinel*, June 3, 1896.
[50] *Sixth Reader*, 246–250; *Second Reader*, 115–118.
[51] *Third Reader*, 203–206.

expected to give according to their means, as illustrated in a poem called "The Philosopher's Scales":

> A long row of alms-houses, amply endow'd
> By a well-esteem'd Pharisee, busy and proud,
> Next loaded one scale; while the other was prest
> By those mites the poor widow dropp'd into the chest;
> Up flew the endowment, not weighing an ounce,
> And down, down the farthing-worth came with a bounce.[52]

Apart from illness and misfortune, no man needed to be poor. As one McGuffey story put the matter, all could find employment and there was no place for idlers and vagrants. Of course, one should be frugal, as the famous story of the string-saving boy proved, and labor was essential to success:

> Shall birds, and bees, and ants, be wise,
>   While I my moments waste?
> O let me with the morning rise,
>   And to my duty haste.[53]

Henry, the orphan boy, illustrated the fruits of rugged individualism. In need of a new grammar book, he shoveled snow to earn the price, thus proving "Where There's a Will, There is a Way." [54]

Newspapers elaborated the same theme. In 1867 the editor of the Algona, Iowa, paper replied sharply to a letter from a local citizen who objected to raising money for foreign missions when Algona had poor and destitute families of its own. The editor doubted if any Algonans were too poor to deny themselves at least one luxury, like owning a worthless cur, smoking or chewing at a cost of twenty-five to fifty dollars a year, or the inordinate use of tea or coffee. A man had recently told a local storekeeper a pitiful tale of hard times and no job, and had been given a sack of flour on credit. Having obtained this, he immediately produced twenty-five cents in cash to buy tobacco. With that style of poverty the editor had no sympathy. Furthermore, he had no sympathy with thievery, since any healthy man could "earn a living in this land of plenty." [55]

Preachers and newspaper editors agreed with McGuffey that individuals could rise in the world through their own efforts. A Centreville, Michigan, preacher, in 1869 affirmed that his community had no rich, no poor, no ignorant citizens save as each individual's own vice or virtue, own energy, or indolence had made him so.[56] When former Senator John J. Ingalls of Kansas expressed similar sentiments in 1893, the editor of the

---

[52] Sixth Reader, 205–206.
[53] See Fourth Reader, 111–112, 63–65; First Reader, 51.
[54] Fourth Reader, 31–32.
[55] Algona, Iowa, The Upper Des Moines, January 10 and February 28, 1867.
[56] Centreville, Michigan, St. Joseph County Republican, November 27, 1869.

Gallatin, Missouri, paper devoted virtually a whole column to summarizing his remarks. According to Ingalls, all men were self-made; even chance and circumstance were made by men and not the other way round. He who was born poor was fortunate. Future leaders of thought, business, and society would not come from the gilded youth of 1893 but from ambitious sons of farmers and laborers.[57]

Near the turn of the century, Markham's famous poem, "The Man with the Hoe," disturbed defenders of the old order because it seemingly condemned the economic system for injuring the common man. Businessmen offered prizes for poetical rebuttals, and William Jennings Bryan lectured on the implications of the poem. Small-town Mid-America was also disturbed. A "goodly contingent" of Brookfield, Missouri, businessmen gathered at the local Congregational church in the fall of 1899 to hear the pastor discuss the poem. According to him, the idea that the hoe could debase mankind was utterly un-American, degenerate, and unpatriotic. The man with the hoe was the man with opportunity; one needed only to keep an eye on the individual who refused to grasp its handle. Our mightiest leaders had been the products of lives of toil with the hoe, axe, crucible, mallet, and saw.[58]

According to McGuffey, the inferior animals made no mistakes and no improvements; man made both.[59] People were inclined to agree, although they accepted progress as so natural as to need no proof or analysis. And, of course, American standards were the measuring sticks. When John E. Young summarized world events in his diary at the close of 1868, he concluded that China was making rapid progress toward civilization and political greatness. American influence was given as the reason. Political revolution in Japan, moreover, gave hope that civilization and human progress would find a lodgment there. Even Abyssinia had been compelled to bow before the prowess of English civilization and Christianity.[60]

Progress was most generally interpreted as growth in material things. When the historian of Kossuth County, Iowa, came to the subject of progress, he followed a very common pattern in telling the story in terms of *growth*—growth of population, of property values, of roads, of the butter and cream industry.[61] Although the editor of a Kossuth County paper was inclined to agree with such measurements, he expressed some doubts in an article published in 1896. After pointing out the great growth in population, fine homes, wealth, and railroads in the short interval since Algona's first New Year's celebration in 1859, he raised the question of whether people locally were any happier. How much, he asked, had such externals added to the zest for life of those pioneers still present? [62] Even

[57] Gallatin, Missouri, *North Missourian*, May 26, 1893.

[58] Brookfield, Missouri, *Brookfield Gazette*, September 2, 1899.

[59] *Fifth Reader*, 88–90.

[60] Entry, December 31, 1868, John E. Young Diaries, 1843–1904, Illinois Historical Society Library, Springfield.

[61] Benjamin F. Reed, *History of Kossuth County, Iowa* (Chicago, 1913), II, Chapter 27, "Some Evidences of Progress."

[62] Algona, Iowa, *The Upper Des Moines*, January 1, 1896.

town boosters could be sentimental about the good old days, but sentiment was not allowed to interfere with the constant itch for bigness, growth, and numbers—in short, with progress.

MAJOR AND MINOR SINS

McGuffey also introduced his young readers to the major moralistic theme of the dominant, middle-class group, the dangers of liquor and its associated evils. In a story called "Touch Not—Taste Not—Handle Not" he described the terrible economic, physical, and moral consequences of drinking. Still other stories told of "intemperate husbands," who abused their first-born sons and brought their wives to a sorrowful death, and of the "venomous worm" which was more deadly than the rattlesnake or the copperhead. In an account filled with suspense, McGuffey described this terrible creature which bit only the human race, and then identified it as the "*Worm of the Still.*" [63] Gambling was also bad, for it grew on one at an insatiable rate and ultimately led to other evils, such as drinking, cheating, and murder.[64] While not condemned outright, dancing obviously found hospitable allies in liquor and cards, and the serious-minded-and-aspiring youngster was taught to avoid all three.

This cluster of moral convictions fascinated later novelists like Don Marquis, who pictured the saloon and church as concrete symbols of the age-old conflict of light and darkness, of evil and good. Church and saloon offered escape and refuge.[65] The swinging doors of a saloon gave sanctuary from too much virtue; the double portals of a church opened avenues to goodness. Neither church nor saloon could win total victory in the eternal struggle of good versus evil.

The Middle West was not unique in supporting both church and saloon. McGuffey himself came from a moralistic, middle-class background farther to the East, and only through his fear that savagery would destroy civilization on the Middle Border frontier did he express sentiments peculiar to that area. Although the battle of church-versus-saloon perhaps was more intense on the Middle Border, the struggle itself was nationwide.

The conflict left no room for halfway measures on either side. Men generally drank to excess or were teetotalers. In this battle of extremes drunkenness often led to disaster. The warden of the Indiana state prison in 1859 reported that 446 of the 556 inmates had been addicted to drink.[66] Newspapers and diarists constantly referred to tragedies resulting from intoxication. John E. Young of the little town of Athens, Illinois, recorded the death of a local physician in 1893 from an overdose of morphine following a drunken spree; the serious injury to a local citizen, who fell off the railroad cars while on a "tare" in Springfield on the Fourth of July in 1894; the loss of an arm by "old man Hess," who fell under a train at the

[63] *Fifth Reader*, 83–85, 155–160, 192–193.
[64] *Ibid.*, 204–208.
[65] Don Marquis, *Sons of the Puritans*.
[66] Logan Esarey, *A History of Indiana from 1850 to 1920* (Bloomington, 1935), 589.

local depot while on a Christmas drunk in 1895; and drunken antics at local saloons during the Christmas season of 1896.[67] Such widespread evidence fired the opponents of liquor to greater efforts in behalf of total prohibition, and this in turn encouraged still heavier drinking by those who dared to transgress.

Dancing, cards, and smoking also continued in spite of moral opposition. William Allen White's father and mother occasionally played euchre and seven-up, but when White caught his son doing the same with other boys in the haymow, he set up a table on the front porch and made them play in full view of citizens passing on the street. That was sufficient to cure his son of the habit for years to come.[68] Chewing and smoking by men were tolerated within limits, but many thought of them as dirty, expensive, and conducive to still greater evils. An exchange item labelled "Boys Beware" in a Michigan paper in 1869 warned youngsters against chewing tobacco, smoking cigars, drinking, and playing cards or billiards. Such habits cost money, led to stealing, and were filthy in nature.[69]

Cigarettes increased greatly in popularity near the turn of the century. Youngsters liked the early cigarette brands like Duke's Cameo and Sweet Caporals. Each packet of the latter contained a picture of an "opera star" dressed in tights, of which Lillian Russell was the favorite. Smokers who preferred Sweet Caporals could assemble a whole collection of twenty-four near-to-nude beauties.[70] In the 1890's papers began to publish material from the National Cigarette Association explaining the evil effects of smoking. According to Dr. David Starr Jordan, president of Stanford University, boys who smoked cigarettes were like wormy apples and very few ever got to college. While other boys pushed ahead, they had need of the undertaker and the sexton. Still, said Dr. Jordan, philosophically, this speeded up the race for the survival of the fittest.[71] One country paper in 1893 mentioned a cigarette "fiend" who, on his way to the World's Fair, missed his train in Brookfield while trying to purchase a nickel's worth of "coffin nails." [72]

The word "sex" was too horrible a thing for McGuffey to bandy about. Others might frighten pubescent youngsters with the dire consequences of "impure thoughts," but McGuffey seemingly preferred to believe that Christian children would concentrate on school books and their duties to parents. McGuffey said that marriage and a family gave men the necessary stimulus to succeed, and that marriage and motherhood constituted the natural and most honored vocation for women.[73]

This attitude harmonized nicely with prevailing opinion on the Middle Border. Since all women were expected to marry, spinsters had no place in society. They could work as domestics for others or live with more fortunate married relatives, but no woman was supposed to have become an "old

[67] John E. Young Diaries 1843–1904, Illinois Historical Society Library.

[68] William Allen White, *Autobiography* (New York, 1946), 52.

[69] Centreville, Michigan, *St. Joseph County Republican*, April 10, 1869.

[70] Fred L. Holmes, *Side Roads Excursions into Wisconsin's Past* (Madison, 1949), 59.

[71] Greencastle, Indiana, *Star-Press*, March 3 and July 28, 1894.

[72] Gallatin, Missouri, *North Missourian*, November 3, 1893.

[73] See, for example, *Fifth Reader*, 169–170, and *Sixth Reader*, 76.

maid" by choice.[74] If no husband was available, a woman could save her pride by pretending that her lover had died on the eve of their marriage and that she had been unable thereafter to think of caring for another man. Idealized love appealed to that sentimental age, partially because it helped conceal the grim practicality surrounding so much of the marriage relationship.

Although circumscribed, the wife's position was important. She prided herself on being a good cook and housekeeper. Company dinners with lavish quantities of food demonstrated her ability as a cook and her husband's success as a "good provider." While guests crammed themselves with food, she bustled about the table to see that all were properly served, and not until the last guest had finished did she permit herself to eat. As an angel of mercy to neighbors in distress and an avenging instrument of gossip, she maintained her family's influence in society and church affairs. She was economical of her husband's worldly goods, condemned the vanities of rouge and the sin of cigarettes, and got her washing on the line at an early hour on Monday morning. Most of all, she sought "advantages" for her children, and operated as a matchmaker in behalf of her marriageable daughters. In carrying out these functions she personified the traits of the successful middle-class housewife.

Marriage itself involved a combination of Rabelaisian humor and prudery. The Christmas season rivalled June for weddings, perhaps because routine activities slackened between Christmas and New Year's. Charivaris, infares, and joshing often marked the occasion. When William Allen White's parents returned from their honeymoon, they found that every chamber pot in their home had been gaily decorated by friends in honor of the occasion. Similarly, the editor of the Gallatin, Missouri, paper honored the marriage of a respectable couple in 1865 with the comment that he was glad to see them obeying the Apostle Paul's injunction that it was better to marry than to burn.[75]

In marriage, as in most aspects of life, the puritanical streak was uppermost. When Tocqueville visited America in the 1830's he was surprised to see how freely unchaperoned young girls went places with men. In his opinion, this very freedom explained in part why American women made excellent wives in a practical sense. At the same time, he felt sure that mothers had to warn girls of the dangers in unrestricted association with men, and he wondered if this did not invigorate judgment at the expense of imagination.[76] A midwestern paper put the matter more bluntly in 1898 in a story headed "Where is Papa?" In this case, an unfortunate girl had been deserted by her lover, and the editor urged mothers to warn their daughters against the falsity of men's promises. Girls should be told that

---

[74] See Zona Gale, *Miss Lulu Bett* (New York, 1920) for an excellent treatment of the plight of the unmarried female, and Rose Wilder Lane, *Old Home Town* (New York, 1935), for a shrewd but sympathetic account of the life of the small-town woman.

[75] Gallatin, Missouri, *North Missourian*, February 23, 1865.

[76] Alexis de Tocqueville, *Democracy in America*, edited by Henry Steele Commager (New York, 1947), 393.

shame could not be covered up no matter how long one lived or how good one became in later life. A woman's entire life could not atone for such a sin.[77]

Mothers apparently needed little urging to instruct their daughters in matters vital to maintaining their purity before marriage. Unfortunately, advice and information seems to have gone no further. Young girls and old maids were excluded from matronly discussions of delicate matters. In watching their elders at home and in society, girls must have concluded that virtue and prudery were synonymous. Married people in small towns carefully avoided any appearance of undue interest in the opposite sex. Social intercourse was stilted and formal, and men and women sat apart at social gatherings to prevent any threat of gossip. Parents avoided displays of affection toward one another in front of their children, and widowed people waited at least a year to remarry in order to escape community censure.

"Sex-warped" attitudes were common enough on the Middle Border. Both Sherwood Anderson and Edgar Lee Masters were obsessed with sex. Both engaged in a series of tawdry sexual alliances, and both had trouble living a normal married life. Although few others wrote equally frank autobiographies, these men were not unique. Still other Midwesterners, seemingly repelled by the sexual crudity which they observed, turned to an impossibly idealized love. The tragedy played out in Ed Howe's *Story of a Country Town* rests basically on Jo Erring's ridiculous and impossible idealization of the gentle and innocent Mateel. Howe's own boyhood was marred by his father's desertion of the family for another woman, and Howe's own marriage in later years came to grief. Idealized love and sex-obsession alike owed something to the puritanical code which permeated much of the Middle Border. But before one joins with Van Wyck Brooks in calling this culture "sex-warped," he must explain the happy marriages which are spelled out in the writings and autobiographies of other men like Garland, Quick, and White. Midwestern culture was complex, composed of several layers, and out of this came markedly different men. . . .

UNCO-OPERATIVE SINNERS

McGuffey and his followers liked to speak of the simple virtues of the village green. A rigorous moral code, closely knit communities in which sinners could easily be exposed, and devoted guardians like the W.C.T.U. supposedly created an ideal environment in which to rear the young. All this, however, ignores a large body of contrary evidence which reduces much of the bucolic theme of rural and small-town purity to the status of folklore. Less than half of the people maintained church membership.[78]

[77] Gallatin, Missouri, *North Missourian*, August 26, 1898.
[78] In 1900 the figures were: Michigan, 40.5%; Ohio, 42%; Iowa, 35.2%; Indiana, 37.4%; Wisconsin, 48.35%; and Missouri, 38.5%, for example. Figures compiled from U. S. Bureau of the Census, *Religious Bodies, 1906*, Part I (Washington, 1910), 308–372.

Many unaffiliated individuals, like the Quick family, were respectable citizens, but virtually every community also had ne'er-do-wells or submarginal families who lived by intermittent day labor. Transient day laborers, bums, and wandering horse traders also invaded small towns at various periods of the year. Boys and girls engaged freely in unsupervised play at school and in outbuildings of family homes. Actually, the environment was both good and bad, as a large body of evidence clearly indicates.

The autobiographies and other published works of Floyd Dell, Edgar Lee Masters, and Sherwood Anderson describe an appalling amount of moral laxity in small towns. A series of slovenly hired girls in his parents' home introduced Masters to sex at an early age. Moreover, the two "Shetland Ponies," as they were widely known, who provided gossip in Sherwood Anderson's boyhood town, had rivals in virtually every midwestern village. One was the daughter of a ne'er-do-well who travelled about exhibiting a stuffed whale, and the other had a drunken tailor for a father. One of them became interested in Sherwood, and asked her confederate to bring him to a rendezvous in the recesses of a rail fence at the edge of town. She had hung her little white pants on a rail and was enticing Sherwood to intimacy at the moment when a barrage of stones was thrown by a young man who, learning of the rendezvous, had followed the couple. Sherwood immediately took off in a wild flight of dismay, yelling as he ran, "Get your pants, Lily. Get your pants, Lily." [79]

Small-town oral tradition contains similar episodes, differing only in details, and the writings of well-balanced, moral men confirm the pattern. William Allen White early acquired a knowledge of basic Anglo-Saxon four-letter words which were scribbled on sidewalks and school toilets. One summer day he and his friends discovered a covered wagon in a wooded camping place near town where strange girls were meeting local men: in his words, "And the knowledge of good and evil came to us, even as to the Pair in the Garden." On another occasion he and his friends discovered the Sunday School Superintendent and a visiting teacher in the woods cooling their toes in the water and rapidly returning to nature. When the boys yelled from a concealed vantage point, the couple rushed hurriedly away. The youngsters were even more astonished, however, when the Superintendent returned to the spot with his wife. Only later in life did White understand the purpose in this. It prevented a divorce when the story circulated in town since the wife naturally believed that she was the woman in question. White's father permitted him to sell cigars and listen to stories by travelling salesmen in the family hotel. As he saw it, there was little to teach a youngster who

> had grown up in a pioneer town around the slaughterhouse and in the livery stable, who had roamed through the romantic woods where the peripatetic strumpets made their camps, who had picked up his sex education from Saxon words chalked on sidewalks and barns, who had taken his Rabelaisian poetry from the walls of backhouses, and who had seen saloons spew out their back door

[79] *Sherwood Anderson's Memoirs* (New York, 1942), 63–64.

their indigestible drunkards, swarming with flies, to furnish amusement and devilment for the entertainment of little boys, as it was in the beginning of civilization.[80]

Anderson and Masters succumbed to the erotic appeal of such influences; White and Quick continued to place girls on a pedestal and to honor chastity in womankind. White knew a boy from an Ohio boarding school with quite a different point of view, and Quick discerned more immediately than did his elders the purpose behind the very embarrassing but seemingly innocent questioning carried on by a young hellion in his own home town who had served a period in a reform school. According to Quick,

> Rural simplicity was supposed to make for a virtuous life. We had this delusion in our family. I have often wondered what city boy ever had more evil associates than did I out there on the prairie. . . . The simple innocence of the Deserted Village was absent. . . . I went with these boys, played with them, and knew them for what they were; but so far as I can see I took little harm from them. They seemed to be mere phenomena, like the weather, interesting but nothing to imitate.[81]

"Social purity" of *thought* was only a myth everywhere on the Middle Border; in practice it varied from individual to individual.

Prudery and frankness went hand in hand. There is truth in the legend that refined women spoke of "lower extremities," while the less refined used the word "limbs," and only those of no standing spoke of "legs." On the other hand, an advertisement of Velpeau's French Female Pills in the Monroe, Wisconsin, paper in 1869 would not be accepted today by village editors. According to the descriptive material, the pills had been kept off the American market until recently because of the ease with which they caused abortion. Pregnant married ladies were warned to avoid them because they invariably caused a miscarriage. Customers could obtain them by mail in packages sealed against the eyes of the curious and they were guaranteed to be entirely safe to take.[82]

Undesirable transients and a rough local element caused trouble everywhere. Itinerant field hands were especially bothersome during the harvest season. Hamlin Garland had to deal with them while operating his father's farm near Osage, Iowa, in the 1870's. They reminded him of a flight of unclean birds. To these former soldiers, errant sons of poor farmers, and unsuccessful mechanics from older states a "girl" was the most desired thing in the world, to be enjoyed without remorse. They furnished local boys with smutty information from South Clark Street in Chicago and the

---

[80] William Allen White, *Autobiography*, 40, 46, 67. Quotations on pages 40 and 67.
[81] Herbert Quick, *One Man's Life* [Indianapolis, 1925], 147–150.
[82] Monroe, Wisconsin, *Monroe Sentinel*, January 6, 1869. See also advertisement of "pessaric remedies" in Chatfield, Minnesota, *Chatfield Democrat*, January 5, 1867.

river front in St. Louis. On rainy days and Saturday nights they fought and caroused with local riffraff in country towns. In Garland's words:

> Saturday night in town! How it all comes back to me! I am a timid visitor in the little frontier village. It is sunset. A whiskey-crazed farmhand is walking bare footed up and down the middle of the road defying the world.—From a corner of the street I watch with tense interest another lithe, pock-marked bully menacing with cat-like action a cowering young farmer in a long linen coat. The crowd jeers at him for his cowardice—a burst of shouting is heard. A trampling follows and forth from the door of a saloon bulges a throng of drunken, steaming, reeling, cursing ruffians followed by brave Jim McCarty, the city marshal, with an offender under each hand. . . .
>
> We are on the way home. Only two of my crew are with me. The others are roaring from one drinking place to another, having a "good time." The air is soothingly clean and sweet after the tumult and the reek of the town.[83]

When a heavy Sunday-night rain stopped harvesting on a Monday in 1876 near Chatfield, Minnesota, nine fights occurred, and hands were "drunk, fighting, raising h—l generally." Some Chatfield residents had participated, and the local paper warned them that order would be maintained, even if it meant a policeman on every corner.[84] Garland's description of such men and their activities applied widely over the Middle West except for a shortage of "brave" Jim McCartys. Constables generally lacked his fortitude and strength, and when a town started boiling over they often failed to meet the crisis.

Nor was the problem limited simply to the harvest season. During one week in December, 1879, the marshal at Mendon, Michigan, accommodated twenty-eight tramps overnight in the village lockup, a part of the immense army, according to a local citizen, which was willing to live by begging and petty thievery.[85] In September, 1897, Centreville, Michigan, had a number of hoboes on its streets daily. They were described as umbrella menders, chimney sweeps, tinkers, and the blind, deaf, lame, lazy, and crazy. The local editor warned that while they seemed harmless, they usually were "whiskey suckers," and would bear watching. Housewives were warned not to leave their washing on the line unguarded.[86]

Local rowdies seem to have been awed only slightly by the better classes. At Athens, Illinois, in the 1890's, the rougher element stole ice cream intended for church socials and slashed harness on teams tied to hitching racks at local churches. At times, officers were called out to

[83] Hamlin Garland, *A Son of the Middle Border* (New York, 1920), 175–176.
[84] Chatfield, Minnesota, *Chatfield Democrat*, August 19, 1876.
[85] Report of Mendon correspondent in Centreville, Michigan, *St. Joseph County Republican*, December 13, 1879.
[86] Centreville, Michigan, *St. Joseph County Republican*, September 10, 1897.

handle rough individuals intent on disrupting revival services. A local group of gamblers and petty thieves engaged in a gun fight with the city marshal and tortured an individual in his isolated home in hopes of learning where his money was hidden.[87]

The activities of this class can be traced in the newspaper files of any midwestern town. Though Gallatin, Missouri, was very proud of its city park in the 1890's, ladies stayed away to avoid the vulgar and profane language being used by male loafers. On Saturday nights, when the "Honey Creekers" tried to "take the town," women remained at home as no section of the business district was immune. At times, the local editor lectured readers on the low respect shown for law and order. According to him, an especially brutal murder aroused only mild resentment. Howling mobs of men and boys surrounded the town marshal in an effort to keep him from taking reluctant drunks to the calaboose. Crap-shooting games and "young blades" intent on injuring school property added to the problem of law enforcement. When "smart" boys pelted a disorderly house near the Windsor hotel one of the women returned the insult with gun fire. Although she left town before arrests could be made, two remaining "soiled doves" had to be brought into court before they would agree to depart. Travelling "crap sharks" had no trouble locating gamblers in Gallatin and neighboring towns.[88]

Twentieth-century cities surpass country towns in crimes against property, but they differ little in crimes of violence. Murder, rape, and manslaughter are sufficiently common in smaller communities to deny them any claim to special purity,[89] and small-town newspaper records indicate that such communities never were better in curbing crimes of violence.[90]

[87] John E. Young Diaries, 1843–1904, entries October 24, 1894, March 27, 1896, March 2, 1898, and March 18, 1900.

[88] Gallatin, Missouri, *North Missourian*, June 2, August 4, and December 29, 1893; March 11, 18, and July 29, 1898.

[89] George B. Vold, "Crime in City and Country Areas," *The Annals of the American Academy of Political and Social Science*, CCXVII (September, 1941), 38–45.

[90] As early as 1900 F. W. Blackmar of the University of Kansas published an article questioning the purity of the village green. Blackmar emphasized the weaknesses leading to "social degeneration" in smaller communities. Village police forces were inadequate to cope with local problems. Gangs of idle village boys loafed on street corners, shot craps and played cards, were guilty of profane language and indecent remarks on Main Street, and engaged in long, leisurely conversations on smutty subjects. Blackmar's article pioneered a sociological trend toward a more realistic appraisal of village morals. F. W. Blackmar, "Social Degeneration in Towns and Rural Districts," *Proceedings of the National Conference of Charities and Correction*, XXVII (1900), 115–124.

A Little Milk, A Little Honey: Jewish Immigration in America

DAVID BOROFF

In the early twentieth century, an American Jewish playwright coined a phrase that entered the common language as a description of American society's absorption of various immigrant streams. The United States was the "melting pot" of nations. Although some authorities, like the Dillingham Commission, questioned the validity of the melting-pot theory, for half a century, this metaphor influenced the popular mind as a fulfillment of the promise of the founding fathers: **e pluribus unum** (out of many, one).

Up until the Civil War period, most voluntary immigrants had been rather easily assimilated into the dominant culture. The major exception among European immigrants had been the large numbers of Irish peasants who migrated during the 1840s and 1850s. Even the German Jews who had come to this country before the late nineteenth century had been largely absorbed. With the coming of the new immigrants from Southern and Eastern Europe in the late nineteenth and early twentieth centuries, however, the assimilation process shifted its intent. The new immigrants, Roman Catholic or Jewish for the most part, were not wanted in the dominant culture. Theories of racial superiority and social evolution were drawn on by the defenders of the traditional American way of life in order to demonstrate the danger these newcomers posed to the older values. As a result of their efforts, restrictive legislation was passed in the 1920s, virtually precluding further migration from the countries of the new immigration. Although the exclusion acts led to a surge of ethnic consciousness on the part of those excluded, the conventional wisdom about the immigration process came to be found in the melting-pot metaphor.

After the Second World War, however, it seemed to many that only the surface had been melted, producing an overlay of general cultural traits developed in the United States, while underneath remained a strong, distinctly traditional ethnic way of life that derived largely from old-world traditions. Beginning with the publication of **Beyond the Melting Pot** by Daniel P. Moynihan and Nathan Glazer in 1963, scholars began to reconsider the nature of ethnic survivals in American society. In the late 1960s, partly in response to the perceived gains of the civil rights and black militant movements of that decade, ethnic consciousness began to grow, and the children and grandchildren of the new immigration started to reevaluate their traditional cultures and to seek a more aggressive stance against an overall culture that they found chauvinistically denying the validity of ethnic pluralism.

The Eastern European Jews provide a special case in this ethnic history. The centuries-long religious and cultural oppression experienced by the Jewish people created in them an exceedingly strong sense of identity that survived intact the transfer to the United States. In addition, because discriminatory laws deprived Jews of access to certain kinds of work and career lines in Eastern Europe, they had learned to fill the interstices in the economic structure as peddlers, small shopkeepers, and artisans. These skills proved useful in America, since these were areas of great need in the rapidly expanding economy of the late nineteenth and early twentieth centuries. Like most of the new immigrants, Jews tended to form distinct communities and were, therefore, in a position to develop special markets for culture-specific items.

Jews provide a special case in another respect. Their relatively high level of literacy, or at least respect for literacy, found outlet and market in the growth of a literary culture, particularly on New York's Lower East Side. It also provided access to upward mobility through the educational process in the public schools. While most of the Jews of the immigrant generation found work in light industry, particularly in the garment business, many in the second generation moved into other areas of employment that proved to be upwardly mobile. In other immigrant groups, there was a greater tendency for children to follow in the line of work of their parents.

The essay reprinted below, by David Boroff, late professor of English at New York University, describes the beginnings of life in the United States for the Jews of the new immigration. The title, "A Little Milk, A Little Honey," suggests the bittersweet quality of life on the Lower East Side. The author concentrates on developments within the Jewish community itself and does not deal with the relationship between Jews and other ethnic groups or the old settlers, although this would be part of the whole picture. What he has written, however, serves as the background for a remarkable story. Jews have so successfully adopted the American Dream that many of their community leaders fear their distinctiveness may be lost through intermarriage and assimilation. Relative to Jewish immigration, perhaps the melting-pot metaphor was right, then, only expressed fifty years ahead of its time.

I t started with a trickle and ended in a flood. The first to come were twenty-three Jews from Brazil who landed in New Amsterdam in 1654, in flight from a country no longer hospitable to them. They were, in origin, Spanish and Portuguese Jews (many with grandiloquent Iberian names) whose families had been wandering for a century and a half. New Amsterdam provided a chilly reception. Governor Peter Stuyvesant at first

"A Little Milk, A Little Honey" by David Boroff. From *American Heritage* 17 (October 1966): 12–14, 74–81. © 1966, American Heritage Publishing Company, Inc. Reprinted by permission from *American Heritage*.

asked them to leave, but kinder hearts in the Dutch West India Company granted them the right to stay, "provided the poor among them . . . be supported by their own nation." By the end of the century, there were perhaps one hundred Jews; by the middle of the eighteenth century, there were about three hundred in New York, and smaller communities in Newport, Philadelphia, and Charleston.

Because of their literacy, zeal, and overseas connections, colonial Jews prospered as merchants, though there were artisans and laborers among them. The Jewish community was tightly knit, but there was a serious shortage of trained religious functionaries. There wasn't a single American rabbi, for example, until the nineteenth century. Jews were well regarded, particularly in New England. Puritan culture leaned heavily on the Old Testament, and Harvard students learned Hebrew; indeed, during the American Revolution, the suggestion was advanced that Hebrew replace English as the official language of the new country. The absence of an established national religion made it possible for Judaism to be regarded as merely another religion in a pluralistic society. The early days of the new republic were thus a happy time for Jews. Prosperous and productive, they were admitted to American communal life with few restrictions. It is little wonder that a Jewish spokesman asked rhetorically in 1820: "On what spot in this habitable Globe does an Israelite enjoy more blessings, more privileges?"

The second wave of immigration during the nineteenth century is often described as German, but that is misleading. Actually, there were many East European Jews among the immigrants who came in the half century before 1870. However, the German influence was strong, and there was a powerful undercurrent of Western enlightenment at work. These Jews came because economic depression and the Industrial Revolution had made their lot as artisans and small merchants intolerable. For some there was also the threatening backwash of the failure of the Revolution of 1848. Moreover, in Germany at this time Jews were largely disfranchised and discriminated against. During this period, between 200,000 and 400,000 Jews emigrated to this country, and the Jewish population had risen to about half a million by 1870.

This was the colorful era of the peddler and his pack. Peddling was an easy way to get started—it required little capital—and it often rewarded enterprise and daring. Jewish peddlers fanned out through the young country into farmland and mining camps, frontier and Indian territory. The more successful peddlers ultimately settled in one place as storekeepers. (Some proud businesses—including that of Senator Goldwater's family—made their start this way.) Feeling somewhat alienated from the older, settled Jews, who had a reputation for declining piety, the new immigrants organized their own synagogues and community facilities, such as cemeteries and hospitals. In general, these immigrants were amiably received by native Americans, who, unsophisticated about differences that were crucial to the immigrants themselves, regarded all Central Europeans as "Germans."

Essentially, the emigration route was the same between 1820 and 1870 as it would be in the post-1880 exodus. The travellers stayed in emigration inns while awaiting their ship, and since they had all their resources with them, they were in danger of being robbed. The journey itself was hazardous and, in the days of the sailing vessels when a good wind was indispensable, almost interminable. Nor were the appointments very comfortable even for the relatively well to do. A German Jew who made the journey in 1856 reported that his cabin, little more than six feet by six feet, housed six passengers in triple-decker bunks. When a storm raged, the passengers had to retire to their cabins lest they be washed off the deck by waves. "Deprived of air," he wrote, "it soon became unbearable in the cabins in which six sea-sick persons breathed." On this particular journey, sea water began to trickle into the cabins, and the planks had to be retarred.

Still, the emigration experience was a good deal easier than it would be later. For one thing, the immigrants were better educated and better acquainted with modern political and social attitudes than the oppressed and bewildered East European multitudes who came after 1880. Fewer in number, they were treated courteously by ships' captains. (On a journey in 1839, described by David Mayer, the ship's captain turned over his own cabin to the Jewish passengers for their prayers and regularly visited those Jews who were ill.) Moreover, there was still the bloom of adventure about the overseas voyage. Ships left Europe amid the booming of cannon, while on shore ladies enthusiastically waved their handkerchiefs. On the way over, there was a holiday atmosphere despite the hazards, and there was great jubilation when land was sighted.

There were, however, rude shocks when the voyagers arrived in this country. The anguish of Castle Garden and Ellis Island was well in the future when immigration first began to swell. But New York seemed inhospitable, its pace frantic, the outlook not entirely hopeful. Isaac M. Wise, a distinguished rabbi who made the journey in 1846, was appalled. "The whole city appeared to me like a large shop," he wrote, "where everyone buys or sells, cheats or is cheated. I had never before seen a city so bare of all art and of every trace of good taste; likewise I had never witnessed anywhere such rushing, hurrying, chasing, running . . . Everything seemed so pitifully small and paltry; and I had had so exalted an idea of the land of freedom." Moreover, he no sooner landed in New York than he was abused by a German drayman whose services he had declined. "Aha! thought I," he later wrote, "you have left home and kindred in order to get away from the disgusting Judaeophobia and here the first German greeting that sounds in your ears is hep! hep!" (The expletive was a Central European equivalent of "Kike.") Another German Jew who worked as a clothing salesman was affronted by the way customers were to be "lured" into buying ("I did not think this occupation corresponded in any way to my views of a merchant's dignity").

After 1880, Jewish immigration into the United States was in flood tide. And the source was principally East Europe, where by 1880 three-quarters of the world's 7.7 million Jews were living. In all, over two million Jews came to these shores in little more than three decades—about one-third of Europe's Jewry. Some of them came, as their predecessors had come, because of shrinking economic opportunities. In Russia and in the Austro-Hungarian empire, the growth of large-scale agriculture squeezed out Jewish middlemen as it destroyed the independent peasantry, while in the cities the development of manufacturing reduced the need for Jewish artisans. Vast numbers of Jews became petty tradesmen or even *luft-menschen* (men without visible means of support who drifted from one thing to another). In Galicia, around 1900, there was a Jewish trader for every ten peasants, and the average value of his stock came to only twenty dollars.

Savage discrimination and pogroms also incited Jews to emigrate. The Barefoot Brigades—bands of marauding Russian peasants—brought devastation and bloodshed to Jewish towns and cities. On a higher social level, there was the "cold pogrom," a government policy calculated to destroy Jewish life. The official hope was that one third of Russia's Jews would die out, one third would emigrate, and one third would be converted to the Orthodox Church. Crushing restrictions were imposed. Jews were required to live within the Pale of Settlement in western Russia, they could not Russify their names, and they were subjected to rigorous quotas for schooling and professional training. Nor could general studies be included in the curriculum of Jewish religious schools. It was a life of poverty and fear.

Nevertheless, the *shtetl*, the typical small Jewish town, was a triumph of endurance and spiritual integrity. It was a place where degradation and squalor could not wipe out dignity, where learning flourished in the face of hopelessness, and where a tough, sardonic humor provided catharsis for the tribulations of an existence that was barely endurable. The abrasions and humiliations of everyday life were healed by a rich heritage of custom and ceremony. And there was always Sabbath—"The Bride of the Sabbath," as the Jews called the day of rest—to bring repose and exaltation to a life always sorely tried.

To be sure, even this world showed signs of disintegration. Secular learning, long resisted by East European Jews and officially denied to them, began to make inroads. Piety gave way to revolutionary fervor, and Jews began to play a heroic role in Czarist Russia's bloody history of insurrection and suppression.

This was the bleak, airless milieu from which the emigrants came. A typical expression of the Jewish attitude towards emigration from Russia —both its hopefulness and the absence of remorse—was provided by Dr. George Price, who had come to this country in one of the waves of East European emigration:

> Should this Jewish emigrant regret his leave-taking of his native land which fails to appreciate him? No! A thousand times no! He must not regret fleeing the clutches of the blood-thirsty crocodile. Sympathy for this country? How ironical it sounds! Am I not despised? Am I not urged to leave? Do I not hear the word *Zhid* constantly? . . . Be thou cursed forever my wicked homeland, because you remind me of the Inquisition . . . May you rue the day when you exiled the people who worked for your welfare.

After 1880, going to America—no other country really lured—became the great drama of redemption for the masses of East European

Jews. (For some, of course, Palestine had that role even in the late nine-teenth century, but these were an undaunted Zionist cadre prepared to endure the severest hardships.) The assassination of Czar Alexander II in 1881, and the subsequent pogrom, marked the beginning of the new influx. By the end of the century, 700,000 Jews had arrived, about one quarter of them totally illiterate, almost all of them impoverished. Throughout East Europe, Jews talked longingly about America as the "goldene medinah" (the golden province), and biblical imagery—"the land of milk and honey" —came easily to their lips. Those who could write were kept busy com-posing letters to distant kin—or even to husbands—in America. (Much of the time, the husband went first, and by abstemious living saved enough to fetch wife and children from the old country.) Children played at "emigrating games," and for the entire *shtetl* it was an exciting moment when the mail-carrier announced how many letters had arrived from America.

German steamship companies assiduously advertised the glories of the new land and provided a one-price rate from *shtetl* to New York. Emi-gration inns were established in Brody (in the Ukraine) and in the port cities of Bremen and Hamburg, where emigrants would gather for the trip. There were rumors that groups of prosperous German Jews would under-write their migration to America; and in fact such people often did help their co-religionists when they were stranded without funds in the port cities of Germany. Within Russia itself, the government after 1880 more or less acquiesced in the emigration of Jews, and connived in the vast business of "stealing the border" (smuggling emigrants across). After 1892, emigration was legal—except for those of draft age—but large num-bers left with forged papers, because that proved to be far easier than get-ting tangled in the red tape of the Czarist bureaucracy. Forged documents, to be sure, were expensive—they cost twenty-five rubles, for many Jews the equivalent of five weeks' wages. Nor was the departure from home en-tirely a happy event. There were the uncertainties of the new life, the fear that in America "one became a gentile." Given the Jewish aptitude for lugubriousness, a family's departure was often like a funeral, lachrymose and anguished, with the neighbors carting off the furniture that would no longer be needed.

For people who had rarely ventured beyond the boundaries of their own village, going to America was an epic adventure. They travelled with pitifully little money; the average immigrant arrived in New York with only about twenty dollars. With their domestic impedimenta—bed-ding, brass candlesticks, samovars—they would proceed to the port cities by rail, cart, and even on foot. At the emigration inns, they had to wait their turn. Thousands milled around, entreating officials for departure cards. There were scenes of near chaos—mothers shrieking, children cry-ing; battered wicker trunks, bedding, utensils in wild disarray. At Ham-burg, arriving emigrants were put in the "unclean" section of the *Aus-wandererhallen* until examined by physicians who decided whether their clothing and baggage had to be disinfected. After examination, Jews could not leave the center; other emigrants could.

The ocean voyage provided little respite. (Some elected to sail by way of Liverpool at a reduction of nine dollars from the usual rate of thirty-four dollars.) Immigrants long remembered the "smell of ship," a distillation of many putrescences. Those who went in steerage slept on mattresses filled with straw and kept their clothes on to keep warm. The berth itself was generally six feet long, two feet wide, and two and a half feet high, and it had to accommodate the passenger's luggage. Food was another problem. Many Orthodox Jews subsisted on herring, black bread, and tea which they brought because they did not trust the dietary purity of the ship's food. Some ships actually maintained a separate galley for kosher food, which was coveted by non-Jewish passengers because it was allegedly better.

Unsophisticated about travel and faced by genuine dangers, Jewish emigrants found the overseas trip a long and terrifying experience. But when land was finally sighted, the passengers often began to cheer and shout. "I looked up at the sky," an immigrant wrote years later. "It seemed much bluer and the sun much brighter than in the old country. It reminded me on [*sic*] the Garden of Eden."

Unhappily, the friendly reception that most immigrants envisioned in the new land rarely materialized. Castle Garden in the Battery, at the foot of Manhattan—and later Ellis Island in New York Harbor—proved to be almost as traumatic as the journey itself. "Castle Garden," an immigrant wrote, "is a large building, a Gehenna, through which all Jewish arrivals must pass to be cleansed before they are considered worthy of breathing freely the air of the land of the almighty dollar. . . . If in Brody, thousands crowded about, here tens of thousands thronged about; if there they were starving, here they were dying; if there they were crushed, here they were simply beaten."

One must make allowances for the impassioned hyperbole of the suffering immigrant, but there is little doubt that the immigration officials were harassed, overworked, and often unsympathetic. Authorized to pass on the admissibility of the newcomers, immigration officers struck terror into their hearts by asking questions designed to reveal their literacy and social attitudes. "How much is six times six?" an inspector asked a woman in the grip of nervousness, then casually asked the next man, "Have you ever been in jail?"

There were, of course, representatives of Jewish defense groups present, especially from the Hebrew Immigrant Aid Society. But by this time, the immigrants, out of patience and exhausted, tended to view them somewhat balefully. The Jewish officials tended to be highhanded, and the temporary barracks which they administered on Ward's Island for those not yet settled soon became notorious. Discontent culminated in a riot over food; one day the director—called The Father—had to swim ashore for his life, and the police were hastily summoned.

Most immigrants went directly from Castle Garden or Ellis Island to the teeming streets of Manhattan, where they sought relatives or *landsleit* (fellow townsmen) who had gone before them. Easy marks for hucksters and swindlers, they were overcharged by draymen for carrying

their paltry possessions, engaged as strikebreakers, or hired at shamelessly
low wages.

"Greenhorn" or "greener" was their common name. A term of vili-
fication, the source of a thousand cruel jokes, it was their shame and their
destiny. On top of everything else, the immigrants had to abide the contempt of their co-religionists who had preceded them to America by forty
or fifty years. By the time the heavy East European immigration set in,
German Jews had achieved high mercantile status and an uneasy integration into American society. They did not want to be reminded of their
kinship with these uncouth and impoverished Jews who were regarded
vaguely as a kind of Oriental influx. There was a good deal of sentiment
against "aiding such paupers to emigrate to these shores." One charitable
organization declared: "Organized immigration from Russia, Roumania,
and other semi-barbarous countries is a mistake and has proved to be a
failure. It is no relief to the Jews of Russia, Poland, etc., and it jeopardizes
the well-being of the American Jews."

A genuine uptown-downtown split soon developed, with condescen-
sion on one side and resentment on the other. The German Jews objected
as bitterly to the rigid, old-world Orthodoxy of the immigrants as they
did to their new involvement in trade unions. They were fearful, too, of
the competition they would offer in the needle trades. (Indeed, the East
Europeans ultimately forced the uptown Jews out of the industry.) On
the other side of the barricades, Russian Jews complained that at the hands
of their uptown brethren, "every man is questioned like a criminal, is
looked down upon . . . just as if he were standing before a Russian official." Nevertheless, many German Jews responded to the call of conscience by providing funds for needy immigrants and setting up preparatory schools for immigrant children for whom no room was yet available
in the hopelessly overcrowded public schools.

Many comfortably settled German Jews saw dispersion as the answer
to the problem. Efforts were made to divert immigrants to small towns in
other parts of the country, but these were largely ineffective. There were
also some gallant adventures with farming in such remote places as South
Dakota, Oregon, and Louisiana. Though the Jewish pioneers were brave
and idealistic, drought, disease, and ineptitude conspired against them. (In
Oregon, for example, they tried to raise corn in cattle country, while in
Louisiana they found themselves in malarial terrain.) Only chicken farming in New Jersey proved to be successful to any great degree. Farm jobs
for Jews were available, but as one immigrant said: "I have no desire to be
a farm hand to an ignorant Yankee at the end of the world. I would rather
work here at half the price in a factory; for then I would at least be able
to spend my free evenings with my friends."

It was in New York, then, that the bulk of the immigrants settled—
in the swarming, tumultuous Lower East Side—with smaller concentra-
tions in Boston, Philadelphia, and Chicago. Far less adaptable than the
German Jews who were now lording it over them, disoriented and frightened, the East European immigrants constituted a vast and exploited proletariat. According to a survey in 1890, sixty per cent of all immigrant
Jews worked in the needle trades. This industry had gone through a proc-

ess of decentralization in which contractors carried out the bulk of production, receiving merely the cut goods from the manufacturer. Contracting establishments were everywhere in the Lower East Side, including the contractors' homes, where pressers warmed their irons on the very stove on which the boss's wife was preparing supper. The contractors also gave out "section" work to families and *landsleit* who would struggle to meet the quotas at home. The bondage of the sewing machine was therefore extended into the tenements, with entire families enslaved by the machine's voracious demands. The Hester Street "pig market," where one could buy anything, became the labor exchange; there tailors, operators, finishers, basters, and pressers would congregate on Saturday in the hope of being hired by contractors.

Life in the sweatshops of the Lower East Side was hard, but it made immigrants employable from the start, and a weekly wage of five dollars—the equivalent of ten rubles—looked good in immigrant eyes. Moreover, they were among their own kin and kind, and the sweatshops, noisome as they were, were still the scene of lively political and even literary discussions. (In some cigar-making shops, in fact, the bosses hired "readers" to keep the minds of the workers occupied with classic and Yiddish literature as they performed their repetitive chores.) East European Jews, near the end of the century, made up a large part of the skilled labor force in New York, ranking first in twenty-six out of forty-seven trades, and serving, for example, as bakers, building-trade workers, painters, furriers, jewellers, and tinsmiths.

Almost one quarter of all the immigrants tried their hands as tradesmen—largely as peddlers or as pushcart vendors in the madhouse bazaar of the Lower East Side. For some it was an apprenticeship in low-toned commerce that would lead to more elegant careers. For others it was merely a martyrdom that enabled them to subsist. It was a modest enough investment—five dollars for a license, one dollar for a basket, and four dollars for wares. They stocked up on pins and needles, shoe laces, polish, and handkerchiefs, learned some basic expressions ("You wanna buy somethin'?"), and were on their hapless way.

It was the professions, of course, that exerted the keenest attraction to Jews, with their reverence for learning. For most of them it was too late; they had to reconcile themselves to more humble callings. But it was not too late for their children, and between 1897 and 1907, the number of Jewish physicians in Manhattan rose from 450 to 1,000. Of all the professions it was medicine that excited the greatest veneration. (Some of this veneration spilled over into pharmacy, and "druggists" were highly respected figures who were called upon to prescribe for minor—and even major—ills, and to serve as scribes for the letters that the immigrants were unable to read and write themselves.) There were Jewish lawyers on the Lower East Side and by 1901 over 140 Jewish policemen, recruited in part by Theodore Roosevelt, who, as police commissioner, had issued a call for "the Maccabee or fighting Jewish type."

The Lower East Side was the American counterpart of the ghetto for Jewish immigrants, as well as their glittering capital. At its peak, around 1910, it packed over 350,000 people into a comparatively small area—

roughly from Canal Street to Fourteenth Street—with as many as 523 people per acre, so that Arnold Bennett was moved to remark that "the architecture seemed to sweat humanity at every window and door." The most densely populated part of the city, it held one sixth of Manhattan's population and most of New York's office buildings and factories. "Uptowners" used to delight in visiting it (as a later generation would visit Harlem) to taste its exotic flavor. But the great mass of Jews lived there because the living was cheap, and there was a vital Jewish community that gave solace to the lonely and comfort to the pious.

A single man could find lodgings of a sort, including coffee morning and night, for three dollars a month. For a family, rent was about ten dollars a month, milk was four cents a quart, kosher meat twelve cents a pound, bread two cents a pound, herring a penny or two. A kitchen table could be bought for a dollar, chairs at thirty-five cents each. One managed, but the life was oppressive. Most families lived in the notorious "dumbbell" flats of old-law tenements (built prior to 1901). Congested, often dirty and unsanitary, these tenements were six or seven stories high and had four apartments on each floor. Only one room in each three or four room apartment received direct air and sunlight, and the families on each floor shared a toilet in the hall.

Many families not only used their flats as workshops but also took in boarders to make ends meet. Jacob Riis tells of a two-room apartment on Allen Street which housed parents, six children, and six boarders. "Two daughters sewed clothes at home. The elevator railway passed by the window. The cantor rehearses, a train passes, the shoemaker bangs, ten brats run around like goats, the wife putters. . . . At night we all try to get some sleep in the stifling, roach-infested two rooms." In the summer, the tenants spilled out onto fire escapes and rooftops, which were converted into bedrooms.

Nevertheless, life on the Lower East Side had surprising vitality. Despite the highest population density in the city, the Tenth Ward had one of the lowest death rates. In part, this was because of the strenuous personal cleanliness of Jews, dictated by their religion. Though only eight per cent of the East European Jews had baths, bathhouses and steam rooms on the Lower East Side did a booming business. There was, of course, a heavy incidence of tuberculosis—"the white plague." Those who were afflicted could be heard crying out, *"Luft! Gib mir luft!"* ("Air! Give me air!"). It was, in fact, this terror of "consumption" that impelled some East Side Jews to become farmers in the Catskills at the turn of the century, thus forerunning the gaudy career of the Catskill Borscht Belt resort hotels. The same fear impelled Jews on the Lower East Side to move to Washington Heights and the Bronx, where the altitude was higher, the air presumably purer.

Alcoholism, a prime affliction of most immigrant groups, was almost unknown among Jews. They drank ritualistically on holidays but almost never to excess. They were, instead, addicted to seltzer or soda water— Harry Golden's "2¢ plain"—which they viewed as "the worker's champagne." The suicide rate was relatively low, though higher than in the *shtetl,* and there was always a shudder of sympathy when the Yiddish press announced that someone had *genumen di ges* (taken gas).

The Lower East Side was from the start the scene of considerable crime. But its inhabitants became concerned when the crime rate among the young people seemed to rise steeply around 1910. There was a good deal of prostitution. The dancing academies, which achieved popularity early in this century, became recruiting centers for prostitutes. In 1908–9, of 581 foreign women arrested for prostitution, 225 were Jewish. There was the notorious Max Hochstim Association, which actively recruited girls, while the New York Independent Benevolent Association—an organization of pimps—provided sick benefits, burial privileges, bail, and protection money for prostitutes. The membership was even summoned to funerals with a two-dollar fine imposed on those who did not attend. Prostitution was so taken for granted that Canal Street had stores on one side featuring sacerdotal articles, while brothels were housed on the other.

Family life on the Lower East Side was cohesive and warm, though there was an edge of shrillness and hysteria to it. Marriages were not always happy, but if wives were viewed as an affliction, children were regarded as a blessing. The kitchen was the center of the household, and food was almost always being served to either family or visitors. No matter how poor they were, Jewish families ate well—even to excess—and mothers considered their children woefully underweight unless they were well cushioned with fat.

It was a life with few conventional graces. Handkerchiefs were barely known, and the Yiddish newspapers had to propagandize for their use. Old men smelled of snuff, and in spite of bathing, children often had lice in their hair and were sent home from school by the visiting nurse for a kerosene bath. Bedbugs were considered an inevitability, and pajamas were viewed as an upper-class affectation. Parents quarrelled bitterly— with passionate and resourceful invective—in the presence of their children. Telephones were virtually unknown, and a telegram surely meant disaster from afar.

The zeal of the immigrants on behalf of their children was no less than awe-inspiring. Parents yearned for lofty careers for their offspring, with medicine as the pinnacle. In better-off homes, there was always a piano ("solid mahogany"), and parents often spent their precious reserves to arrange a "concert" for their precocious youngsters, often followed by a ball in one of the Lower East Side's many halls.

To be sure, the children inspired a full measure of anxiety in their parents. "Amerikane kinder" was the rueful plaint of the elders, who could not fathom the baffling new ways of the young. Parents were nervous about their daughters' chastity, and younger brothers—often six or seven years old—would be dispatched as chaperones when the girls met their boy friends. There was uneasiness about Jewish street gangs and the growing problem of delinquency. The old folks were vexed by the new tides of secularism and political radicalism that were weaning their children from traditional pieties. But most of all, they feared that their sons would not achieve the success that would redeem their own efforts, humiliations, and failures in the harsh new land. Pressure on their children was relentless. But on the whole the children did well, astonishingly well. "The ease and rapidity with which they learn," Jacob Riis wrote, "is equalled only by their good behavior and close attention while in school. There is no whispering and no rioting at these desks." Samuel Chotzinoff, the music critic, tells a story which reveals the attitude of the Jewish schoolboy. When an altercation threatened between Chotzinoff and a classmate, his antagonist's reaction was to challenge him to spell "combustible."

The Lower East Side was a striking demonstration that financial want does not necessarily mean cultural poverty. The immigrant Jews were nearly always poor and often illiterate, but they were not culturally deprived. In fact, between 1890 and World War I, the Jewish community provides a remarkable chapter in American cultural history. Liberated from the constrictions of European captivity, immigrant Jews experienced a great surge of intellectual vitality. Yiddish, the Hebrew-German dialect which some people had casually dismissed as a barbarous "jargon," became the vehicle of this cultural renascence. Between 1885 and 1914, over 150 publications of all kinds made their appearance. But the new Yiddish journalism reached its apogee with the *Jewish Daily Forward* under the long editorial reign of Abraham Cahan. The *Forward* was humanitarian, pro-labor, and socialistic. But it was also an instrument for acclimatizing immigrants in the new environment. It provided practical hints on how to deal with the new world, letters from the troubled (*Bintel Brief*), and even, at one time, a primer on baseball ("explained to nonsports"). The *Forward* also published and fostered an enormous amount of literature in Yiddish—both original works by writers of considerable talent, and translations of classic writers.

In this cultural ferment, immigrants studied English in dozens of night schools and ransacked the resources of the Aguilar Free Library on East Broadway. "When I had [a] book in my hand," an immigrant wrote, "I pressed it to my heart and wanted to kiss it." The Educational Alliance, also on East Broadway, had a rich program designed to make immigrant Jews more American and their sons more Jewish. And there were scores of settlement houses, debating clubs, ethical societies, and literary circles which attracted the young. In fact, courtships were carried on in a rarefied atmosphere full of lofty talk about art, politics, and philosophy. And though there was much venturesome palaver about sexual freedom, actual behavior tended to be quite strait-laced.

But the most popular cultural institution was the café or coffee house, which served as the Jewish saloon. There were about 250 of them, each with its own following. Here the litterateurs sat for hours over steaming glasses of tea; revolutionaries and Bohemians gathered to make their pronouncements or raise money for causes; actors and playwrights came to hold court. For immigrant Jews, talk was the breath of life itself. The passion for music and theatre knew no bounds. When Beethoven's Ninth Symphony was performed one summer night in 1915, mounted police had to be summoned to keep order outside Lewisohn Stadium, so heavy

was the press of crowds eager for the twenty-five-cent stone seats.
Theatre (in Yiddish) was to the Jewish immigrants what Shakespeare and
Marlowe had been to the groundlings in Elizabethan England. Tickets
were cheap—twenty-five cents to one dollar—and theatregoing was universal. It was a raucous, robust, and communal experience. Mothers
brought their babies (except in some of the "swellest" theatres, which for-
bade it), and peddlers hawked their wares between the acts. There were
theatre parties for trade unions and *landsmanschaften* (societies of fellow
townsmen), and the audience milled around and renewed old friendships
or argued the merits of the play. The stage curtain had bold advertisements
of stores or blown-up portraits of stars.

There was an intense cult of personality in the Yiddish theatre and a
system of claques not unlike that which exists in grand opera today. The
undisputed monarch was Boris Thomashefsky, and a theatre program of
his day offered this panegyric:

> Tomashefsky! Artist great!
> No praise is good enough for you!
> Of all the stars you remain the king
> You seek no tricks, no false quibbles;
> One sees truth itself playing.
> Your appearance is godly to us
> Every movement is full of grace
> Pleasing is your every gesture
> Sugar sweet your every turn
> You remain the king of the stage
> Everything falls to your feet.

Many of the plays were sentimental trash—heroic "operas" on historical themes, "greenhorn" melodramas full of cruel abandonments and
tearful reunions, romantic musicals, and even topical dramas dealing with
such immediate events as the Homestead Strike, the Johnstown Flood, and
the Kishinev Pogrom of 1903. Adaptability and a talent for facile plagiar-
ism were the essence of the playwright's art in those days, and "Professor"
Moses Horwitz wrote 167 plays, most of them adaptations of old operas
and melodramas. The plays were so predictable that an actor once admitted he didn't even have to learn his lines; he merely had to have a
sense of the general situation and then adapt lines from other plays.

There was, of course, a serious Yiddish drama, introduced principally by Jacob Gordin, who adapted classical and modernist drama to the
Yiddish stage. Jewish intellectuals were jubilant at this development. But
the process of acculturation had its amusing and grotesque aspects. Shakespeare was a great favorite but *"verbessert und vergrossert"* (improved and
enlarged). There was the Jewish *King Lear* in which Cordelia becomes
Goldele. (The theme of filial ingratitude was a "natural" on the Lower
East Side, where parents constantly made heroic sacrifices.) *Hamlet* was
also given a Jewish coloration, the prince becoming a rabbinical student
who returns from the seminary to discover treachery at home. And *A
Doll's House* by Ibsen was transformed into *Minna*, in which a sensitive

and intelligent young woman, married to an ignorant laborer, falls in love with her boarder and ultimately commits suicide.

Related to the Jewish love of theatre was the immigrant's adoration of the cantor, a profession which evoked as much flamboyance and egotistical preening as acting did. (In fact, actors would sometimes grow beards before the high holydays and find jobs as cantors.) Synagogues vied with each other for celebrated cantors, sometimes as a way of getting out of debt, since tickets were sold for the high-holyday services.

The Lower East Side was a vibrant community, full of color and gusto, in which the Jewish immigrant felt marvelously at home, safe from the terrors of the alien city. But it was a setting too for fierce conflict and enervating strain. There were three major influences at work, each pulling in a separate direction: Jewish Orthodoxy, assimilationism, and the new socialist gospel. The immigrants were Orthodox, but their children tended to break away. *Cheders* (Hebrew schools) were everywhere, in basements and stores and tenements, and the old custom of giving a child a taste of honey when he was beginning to learn to read—as symbolic of the sweetness of study—persisted. But the young, eager to be accepted into American society, despised the old ways and their "greenhorn" teachers. Fathers began to view their sons as "free-thinkers," a term that was anathema to them. Observance of the Law declined, and the Saturday Sabbath was ignored by many Jews. A virulent antireligious tendency developed among many "enlightened" Jews, who would hold profane balls on the most sacred evening of the year—Yom Kippur—at which they would dance and eat nonkosher food. (Yom Kippur is a fast day.) And the trade-union movement also generated uneasiness among the pious elders of the Lower East Side. "Do you want us to bow down to your archaic God?" a radical newspaper asked. "Each era has its new Torah. Ours is one of freedom and justice."

But for many immigrants the basic discontent was with their American experience itself. The golden province turned out to be a place of tenements and sweatshops. A familiar cry was *"a klug af Columbus!"* ("a curse on Columbus") or, "Who ever asked him, Columbus, to discover America?" Ellis Island was called *Trernindzl* (Island of Tears), and Abraham Cahan, in his initial reaction to the horrors of immigration, thundered: "Be cursed, immigration! Cursed by those conditions which have brought you into being. How many souls have you broken, how many courageous and mighty souls have you shattered." The fact remains that most Jewish immigrants, in the long run, made a happy adjustment to their new land.

After 1910, the Lower East Side went into a decline. Its strange glory was over. New areas of Jewish settlement opened up in Brooklyn, the Bronx, and in upper Manhattan. By the mid-twenties, less than ten per cent of New York's Jews lived on the Lower East Side, although it still remained the heartland to which one returned to shop, to see Yiddish theatre, and to renew old ties. By 1924 Jewish immigration into the United States was severely reduced by new immigration laws, and the saga of mass immigration was done. But the intensities of the Jewish immigrant experience had already made an indelible mark on American culture and history that would endure for many years.

Patent Medicine Advertising in the Late Nineteenth Century

JAMES HARVEY YOUNG

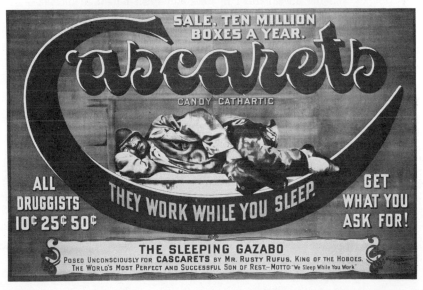

Most Americans at one time or another in their lives use proprietary medicines—remedies for ill health that are dispensed without a
doctor's prescription. These medicines run from the simple, like milk
of magnesia, to the complex. Their primary function, and the characteristic that they share in common, is to make a profit for the manufacturer. The term "patent medicine" is often used for these preparations because the manufacturer holds a patent for the formula that
prohibits its duplication by others, unlike the standard prescription
compounds that can be prepared by any licensed pharmacist.

In simpler times most medicines were composed of natural substances, usually herbs or roots, and had evolved after years of trial
and error. The formulas for these medicines were passed down from
generation to generation, and their possession often elevated their
owners to special status in the communities in which they lived. These
people were the medicine men, or doctors, in their cultures, and,
given the low level of scientific medical knowledge prior to the twentieth century, people were usually better off in consulting an herbal
doctor than one who claimed to be more scientific.

The growth of scientific medicine in the late nineteenth century,
however, led to a corresponding growth in scientific pharmacology in
the United States. Doctors and pharmacists attempted to control the
quality and quantity of the medicines ingested by the public and developed the now widespread practice of prescription medicine. But at
the same time there was a tremendous growth in the patent medicine
field. Part of this growth can be credited to the cultural nationalism of
the early nineteenth century that led to the rejection of imported compounds and the development of new, American patent medicines—
made in America for Americans—which were produced and promoted
with the classic nineteenth-century entrepreneurial skill. Among other
things, this meant that while a few manufacturers got rich, very rich,
most either failed or managed a bare existence in the proprietary
medicine industry.

In his history of the patent medicine business in nineteenth-
century America, James Harvey Young of Emory University, stresses
the importance of advertising. As the middle of the nineteenth century approached, it was clear that the key to success was not to be in
the efficacy of the nostrum, but in the effectiveness of the advertising.
And after the advent of the penny press and the popular magazines
the advertising budget became the most important item in the
production process. In the selection reprinted below, Young analyzes
the advertising appeals of the proprietary medicine industry, showing
the variety of nostrums offered to the public and giving some idea of

the extravagant claims made for the products. Many of the advertising devices employed in the nineteenth century—testimonials of near miraculous cures; statements of endorsement by doctors, either real or fraudulent; dubious medical advice; and so forth—continue in use in patent medicine advertising today.

While many of the patent medicines of the nineteenth century were relatively harmless, some of the most popular contained either addictive or dangerous substances—mercury, opium, alcohol, or cocaine. Alcohol was the basic ingredient of many patent medicines well into the twentieth century. In fact, in the early days of liquor regulations, it was determined that some nostrums could be sold by the bottle as medicine or by the drink as liquor.

The first stage in federal regulation of proprietary medicines came in 1906 with passage of the Pure Food and Drug Act. This act required that manufacturers not lie about the contents of their product and that they list on the label the dangerous substances in the medicine. Further than that the law did not go.

While patent medicine advertising is not as excessive in content today as it was a century ago, it is, at the least, as ubiquitous, and the advertising budget remains an important item in the production process. The American people seem determined to continue to enrich the proprietary medicine manufacturers even in the face of increasingly scientific and effective medical practice.

"The advertising quack . . . is the black wolf, aye, the Bengal tiger of the profession. . . . He is full of shrewdness and cunning, and knows poor, weak human nature like a book."

—DR. WILLIS P. KING, 1882 [1]

The next stage in the narrative of patent medicines in America concerns an expanding criticism that leads to restrictive laws. Before turning to these events, let us pause for some analysis. The psychology of patent medicine advertising is important because of both its priority and its variety.

Nostrum manufacturers turned to ingenious advertising before other manufacturers did because they had to. So long as the demand for a product exceeded the supply, as David Potter has pointed out, the role

"The Pattern of Patent Medicine Appeals" (Editor's title: "Patent Medicine Advertising in the Late Nineteenth Century"), in James Harvey Young, *The Toadstool Millionaires: A Social History of Patent Medicines in America Before Federal Regulations* (copyright © 1961 by Princeton University Press; Princeton Paperback, 1972), pp. 165–89. Reprinted by permission of Princeton University Press.

[1] King, *Quacks and Quackery in Missouri* (St. Louis, 1882), 6.

of advertising could be simple and unsophisticated.[2] Retailers could insert into newspapers the simple message: "Here it is. Come and get it." Customers would hurry to the store. Manufacturers, disposing of their output easily, had no need to go to the expense of advertising and of differentiating their products from those of other producers making the same things. Not until the amazing development of manufacturing capacity brought supply abreast of demand, in the decades following the Civil War, were most American producers really confronted with the problem of competitive selling in an economy of abundance. Then those who processed food and made soap and manufactured bicycles began to take lessons from the remedy vendor.

The medicine man had something to teach because he had operated in an economy of abundance almost from the start. Since sickness was well-nigh universal, the demand for his wares was potentially inexhaustible. But then, so also was the supply. At least from the days of the four Lees and Thomas Dyott, American production of proprietary remedies was off to a fast start. There was no end to the variety and quantity of ingredients available, and there were soon more pills and potions than Americans could swallow conveniently. The medicine man's key task quickly became not production but sales, the job of persuading ailing citizens to buy his particular brand from among the hundreds offered. Whether unscrupulous or self-deluded, nostrum makers set about this task with cleverness and zeal.

Another reason for pioneering by patent medicine promoters in the psychology of advertising lay in the goal of the customers. They wanted to regain or to preserve their health. Problems relating to disease are complex, and the thinking about them in the 19th century was extremely confused. There was more to the matter than whether a hat fit or an axe cut. These circumstances gave the remedy maker plenty of elbow room for subtlety.

Many examples of the remedy promoter's ingenuity have been cited in the preceding pages. Here the purpose is to present in a systematic way the pattern of appeals made to would-be customers, as that pattern emerges from a study of the nostrum advertising of more than a century. There were fads and vogues in the presentation of packaged remedies to the public, as earlier chapters reveal, yet these were often changes rung on basic themes. Certain fundamental appeals appeared over and over again.

The first requirement for success in a competitive world, as Dyott and Swaim, Brandreth and Helmbold, were quick to realize, was: Be known. Unless the identity of the product was firmly fixed in the minds of those who might buy, there was no hope. This called for lavish advertising. Patent medicine men confronted the American citizen as he read his mail, as he perused the paper, as he strolled the streets, as he traversed the countryside. They devised schemes to slip up on him unaware—the plain envelope, the fake news story. They struck not only slyly but often. One pill was advertised thirty-seven times in the same

[2] Potter, *People of Plenty, Economic Abundance and the American Character* (Chicago, 1954), 166–88.

issue of a paper. Dr. Donald Kennedy's Medical Discovery and Dr. T. Felix Gourard's complexion cure were promoted, year in and year out, without the slightest change in copy, for over forty years.[3]

The impact of repetition was strengthened if the product name was memorable. Some proprietors turned to alliteration, and the sick could dose themselves well-nigh through the alphabet, from Burdock Blood Bitters to Swift's Sure Specific. That the names of medicines, year after year, were printed in the same distinctive type induced a feeling of familiarity. Pictorial symbols served the same function. The trade-mark, indeed, was a fixed star in a universe of flux. The ownership of medicines might change again and again, and so might the formula. The diseases for which medicines were advertised might vary over time, and sometimes even names were altered. Trade-marks, however, protected first by common law and then by federal statute, endured forever. Radway's ministering angel and Lydia Pinkham's maternal countenance were known to generations.[4]

The would-be purchaser of any product wants assurance that it will serve the purpose for which intended. Would a remedy cure? The proprietor answered, of course, with a resounding yes. And he often added that the cure was sure, swift, and safe. In the very names of nostrums these basic traits were underlined: Dr. Sweet's Infallible Liniment, Comstock's Dead Shot Pellets, Pronto, Warner's Safe Cure.[5] Many lines of copy were devoted to reiterating the same assurances. Merely to state, no matter how emphatically, that a remedy could cure, was not enough. The reader was a cagey customer, and he wanted proof.

The manufacturer was called upon, in one way or another, to trot out his credentials. Flamboyance of personality could be a sales asset, as the antics of Henry T. Helmbold reveal. Yet no matter how lively the promoter or how lavish his headquarters, persuasiveness has seemed to require that he stand with at least one foot planted somewhere within the broad domain of medicine.

This remedy is worthy, countless advertisements have claimed, because its proprietor is a member of one of the healing professions, a doctor, a druggist, a nurse. Many patent medicines, in truth, were made by physicians and pharmacists—to the despair of their colleagues—and other proprietary formulas did not vary significantly from formulas in official volumes. By no means all, however, of the packaged remedies seeking shelter under reputable medicine's tent have had even these slim excuses for being there. The title of doctor has been appropriated, time and time again, with no justification whatever. The name and fame of noted scientists have been stolen to give the posture of greatness to the quack. Soon

[3] Ticknor, *A Popular Treatise on Medical Philosophy* [New York, 1838], 277; Rowell, *Forty Years an Advertising Agent* [New York, 1926], 387; Hower, *The History of an Advertising Agency* [Cambridge, rev. ed., 1949], 296, 298.

[4] Rowell, 390; Paul, *The Law of Trade-Marks* [St. Paul, 1903].

[5] Advertising materials in the Landauer Coll., N.-Y. Hist. Soc.; Pronto listed in Amer. Med. Assoc., *Nostrums and Quackery*, III, 140. In this chapter the three volumes in this set are cited as N&Q with the appropriate volume number.

after Paul Ehrlich announced the discovery of salversan for treating venereal disease, a New York charlatan marketed a blood poison cure,
usurping not only the German bacteriologist's name, but even his famous
formula number, "606." [6]

By many ruses have quacks sought to convince the public of their
medical respectability. "The common method of supporting barefaced
imposture at the present day . . . ," wrote Oliver Wendell Holmes in the
1840's, "consists in trumping up 'Dispensaries,' 'Colleges of Health,' and
other advertising charitable clap-traps, which use the poor as decoy-ducks
for the rich." James Morison, in selling his Vegetable Universal Medicines
in America, boasted of his British College of Health. Even if no son of
Uncle Sam could equal the London grocer who swore in court that he
had taken 18,000 of Morison's pills, still the American market was flourishing. American nostrum makers, imitating Morison, institutionalized
themselves into medical dignity. In Philadelphia William Wright had a
North American College of Health, and in Cleveland W. H. Libby had
an Indian Medical Infirmary.[7]

Another practice widespread among quacks was the distribution of
books and pamphlets giving medical advice. Since colonial days Americans had been accustomed to consult home treatment volumes compiled
by doctors and sold by apothecaries. Early in the 19th century, nostrum
makers began to trespass on this field. Selling the booklets cheaply, or
giving them away, proprietors followed the familiar format, listing health
hazards from ague to wounds. When it came to suggested therapy, of
course, something besides the customary simples was prescribed. Moffat's
Medical Manual and Haas' Every Man His Own Physician are examples
of the art, and in 1875 came The People's Common Sense Medical Adviser
in Plain English. Published by Ray Vaughn Pierce of Buffalo, a doctor
who had a Favorite Prescription and was responsible for a Golden Medical Discovery, this compilation of "common sense" was to go through a
hundred editions in the course of sixty years.[8]

Nostrum makers donned the medical mantle in other ways. They
larded their advertising with quotations—or misquotations—from medical
authorities. They simulated "The Doctor's Advice" columns in the newspapers. They buried in what appeared to be straightforward counsel on
health a purportedly innocent formula, although one of the ingredients,
with a high-sounding pharmacopoeial name, was really a proprietary article. They stood with the angels and shouted, in tones of loftiest medical
rectitude, anathemas at the devilish quacks. In 1890 the makers of Vin

[6] Daniel Drake, a letter on quackery, Sep. 15, 1846, printed in an unidentified journal,
    1858, clipping in Toner Coll., Rare Book Div., Library of Congress; N&Q, II,
    114–16.
[7] Holmes, Medical Essays [Boston, 1892], 87; Morison, Practical Proofs of the Sound-
    ness of the Hygeian System (3rd ed., N.Y., 1832), in N.Y. Academy of Med.; N.Y.
    Sun, Mar. 30, 1837; Wright brochure in Rare Book Div., Library of Congress;
    Libby, The Indian Hygiena (Cleveland, 1865).
[8] Moffat (N.Y., 1839); Haas (N.Y., 1853); Pierce, 1st ed. in N.Y. Academy of Med.
    and 100th in Ntl. Library of Med.

Mariani mailed to doctors a pamphlet entitled "The Effrontery of Proprietary Medicine Advertisers." What at first glance looked like another professional blast at the enemy turned out to be an ingenious self-bestowed blessing upon an alcoholic concoction containing coca leaves.[9]

Yet, in their concern for medical science, the nostrum makers displayed a curious ambivalence. While seeking to ally with it, they must at the same time condemn. While borrowing the prestige of the physician, the patent medicine men must also traduce him. While appropriating the merits of medical knowledge, they need not feel responsible for its shortcomings. Quackery, as usual, could have things both ways.

Year after year nostrum advertisers told the layman about the failings of the doctors. Wherever regular physicians were weak, lo, there the nostrum maker was strong. Their therapy was brutal, his was mild. Their treatment was costly, his was cheap. Their procedures were mysterious, his were open. Their prescriptions were in Latin, his label could be read by all. Their attack on illness was temporizing, his was quick. Their approaches were cumbersome, his were simple. Their techniques led to the grave, his never failed. Most nostrums were like Louis Goelicke's Matchless Sanative, the very "Conqueror of Physicians." [10]

Why, if a nostrum was as sure and swift at curing as its maker kept asserting, did not regular physicians quickly adopt it? Because doctors—at least some of them—did not want to cure people. They got more profit from keeping the patient sick. "Most doctors prescribe BAD-EM SALZ," its manufacturer told the public, "but some of them don't. One doctor, more honest than the rest, explained it this way: 'BAD-EM SALZ? Yes, I used to prescribe it a great deal, but I stopped. Why? Simply because the patients didn't come back to me. If I had kept on they would all have been taking BAD-EM SALZ and getting well without my assistance!' " [11]

Thus many regular physicians, as the quacks would have it, were deliberately selfish in opposing patent medicines. Others were enmeshed in the tangled coils of their stodgy profession, practicing by rote what they had learned, unable to detect a new idea when they saw one. Hence they were blind to the one dazzling new discovery that was destined to end forever the pain and suffering of disease.

Over and over again, throughout the history of patent medicines, promoters have pierced through the darkness yet enshrouding illness and come up with the perfect remedy. They have done so, often, by conceiving a completely new theory of disease, a monistic theory with a one-shot therapy, and the panacea is the medicine advertised. Benjamin Brandreth had found the root of all illness in constipation, and he sought to purge mankind to health. Dr. Donald Kennedy advanced a bloodhound theory of medicine. "My Medical Discovery," he advertised, "seldom takes hold of two people alike! Why? Because no two people have the same weak spot. Beginning at the stomach, it goes searching through the

[9] N&Q, I, 628; II, 186, 203; the Vin Mariani pamphlet in Toner Coll.
[10] Goelicke poster in Landauer Coll.
[11] N&Q, II, 185.

body for any hidden humor. . . . Perhaps it's only a little sediment left on a nerve or in a gland; the Medical Discovery slides it right along, and you find quick happiness from the first bottle. Perhaps it's a big sediment or open sore, well settled somewhere, ready to fight. The Medical Discovery begins this fight, and you think it pretty hard; but soon you thank me for making something that has reached your weak spot."[12]

Hundreds of similar theories have bestrewn the pathway of American pseudo-medicine, each of them a discovery "of far more reaching importance than those obtained by Koch or Pasteur" [13] or whatever genuine scientist held highest public esteem at the moment of bottling. The springboard for the leap to truth has not always been located within the human body, in bowel or kidney or blood. Science is a broad domain, and the nostrum man has been quick to base his monistic concept on an exciting event occurring in any of science's provinces. He has dogged the botanist's footsteps, grabbing a new plant or seeing new virtue in an old one. Tobacco and coffee, maple sugar and pineapple, asparagus and celery, are among the bounties from nature exploited by the patent medicine man. Dr. Miles' Compound Extract of Tomato, a big seller in the 1830's, made catsup a sovereign remedy for mankind's ills.[14]

The mineral realm, too, provided the nostrum maker with happy inspirations. "So deep was the faith in iron" during the early Industrial Revolution, Lewis Mumford has written, "that it was . . . a favorite form of medicine, chosen as much for its magical association with strength as for any tangible benefits." In this spirit American males were urged to overcome sexual weakness by swallowing Aromatic Lozenges of Steel. Creosote had earlier been exploited as a cure for cancer, but as a panacea it did not rank with petroleum. In the 1840's when the dark greasy liquid began to foul his salt wells, Samuel M. Kier hauled it twenty miles to Pittsburgh, poured it into bottles, and called it "THE MOST WONDERFUL REMEDY EVER DISCOVERED!" "The lame . . . were made to walk—the blind to see." Kier soon had more oil than he could handle medicinally, and he succeeded in refining some so that it would burn and cast a light. Thus he became a pioneer in an industry much greater than he could have imagined when he issued a circular praising petroleum in verse:

> The healthful balm from Nature's secret spring,
> The bloom of health, and life, to man will bring;

[12] *Frank Leslie's Popular Monthly*, 43 (1897), back cover.
[13] N&Q, ii, 145.
[14] Wyndham B. Blanton, *Medicine in Virginia in the Seventeenth Century* (Richmond, 1930), 111; Turner, *The Shocking History of Advertising!* [New York, 1953], 24, 54–55, 282–83; Shryock, *The Development of Modern Medicine* [New York, 1947], 20; Dr. Talbot's Concentrated Medical Pineapple Cider, *Harper's Wkly.*, 8 (1864), 687; Dr. Butler's Asparagus Bitters, Thompson, *Bitters Bottles* [Watkins Glen, N.Y., 1947], 21; Celery Compound handbill, Landauer Coll.; Pickard and Buley, *The Midwest Pioneer* [New York, 1946], 282–83.

As from her depths the magic liquid flows,
To calm our sufferings, and assuage our woes.[15]

Elisha Perkins' metallic tractors had many heirs. The advertising pages of American history abound with Magnetic Fluids and Galvanic Belts, Electric Insoles and Electro-Magnetic Wrist-Bands, plus an infinite variety of cravats, pillows, anklets, elbow pads, necklaces, head-caps, corsets, combs, and infernal machines by which magnetic entrepreneurs have tried to transmit healing potency to the ailing human frame. The young lady suffering from sick headache who sought help in the late 19th century from the Electrikure, put the shiny silver cylinder in a crock of water, moved the switch to position six, attached coin-sized discs to her wet ankle with elastic bands, and leaned back in a chair. She did not know that the green wires carried no current, that the metal cylinder was heavy from crushed rock.[16]

The apparatus of the chemist, with its bubbling retorts and test tubes filled with bright and foaming liquids, has brought to nostrum advertising the awesome authority of the laboratory. Not only complicated formulas of the chemist's compounding, but also simplified essences of his analysis, have poured into patent medicine bottles. The basic elements of the universe itself have gone to the aid of suffering humanity. Dr. Judge's Oxy-Hydrogenated Air cured catarrh, deafness, and consumption when sucked or sniffed through a tube from the bottle in which it was confined. The National Ozone Company prepared twenty-four different remedies ranging from an ozone specific for cholera to an ozone tonic for the uterus.[17]

Oxygen has had its tens, but radium has had its hundreds. Quick to exploit the discovery of the Curies was Dr. Rupert Wells, and even his name was fake. He called his medicine Radol, labeled it as "radium impregnated," and advertised it as a "marvelous radiotized fluid" which

---

[15] Mumford, *Technics and Civilization* (N.Y., 1934), 164; Wootton, *Chronicles of Pharmacy*, II |London, 1910|, 367; *N.Y. Eve. Post*, Jan. 5, 1804; Pickard and Buley, 282; *Carpenter's Annual Medical Advertiser* (Phila., 1836); John F. Fulton, "The Impact of Science on American History," *Isis*, 42 (1951), 187–88; *Dictionary of American Biography*, x, 371–72; Paul H. Giddens, *Early Days of Oil* (Princeton, 1948), 3; Giddens, *Pennsylvania Petroleum, 1750–1872* (Titusville, 1947), xi, xii, 17; *Frederick* |Md.| *Examiner*, Jan. 19, 1853; circular reproduced in Giddens, *Early Days*, 3.

[16] *A Treatise on the Application of John H. Tesch & Co.'s Electro-Magnetic Remedies* (Milwaukee, 1866), in the Rare Book Div., Library of Congress; Boston Electro-Pathy Institute broadside, 1859, in Amer. Antiquarian Soc.; Dr. Wm. O. Parmenter's Magnetic Oil poster from the 1840's in the Landauer Coll. The Electrikure No. 2 was made in New York City, rediscovered in Mississippi, and given to the author by Eugene B. Antley.

[17] Dr. Cullen's Vegetable Remedy poster, Rare Book Div., Library of Congress; Judge pamphlet (Boston, 1878), in Ntl. Library of Med.; Oxydonor ad, *Frank Leslie's Popular Monthly*, 43 (1897), 630; *Ozone Era, and Family Physician* (Chicago, 1885), in Chicago Hist. Soc.

would cure cancer in all forms, locations, and stages. Samuel Hopkins Adams, writing in *Collier's*, demurred. "Radol," he said, "contains exactly as much radium as dishwater does, and is about as efficacious in cancer or consumption." The liquid was an acid solution of quinine sulphate with alcohol added, and such a product could be expected to exhibit the bluish fluorescent glow which Wells attributed to radium. Radol was eventually put out of business. But the mysterious and potent new element continued to shed its emanations into the well-filled ranks of quackery. The radium nostrums are a case example of a broader phenomenon in quackery. "For each step forward which science makes, cautiously and limited," wrote Haven Emerson, "there is a curiously distorted shadow of pseudo-science, claiming blindly that now at last the goal is reached, warping out of all proportion the added bit of knowledge." [18]

Botany, chemistry, and electricity have all served their turn. Yet, to the nostrum maker, science has been an even more elastic word. It has encompassed not only the genuinely new but also the old newly rediscovered. The whole realm of the exotic has been a happy hunting ground in which the adventuresome promoter has trapped alluring lore. Millions of medicine bottles have been vended on the authority of faraway places and ancient times.

The itinerant mountebank of the 1740's who persuaded colonists to buy his Chinese Stones was the honored ancestor of a host of oriental descendants. Especially in the mid-19th century, when the European powers were opening up the ancient country, did nostrums flourish bearing such names as Dr. Lin's Celestial Balm of China, Dr. Drake's Canton Chinese Hair Cream, and Carey's Chinese Catarrh Cure. The advertising and labels caught the strangeness of it all. Dr. Lin presented an exquisite engraving of a Chinese sage sitting in an elaborate chair; one servant held a parasol over his worthy head while another brought a bottle of the Balm. Dr. Drake also pictured an oriental scene, bolstered, however, with American verse:

> Our distant brothers, the *Chinese*,
> Long fam'd for their refreshing Teas,
> Produce a *Cream*, so rich and full,
> That clothes with hair the baldest skull.[19]

(The Consul General in Shanghai gave this advice some decades later to would-be American exporters of proprietary remedies: "The favorite

[18] N&Q, I, 68–75; typed ms. entitled "Drug Inspection and Correlated Studies," in folder "Drug Lab (243)," Bur. of Chem., General Correspondence, 1909, Record Group 97, Ntl. Archives; Samuel Hopkins Adams, *The Great American Fraud* (Chicago, 1906), 91. For other versions see N&Q, II, 616; *Radium Water* (East Orange, N.J., 1926), in Yale Med. Library. Emerson cited in Harry H. Moore, *Public Health in the United States* (N.Y., 1923), 167.

[19] *S.C. Gaz.*, Nov. 21, 1743; *Pa. Gaz.*, Oct. 17, 1745; Lin label in Landauer Coll.; Drake pamphlet in Rare Book Div., Library of Congress; a bottle of Carey's remedy in the Rochester (N.Y.) Museum.

design for calendars [advertising patent medicines] used to be an illustration of an old classic tale, but now the Chinese prefer a girl picture either
in semi-Western or Chinese dress.")[20]

In the meantime, however, Americans continued to be fascinated by
the remote. While excitement was high over the depredations of the
Barbary pirates, Ibraham Adam Ben Ali, a Turk or (as an editor thought
more likely) "some crafty native, who has assumed a Turkish name"
went about selling the Incomparable Algerine Medicine for the scurvy.
On the heels of the Mexican War, the Mexican Mustang Liniment became a popular product. At the same time a patent medicine man discovered the exoticism of that distant spoil of war called California. In
the same year that gold was discovered in Sutter's stream, Frederick Fay
sought gold through marketing a proprietary version of a California plant
called Canchalagua. Soon after Commodore Perry had ended Japan's
feudal isolation, an American named Grindle began to sell Japanese Life
Pills, a blood purifier made from a recipe discovered—so he said—by a
common sailor who had been cast away "upon the *mysterious shores of
Japan*" eight years before the Commodore arrived. The Japanese Emperor
was shortly to be one of the recipients of ornate boxes of Cherry Pectoral
especially prepared for donation to foreign sovereigns by James C. Ayer.
Other dignitaries so honored included the Sultan of Turkey, the Queen
of Spain, the King of Siam, the Emperor of China, the President of Peru,
and the Czar of Russia. For the armies of the Czar, Ayer added several
bushels of cathartic pills.[21]

The list of alien areas with which nostrums have been christened
reads like a gazetteer. The hardy soul could dose himself around the
world. What combination of diseases, howsoever dire, could hold out
against such an international therapeutic arsenal as Bragg's Arctic Lini-
ment, Hayne's Arabian Balsam, Bavarian Malt Extract, Brazilian Bitters,
Carpathian Bitters, Castillian Bitters, Crimean Bitters, Kennedy's East
India Bitters, Hoofland's German Tonic, Good Hope Bitters, Hoofland's
Greek Oil, Buchan's Hungarian Balsam, Wyncoop's Iceland Pectoral, Os-
good's Indian Cholagogue, Mecca Compound, Peruvian Syrup, Persian
Balm, Roman Eye Balsam, Redding's Russian Salve, South American
Fever and Ague Remedy, Jayne's Spanish Alterative, Hart's Swedish
Asthma Medicine, Tobias' Venetian Liniment, and Westphalia Stomach
Bitters? [22]

To the ordinary American looking for a remedy to cure his aches
and pains, distance seemed to lend enchantment. Sometimes the magic of

---

[20] Thomas Sammons, "Proprietary Medicine and Ointment Trade in China" (Special
Consular Reports, No. 76, Wash., 1917), 7–8.

[21] *N.Y. Daily Advertiser*, Sep. 18, 1800; *Mexican Mustang Liniment* (n.p., 1850), N.Y.
Academy of Med.; Frederick A. Gay, *Sketches in California . . . also Interesting
Information in Relation to Canchalagua* (n.p., 1848), in the Collection of William
Robertson Coe, Yale Univ. Library; Grindle's brochure in Prints and Photographs
Div., Library of Congress; N&Q, 1, 588; Holcombe, "Private Die Proprietary Stamp
Notes," *Scott's Monthly Jnl.*, Dec. 1937, 348–49.

[22] Many sources, with the bitters chiefly from Thompson.

the faraway was buttressed by folk beliefs to which medicine men could appeal. Everyone knew about Chinese longevity, and Dr. Lin could tout his Chinese Blood Pills by asserting that "such immense ages" resulted from purification of the blood. Everyone knew, too, that Chinese hair was long and black and beautiful, and this gave Dr. Drake a cue in promoting his Canton Chinese Hair Cream. Nor did it take much perception to get the point about Turkish Wafers, advertised with the device of star and crescent and phrases like "For Men Only / Turkish Method / The Sultans / and Harems." [23]

The long ago also had its mysterious appeal. Yadil was an esoteric form of garlic with a history of marvelous cures running back five and a half millennia. Almost as ancient was a Druid Ointment "handed down from . . . mystic days when Stonehenge was a busy temple." Jew David's Honey Coated Pills were imbued with the sanctity of the Holy Land. Dr. M. S. Watson's Great Invincible Birgharmi Stiff Joint Panacea had been recently rediscovered along the Nile. When, in 1880, a genuine Egyptian obelisk was erected in New York's Central Park, a new interest in Egyptology made itself evident among the nostrum makers. Vaseline put out a trade card picturing the obelisk, and Ayer's Sarsaparilla issued a pamphlet describing "A Night with Rameses II." [24]

The glamor of the long ago and the fascination of the faraway united in the American Indian. The Indian, to be sure, had once been both here and now. The fact that he had really contributed so bountifully of his own healing lore to the white European, enriching regular medicine (even unto today) with therapeutic plants, would in itself have prompted a whole host of imitative quacks. Yet the heyday of the Indian vogue in quackery was not to come until the red man had been pushed far to the west. People who dosed themselves with patent "Indian" remedies had never or seldom seen an Indian. If not quite so distant as a Japanese Emperor or so long gone as a Pharaoh, the Indian profited from the same sort of glamor, with a fillip of patriotism—for he was an American —to boot. As earlier he had been for Europeans, so now he became for non-frontier Americans, the noble savage. The romanticizing process represented in the novels of James Fenimore Cooper took place, and at about the same time, on a lower literary level, in patent medicine promotion. Unspoiled creature of Nature's original domain, the Indian was strong, virile, healthy. "The Art of Healing had its origin in the Woods," opined the author of a nostrum pamphlet, "and the Forest is still the best Medical School." From it had come Wright's Indian Vegetable Pills. Upon the wrapper was engraved a symbolical scene: a majestic Indian sat against a mighty tree and gazed across a river, on which churned a side-wheeler, toward a thriving city on the opposite shore. The gift from Nature to Civilization was made explicit, for on a banner held by the Indian were

[23] Turkish Wafer brochure, Landauer Coll.
[24] N&Q, III, 136–37; Thomas H. Jones, "Patent Medicines," *Good Words*, 2 (1861), 371–75; *Frederick* [Md.] *Wkly. Times*, Oct. 4, 1832; Jew David's Pill Wrapper, Rare Book Div., Library of Congress; Pickard and Buley, 280; obelisk items in Landauer Coll.

the words, "Wright's Pills." Another remedy, Southern Balm, made the same point in a different way. It pictured an Indian handing a healing plant to Aesculapius.[25]

Another folk notion was used to bolster the Indian's prowess. Since the best cures for diseases native to a country are always to be found within its borders, and since venereal disease was discovered in America by the sailors of Columbus, then America must be the source of the sovereign remedy for syphilis. After centuries of search, proclaimed one nostrum maker, that blessed cure had now been found. He did not explain why, considering that the sailors had met the ailment in the West Indies, the cure was continental, discovered among "the remnant of the once powerful Cherokee." [26]

From the 1820's onward for a century the Indian strode nobly through the American patent medicine wilderness. Hiawatha helped a hair restorative and Pocahontas blessed a bitters. Dr. Fall spent twelve years with the Creeks to discover why no Indian had ever perished of consumption. Edwin Eastman found a blood syrup among the Comanches, Texas Charley discovered a Kickapoo cure-all, and Frank Cushing pried the secret of a stomach renovator from the Zuni. (Frank, a famous ethnologist, had gone West on a Smithsonian expedition.) Besides these notable accretions to pharmacy, there were Modoc Oil, Seminole Cough Balsam, Nez Perce Catarrh Snuff, and scores more, all doubtless won for the use of white men by dint of great cunning and valor.[27]

Indeed, the Indian vogue in the last half of the 19th century conformed to the traditions of the Wild West and often revealed itself in documents at first glance indistinguishable from dime novels about savages not always quite so noble as they once had been. Both bad Indians and good Indians peopled the pages of the adventure story *The Rescue of Tula* issued in 1859.[28] The hero of this paperback was Dr. Cunard. Son of a wealthy father, the physician had traveled throughout the world seeking cures for the ailments of men. He became fluent in more than thirty languages. He classified more than 10,000 plants in the Rocky Mountains alone. Living for years with various Indian tribes, Cunard met "unheard of perils and hardships, hoping only to benefit his race."

One day while among the Navajoes within the borders of Mexico, the doctor came upon a fearful spectacle. "An Indian girl, with her hair floating in the wind was bound to a stake, and around her was piled the

---

25 Kremers and Urdang, *History of Pharmacy* [Philadelphia, 1940], 128; Wright's pamphlet, Rare Book Div., Library of Congress; Wright wrapper in author's possession; Southern Balm brochure, Prints and Photographs Div., Library of Congress.
26 Cherokee Medicines pamphlet, Landauer Coll.
27 *Harper's Wkly.*, 8 (1864), 128; *Frank Leslie's Popular Monthly*, 43 (1897), 5; *Springfield Ill. State Register*, Nov. 2, 1839; *Captured and Branded by the Comanches* (n.p., 1876), Landauer Coll.; *Life and Scenes among Kickapoo Indians* (New Haven, 189–), and *Almost a Life* (New Haven, 1882?), Coll. of William Robertson Coe, Yale Univ. Library; Oregon Indian Medicine Co. pamphlet, Landauer Coll.; Florida Balm brochure, Prints and Photographs Div., Library of Congress.
28 B. L. Judson & Co., N.Y., in Library of Congress.

fuel, soon to be lighted for her torture." Cunard was frozen by her beauty. "The chisel of Praxiteles never formed a lovelier shape, her face and form were of faultless beauty; but the crowning beauty was her eye; before its lightning glance, her tormentors (soon to be) stood abashed. . . . The chief of the captors begged her to be his squaw."

"Dog of a Navajoe," she replied, "I defy thee. I am the daughter of an Aztec Chief. The Eagle mates not with the thieving Hawk."

The sound of this proud voice awoke Cunard from his rigid trance just as the chief applied the torch. Casting aside botanical specimens, the doctor bounded down the mountainside, scattered the startled Navajoes, hurled aside the burning faggots, cut the binding thongs, and carried the princess to the lodge of the medicine man. Then he turned and confronted the astounded Indians.

"It was well that he did so." For the amazed quiet produced by his bold action had ebbed, and the chief was already fitting an arrow to his bow.

"I demand her for my squaw," Dr. Cunard cried. "The Great Spirit has said it, and I say to you, that if you dare refuse, tomorrow you shall see sudden darkness come at noon-day, and the sun shall change to blood —nay, for a sign that I speak truly, the great sun shall be darkened to-morrow, whether you consent or not. Then keep the girl but twenty-four hours unharmed, and if it does not happen as I say, commit us both to the flames; but if it does so come about, know ye me as the 'Benisontan,' the Great Judge of the pale faces, over whom the 'Manitou' spreads his wing, and whom you cannot harm."

Cunard, of course, had perused an almanac, and when next day his prediction was borne out and his gestures seemed to restore the sun, ceremonies were held in his honor. Then Cunard and Tula set out for her home in a secluded mountain valley. Welcomed for his heroism, the doctor dwelt with the Aztecs for nearly a year. He observed that a powder dispensed by the medicine man prevented any serious sickness among members of the tribe. Begging the formula of the Sachem Tezucho as a boon for having saved his daughter, Cunard was taken in the dark of night through labyrinthine mountain passages to the aged sorceress who alone possessed the secret. Because of his courage, she yielded to his entreaties.

"[It is] a secret," the doctor cries, "that once in my possession, shall *bring healing and strength upon its wings to all the world.*"

Deeper into the mountain must they yet go, to a gloomy cavern containing an altar bearing a golden image of the Sun. Here Cunard takes an oath never to reveal the location of the hidden valley, and here he is shown the six herbs composing the remedy and told their proper proportions. Then, bidding farewell to the last unconquered Aztecs, he departs for the East.

Cunard returns home to find his mother on her deathbed, but the miraculous herbs effect an immediate cure. The news spreads and the demand expands. The doctor cannot compound the remedy fast enough. In order that all who suffer may be healed, Cunard conveys the secret to

B. L. Judson & Co., who now compound it as Judson's Mountain Herb Pills.

According to the pamphlet, Dr. Cunard resumes his investigations "for the cause of science and humanity." But is it too much to hope that he has really returned to Tula, the proud Aztec princess, in her secluded mountain valley, where both of them, partaking now and again of the six magic herbs, remain even now glowing with happiness and radiant with health?

The Indian as symbol for hardihood, the Chinese as symbol for longevity, are but two of many figures from history and mythology who have been called upon to vouch for patent medicines. In word and picture, the blessed name of mother has been invoked, nor has grandmother's proverbial wisdom been neglected. The strength of the ox, the power of the elephant, the mystic potency of the unicorn, the recuperative zeal of the phoenix—all have served their turn. Angels great and small, though mostly female, have borne glad tidings. Ben Hur has fought for kidney vigor; Ponce de Leon has promised youth's renewal; Jack has killed the Giant Constipation. Knights have gone forth to battle, sometimes with Red Cross emblazoned on their shields.[29]

The mighty of mythology have been invoked. There was a Minerva Pill to conquer syphilis, a Juno Cordial to banish barrenness. Mars and Jupiter were also called upon. Hercules was an impartial hero, going forth to battle in many a nostrum cause besides that of William Swaim. With equal impartiality Hygeia hovered at the elbows of numerous proprietors, and Aesculapius bestowed his blessing far and wide.[30]

As there are symbols of strength to encourage, so are there symbols of evil to frighten. A fearsome array of creatures have slithered and crept through patent medicine advertising, serpents and dragons, fantastic misshapen imps from the nightmares of the damned, even old Beelzebub himself. The demonic might be subtly suggested with mere words. Under the headline, "Reverend Imposter!!!" an advertisement for the Matchless

---

[29] Mother's Friend brochure, Rare Book Div., Library of Congress; N&Q, III, 25; Belmont Med. Soc., *Transactions, for 1850–51,* 50; *Davy's lac-elephantis,* pamphlet cited in *Index-Catalogue of the Library of the Surgeon-General's Office,* series I, IX (Wash., 1888), 57; Unicorn Drops brochure, Prints and Photographs Div., Library of Congress; Moffat's Phoenix Bitters brochure and Baldwin's Infallible Embrocation brochure, Rare Book Div., Library of Congress; *Ayer's American Almanac, 1885;* N&Q, I, 587, and III, 102; Pierce's Pleasant Purgative Pellets poster (Jack) and Dorman's Original Red Cross Bitters brochure, Prints and Photographs Div., Library of Congress.

[30] *Phila. Democratic Press,* Oct. 25, 1827; Dr. Larzetti's Juno Cordial brochure, Rare Book Div., Library of Congress; Mars and Jupiter referred to in Proprietary Assoc., *18th Annual Report,* 184; Potter's Vegetable Catholicon handbill, Landauer Coll.; wrapper for Force, The Master Rebuilder Tonic, Museum of the State Hist. Soc. of Wis.; Morison ad in back of part 20 (May 1855) of William M. Thackeray, *The Newcomes;* Jewett's Health Restoring Bitters poster, Prints and Photographs Div., Library of Congress; Holcombe, "Private Die Proprietaries," *Wkly. Philatelic Gossip,* Aug. 1, 1942, 490, 497.

Sanative told of a New York minister who had been ejected from his church because of improper conduct. This devil's disciple had begun the manufacture, "with his own unholy hands," of a spurious sanative, which he was employing swindling peddlers to palm off on the public. The ex-minister, moreover, had a cloven foot.[31]

The realm of death was replete with symbols, none more awesome than the grim reaper. Whatever dread disease he represented, the robed skeleton, escorting his victim toward an open grave, was a sobering fig-ure. Tombstones stood watch, engraved with skull and crossbones. Yet, despite the atmosphere of almost overwhelming disaster, there still was hope. A knight stood by with sword unsheathed, or an angel hovered ready to reach across the grave to any mortal willing to pay a dollar for the saving remedy.[32]

One gloomy proprietor felt impelled to ransack the caverns of the foreboding. A man is collapsed on the ground, one hand holding his stomach, the other pressed to his despairing face. He lies at the edge of a murky stream, in which crocodiles swim and from which protrudes the skull of a steer. A snake slithers along the bank amidst noxious weeds. Vultures soar overhead, and jagged lightning rends a russet sky, clouds veiling the sun. A grinning skeleton, robed and with scythe, approaches. But, behold, barring his path stands a sturdy maiden, her face aglow, her left arm boldly pushing death away. She is wrapped in a diaphanous robe, but her bosom and midriff are bare, and around the latter she wears Parr's English Pad.[33]

The symbol of evil—simple or compounded—was only one way of frightening a customer into buying a medicine. Nostrum makers found more direct ways of confronting the layman with the grim consequences of inattention to his symptoms. Neglect might bring embarrassment, pain, moral decay, even death itself.

"Humiliating Eruptions" or foul breath could offend friends and lead to social isolation. Baldness could shatter prestige. "How strangely," began an ad for Aldridge's Balm of Columbia, "the loss of . . . [the hair] changes the countenance, and prematurely brings on the appearance of old age, which causes many to recoil at being uncovered, and sometimes even shun society to avoid the jests and sneers of their acquaintance." Maladies of this sort might hurt the purse; an anti-eczema treatment head-lined one appeal: "Preacher Itched So He Had to Quit." Even romance might be jeopardized. Witness the poignant tale of Kate.[34]

---

[31] Dr. Cheever's Life-Root Mucilage brochure, Rare Book Div., Library of Congress; *Ayer's American Almanac, 1859* and *1885*; Dr. Carter broadside, 1844, Amer. Anti-quarian Soc.; Potter's Vegetable Catholicon poster, Landauer Coll.; N&Q, I, 39; Rowell, 388–89; Dr. Jayne's Alterative poster and Wolcott's Instant Pain Annihi-lator poster, Prints and Photographs Div., Library of Congress; *Vandalia Ill. Sentinel*, Mar. 14, 1840.

[32] N&Q, I, 96, and II, 96; Von Graef Sexual Troche pamphlet, Toner Coll.; Folger's Hygeiangelos pamphlet, Ntl. Library of Med.

[33] Landauer Coll.

[34] *Harper's Wkly.*, 29 (1885), 414; *Springfield Ill. State Register*, Oct. 12, 1839; N&Q, II, 622; Dr. I. J. O'Brien ad, *N.Y. Herald*, Mar. 1, 1860.

Kate never smiles, no happy thought
  Lights up her pensive eye,
The merry laugh from lip to lip
  Passes unheeded by.
Frozen forever is her heart,
  The sparkling fount of gladness,
And o'er it pours in rapid flood
  The ebon wave of sadness.

She never smiles, has frowning grief
  With her stern magic bound her?
Has care her long lean finger raised,
  To cast her fetter round her?
Has one so young the lesson learned,
  That love is oft betrayed?
Ah no! she never smiles because—
  Her front teeth are decayed!

Worse than humiliation was pain. In vivid prose and grim picture, nostrum makers displayed the epileptic falling in the path of a speeding vehicle, the heart sufferer tumbling from a ladder, the madman flailing his arms against the bars of his cell, the cancer victim with nose and cheek eaten away. Nor were externals enough. The body was entered, explored, dissected, its hideous lesions revealed for all to see. It mattered not that Dr. Haines, whose Golden Remedy would "cure" the liquor habit, had stolen his hob-nailed liver from a temperance poster; it was just as sobering for all that. The many worms that dwelt in man's insides were displayed with all their sinuous convolutions, staring at the reader with big round eyes. Happily there was no cut to illustrate one advertising headline: "Another Monster Parasite Over Sixty Feet Long." Expert illustrators were well paid to draw horrendous worms and germs, and to change photographs so as to fake or intensify the ravages of cancer and other dire maladies.[35]

Diseased organs printed on a flat surface in black and white were frightening enough. In three dimensions and with color added they were worse. Profiting from such a morbid lure were anatomical museums, a quack venture that flourished in the dingier streets of cities. The New-York Museum of Anatomy issued a catalog in 1868 listing its 2,167 exhibits. "Here . . . are presented," the proprietors announced, "the nu-

---

[35] McAlister's Ointment pamphlet and Beekman's Pumonic Syrup poster, Rare Book Div., Library of Congress; *Alarming Truths* (N.Y., 1891), Toner Coll.; N&Q, I, 56, 109, and II, 158, 281, 615; *Life and Scenes among Kickapoo Indians,* inside front cover; Dr. Sherman's Messenger of Health pamphlet, Landauer Coll.; Dr. Stanway's Professional Mark brochure, Prints and Photographs Div., Library of Congress; Secy. of Agric. to Postmaster Gnl., Dec. 9, 1908, Letterbook, Records of the Office of the Secy. of Agric., RG 16, Ntl. Archives; Alvin F. Harlow, "The Career of an Artist," *Amer. Mercury,* 4 (1925), 305–18.

merous lesions, contagions, and disorders which infect all parts of this beautiful mechanism—maladies belonging to the skin, the muscles, the joints, the glands, and to all the internal viscera—every disease deranging the functions, corrupting the blood, decomposing the tissues, deforming the structure and defacing the beauty of the human form divine." Along with exhibits of sickness went samples of sin, sadism, and sex to lure the curious to the waxworks show—the deformed foot of a man executed for murdering his wife and mother-in-law, the French general who lingered on awhile in agony though flayed alive, the female generative organs before and after copulation. But the main stress was upon gruesome renditions of all parts of the body ruined by disease, especially private parts ravaged by unmentionable maladies. Agents haunted the gallery to watch the spectators and exhort those who appeared shamed and stricken back behind scenes where the "doctor" waited with his high-priced "cures." [36]

The fear of death was preyed upon in numerous ways. Deathbed scenes pointed up the utter anguish of the earthly parting. Vivid cuts pictured men putting bullets through their brains—in one case "the result of neglected nervousness." One ad showed a corpse sitting bolt upright in a coffin, with the legend "Killed by Catarrh!" And how much more maudlin was it possible to get than in this verse?

> Grim death has taken darling little Jerry,
>   The son of Joseph and Seveva Vowels;
> Seven months he suffered with the dysentery,
>   And then he perished with his little bowels.
> Perhaps 'twas weaning little Jerry,
>   His bottle seemed to hurt his stomach's tone;
> But with the angels he'll get plump and merry,
>   For there's no nursing bottles where he's gone.[37]

"Oh, what a pity," the moral is pointed, "that Mrs. Vowels did not know about CASTORIA."

"The medical ad," opined an advertising executive at the turn of the century, "which gives symptoms and tells the progressive stages of a disease, saying plainly what it will lead to if it is not checked, is the one which will produce the most effect on the ordinary mind. I believe most ailing people get a morbid satisfaction from reading vivid descriptions of the symptoms of their sickness." [38]

Disease may indeed lead to pain and death, but not infrequently nostrum promoters predicted these dire consequences when they were by no

---

[36] N&Q, I, 23, and II, 375; *Catalogue of the New-York Museum of Anatomy* (N.Y., 1868), Emory Univ. Library.

[37] N&Q, II, 95, 300, and III, 183; *Standard Remedies*, 17 (1930), 6; *Alarming Truths; Nation*, 20 (May 20, 1875), 343; poem cited in Holcombe, "Private Die Proprietaries," *Wkly. Philatelic Gossip*, June 27, 1942, 375.

[38] Charles A. Bates, *Good Advertising* (N.Y., 1896), 439.

means the logical outcome of symptoms listed in the advertising. All back-pains did not denote kidney disease, all pimples did not signify poisoned blood, all coughs did not indicate consumption. Quacks exaggerated small symptoms and turned normal physiological phenomena into dread signs of incipient pain and death. They recognized that nearly every man is vulnerable to the power of suggestion and sought to make him sick so they could make him well. When sickness was widespread and men more than usually worried, nostrum makers worked overtime. From yellow fever epidemics in the 18th century to sieges of influenza in the 20th, promoters tied their remedies to the prevailing fear. "Scare" advertising indeed sold medicine. Now and then a healthy person, brooding over the agonized future which his symptoms foretold—according to the quack—turned to suicide.[39]

It was all very well to frighten the customer, but it was also neces-sary to reassure him. The two moods were often combined in the before-and-after sequence, and not infrequently Miss After-Using might have luxuriant tresses whereas her alter ego, Miss Before-Using, had been bald as a billiard ball. In this field of the before-and-after, tampering with photographs was particularly rife.[40]

Even stronger bastions for encouragement were deemed necessary. As nostrum advertisers bolstered their appeals with the magic name of science and the lure of the exotic, so they seized the symbols of patriotism. Early in the 19th century, the American eagle appeared in nostrum ad-vertising. So too did the Stars and Stripes, until the practice was declared illegal by that same Congress whose place of meeting was represented on a bitters label. One firm printed the text of the Constitution in small type and black ink. Advertising slogans were added along the borders and run into the main body, in larger type and red ink. Thus the powers of Con-gress were interrupted for the message: "Pendleton's Calisaya Tonic Bit-ters Is used by the most delicate Females." Joined to the article on the judiciary was the counsel that the Bitters be used "for Impaired or Ex-hausted Vital Energy." During the Spanish-American War, a pamphlet cover displayed a sailor and a soldier flanking a man-sized bottle of Pe-Ru-Na. "The Three Safeguards of Our Country," the legend said. "The Navy protects our Country against foreign invasion, The Army protects our Country against internal Dissension, PE-RU-NA protects our Country against Catarrhal Diseases." [41]

Uncle Sam, after his invention, became a favorite figure in patent medicine advertising. For one proprietor he sat at a table and affixed his

39 N&Q, i, 802–803, ii, 432–33, and iii, 120; N.Y. Eve. Post, Aug. 18, 1804; Food and Drug Bull. of the [N.Y. City] Dept. of Health, 2, (1920), [2]; Printer's Ink, 240 (Sep. 26, 1952), 10.
40 Black Cat, Mar. 1898, xx; Harlow, 307–308.
41 Benjamin Morange Medicated Oil Silk broadside [1826], N.Y. Academy of Med.; Brandreth Pills glass sign, Landauer Coll.; Congress Bitters card, Marion W. Sterling Coll. of Advertising Cards, Enoch Pratt Free Library, Baltimore; Clark, The Southern Country Editor, 73; Pendleton brochure, Map and Print Room, N.-Y. Hist. Soc.; Pe-Ru-Na pamphlet, Ntl. Library of Med.

signature to a document which read: "This is to certify that I am using 100,000 boxes of Ex-Lax every month." [42]

So much for patriotism.

Religion was also a mighty fortress in which the nostrum maker took refuge. Testimonials from ministers continued to rank with those from physicians at the summit of prestige. By eating a bowl of Grape-Nuts "after my Sabbath work is done," observed one pastor, ". . . my nerves are quieted and rest and refreshing sleep are ensured me." Whether those among the clergy who had wandered farthest from the decrees of the Council of Trent were the most susceptible to quackery, as Sir William Osler postulated, might be difficult to demonstrate. Ayer's Sarsaparilla managed to get a testimonial from the Sisters of Charity who ran St. Mary's Infant Asylum in Massachusetts. Remedies were named for St. Anne and St. Joseph, not to mention Pastor Koenig and Father John. [43]

Failure turned to success for one proprietor when he began to tell the public that his formula had been "revealed in a providential manner." Dr. Munyon, the purveyor of a kidney cure, confronted millions of Americans with his grim visage, lifted arm, and elevated finger. "If the Sign of the Cross Were to Be Destroyed," he cried, "the Next Best Sign Would Be 'The Index Finger Pointing Heavenward.' " Signs and symbols abounded from the religious realm. Besides angels, Eve also appeared, picking fruit in a garden. The Good Samaritan had a career that spanned the centuries. Nostrums were marketed bearing such names as Balm of Gilead, Paradise Oil, Resurrection Pills, and 666 (see Revelation 13:18). [44]

The Bible was often quoted. One proprietor reprinted the sermon of a noted Brooklyn divine on a text from the Proverbs (7:23): "Till a dart strike through his liver." Whenever this organ was mentioned in the sermon, Warner broke in with a plug for his Safe Cure for liver ailments. [45]

Even the troublesome factors in religious life could be turned to account. The makers of a multi-purpose liniment called Merchant's Gargling Oil got out a trade card showing a grinning gorilla who boldly announced:

> If I am Darwin's Grandpapa,
> It follows don't you see,
> That what is good for man and beast,
> Is doubly good for me. [46]

[42] Landauer Coll.

[43] *The Commoner*, July 14, 1906; Osler cited in *British Med. Jnl.*, 1 (May 27, 1911), 1250; *Ayer's American Almanac, 1885*; N&Q, II, 16, 91, 144, 622.

[44] Rowell, 384; N&Q, I, 513; Eve in Proprietary Assoc., *18th Annual Report*, 184, and *Woman's A, B, C of Health* (n.p., 1860), Rare Book Div., Library of Congress; Moffat's *The Good Samaritan* (1842), *ibid.;* Dr. Peabody's *The Good Samaritan* (1865), Chicago Hist. Soc.; *N.Y. Eve. Post*, Aug. 25, 1804; Resurrection Pills, Radway & Co. circular in author's possession; N&Q, III, 70; *N.Y. PM*, Apr. 23, 1944.

[45] Landauer Coll.

[46] *Ibid.*

Found more frequently than doggerel in nostrum advertising has been the appeal to statistics: the proofs of time and territory and total cures. Indian Balsam of Liverwort had proved its efficacy for ten years, LaMott's Cough Drops for a full score, and Pond's Extract, "The Universal Pain Extractor," (as of 1878) for over thirty. In frontier Illinois, the purveyors of Garlegant's Balsam boasted of its success in Maryland, Virginia, Pennsylvania, Ohio, New York, Kentucky, Missouri, South Carolina, Alabama, Georgia, and New Orleans. A later proprietor issued a pamphlet suggesting an amazingly expansive therapy, *Half the People in the World*. This was, nonetheless, only half as encompassing as the odyssey of pain-killing circumnavigation undertaken by Perry Davis.[47]

Potter's Vegetable Catholicon, in the 1830's, produced cures so numerous "as to preclude insertion in any newspaper." In the next decade Dr. Townsend of Sarsaparilla fame was bold enough to try. Within two years, he said, his remedy had cured over 35,000 cases of severe disease, of which at least 5,000 had been deemed incurable. Included were more than 3,000 cases of chronic rheumatism, 2,000 of dyspepsia, 5,000 of consumption, 2,000 of scrofula, 2,500 of kidney disease and dropsy, 1,500 of liver ailments, 1,000 of female complaints, 400 of general debility and want of energy, and thousands more of ulcers, erysipelas, pimples, headache, spinal afflictions, etc., etc. Countless other proprietors resorted to the overwhelming impact of huge numbers in the hope of luring individual readers to join the crowd.[48]

Big numbers were impressive, but—by themselves, at any rate—they did not have the emotional impact of the individual case. The face was made to stand out in the crowd through the drama of the testimonial. President Jackson spoke well of an ointment, and Vice-President Colfax praised a throat lozenge. "Congressmen," observed a 20th-century commentator, "are notoriously easy to get, and senators by no means beyond range." Peruna managed to get out an ad naming fifty members of Congress who were voting its anti-catarrhal ticket. Doctors and ministers, authors and athletes, have testified. Vin Mariani ventured into the arts, citing compliments from Charles Gounod and Emile Zola. From the theater Edwin Booth and William Gillette, Julia Marlowe and Sarah Bernhardt—all spoke their lines for various remedies.[49]

Not all the testifying by the famous, to be sure, could be taken at face value. Muckraking journalists were to discover that praise might be

---

[47] *Springfield Ill. State Register*, Aug. 4, 1837, and Sep. 21, 1839; *Alton* [Ill.] *Spectator*, Nov. 5, 1834; *N.Y. Spirit of the Times*, Nov. 16, 1878; Pineoline pamphlet, *Half the People in the World* (St. Louis, 1896), Toner Coll.; Davis pamphlet, *Around the World in 40 Years*.

[48] *Shawneetown Ill. Gaz.*, May 29, 1830; *Frederick* [Md.] *Republican Citizen*, Apr. 7, 1848.

[49] *Standard Remedies*, 8 (June 1922), 8–9, and (July 1922), 8, 10, 12; Adams, *Great American Fraud*, 65; *Harper's Wkly.*, 24 (1880), 112, and 39 (1895), 1,101, 1,122; Holcombe, "Private Proprietary Stamp Notes," *Stamp and Cover Collectors' Review*, Oct. 1938, 249–50; Adams in *N.Y. Tribune*, Feb. 21, 1915, reprinted in Amer. Med. Assoc. pamphlet, *Testimonials Medical and Quasi-Medical*.

bought, or pried from the reluctant by various shrewd ruses, some of them smacking of blackmail. Outright fakery was sometimes resorted to, with testimonials from famous men fabricated out of whole cloth. The German bacteriologist Robert Koch was one of many treated to this indignity.[50]

The same sort of trickery was used by nostrum makers in printing praise from humble citizens. Some simply did not exist, except in the imagination of the copywriter. There was one touching tale of an old resident who had been given up by five physicians until cured by Mayr's Wonderful Remedy. This cheering narrative was sent out to newspapers all over the nation, with a headline containing a blank space in which to insert the name of the city in which the ad was run. But these extremes were not really necessary. Patent medicine men knew from the beginning that they could get all the genuine certificates of cure they needed. Testimonials could be purchased for a pittance. More often they were given free. Men and women, persuaded they had been cured, were eager to volunteer their thanks. Others among the unsung, whether or not they were quite aware of it, were looking for a boost in self-esteem, attention from the neighbors. "If your brains won't get you into the papers," advised a newspaper editor, "sign a 'patent medicine' testimonial. Maybe your kidneys will." [51]

Commendation from representatives of America's millions, on farm and in factory, has been much esteemed by nostrum makers. "It is generally agreed among experts," noted a newspaper writer at the beginning of the 20th century, "that nothing is more effective as a business getter than the much derided 'testimonial.' Personal statements of that kind have a tremendous influence in small communities, and those signed by plain, everyday working people are at present regarded as more valuable than the indorsement of celebrities." So it had been two centuries before with Bateman's Pectoral Drops.[52]

With thousands of testimonials appearing in hundreds of papers, it is not surprising that now and then the same page of the same issue of the same paper should reveal both the testimonial and the obituary of the testator. More often, testimonials continued running in newspaper columns long after the satisfied users had gone to their graves.[53]

If greater stress was placed on the authority of the other fellow in nostrum advertising, there were proprietors willing to let the reader himself be judge. Few have had courage enough to suggest so dramatic a demonstration of therapeutic merit as that proposed by the maker of Riga Balsam in 1801. "The trial of it is this," he advertised in a Savannah paper. "Take a hen, drive a nail through it's scull, brains and [t]ongue, then pour some of it into the wound it will directly stop the bleeding, cure it

[50] N&Q, I, 686; Mark Sullivan, "The Inside Story of a Sham," *Ladies' Home Jnl.*, 23 (Jan. 1906), 14.

[51] N&Q, II, 528–32; *Toronto Star*, cited in *ibid.*, III, 197.

[52] *New Orleans Time-Democrat*, cited in *Druggists Circular*, 45 (1901), xi.

[53] N&Q, I, 139, 644, II, 178, and III, 198–200; *Testimonials Medical and Quasi-Medical; Printer's Ink*, 172 (Sep. 5, 1935), 106.

in 8 or 6 minutes, and it will eat as before." On the whole, advertisers wanted readers to try the medicine out not on chickens but on themselves. If the remedy did not work, money would be cheerfully refunded. As one proprietor slyly put it:

> While Quacks are robbing mortal clay,
> My motto is *"No cure, no pay."*

The money-back guarantee was a perennial pitch. Sometimes the ante was raised. The manufacturer of a hair restorer went so far as to announce that his product could grow hair on John D. Rockefeller's head or he would forfeit $1,000.[54]

Thus the patent medicine fraternity ran the gamut of appeals to human psychology. Critics might rant, the judicious might grieve, but the nostrum promoter pursued his wily way. "Advertisers and flourishers know perfectly well," wrote an editorialist in 1871, "that even the gravest and most cautious are to a certain extent touched by their appeals, and that even in the act of denunciation, the most careful often find themselves seduced." [55]

---

[54] *Columbian Museum & Savannah Advertiser*, Mar. 3, 1801; *Phila. Public Ledger*, Sep. 26, 1836; *Standard Remedies*, 23 (June 1937), 13; *Amer. Druggist*, 47 (1905), 358.

[55] "Thoughts on Puffing," *All the Year Round*, 25 (Mar. 4, 1871), 330.

The Social Insulation of the Traditional Elite

E. DIGBY BALTZELL

The myth of equality has had a powerful influence in shaping American attitudes. Beginning in the colonial period and continuing until today, foreign visitors as well as native writers have commented on what they have perceived as the high degree of social mobility available to Americans as a result of the basic equality of opportunity that is their birthright. Of course, many of these same writers have also pointed out that certain elements of the population were left out of the equality scheme by definition, for example, women and non-whites. But the myth persisted, even among those denied access to its rewards.

At least one group of Americans, however, knew better—the wealthy traditional elite (which did assimilate newcomers, but slowly). From the colonial period to the Civil War, many wealthy citizens of WASP ancestry believed they had a special place in society. Their wealth and traditions insulated them from the entrepreneurial clamor of the Jacksonian period, and they maintained a castelike existence in the cities of the Eastern seaboard.

After the Civil War, however, traditions and family connections were no longer sufficient to maintain the exclusivity of the caste structure. The route to riches had shifted, and holders of the new wealth aspired to the life-style previously available primarily to the WASP elite. The homogeneous quality of upper-class existence began to break down under the onslaught of rapid economic growth and the extraordinary financial success of an increasing number of non-WASP families.

Initially, the traditional elite had supported open immigration from Eastern and Southern European countries in order to insure an overabundance of common laborers that would tend to keep wages down, but as participants in this new immigration began to rise in economic status, and in some cases to become actually wealthy, the elite began to reconsider their position. Although they were unable to restrict immigration until well into the twentieth century, they were able to take steps soon after the Civil War to insulate themselves from the society of wealthy non-WASPs.

E. Digby Baltzell, a sociologist at the University of Pennsylvania, has taken as his field of study the traditional elite of the Eastern seaboard. After publishing a book on the upper-class families of Philadelphia, he enlarged his focus to consider the exclusionary tactics of the WASP elite through the last hundred years. In the chapter reprinted below, he focuses on the anti-Semitic practices of the traditional families and enumerates the various devices by which the traditional upper class insulated itself socially from non-WASP wealth. Several features of the social life of the upper class taken so much for

71

granted today have their origin in this period. Exclusive prep schools, college societies, restricted suburbs, summer resorts, and city clubs were founded in order to enable the traditional elite to protect what they saw as their caste privileges. Consequently, the excluded wealthy families formed their own parallel network of social organizations that were designed to reflect the class, if not the caste, prerogatives of upper-class existence.

We are still in power, after a fashion. Our sway over what we call society is undisputed. We keep the Jew far away, and the anti-Jew feeling is quite rabid.

HENRY ADAMS

The Civil War was fought, by a nation rapidly becoming centralized economically, in order to preserve the political Union. Although the Union was preserved and slavery abolished, the postwar Republic was faced with the enormously complex and morally cancerous problem of caste, as far as the formally free Negroes were concerned. The solution to this problem has now become the central one of our own age. But the more immediate effect of the Civil War was that, in the North at least, the nation realized the fabulous potential of industrial power. The Pennsylvania Railroad, for instance, began to cut back operations at the beginning of the war, only to realize a tremendous boom during the remainder of the conflict (total revenue in 1860: $5,933 million; in 1865: $19,533 million). But the profits of the war were nothing compared to those of the fabulous postwar years. Between 1870 and 1900, the national wealth quadrupled (rising from $30,400 million to $126,700 million and doubled again by 1914—reaching $254,200 million).[1]

During this same period, wealth became increasingly centralized in the hands of a few. In 1891, *Forum* magazine published an article, "The Coming Billionaire," which estimated that there were 120 men in the nation worth over $10 million. The next year, the *New York Times* published a list of 4,047 millionaires, and the Census Bureau estimated that 9 per cent of the nation's families owned 71 per cent of the wealth. By 1910 there were more millionaires in the United States Senate alone than there were in the whole nation before the Civil War. This new inequality was dramatized by the fact that, in 1900, according to Frederick Lewis Allen, the former immigrant lad Andrew Carnegie had an *income* of between $15

"The Social Defense of Caste" (Editor's title: "The Social Insulation of the Traditional Elite"). From *The Protestant Establishment*, by E. Digby Baltzell, pp. 109–42. Copyright © 1964 by E. Digby Baltzell. Reprinted by permission of Random House, Inc.

[1] Here I have followed Richard Hofstadter, *The Age of Reform*. New York: Vintage Books, 1960, Chap. IV.

and $30 million (the income tax had been declared unconstitutional in a test case in 1895), while the average unskilled worker in the North received less than $460 a year in wages—in the South the figure was less than $300. It is no wonder that the production of pig iron rather than poetry, and the quest for status rather than salvation, now took hold of the minds of even the most patrician descendants of Puritan divines.

This inequality of wealth was accompanied by an increasing centralization of business power, as the nation changed, in the half century after Appomattox, from a rural-communal to an urban-corporate society. President Eliot of Harvard, in a speech before the fraternity of Phi Beta Kappa in 1888, noted this new corporate dominance when he pointed out that, while the Pennsylvania Railroad had gross receipts of $115 million and employed over 100,000 men in that year, the Commonwealth of Massachusetts had gross receipts of only $7 million and employed no more than 6,000 persons.[2] And this corporate economy was further centralized financially in Wall Street. The capital required to launch the United States Steel Corporation, for example, would at that time have covered the costs of all the functions of the federal government for almost two years. J. P. Morgan and his associates, who put this great corporate empire together in 1901, held some three hundred directorships in over one hundred corporations with resources estimated at over $22 billion. This industrial age, in which the railroads spanned the continent and Wall Street interests controlled mines in the Rockies, timber in the Northwest, and coal in Pennsylvania and West Virginia, brought about a national economy and the emergence of a national mind.

And the prosperity of this new urban-corporate world was largely built upon the blood and sweat of the men, and the tears of their women, who came to this country in such large numbers from the peasant villages of Southern and Eastern Europe. Whereas most of the older immigrants from Northern and Western Europe had come to a rural America where they were able to assimilate more easily, the majority of these newer arrivals huddled together in the urban slums and ghettos which were characteristic of the lower levels of the commercial economy which America had now become.

Except for the captains of industry, whose money-centered minds continued to welcome and encourage immigration because they believed it kept wages down and retarded unionization, most old-stock Americans were frankly appalled at the growing evils of industrialization, immigration and urbanization. As we have seen, the closing decades of the nineteenth century were marked by labor unrest and violence; many men, like Henry Adams, developed a violent nativism and anti-Semitism; others, following the lead of Jane Addams, discovered the slums and went to work to alleviate the evils of prostitution, disease, crime, political bossism and grinding poverty; both Midwestern Populism and the Eastern, patrician-led Progressive movement were part of the general protest and were, in turn, infused with varying degrees of nativism; and even organized labor,

[2] Charles William Eliot, *American Contributions to Civilization*. New York: The Century Company, 1897, pp. 85–86.

many of whose members were of recent immigrant origin, was by no means devoid of nativist sentiment.

In so many ways, nativism was part of a more generalized anti-urban and anti-capitalist mood. Unfortunately, anti-Semitism is often allied with an antipathy toward the city and the money-power. Thus the first mass manifestations of anti-Semitism in America came out of the Midwest among the Populist leaders and their followers. In the campaign of 1896, for example, William Jennings Bryan was accused of anti-Semitism and had to explain to the Jewish Democrats of Chicago that in denouncing the policies of Wall Street and the Rothschilds, he and his silver friends were "not attacking a race but greed and avarice which know no race or religion." [3] And the danger that the Populist, isolationist and anti-Wall Street sentiment in the Middle West might at any time revert to anti-Semitism continued. As we shall see in a later chapter, Henry Ford, a multimillionaire with the traditional Populist mistrust of the money-power, was notoriously anti-Semitic for a time in the early 1920's.

Nativism was also a part of a status revolution at the elite level of leadership on the Eastern Seaboard. "The newly rich, the grandiosely or corruptly rich, the masters of the great corporations," wrote Richard Hofstadter, "were bypassing the men of the Mugwump type—the old gentry, the merchants of long standing, the small manufacturers, the established professional men, the civic leaders of an earlier era. In scores of cities and hundreds of towns, particularly in the East but also in the nation at large, the old-family, college-educated class that had deep ancestral roots in local communities and often owned family businesses, that had traditions of political leadership, belonged to the patriotic societies and the best clubs, staffed the government boards of philanthropic and cultural institutions, and led the movements for civic betterment, were being overshadowed and edged aside in making basic political and economic decisions. . . . They were less important and they knew it." [4]

Many members of this class, of old-stock prestige and waning power, eventually allied themselves with the Progressive movement. Many also, like Henry Adams, withdrew almost entirely from the world of power. The "decent people," as Edith Wharton once put it, increasingly "fell back on sport and culture." And this sport and culture was now to be reinforced by a series of fashionable and patrician protective associations which, in turn, systematically and subtly institutionalized the exclusion of Jews.

The turning point came in the 1880's, when a number of symbolic events forecast the nature of the American upper class in the twentieth century. Thus, when President Eliot of Harvard built his summer cottage at Northeast Harbor, Maine, in 1881, the exclusive summer resort trend was well under way; the founding of The Country Club at Brookline, Massachusetts, in 1882, marked the beginning of the country-club trend; the founding of the Sons of the Revolution, in 1883, symbolized the birth of the genealogical fad and the patrician scramble for old-stock roots; Endicott Peabody's founding of Groton School, in 1884, in order to rear

---

[3] Richard Hofstadter, op. cit., p. 80.
[4] Ibid., p. 137.

young gentlemen in the tradition of British public schools (and incidentally to protect them from the increasing heterogeneity of the public school system) was an important symbol of both upper-class exclusiveness and patrician Anglophilia; and finally, the Social Register, a convenient index of this new associational aristocracy, was first issued toward the end of this transitional decade in 1887 (the publisher also handled much of the literature of the American Protective Association, which was active in the nativist movement at that time).

The Right Reverend Phillips Brooks—the favorite clergyman among Philadelphia's Victorian gentry, who was called to Boston's Trinity Church in 1869, the year Grant entered the White House and Eliot accepted the presidency at Harvard—was one of the most sensitive barometers of the brahmin mind. Thus, although he himself had graduated from the Boston Latin School along with other patricians and plebeian gentlemen of his generation, he first suggested the idea of Groton to young Peabody in the eighties and joined the Sons of the Revolution in 1891, because, as he said at the time, "it is well to go in for the assertion that our dear land at least used to be American." [5]

* ### ANCESTRAL ASSOCIATIONS AND THE QUEST FOR OLD-STOCK ROOTS

The idea of caste dies hard, even in a democratic land such as ours. Our first and most exclusive ancestral association, the Society of the Cincinnati, was formed in 1783, just before the Continental Army disbanded. Its membership was limited to Washington's officers and, in accord with the rural traditions of primogeniture, was to be passed on to the oldest sons in succeeding generations. The society's name reflects the ancient tradition of gentlemen-farmers, from Cincinnatus to Cromwell, Washington and Franklin Roosevelt, who have served their country in times of need. Just as the founding of the Society of Cincinnati reflected the rural values of the gentleman and his mistrust of grasping city ways, it was quite natural that the new wave of ancestral associations which came into being at the end of the nineteenth century was a reaction to the rise of the city with its accompanying heterogeneity and conflict. As Wallace Evan Davies, in *Patriotism on Parade*, put it:

> "The great Upheaval," the Haymarket Riot, the campaigns of Henry George, and the writings of Edward Bellamy crowded the last half of the eighties. The nineties produced such proofs of unrest as the Populist Revolt, the Homestead Strike with the attempted assassination of Henry Clay Frick, the Panic of 1893, the Pullman Strike, Coxey's Army, and, finally, the Bryan campaign of 1896. Throughout all this the conservative and propertied classes watched apprehensively the black cloud of anarchism, a menace as produc-

[5] Barbara Miller Solomon, *Ancestors and Immigrants: A Changing New England.* Cambridge, Mass.: Harvard University Press, 1956, p. 87.

tive of alarm and hysteria as bolshevism and communism in later
generations.[6]

These old-stock patriots, desperately seeking hereditary and historical
roots in a rapidly changing world, flocked to the standards of such newly
founded societies as the Sons of the Revolution (1883), the Colonial Dames
(1890), the Daughters of the American Revolution (1890), Daughters of
the Cincinnati (1894), the Society of Mayflower Descendants (1894), the
Aryan Order of St. George or the Holy Roman Empire in the Colonies of
America (1892), and the Baronial Order of Runnymede (1897). It is no
wonder that genealogists, both amateur and professional, rapidly came
into vogue. Several urban newspapers established genealogical departments;
the Lenox Library in New York purchased one of its largest genealogical
collections, in 1896, setting aside a room "for the convenience of the large
number of researchers after family history"; the *Library Journal* carried
articles on how to help the public in ancestor hunting; and, as of 1900, the
Patriotic Review listed seventy patriotic, hereditary and historical associations, exactly *half* of which had been founded during the preceding decade
alone.

This whole movement was, of course, intimately bound up with anti-
immigrant and anti-Semitic sentiments. Thus a leader of the D.A.R. saw
a real danger in "our being absorbed by the different nationalities among
us," and a president-general of the Sons of the American Revolution reported that: "Not until the state of civilization reached the point where
we had a great many foreigners in our land . . . were our patriotic societies successful." [7] The Daughters of the American Revolution was indeed extremely successful. Founded in 1890, it had 397 chapters in 38
states by 1897. That the anti-immigrant reaction was most prevalent in the
urban East, however, was attested to by the fact that the Daughters made
slow headway in the West and South and had a vast majority of its chapters in New York and Massachusetts.

But, as Franklin Roosevelt once said, "we are all descendants of immigrants." While old-stock Americans were forming rather exclusive associations based on their descent from Colonial immigrants, newer Americans were also attempting to establish their own historical roots. Such
organizations as the Scotch-Irish Society (1889), the Pennsylvania-German
Society (1891), the American Jewish Historical Society (1894), and the
American Irish Historical Society (1898) were concerned to establish ethnic recognition through ancestral achievement. "The Americanism of all
Irishmen and Jews," writes Edward N. Saveth, "was enhanced because of
the handful of Irishmen and Jews who may have stood by Washington
in a moment of crisis." [8]

---

[6] Wallace E. Davies, *Patriotism on Parade: The Story of Veterans' and Hereditary
Organizations in America, 1783–1900*. Cambridge, Mass.: Harvard University Press,
1956.

[7] *Ibid.*, p. 48.

[8] Edward N. Saveth, *American Historians and European Immigrants, 1875–1925*. New
York: Columbia University Press, 1948, p. 194.

The genealogically minded patrician has remained a part of the American scene down through the years. The front page of any contemporary copy of the Social Register, for instance, lists a series of clubs, universities and ancestral associations, with proper abbreviations attached, in order that each family may be identified by its members' affiliations. A recent Philadelphia Social Register listed an even dozen such societies, and a venerable old gentleman of great prestige (if little power) was listed in a later page as follows:

> Rittenhouse,   Wm.   Penn—Ul.Ph.Myf.Cc.Wt.Rv.Ll.Fw.P'83 . . .
>   Union League

It was indeed plain to see (after a bit of research on page 1) that this old gentleman was nicely placed as far as his ancestral, college and club affiliations were concerned. He belonged to the Union League (Ul) and Philadelphia clubs (Ph), had graduated in 1883 from Princeton University (P'83), and was apparently devoting himself to some sort of patriotic ancestor worship in his declining years, as suggested by his ancestral association memberships: Mayflower Descendants (Myf); Society of Cincinnati (Cc); Society of the War of 1812 (Wt); Sons of the Revolution (Rv); Military Order of the Loyal Legion (Ll); and the Military Order of Foreign Wars (Fw). And, as the final entry shows, he was living at the Union League.

THE SUMMER RESORT AND THE QUEST
FOR HOMOGENEITY

Americans have always longed for grass roots. In a society of cement, the resort movement in America paralleled the genealogical escape to the past. The physiological and physical ugliness of the city streets gradually drove those who could afford it back to nature and the wide-open spaces. Men like Owen Wister, Theodore Roosevelt and Madison Grant went out to the West, and the more timid, or socially minded, souls sought refuge at some exclusive summer resort. In spite of the efforts of men like Frederick Law Olmstead and Madison Grant to bring rural beauty into the heart of the city (Olmstead built some fifteen city parks from coast to coast, Central Park in New York City being the most well known), first the artists and writers, then the gentry, and finally the millionaires were seeking the beauty of nature and the simple life among the "natives" of coastal or mountain communities along the Eastern Seaboard. President Eliot and his sons spent the summers during the seventies camping in tents before building the first summer cottage in Northeast Harbor, Maine, in 1881.[9] Charles Francis Adams, Jr., saw his native Quincy succumb to industrialism and the Irish (the Knights of Labor gained control of the

---

[9] Henry James, *Charles W. Eliot.* Vol. I. Boston: Houghton Mifflin Company, 1940, p. 344.

Adams "race-place" in 1887), gave up his job with the Union Pacific in 1890, and finally escaped to the simple life at Lincoln, Massachusetts, in 1893.

The summer resort increased in popularity after the Civil War and went through its period of most rapid growth between 1880 and the First War. Long Branch, New Jersey, summer capital of presidents from Grant to Arthur, was filled with proper Philadelphians and New Yorkers. Further south, Cape May—where Jay Cooke, financier of the Civil War, spent every summer—was the most fashionable Philadelphia summer resort until well into the twentieth century. Boston's best retreated to the simple life at Nahant. Others went to the Berkshires, where large "cottages," large families and large incomes supported the simple life for many years (Lenox boasted thirty-five of these cottages as of 1880, and seventy-five by 1900).[10] Between 1890 and the First War, Bar Harbor became one of America's most stylish resorts. By 1894, the year Joseph Pulitzer built the resort's first hundred-thousand-dollar "cottage," Morgan and Standard Oil partners were the leaders of the community (when a Vanderbilt bought a cottage in 1922, it was the first to change hands in fifteen years; within the next three years, forty-seven such cottages changed hands). Less fashionable, but no less genteel, Northeast Harbor grew at the same time. Anticipating modern sociology, President Eliot made a study of the community in 1890. Among other things, he found that, as of 1881, non-resident summer people owned less than one-fifth of the local real property; only eight years later, in 1889, they owned over half (and total property values had almost doubled).[11]

Just as the white man, symbolized by the British gentleman, was roaming round the world in search of raw materials for his factories at Manchester, Liverpool or Leeds, so America's urban gentry and capitalists, at the turn of the century, were imperialists seeking solace for their souls among the "natives" of Lenox, Bar Harbor or Kennebunkport. Here they were able to forget the ugliness of the urban melting pot as they dwelt among solid Yankees (Ethan Frome), many of whom possessed more homogeneous, Colonial-stock roots than themselves. And these rustic "types" kept up their boats, taught their children the ways of the sea, caught their lobsters, served them in the stores along the village streets, and became temporary servants and gardeners on their rustic estates. But although most old-time resorters were patronizingly proficient with the "Down East" accent, and appreciated the fact that the "natives" were their "own kind" racially, sometimes the idyllic harmony was somewhat superficial, at least as far as the more sensitive "natives" were concerned. Hence the following anecdote circulating among the "natives" at Bar Harbor: "They emptied the pool the other day," reported one typical "type" to another. "Why?" asked his friend. "Oh, one of the natives fell in."

But the simple life was, nevertheless, often touching and always relax-

---

[10] Cleveland Amory, *Last Resorts*. New York: Harper & Brothers, 1952, p. 21.
[11] Henry James, *op. cit.*, p. 111.

ing. All one's kind were there together and the older virtues of communal life were abroad; Easter-Christmas-Wedding Christians usually went to church every Sunday; millionaires' wives did their own shopping in the village, and walking, boating and picnicking brought a renewed appreciation of nature. And perhaps most important of all, one knew who one's daughter was seeing, at least during the summer months when convenient alliances for life were often consummated.

When J. P. Morgan observed that "you can do business with anyone, but only sail with a gentleman," he was reflecting the fact that a secure sense of homogeneity is the essence of resort life. It is no wonder that anti-Semitism, of the gentlemanly, exclusionary sort, probably reached its most panicky heights there. Thus one of the first examples of upper-class anti-Semitism in America occurred, in the 1870's, when a prominent New York banker, Joseph Seligman, was rudely excluded from the Grand Union Hotel in Saratoga Springs. This came as a shock to the American people and was given wide publicity because it was something new at that time. Henry Ward Beecher, a personal friend of the Seligmans, reacted with a sermon from his famous pulpit at Plymouth Church: "What have the Jews," he said, "of which they need be ashamed, in a Christian Republic where all men are declared to be free and equal? . . . Is it that they are excessively industrious? Let the Yankee cast the first stone. Is it that they are inordinately keen on bargaining? Have they ever stolen ten millions of dollars at a pinch from a city? Are our courts bailing out Jews, or compromising with Jews? Are there Jews lying in our jails, and waiting for mercy. . . . You cannot find one criminal Jew in the whole catalogue. . . ." [12]

The Seligman incident was followed by a battle at Saratoga Springs. Immediately afterwards, several new hotels were built there by Jews, and by the end of the century half the population was Jewish; as a result, it is said that one non-Jewish establishment boldly advertised its policies with a sign: "No Jews and Dogs Admitted Here." At the same time, other prominent German Jews were running into embarrassing situations elsewhere. In the 1890's, Nathan Straus, brother of a member of Theodore Roosevelt's Cabinet and a leading merchant and civic leader himself, was turned down at a leading hotel in Lakewood, New Jersey, a most fashionable winter resort at that time. He promptly built a hotel next door, twice as big and for Jews only. And the resort rapidly became Jewish, as kosher establishments multiplied on all sides.

Even the well-integrated and cultivated members of Philadelphia's German-Jewish community eventually had to bow to the trend. As late as the eighties and nineties, for instance, leading Jewish families were listed in the Philadelphia Blue Book as summering at fashionable Cape May, along with the city's best gentile families. But this did not continue, and many prominent Philadelphia Jews became founding families at Long Branch, Asbury Park, Spring Lake or Atlantic City, where the first resort

---

[12] Quoted in Carey McWilliams, *A Mask for Privilege*. Boston: Little, Brown & Company, 1948, p. 6.

synagogues were established during the nineties: Long Branch (1890),
Atlantic City (1893), and Asbury Park (1896).[13]

As the East European Jews rapidly rose to middle-class status, resort-
hotel exclusiveness produced a running battle along the Jersey coast and
up in the Catskills. One resort after another changed from an all-gentile
to an all-Jewish community. Atlantic City, for example, first became a
fashionable gentile resort in the nineties. By the end of the First War,
however, it had become a predominantly Jewish resort, at least in the
summer months (the first modern, fireproof hotel was built there in 1902;
there were a thousand such hotels by 1930). According to Edmund Wilson, it was while visiting Atlantic City in the winter of 1919 that John Jay
Chapman first became anti-Semitic. "They are uncritical," he wrote to
a friend after watching the boardwalk crowd of vacationing Jews. "Life
is a simple matter for them: a bank account and a larder. . . . They strike
me as an inferior race. . . . These people don't know anything. They have
no religion, no customs except eating and drinking." [14]

Just before the First World War, resort establishments began to advertise their discriminatory policies in the newspapers. The situation became so embarrassing that New York State passed a law, in 1913, forbid-
ding places of public accommodation to advertise their unwillingness to
admit persons because of race, creed or color.

Although the high tide of formal resort society has declined in recent years, the rigid exclusion of Jews has largely continued. As Cleveland
Amory has put it:

> Certain aspects of the narrowness of the old-line resort society
> have continued, not the least of which is the question of anti-
> Semitism. Although certain Jewish families, notably the Pulitzers,
> the Belmonts and the Goulds have played their part in resort
> Society—and Otto Kahn, Henry Seligman, Jules Bache and Fred-
> erick Lewison have cut sizeable figures—the general record of resort
> intolerance is an extraordinary one; it reached perhaps its lowest
> point when Palm Beach's Bath and Tennis Club sent out a letter
> asking members not to bring into the club guests of Jewish extrac-
> tion. Among those who received this letter was Bernard Baruch,
> then a member of the club and a man whose father, Dr. Simon
> Baruch, pioneered the Saratoga Spa. Several of Baruch's friends ad-
> vised him to make an issue of the affair; instead, he quietly resigned.
> "No one," he says today, "has had this thing practiced against him
> more than I have. But I don't let it bother me. I always remember
> what Bob Fitzsimmons said to me—he wanted to make me a
> champion, you know—'You've got to learn to take it before you
> can give it out.' " [15]

13 E. Digby Baltzell, *Philadelphia Gentlemen*. Glencoe, Ill.: The Free Press, 1958,
p. 285.
14 Edmund Wilson, *A Piece of My Mind*. New York: Doubleday Anchor Books,
1958, p. 97.
15 Cleveland Amory, *op. cit.*, p. 48.

THE SUBURBAN TREND, THE COUNTRY CLUB
AND THE COUNTRY DAY SCHOOL

The resort and the suburb are both a product of the same desire for homogeneity and a nostalgic yearning for the simplicities of small-town life. Just as, today, white families of diverse ethnic origins and newly won middle-class status are busily escaping from the increasingly Negro composition of our cities, so the Protestant upper class first began to flee the ugliness of the urban melting pot at the turn of the century. In Philadelphia, for instance, the majority of the Victorian gentry lived in the city, around fashionable Rittenhouse Square, as of 1890; by 1914, the majority had moved out to the suburbs along the Main Line or in Chestnut Hill. And this same pattern was followed in other cities.

In many ways Pierre Lorillard was the Victorian aristocrat's William Levitt. Just as Levittown is now the most famous example of a planned community symbolizing the post World War II suburban trend among the middle classes, so Tuxedo Park, New York, established on a site of some 600,000 acres inherited by Pierre Lorillard in 1886, was once the acme of upper-class suburban exclusiveness. According to Cleveland Amory, the Lorillards possessed a foolproof formula for business success which, in turn, was exactly reversed when they came to promoting upper-class exclusiveness. He lists their contrasting formulas as follows:

For Business Success:
   1) Find out what the public wants, then produce the best of its kind.
   2) Advertise the product so that everybody will know it is available.
   3) Distribute it everywhere so that everybody can get it.
   4) Keep making the product better so that more people will like it.

For Snob Success:
   1) Find out who the leaders of Society are and produce the best place for them to live in.
   2) Tell nobody else about it so that nobody else will know it's available.
   3) Keep it a private club so that other people, even if they do hear about it, can't get in.
   4) Keep the place exactly as it was in the beginning so that other people, even if they do hear about it and somehow do manage to get in, won't ever like it anyway.[16]

At Tuxedo Park, Lorillard produced almost a caricature of the Victorian millionaire's mania for exclusiveness. In less than a year, he surrounded seven thousand acres with an eight-foot fence, graded some thirty miles of road, built a complete sewage and water system, a gate house

[16] *Ibid.*, p. 83.

which looked like "a frontispiece of an English novel," a clubhouse staffed with imported English servants, and "twenty-two casement dormered English turreted cottages." On Memorial Day, 1886, special trains brought seven hundred highly selected guests from New York to witness the Park's opening.

Tuxedo was a complete triumph. The physical surroundings, the architecture and the social organization were perfectly in tune with the patrician mind of that day. In addition to the English cottages and the clubhouse, there were "two blocks of stores, a score of stables, four lawn-tennis courts, a bowling alley, a swimming tank, a boathouse, an icehouse, a dam, a trout pond and a hatchery. . . . The members sported the club badge which, designed to be worn as a pin, was an oakleaf of solid gold; club governors had acorns attached to their oakleafs and later all Tuxedo-ites were to wear ties, hatbands, socks, etc., in the club colors of green and gold. . . . No one who was not a member of the club was allowed to buy property."

Tuxedo Park was perhaps a somewhat exaggerated example of an ideal. It certainly would have suggested the conformity of a Chinese commune to many aristocrats seeking real privacy (in the eighties at Nahant, for example, Henry Cabot Lodge built a high fence between his place and his brother-in-law's next door). The upper-class suburban trend as a whole, nevertheless, was motivated by similar, if less rigid, desires for homogeneity. Unlike Tuxedo, however, the country club and the country day school, rather than the neighborhood *per se*, were the main fortresses of exclusiveness. Thus the beginning of a real suburban trend can conveniently be dated from the founding of *The* Country Club, at Brookline, Massachusetts, in 1882. In the next few decades similar clubs sprang up like mushrooms and became a vital part of the American upper-class way of life. Henry James, an expert on Society both here and abroad, found them "a deeply significant American symbol" at the turn of the century, and an English commentator on our mores wrote:

> There are also all over England clubs especially devoted to particular objects, golf clubs, yacht clubs, and so forth. In these the members are drawn together by their interest in a common pursuit, and are forced into some kind of acquaintanceship. But these are very different in spirit and intention from the American country club. It exists as a kind of center of the social life of the neighborhood. Sport is encouraged by these clubs for the sake of general sociability. In England sociability is a by-product of an interest in sport.[17]

This English commentator was, of course, implying that the real function of the American country club was not sport but social exclusion. And throughout the twentieth century the country club has remained, by and

[17] George Birmingham, "The American at Home and in His Club," in *America in Perspective*, edited by Henry Steele Commager. New York: New American Library, 1947, p. 175.

large and with a minority of exceptions, rigidly exclusive of Jews. In response to this discrimination, elite Jews have formed clubs of their own.[18] When many wealthy German Jews in Philadelphia first moved to the suburbs, as we have seen, the famous merchant Ellis Gimbel and a group of his friends founded one of the first Jewish country clubs in the nation, in 1906.[19] After the Second War, when many Jewish families began to move out on the city's Main Line, another elite club, largely composed of East European Jews, was opened.

If the country club is the root of family exclusiveness, the suburban day school provides an isolated environment for the younger generation. Thus a necessary part of the suburban trend was the founding of such well-known schools as the Chestnut Hill Academy (1895) and Haverford School (1884) in two of Philadelphia's most exclusive suburbs; the Gilman School (1897) in a Baltimore suburb; the Browne and Nichols School (1883) in Cambridge, Massachusetts; the Morristown School (1898), the Tuxedo Park School (1900), and the Hackley School (1899) in Tarrytown, to take care of New York suburbia.[20] While not as rigidly exclusive as the country club as far as Jews are concerned, these schools have been, of course, overwhelmingly proper and Protestant down through the years. Few Jews sought admission before the Second War, and since then some form of quota system has often been applied (this is especially true of the suburban schools run by the Quakers in Philadelphia, largely because of their extremely liberal policies of ethnic, racial and religious tolerance).

The greatest monuments are often erected after an era's period of greatest achievement. Versailles was completed after the great age of Louis XIV, the finest Gothic cathedrals after the height of the Catholic synthesis, and the neoclassic plantation mansions after the South had begun to decline. As we shall see below, upper-class suburban homogeneity and exclusiveness are rapidly vanishing characteristics of our postwar era. And when the upper class reigned supreme in its suburban glory (1890–1940), discriminatory practices were genteel and subtle when compared, for example, with the methods of modern automobile magnates in Detroit. The grosser, Grosse Pointe methods, however, will serve to illustrate (in the manner of our discussion of Tuxedo Park) the anti-Semitic and anti-ethnic values of suburban upper class, especially at the height of its attempted escape from the motley urban melting pot. As a somewhat tragic, and slightly ludicrous, monument to the mind of a fading era, the following paragraphs from *Time* magazine must be reproduced in full:

> Detroit's oldest and richest suburban area is the five-community section east of the city collectively called Grosse Pointe (pop. 50,000). Set back from the winding, tree-shaded streets are fine,

[18] John Higham, *Social Discrimination Against Jews in America, 1830–1930.* Publication of the American Jewish Historical Society, Vol. XLVII, No. 1, September 1957, 13.

[19] Mr. Gimbel had only recently been "blackballed" by the Union League Club in the city.

[20] Porter Sargent, *Private Schools.* Boston: Porter Sargent, 1950.

solid colonial or brick mansions, occupied by some of Detroit's oldest (pre-automobile age) upper class, and by others who made the grade in business and professional life. Grosse Pointe is representative of dozens of wealthy residential areas in the U. S. where privacy, unhurried tranquility, and unsullied property values are respected. But last week, Grosse Pointe was in the throes of a rude, untranquil exposé of its methods of maintaining tranquility.

The trouble burst with the public revelation, during a court squabble between one property owner and his neighbor, that the Grosse Point Property Owners Association (973 families) and local real estate brokers had set up a rigid system for screening families who want to buy or build homes in Grosse Pointe. Unlike similar communities, where neighborly solidarity is based on an unwritten gentleman's agreement, Grosse Pointe's screening system is based on a written questionnaire, filled out by a private investigator on behalf of Grosse Point's "owner vigilantes."

The three-page questionnaire, scaled on the basis of "points" (highest score: 100), grades would-be home owners on such qualities as descent, way of life (American?), occupation (Typical of his own race?), swarthiness (Very? Medium? Slightly? Not at all?), accent (Pronounced? Medium? Slight? None?), name (Typically American?), repute, education, dress (Neat or Slovenly? Conservative or Flashy?), status of occupation (sufficient eminence may offset poor grades in other respects). Religion is not scored, but weighted in the balance by a three-man Grosse Pointe screening committee. All prospects are handicapped on an ethnic and racial basis: Jews, for example, must score a minimum of 85 points, Italians 75, Greeks 65, Poles 55; Negroes and Orientals do not count.[21]

On reading this questionnaire, one could not fail to see that these Detroit tycoons were, after all, only reflecting their training in the methodology of modern social science. One might prefer the less-amoral world of William James, who once said: "In God's eyes the difference of social position, of intellect, of culture, of cleanliness, of dress, which different men exhibit . . . must be so small as to practically vanish." But in our age, when the social scientist is deified, several generations of young Americans have now been scientifically shown that men no longer seek status "in God's eyes." Instead they are asked to read all sorts of status-ranking studies, often backed by authoritative "tests of significance," which show how one is placed in society by one's cleanliness, dress, and drinking mores. How, one may ask, can one expect these suburbanites, most of whom have been educated in this modern tradition, not to use these methods for their own convenience.

[21] *Time*, April 25, 1960. [Reprinted by permission from *Time*, The Weekly News-Magazine; Copyright Time Inc.]

THE NEW ENGLAND BOARDING SCHOOL

The growth in importance of the New England boarding school as an upper-class institution coincided with the American plutocracy's search for ancestral, suburban and resort-rural roots. At the time of Groton's founding in 1884, for example, these schools were rapidly becoming a vital factor in the creation of a national upper class, with more or less homogeneous values and behavior patterns. In an ever more centralized, complex and mobile age, the sons of the new and old rich, from Boston and New York to Chicago and San Francisco, were educated together in the secluded halls of Groton and St. Paul's, Exeter and Andover, and some seventy other, approximately similar, schools. While Exeter and Andover were ancient institutions, having been founded in the eighteenth century, and while St. Paul's had been in existence since before the Civil War, the boarding school movement went through its period of most rapid growth in the course of the half century after 1880. Exeter's enrollment increased from some 200 boys in 1880, to over 400 by 1905. The enrollment reached 600 for the first time in 1920, rose to 700 in the 1930's, and has remained below 800 ever since. St. Paul's went through its period of most rapid growth in the two decades before 1900 (the school graduated about 45 boys per year in the 1870's and rose to 100 per year by 1900, where it has remained ever since).

It is interesting in connection with the growth of a national upper class that the founding of many prominent schools coincided with the "trust-founding" and "trust-busting" era. Thus the following schools were founded within a decade of the formation of the United States Steel Corporation, in 1901:

> The Taft School in Watertown, Connecticut, was founded by Horace Dutton Taft, a brother of President Taft, in 1890; the Hotchkiss School, Lakeville, Connecticut, was founded and endowed by Maria Hotchkiss, widow of the inventor of the famous machine-gun, in 1892; St. George's School, Newport, Rhode Island, which has a million-dollar Gothic chapel built by John Nicholas Brown, was founded in 1896; in the same year, Choate School, whose benefactors and friends include such prominent businessmen as Andrew Mellon and Owen D. Young, was founded by Judge William G. Choate, at Wallingford, Connecticut; while the elder Morgan was forming his steel company in New York and Pittsburgh in 1901, seven Proper Bostonians, including Francis Lowell, W. Cameron Forbes; and Henry Lee Higginson, were founding Middlesex School, near Concord, Massachusetts; Deerfield, which had been a local academy since 1797, was reorganized as a modern boarding school by its great headmaster, Frank L. Boydon, in 1902; and finally, Father Sill of the Order of the Holy Cross, founded Kent School in 1906.[22]

[22] E. Digby Baltzell, *op. cit.,* p. 302.

While the vast majority of the students at these schools were old-stock Protestants throughout the first part of the twentieth century at least, it would be inaccurate to suppose that the schools' admission policies rigidly excluded Catholics or even Jews. Few Catholics and fewer Jews applied (Henry Morgenthau attended Exeter. As he never referred to the fact, even in his *Who's Who* biography, he probably had a pretty lonely time there). As a matter of historical fact, these schools were largely preoccupied, during the first three decades of this century, with assimilating the sons of America's newly rich Protestant tycoons, many of whom were somewhat spoiled in the style of the late William Randolph Hearst, who had been asked to leave St. Paul's.

On the whole . . . , these schools have continued to assimilate the sons of the newly rich down through the years. John F. Kennedy, for example, was graduated from Choate School in the thirties, after spending a year at Canterbury. In this connection, it was a measure of the increasingly affluent status of American Catholics that the nation's two leading Catholic boarding schools, Portsmouth Priory and Canterbury, were founded in 1926 and 1915 respectively.

THE COLLEGE CAMPUS IN THE GILDED AGE: GOLD COAST AND SLUM

The excluding mania of the Gilded Age was of course reflected on the campuses of the nation, especially in the older colleges in the East. In his book, *Academic Procession*, Ernest Earnest begins his chapter entitled "The Golden Age and the Gilded Cage" as follows:

> It is ironic that the most fruitful period in American higher education sowed the seeds of three of the greatest evils: commercialized athletics, domination by the business community, and a caste system symbolized by the Gold Coast. . . . A smaller percentage of students came to prepare for the ministry, law, and teaching; they came to prepare for entrance into the business community, especially that part of it concerned with big business and finance. And it was the sons of big business, finance, and corporation law who dominated the life of the campus in the older Eastern colleges. To an amazing degree the pattern set by Harvard, Yale and Princeton after 1880 became that of colleges all over the country. The clubs, the social organization, the athletics—even the clothes and the slang—of "the big three" were copied by college youth throughout the nation. In its totality the system which flowered between 1880 and World War I reflected the ideals of the social class which dominated the period.[23]

[23] Ernest Earnest, *Academic Procession*. New York: Bobbs-Merrill Company, Inc., 1953.

It is indeed appropriate that Yale's William Graham Sumner added the term "mores" to the sociological jargon, for the snobbish mass mores of the campuses of the Gilded Age were nowhere more binding than at New Haven. In the nineties, Yale became the first football factory and led the national trend toward anti-intellectualism and social snobbishness. Between 1883 and 1901, Yale plowed through nine undefeated seasons, piled up seven hundred points to its opponents' zero in the famous season of 1888, and produced Walter Camp, who picked the first All-American eleven and who produced Amos Alonzo Stagg, who, in turn, taught Knute Rockne everything he knew about football. By the turn of the century, "We toil not, neither do we agitate, but we play football" became the campus slogan. And cheating and the use of purchased papers almost became the rule among the golden boys of Yale, most of whom lived in "The Hutch," an expensive privately owned dormitory where the swells patronized private tailors, ruined expensive suits in pranks, sprees and rioting, ordered fine cigars by the hundred-lot, and looked down on those poorer boys who had gone to public high schools. The Yale Class Book of 1900, appropriately enough, published the answer to the following question: Have you ever used a trot? Yes: 264, No: 15. At the same time, in a survey covering three floors of a dormitory, it was found that not a single student wrote his own themes. They bought them, of course. After all, this sort of menial labor was only for the "drips," "grinds," "fruits," "meatballs," and "black men" of minority ethnic origins and a public school education. But at least one gilded son was somewhat horrified at the mores of Old Eli in those good old days before mass democracy had polluted gentlemenly education. A member of the class of 1879, this young gentleman asked an instructor in history to recommend some outside reading. The reply was "Young man, if you think you came to Yale with the idea of reading you will find out your mistake very soon." [24]

This anti-intellectual crowd of leading Yale men was composed primarily of boarding school graduates who began to dominate campus life at this time. Owen Johnson, graduate of Lawrenceville and Yale (1900), wrote about this generation in his best seller, *Stover at Yale*.[25] Stover soon learned that the way to success at Yale meant following the mores established by the cliques from Andover, Exeter, Hotchkiss, Groton and St. Paul's: "We've got a corking lot in the house—Best of the Andover crowd." Even in the famous senior societies, caste replaced the traditional aristocracy of merit. Thus a committee headed by Professor Irving Fisher found that, whereas twenty-six of the thirty-four class valedictorians had been tapped by the senior societies between 1861 and 1894, after 1893 not a single one had been considered.[26]

By the turn of the century, the College of New Jersey which had only recently changed its name to Princeton was far more homogeneously upper class than Yale. "The Christian tradition, the exclusiveness of the

---

[24] *Ibid.*, p. 232.
[25] *Ibid.*, p. 208.
[26] *Ibid.*, p. 230.

upper-class clubs, and the prejudices of the students," wrote Edwin E. Slosson in *Great American Universities* in 1910, "kept away many Jews, although not all—there are eleven in the Freshman class. Anti-Semitic feeling seemed to me to be more dominant at Princeton than at any of the other universities I visited. 'If the Jews once get in,' I was told, 'they would ruin Princeton as they have Columbia and Pennsylvania.' " [27]

Football mania and the snobberies fostered by the eating-club system gradually dominated campus life at Princeton. Thus in 1906, Woodrow Wilson, convinced that the side shows were swallowing up the circus, made his famous report to the trustees on the need for abolishing the clubs. Although many misunderstood his purpose at the time, Wilson actually desired to make Princeton an even more homogeneous body of gentlemen-scholars. His preceptorial and quadrangle plans envisioned a series of small and intimate groups of students and faculty members pursuing knowledge without the disruptive class divisions fostered by the existing club system. Wilson was defeated in his drive for reform (partly because of his tactlessness) and was eventually banished to the White House, where he would be less of a threat to the system so dear to the hearts of many powerful trustees.

One should not dismiss Princeton's idea of homogeneity without mentioning one of its real and extremely important advantages. Princeton is one of the few American universities where an honor system is still in force, and presumably works. In this connection, Edwin E. Slosson's observations on the system as it worked in 1910 should be quoted in full:

> At Harvard I saw a crowd of students going into a large hall, and following them in, I found I could not get out, that no one was allowed to leave the examination room for twenty minutes. The students were insulated, the carefully protected papers distributed, and guards walked up and down the aisles with their eyes rolling like the search lights of a steamer in a fog. Nothing like this at Princeton; the students are on their honor not to cheat, and they do not, or but rarely. Each entering class is instructed by the Seniors into the Princeton code of honor, which requires any student seeing another receiving or giving assistance on examination to report him for a trial by his peers of the student body. . . . I do not think the plan would be practicable in the long run with a very large and heterogeneous collection of students. It is probable that Princeton will lose this with some other fine features of its student life as the university grows and becomes more cosmopolitan. The semi-monastic seclusion of the country village cannot be long maintained. [28]

In contrast to Princeton, and even Yale, Harvard has always been guided by the ideal of diversity. A large and heterogeneous student body,

---

[27] Edwin E. Slosson, *Great American Universities*. New York: The Macmillan Company, 1910, p. 105.

[28] *Ibid.*, p. 106.

however, is always in danger of developing class divisions. Like his friend Woodrow Wilson, A. Lawrence Lowell was disturbed by this trend at Harvard at the turn of the century. In a letter to President Eliot, written in 1902, he mentioned the "tendency of wealthy students to live in private dormitories outside the yard" and the "great danger of a snobbish separation of the students on lines of wealth." [29] In a committee report of the same year, he noted how one of the finest dormitories was becoming known as "Little Jerusalem" because of the fact that some Jews lived there.

Samuel Eliot Morison, in his history of Harvard, shows how the college gradually became two worlds—the "Yard" and the "Gold Coast"—as Boston society, the private schools, the club system and the private dormitories took over social life at the turn of the century.[30] "In the eighties," he writes, "when the supply of eligible young men in Boston was decreased by the westward movement, the Boston mammas suddenly became aware that Harvard contained many appetizing young gentlemen from New York, Philadelphia, and elsewhere. One met them in the summer at Newport, Beverly, or Bar Harbor; naturally one invited them to Mr. Papanti's or Mr. Foster's 'Friday Evenings' when they entered College, to the 'Saturday Evening Sociables' sophomore year, and to coming-out balls thereafter." [31] These favored men were, at the same time, living along Mount Auburn Street in privately run and often expensive halls, and eating at the few final clubs which only took in some 10 to 15 per cent of each class. Closely integrated with the clubs and Boston Society were the private preparatory schools. Until about 1870, according to Morison, Boston Latin School graduates still had a privileged position at Harvard, but "during the period 1870–90 the proportion of freshmen entering from public high schools fell from 38 to 23 per cent." About 1890 the Episcopal Church schools and a few others took over. "Since 1890 it has been almost necessary for a Harvard student with social ambition to enter from the 'right' sort of school and be popular there, to room on the 'Gold Coast' and be accepted by Boston society his freshman year, in order to be on the right side of the social chasm . . . conversely, a lad of Mayflower or Porcellian ancestry who entered from a high school was as much 'out of it' as a ghetto Jew." [32]

During most of Harvard's history, according to Morison, a solid core of middle-class New Englanders had been able to absorb most of the students into a cohesive college life which was dominated by a basic curriculum taken by all students. The increasing size of the classes (100 in the 1860's to over 600 by the time Franklin Roosevelt graduated in 1904), the elective system which sent men off to specialize in all directions, and the increasing ethnic heterogeneity of the student body, paved the way for exclusiveness and stratification. By 1893, for example, there were enough Irish Catholics in the Yard to support the St. Paul's Catholic Club, which

[29] Ernest Earnest, *op. cit.,* p. 216.
[30] Samuel Eliot Morison, *Three Centuries of Harvard, 1636–1936.* Cambridge, Mass.: Harvard University Press, 1937.
[31] *Ibid.,* p. 416.
[32] *Ibid.,* p. 422.

acquired Newman House in 1912. The situation was similar with the Jews.
"The first German Jews who came were easily absorbed into the social
pattern; but at the turn of the century the bright Russian and Polish lads
from the Boston public schools began to arrive. There were enough of
them in 1906 to form the Menorah Society, and in another fifteen years
Harvard had her 'Jewish problem.' "[33]

The "Jewish problem" at Harvard will be discussed below. Here it is
enough to emphasize the fact that it grew out of the general development
of caste in America at the turn of the century. And this new type of caste
system was supported by all kinds of associations, from the suburban
country club to the fraternities and clubs on the campuses of the nation.
Not only were two worlds now firmly established at Harvard and Yale and
to a lesser extent at Princeton; at other less influential state universities and
small colleges, fraternities dominated campus life.

Although fraternities grew up on the American campus before the
Civil War, they expanded tremendously in the postwar period. By the late
1880's, for instance, the five hundred undergraduates at the University of
Wisconsin were stratified by a fraternity system which included no less
than thirteen houses.[34] As class consciousness increased, campus mores of
course became more rigidly anti-Semitic and often anti-Catholic. Bernard
Baruch, who entered the College of the City of New York in 1884 (as he
was only fourteen at the time, his mother would not let him go away to
Yale, which was his preference), felt the full weight of campus anti-
Semitism. Although he was extremely popular among the small group of
less than four hundred undergraduates, and although he was elected president of the class in his senior year, young Baruch was never taken into a
fraternity at C.C.N.Y. "The Greek-letter societies or fraternities," he
wrote years later in his autobiography, "played an important part at the
college. Although many Jews made their mark at the college, the line was
drawn against them by these societies. Each year my name would be proposed and a row would ensue over my nomination, but I never was elected.
It may be worth noting, particularly for those who regard the South as
less tolerant than the North, that my brother Herman was readily admitted
to a fraternity while he attended the University of Virginia." [35] In response to the "Anglo-Saxon-Only" mores which accompanied the fraternity boom in the eighties and nineties, the first Jewish fraternity in
America was founded at Columbia, in 1898.

The campus mores were, of course, modeled after the adult world
which the students in the Gilded Age were preparing to face. For the large
corporations, banks and powerful law firms—in the big-city centers of
national power—increasingly began to select their future leaders, not on
the basis of ability alone, but largely on the basis of their fashionable university and club or fraternity affiliations. "The graduate of a small college
or a Western university," writes Ernest Earnest, "might aspire to a judge-

[33] *Ibid.*, p. 417.
[34] Ernest Earnest, *op. cit.*, p. 207.
[35] Bernard M. Baruch, *Baruch: My Own Story*. New York: Pocket Books, Inc., 1958,
   p. 54.

ship or bank presidency in the smaller cities and towns; he might get to Congress, become a physician or college professor. Particularly west of the Alleghenies he might become a governor or senator. But he was unlikely to be taken into the inner social and financial circles of Boston, New York or Philadelphia." [36] In the first half of the twentieth century, five of our eight Presidents were graduates of Harvard, Yale, Princeton and Amherst. A sixth came from Stanford, "the Western Harvard," where the social system most resembled that in the East.

THE METROPOLITAN MEN'S CLUB: STRONGHOLD OF PATRICIAN POWER

When the gilded youths at Harvard, Yale and Princeton finally left the protected world of the "Gold Coast" to seek their fortunes in the Wall streets and executive suites of the nation, they usually joined one or another exclusive men's club. Here they dined with others of their kind, helped each other to secure jobs and promotions, and made friends with influential older members who might some day be of help to them in their paths to the top. Proper club affiliation was, after all, the final and most important stage in an exclusive socializing process. As a character in a novel about Harvard, published in 1901, put it: "Bertie knew who his classmates in college were going to be at the age of five. They're the same chaps he's been going to school with and to kid dancing classes . . . it's part of the routine. After they get out of college they'll all go abroad for a few months in groups of three or four, and when they get back they'll be taken into the same club (their names will have been on the waiting list some twenty-odd years) . . . and see one another every day for the rest of their lives." [37] But, by the century's turn, the metropolitan club was gradually becoming more than a congenial gathering-place for similarly bred gentlemen.

British and American gentlemen, especially after the urban bourgeoisie replaced the provincial aristocracy, soon realized that the club was an ideal instrument for the gentlemanly control of social, political and economic power. For generations in England, top decisions in the City and at Whitehall have often been made along Pall Mall, where conservatives gathered at the Carlton and liberals at the Reform. But perhaps the best illustration of the role of the club in the making of gentlemen, and its use as an instrument of power, was a "gentlemanly agreement" which was made in the late nineteenth century at the frontiers of empire. And it is indeed symbolic and prophetic that it should have been made in racialist South Africa by the great Cecil Rhodes, that most rabid of racialists who dreamed of forming a Nordic secret society, organized like Loyola's, and devoted to world domination. The club served Rhodes well on his way to wealth.[38]

[36] Ernest Earnest, *op. cit.,* p. 218.

[37] *Ibid.,* p. 217.

[38] See Hannah Arendt, *The Origins of Totalitarianism.* New York: Harcourt, Brace and Company, 1951, p. 203. And S. Gertude Millin, *Cecil Rhodes.* London: Harper & Brothers, 1933, pp. 99–100.

The exploitation of Africa became a full-fledged imperialist enterprise only after Cecil Rhodes dispossessed the Jews. Rhodes' most important competitor in the fight for control of the Kimberley diamond mines was Barney Barnato, son of a Whitechapel shopkeeper, who was possessed by a passionate desire to make his pile and, above all, to become a gentleman. Both Rhodes and Barnato were eighteen years of age when they arrived in Kimberley in the early seventies. By 1885 Rhodes was worth fifty thousand pounds a year, but Barnato was richer. At that time Rhodes began his "subtle" and persistent dealings with Barnato in order to gain control of de Beers. Nearly every day he had him to lunch or dinner at the "unattainable," at least for Barnato, Kimberley Club (he even persuaded the club to alter its rules which limited the entertainment of nonmembers to once-a-month). At last, Barnato agreed to sell out to Rhodes for a fabulous fortune, membership in the Kimberley Club, and a secure place among the gentlemanly imperialists. While Rhodes had perhaps used his club and his race with an ungentlemanly lack of subtlety, "no American trust, no trust in the world, had such power over any commodity as Rhodes now had over diamonds." But in the end, his dream that "between two and three thousand Nordic gentlemen in the prime of life and mathematically selected" should run the world became the very respectable Rhodes Scholarship Association, which supported selected members of all "Nordic Races," such as Germans, Scandinavians and Americans, during a brief stay in the civilizing atmosphere of Oxford University (the "Nordic" criterion for selection has since been abandoned). In the meantime, his friend Barney Barnato, soon after realizing his dream of becoming both a millionaire and a gentleman, drowned himself in the depths of the sea.

Many such dreams of corporate and financial empire-building have been consummated within the halls of America's more exclusive clubs. The greatest financial imperialist of them all, J. Pierpont Morgan, belonged to no less than nineteen clubs in this country and along Pall Mall. One of his dreams was realized on the night of December 12, 1900, in the course of a private dinner at the University Club in New York. Carnegie's man, Charles M. Schwab, was the guest of honor and the steel trust was planned that night.

In the 1900's the metropolitan club became far more important than the country club, the private school and college, or the exclusive neighborhood as the crucial variable in the recruitment of America's new corporate aristocracy. Family position and prestige, built up as a result of several generations of leadership and service in some provincial city or town, were gradually replaced by an aristocracy by ballot, in the hierarchy of metropolitan clubdom. In New York, for example, this process can be illustrated by the club affiliations of successive generations of Rockefellers: John D. Rockefeller belonged to the Union League; John D., Jr., to the University Club; and John D. III to the Knickerbocker. Thus is a business aristocracy recruited.

And this associational, rather than familistic, process was certainly democratic, except for one thing. That is the fact that, almost without exception, every club in America now developed a castelike policy toward the Jews. They were excluded, as a people or race, regardless of their personal qualities such as education, taste or manners. It is important, more-over, to stress the fact that this caste line was only drawn at the end of the nineteenth century, when, as we have seen, the members of the upper class were setting themselves apart in other ways. Joseph Seligman's experience at Saratoga Springs was part of a general trend which came to a head again when Jesse Seligman, one of the founders of New York's Union League, resigned from the club in 1893, when his son was blackballed because he was a Jew. Apparently this sort of anti-Semitism was not yet a norm when the club was founded during the Civil War.

Nor was it the norm among the more exclusive clubs in other cities. The Philadelphia Club, the oldest and one of the most patrician in America, was founded in 1834, but did not adhere to any anti-Semitic policy until late in the century. During the Civil War, for instance, Joseph Gratz, of an old German-Jewish family and a leader in his synagogue, was president of the club. The membership also included representatives of several other prominent families of Jewish origin. Yet no other member of the Gratz family has been taken into the Philadelphia Club since the nineties, a period when countless embarrassing incidents all over America paralleled the Seligman incident at the Union League.[39] The University Club of Cincin-nati finally broke up, in 1896, over the admission of a prominent member of the Jewish community. Elsewhere, prominent, cultivated and powerful Jews were asked to resign, or were forced to do so by their sense of pride, because of incidents involving their families or friends who were refused membership solely because of their Jewish origins. Gentlemanly anti-Semitism even invaded the aristocratic South. As late as the 1870's one of the more fashionable men's clubs in Richmond, the Westmoreland, had members as well as an elected president of Jewish origins. But today all the top clubs in the city follow a policy of rigid exclusiveness as far as Jews are concerned. This is the case even though the elite Jewish community in Richmond, as in Philadelphia, has always been a stable one with a solid core of old families whose members exhibit none of the aggressive, *parvenu* traits given as a reason for the anti-Semitic policies of clubs in New York, Chicago or Los Angeles.

Yet the inclusion of cultivated Jews within the halls of the Phila-delphia or Westmoreland clubs in an earlier day was characteristic of a provincial and familistic age when the men's club was really social, and membership was based on congeniality rather than, as it has increasingly become, on an organized effort to retain social power within a castelike social stratum. George Apley, whose values were the product of a rapidly departing era, threatened to resign from his beloved Boston Club when he thought it was being used, somewhat in the style of Cecil Rhodes, as an agency for the consolidation of business power. At a time when his club-mates Moore and Field were apparently violating his gentlemanly code in seeking the admission of their business associate Ransome, Apley wrote the admissions committee as follows:

[39] As a matter of "subtle" fact, there were no "Jewish" members of the Gratz family left in the city by this time.

I wish to make it clear that it is not because of Ransome personally that I move to oppose him.

Rather, I move to oppose the motive which actuates Messrs. Moore and Field in putting this man up for membership. They are not doing so because of family connections, nor because of disinterested friendship, but rather because of business reasons. It is, perhaps, too well known for me to mention it that Mr. Ransome has been instrumental in bringing a very large amount of New York business to the banking house of Moore and Fields. This I do not think is reason enough to admit Mr. Ransome to the Province Club, a club which exists for social and not for business purposes.[40]

Today many other clubs like Apley's Province, but unlike Pittsburgh's Duquesne, are fighting the intrusion of business affairs into a club life supposedly devoted to the purely social life among gentlemen. "A year or two ago," wrote Osborn Elliott in 1959, "members of San Francisco's sedate Pacific Union Club (known affectionately as the P.U.) received notices advising them that briefcases should not be opened, nor business papers displayed, within the confines of the old club building atop Nob Hill." [41] At about the same time, patrician New Yorkers were shocked at a *Fortune* article which reported that "at the Metropolitan or the Union League or the University . . . you might do a $10,000 deal, but you'd use the Knickerbocker or the Union or the Racquet for $100,000, and then for $1 million you'd have to move on to the Brook or the Links." [42]

In this chapter I have shown how a series of newly created upper-class institutions produced an associationally insulated national upper class in metropolitan America. I have stressed their rise in a particular time in our history and attempted to show how they were part of a more general status, economic and urban revolution which, in turn, was reflected in the Populist and Progressive movements. All this is important as a background for understanding the present situation, primarily because it shows that upper-class nativism in general and anti-Semitism in particular were a product of a particular cultural epoch and, more important, had not always been characteristic of polite society to anywhere near the same extent. This being the case, it may well be true, on the other hand, that new social and cultural situations may teach new duties and produce new upper-class mores and values. As a measure of the success of these caste-creating associations, the following remarks made by the late H. G. Wells after a visit to this country soon after the turn of the century are interesting.

In the lower levels of the American community there pours perpetually a vast torrent of strangers, speaking alien tongues, inspired by alien traditions, for the most part illiterate peasants and working-people. They come in at the bottom: that must be insisted

---

[40] John P. Marquand, *The Late George Apley*. New York: The Modern Library, 1940, p. 189.

[41] Osborn Elliott, *Men at the Top*. New York: Harper & Brothers, 1959, p. 163.

[42] *Ibid.*, p. 164.

upon. . . . The older American population is being floated up on the top of this influx, a sterile aristocracy above a racially different and astonishingly fecund proletariat. . . .

Yet there are moments in which I could have imagined there were no immigrants at all. All the time, except for one distinctive evening, I seem to have been talking to English-speaking men, now and then, but less frequently, to an Americanized German. In the clubs there are no immigrants. There are not even Jews, as there are in London clubs. One goes about the wide streets of Boston, one meets all sorts of Boston people, one visits the State-House; it's all the authentic English-speaking America. Fifth Avenue, too, is America without a touch of foreign-born; and Washington. You go a hundred yards south of the pretty Boston Common, and, behold! you are in a polyglot slum! You go a block or so east of Fifth Avenue and you are in a vaster, more Yiddish Whitechapel.[43]

At this point, it should be emphasized that it was (and still is) primarily the patrician without power, the clubmen and resorters and the functionless genteel who, as Edith Wharton wrote, "fall back on sport and culture." It was these gentlemen with time on their hands who took the lead in creating the "anti-everything" world which Henry Adams called "Society." So often, for example, it was the men of inherited means, many of them bachelors like Madison Grant, who served on club admission committees, led the dancing assemblies and had their summers free to run the yacht, tennis and bathing clubs at Newport or Bar Harbor. And these leisurely patricians were, in turn, supported by the new men, and especially their socially ambitious wives, who had just made their fortunes and were seeking social security for their children. In all status revolutions, indeed, resentment festers with the greatest intensity among the new rich, the new poor, and the functionless genteel. And these gentlemen of resentment responded to the status revolution at the turn of the century by successfully creating, as H. G. Wells so clearly saw, two worlds: the patrician and Protestant rich, and the rest.

[43] H. G. Wells, *The Future in America*. New York: Harper & Brothers, 1906, p. 134.

Suggestions for Further Reading

Few general works try to cover this period from the perspective of everyday life. One popular and entertaining work that attempts this view is J. C. Furnas, *The Americans: A Social History of the United States, 1587–1914* * (New York, 1969), available in a two-volume paperback edition. Other works that present some coverage of everyday life during the Gilded Age are Ray Ginger, *Age of Excess: The United States from 1877–1914* * (New York, 1965); Henry F. May, *Protestant Churches and Industrial America** (New York, 1949); and Thomas Cochran and William Miller, *The Age of Enterprise: A Social History of Industrial America** (New York, 1961). For a view of the closing decade, see Larzer Ziff, *The American 1890's: Life and Times of a Lost Generation** (New York, 1966). Tamara Hareven has edited a useful collection of essays in *Anonymous Americans: Explorations in Nineteenth Century Social History** (Englewood Cliffs, N.J., 1971). Fictional treatments of the period that are revealing are Mark Twain and Charles Warner, *The Gilded Age** (New York, 1874), and two works by William Dean Howells, *The Rise of Silas Lapham** (Boston, 1884) and *The Hazard of New Fortunes** (New York, 1889).

For material on everyday life on the Middle Border and Great Plains, see Robert Dykstra, *The Cattle Towns** (New York, 1968); Merle Curti, *The Making of an American Community: A Case Study of Democracy in a Frontier County** (Stanford, 1959); and Everett Dick, *The Sod-House Frontier, 1854–1890: A Social History of the Northern Plains from the Creation of Kansas and Nebraska to the Admission of the Dakotas* (New York, 1937). Developments in agriculture are covered in Fred A. Shannon, *The Farmer's Last Frontier, Agriculture, 1860–1897* * (New York, 1945). Ruth Miller Elson has analyzed the books used in the schools in *Guardians of Tradition: American Schoolbooks of the Nineteenth Century** (Lincoln, Neb., 1964). The role of popular literature in shaping values throughout American history is explored in Russell Nye, *The Unembarrassed Muse: Popular Arts in America** (New York, 1970). Fiction provides an excellent source of information about life in the Midwest. Classic works of American literature on this subject are Mark Twain, *Life on the Mississippi** (Boston, 1883), *Huckleberry Finn** (New York, 1885), *Tom Sawyer** (Hartford, Conn., 1892); Sherwood Anderson, *Winesburg, Ohio** (New York, 1919); Sinclair Lewis, *Main Street** (New York, 1920); and, most sympathetically, Willa Cather, *My Antonia** (Boston, 1926); and Hamlin Garland's autobiographical *A Son of the Middle Border* (New York, 1918).

* Available in paperback edition.

For background on life in the cities, see Robert Ernst, *Immigrant Life in New York City, 1825–1863* (New York, 1949), and Stephan Thernstrom and Richard Sennett, eds., *Nineteenth-Century Cities: Essays in the New Urban History** (New Haven, 1969). On immigration, see Oscar Handlin, *The Uprooted** (Boston, rev. ed., 1973). The basic theoretical work on assimilation is Milton Gordon, *Assimilation in American Life** (New York, 1964). Other works dealing with the Jewish community are Moses Rischin, *The Promised City: New York's Jews, 1870–1914** (Cambridge, Mass., 1962); Arthur A. Cohen, *New York Jews and the Quest for Community: The Kehillah Experiment, 1908–1922* (New York, 1970); and a novel by Abraham Cahan, *The Rise of David Levinsky** (New York, 1917). Two contemporary works that provide interesting insights into city living are Edward Bellamy's utopian novel, *Looking Backward, 2000–1887** (Boston, 1888), and Jacob Riis, *How the Other Half Lives: Studies Among the Tenements of New York** (New York, 1890).

For a study of the Philadelphia elite, see E. Digby Baltzell, *Philadelphia Gentleman: The Making of a National Upper Class* (Glencoe, Ill., 1958). Glimpses of the life-style of the wealthy are found in Stewart Holbrook, *The Age of the Moguls* (Garden City, N.Y., 1953), and Stephen Birmingham, *The Right People: A Portrait of America's Social Establishment* (Boston, 1968). A contemporary critical analysis is Thorstein Veblen, *The Theory of the Leisure Class** (New York, 1899), and a recent critique is C. Wright Mills, *The Power Elite** (New York, 1956). Popular treatments of non-Anglo-Saxon wealth are found in Stephen Birmingham, *Our Crowd: The Great Jewish Families of New York** (New York, 1967), *The Grandees: America's Sephardic Elite** (New York, 1971), and *Real Lace: America's Irish Rich** (New York, 1973). Higher education is scrutinized in Richard Hofstadter and Walter P. Metzger, *The Development of Academic Freedom in the United States** (New York, 1955), available in a two-volume paperback edition.

The standard history of medical practice in the United States, badly in need of updating, is Richard Shryock, *The Development of Modern Medicine* (Philadelphia, 1936; rev. and enl. ed., 1947). Specialized treatments of earlier aspects of health care are found in Charles F. Rosenberg, *The Cholera Years: The United States in 1832, 1849, and 1866** (Chicago, 1962), and John Duffy, *A History of Public Health in New York City, 1625–1866* (New York, 1968). Quackery is dealt with in Stewart Holbrook, *The Golden Age of Quackery* (New York, 1959); James Harvey Young, *The Medical Messiahs: A Social History of Health Quackery in Twentieth-Century America* (Princeton, N.J., 1967); and two older works by Morris Fishbein, *The Medical Follies* (New York, 1925) and *Fads in Quackery and Healing* (New York, 1932). A work on recent patent medicines is James Cook, *Remedies and Rackets: The Truth about Patent Medicines Today* (New York, 1958). Medical theory and practice in the nineteenth century with regard to the differences between men and women is a growing field of research. Two pioneering articles on this subject are Ben Barker-Benfield, "The Spermatic Economy: A Nineteenth Century View of Sexuality," *Feminist Studies* 1 (1972), reprinted in Michael Gordon, ed., *The American Family in Social-Historical Perspective** (New York, 1973), and Ann Douglas Wood, " 'The Fashionable Diseases'. Women's Complaints and their Treatment in Nineteenth Century America," *Journal of Interdisciplinary History* 4 (Summer 1973); 25–52. See also Barbara Ehrenreich and Deirdre English, *Complaints and Disorders: The Sexual Politics of Sickness** (Old Westbury, N.Y., 1973), and Lois Banner and Mary Hartman, eds., *Clio's Consciousness Raised** (New York, 1974).

1900–1930
The Early Twentieth Century

The Family, Feminism, and Sex
at the Turn of the Century

DAVID M. KENNEDY

Although recent historical research has clearly demonstrated that the nuclear family structure (parents and children) has existed widely in England and the United States since at least the seventeenth century, changing social and economic conditions led the late Victorians to assume it was a product of their own times. They were led, then, to believe that the problems of family life were caused by the emergence of a new family structure rather than by the changing environment. The growth of the industrial city, the separation of home and workplace, the shift in the role of children from units of production to units of consumption all led middle-class Americans to change certain generally accepted standards of family life. Perhaps the most widely noted of these changes was the reduced birthrate. While immigrants were continuing to have large families, many old-stock Americans were limiting the size of their families to two or three children. The implication seemed clear, and Theodore Roosevelt pronounced the words for it—"race suicide." To Roosevelt and others like him, the traditional stock that had made this nation great was about to be overrun by the children of the foreign born.

What was not seen at the time is what since has been called the process of stratification diffusion—a process that made the birthrate a function of social mobility. As the immigrants began to move up the social scale, they sought the advantages of a small family for themselves and their offspring, and their birthrate dropped. For example, Russian Jewish immigrants had the largest birthrate among the immigrant groups in the early twentieth century, but, by 1970, their descendants had the lowest birthrate among American ethnic groups.

The changing life-style of the middle-class family led to a changed role for the women in these families. Or perhaps it was the other way around—the changing role of women led to a new family life-style. But to traditionalists at the time, the relationship was clear —the women's new attitude attacked the basic structure of the family and led not only to race suicide but also to an increase in the divorce rate.

One outcome of the changing role of middle-class women was the turn-of-the-century feminist movement, which is well known for its espousal of suffrage and equal opportunities in education and employment for women. Another, but less well known, development is only now being seriously studied—the changing viewpoint toward the erotic, or sex. It was evident around the turn of the century that more women, and men as well, were marrying for reasons of personal satisfaction, although few talked about the erotic dimension of their choice. Only with the advent of Freudian terminology and the writings of sexologists such as Havelock Ellis did people begin to discuss openly the role of sex in human relations.

In his book on the career of Margaret Sanger and the birth control movement in the United States, David Kennedy, of Stanford University, includes a chapter, reprinted here, that summarizes the background of the movement. Kennedy, in placing Sanger's work in perspective, briefly discusses many of the controversies referred to above. Much of the opposition to the birth control movement couched its objections in the language of "the nature of woman" and, in some cases, religion. But, clearly, concern with the race-suicide notion was paramount. The closing of the immigrant stream in the 1920s reduced somewhat the furor over race suicide.

The nineteenth-century American considered the family, as Henry James put it, "the original germ-cell which lies at the base of all that we call society." That view drew support from the findings of American social scientists, who, in their Germanic search for the origins of all institutions, repeatedly demonstrated the initial formation of society in the microcosm of the family. And the sacredness of the idea of the family had more than an evolutionary derivation. In a country plagued by the divisive effects of civil war, territorial expansion, and the birth of modern industrialism, men put a high premium on the forces working for order and cohesion. The family, they thought, was such a force. Its significance, therefore, was less personal than social. The happiness of its members was well and good, but as James pointed out, "the true sanctity of marriage inheres at bottom in its social uses: It is the sole nursery of the social sentiment in the human bosom." [1] Since the family was both germ cell and nursery, any attempts to tamper with it contradicted nature and threatened the entire moral order. As a woman writer said in 1873: "Whatever tends to deteriorate the marriage relation and consequently the home, tends to deteriorate the whole machinery of life, whether social or political." [2]

By the beginning of the twentieth century, the very forces against which the home had been deemed the most effective defense appeared to many to be undermining the home itself. Critics blamed especially the recrudescence of primitive individualism, as evidenced by growing divorce rates, for the destruction of the traditional family. Several observers

"The Nineteenth-Century Heritage: The Family, Feminism, and Sex" (Editor's title: "The Family, Feminism, and Sex at the Turn of the Century"). From *Birth Control in America: The Career of Margaret Sanger* by David M. Kennedy (New Haven: Yale University Press, 1970), pp. 36–69.

1 Henry James, "Is Marriage Holy?" *Atlantic Monthly*, March 1870, p. 363.
2 Abba Goold Woolson, *Woman in American Society* (Boston: Roberts Brothers, 1873), p. 82.

saw that ruinous spirit best typified in the dramas of Henrik Ibsen, whose philosophy was described as "bold and uncompromising selfishness." Many Americans agreed with the literary critic Chauncey Hawkins that in the face of such egotism, "the family, that institution which we have long regarded as the unit of civilization, the foundation of the state," could not long survive.[3]

The alarm had little substance. The nineteenth-century family, which the Victorians regarded as a contemporary embodiment of the primeval social unit, was in fact a relatively modern institution. As the French historian Phillipe Ariés has convincingly shown, the concept of the family did not emerge until the late Renaissance, and then only among the upper classes. The apparent disintegration of the family which the late Victorians decried in fact represented its adjustment to new living conditions brought about by urbanization and industrialization. But those processes by no means spelled the death of the family.[4]

As Americans moved increasingly to cities in the nineteenth century, old patterns of family life had to change. Separated in most instances from the protective and preceptive influences of kin groups and village culture, men and women newly arrived in American cities began family life without precedents and with only vague prospects. As the sociologist Arthur W. Calhoun commented, America was the first civilization that in any large way experimented with "placing the entire burden of securing the success of marriage and the family life upon the characters and capacities of two persons. . . . American marriage is a union of two people and not an alliance between two families." In that new atomistic union, marital partners took on new roles and marriage itself assumed new character and functions. On the farm, the family had been an integral producing unit. In the city, families no longer worked together. The factory or the office kept the father away from the home most of the day. The urban economy forced the housewife out of the agricultural producing unit and, by emphasizing pecuniary rewards, tended to devalue household labor. Moreover, industry itself usurped many of the functions the housewife had once been accustomed to performing. "The machine," wrote E. A. Ross, "has captured most of the domestic processes." Thus the urban home by the early twentieth century had lost nearly all its economic cogency.[5]

---

[3] Chauncey J. Hawkins, *Will the Home Survive? A Study of Tendencies in Modern Literature* (New York: Thomas Whittaker, 1907), pp. 7, 56.

[4] Philippe Ariés, *Centuries of Childhood* (New York: Alfred A. Knopf, 1962); Christopher Lasch, "Divorce and the Family in America," *Atlantic*, November 1966, pp. 57–61; see also William L. O'Neill, *Divorce in the Progressive Era* (New Haven: Yale University Press, 1967).

[5] Arthur W. Calhoun, *A Social History of the American Family*, vol. 3, *Since the Civil War* (Cleveland: Arthur H. Clark, 1919), p. 169; E. A. Ross, "The Significance of Increasing Divorce," *Century Magazine*, May 1909, p. 151; see also Robert W. Smuts, *Women and Work in America* (New York: Columbia University Press, 1959).

As industry deprived the family of many of its economic functions, the state took over many of its welfare functions by enacting laws creating compulsory education, maternal health programs, and juvenile court systems. Social critics from John Spargo to Theodore Roosevelt endorsed the Socialist idea of the state as an "over-parent" which should provide schools, housing, sanitation, and recreation in the crowded cities. "If this be Socialism," Roosevelt said, "make the most of it!" Thus with little dissent, the state substituted its services for the old self-sufficiency of the family.[6]

Paradoxically, many of the same critics who blamed "individualism" for the destruction of the Victorian family also observed a "new solidarity of the state" being built "at the expense of the old solidarity of the family." Somehow, the individualism that destroyed one institution was supposed to give birth to the collectivism that strengthened another.[7] The confusion reflected the Victorian failure to recognize the transformation of the family not as a collapse but as an adjustment. The family did not retreat before new social forces. Indeed, the late nineteenth century saw a continuation of the strengthening of the notion of the family, especially among the middle and upper classes. As Ariés has remarked, "the whole evolution of our contemporary manners is unintelligible if one neglects this astonishing growth of the concept of the family. It is not individualism which has triumphed, but the family." [8]

But in that triumph the family took on a new vital center. "The old economic framework of the family has largely fallen away," noted E. A. Ross in 1909, "leaving more of the strain on the personal tie." Ross did not mean that husbands and wives had never before loved each other or that personal relations had not always figured importantly in marriage. But when urban industrialism displaced economic partnership from the matrix of marriage, such factors as congeniality and affection assumed greater importance. "Essentially," said George Elliott Howard, a sociologist who wrote frequently on the divorce problem, "the family society is becoming a psychic fact." The family, in other words, had taken on increased, rather than diminished, emotional significance. Husbands now had to be more than mere providers. And wives, having lost the role of economic partner, had to assume several new ones. "In the old days," commented a woman in 1907, "a married woman was supposed to be a frump and a bore and a physical wreck. Now you are supposed to keep up intellectually, to look young and well and be fresh and bright and entertaining." Rising divorce rates signaled more than the ease of separa-

---

[6] John Spargo, *Socialism and Motherhood* (New York: B. W. Huebsch, 1914); Theodore Roosevelt, *The Foes of Our Own Household* (New York: George H. Doran, 1917), p. 183.

[7] George Elliott Howard, "Changed Ideals and Status of the Family and the Public Activities of Women," *Annals of the American Academy of Political and Social Science* 56 (November 1914): 29.

[8] Ariés, *Centuries of Childhood*, p. 406.

tion in a free and rich society. They also bespoke the difficulty of adjustment to the intensified emotional demands of family life.[9]

The new industrial economy also demanded a new work discipline which denied emotion and encouraged exclusively cognitive behavior in the interests of production. That compartmentalization of experience made the home the exclusive arena for the play of emotion. And the growth of the family's emotional exclusiveness made the home an increasingly private place. As the urban family became less self-sufficient, therefore, it simultaneously grew more committed to self-determination. Ariés has shown that "in the 18th century, the family began to hold society at a distance, to push it back beyond a steadily extending zone of private life." Nineteenth-century industrialism quickened that development, and by 1906 an American sociologist frankly acknowledged "the manifest conflict of interests between the individual family and the community at large." That conflict was most marked, the writer said, when the family refused to produce enough children for the service of the state.[10]

A new attitude toward childhood, along with the development of the family as a "psychic fact" and as a progressively more private institution, completed the list of characteristics that distinguished the modern family. Again, as Ariés has demonstrated, "the concept of the family, which thus emerges in the 16th and 17th centuries, is inseparable from the concept of childhood." Before the sixteenth century, children were considered "little adults," who were loved, to be sure, but whose primary value to the producing family was economic. After that time, in line with the general restructuring of the family, children took on a greater emotional value. Moreover, childhood came increasingly to be regarded as a special age of life, and the child as a special being with his own distinctive qualities. Foremost among those qualities was the child's capacity for formation and development. When that quality was recognized, as Christopher Lasch has said, "child-rearing ceased to be simply one of many activities and became the central concern—one is tempted to say the central obsession—of family life." The late nineteenth century made that concern explicit, as in the novelist Margaret Deland's proclamation of "the right of children *not* to be born." When parents, she said, "unable to support a child in physical and moral and intellectual well-being, bring such a child into the world . . . they are socially criminal." And when Charlotte Perkins Gilman said in 1911 that the duty of the family was to ensure children "an ever longer period of immaturity," by extending their education as long as possible, she was acknowledging the new status of the child not as an economic asset, but as an economic liability. In that way the oft-noted shift from a producing to a consuming psychology affected even the affairs of the family. Parents no longer produced chil-

---

[9] Ross, "Increasing Divorce," p. 151; Howard, "Changed Ideals," p. 29; Lydia K. Commander, *The American Idea* (New York: A. S. Barnes, 1907), p. 182.

[10] Ariés, *Centuries of Childhood*, p. 398; American Sociological Society, *Papers and Proceedings* 1 (1906): 53. See also Kenneth Keniston, *The Uncommitted: Alienated Youth in American Society* (New York: Harcourt, Brace and World, 1965), pp. 241–81.

dren in the greatest quantity possible. They had fewer children in order to provide each with a better quality of upbringing.[11]

The shrinking size of the American family—especially among the genteel classes—caused at least as much alarm at the turn of the century as did the growing divorce rate. Benjamin Franklin had predicted in 1755 that the abundance of the New World would cause the American people to double their numbers every twenty years. At that rate, there should have been nearly 130 million Americans by 1900; in fact, there were scarcely 76 million. In Franklin's day, families commonly had eight or ten children. By 1900, the average number of children per family was closer to three. The birthrate of American women had been falling steadily since at least 1820. While 1,000 mothers in 1800 had 1,300 children under five years of age, the same number of mothers in 1900 had fewer than 700 such children. The trend indicated, said Theodore Roosevelt, that the American people were committing "race suicide." With that utterance in 1903, Roosevelt minted the phrase which for the next forty years was a frequent rallying cry for the opponents of birth control.[12]

President Roosevelt, in his annual message to Congress in 1905, described the transformation of family life "as one of the greatest sociological phenomena of our time; it is a social question of the first importance, of far greater importance than any merely political or economic question can be." Yet much of Roosevelt's concern for the condition of the family proceeded from his political assumptions. In his view, the family should be the servant of the state; it should provide children to build national strength. Germany dominated Europe, Roosevelt wrote, because she had won "the warfare of the cradle . . . during the nineteenth century." If America aspired to ascendancy in world affairs, American parents must breed larger families.[13]

The race suicide alarm, however, fed more on ethnocentric fears than on nationalist ambition. Though Roosevelt complained because American population statistics did not keep pace with his jingoistic appetite, he considered the "worst evil" to be the greater infertility of "the old native American stock, especially in the North East," as compared with the immigrant population. In 1902 R. R. Kuczynski demonstrated what everyone had suspected for a long time—that the immigrant birthrate was 70 to 80 percent higher than the native birthrate. Worse, Kuczynski concluded, it was "probable that the native population cannot hold its own. It seems to be dying out." In a study a few years later, the United States Immigration Commission found that "the rate of childbearing on the part

11 Ariés, *Centuries of Childhood*, p. 353; Lasch, "Divorce and the Family," p. 59; Margaret Deland, "The Change in the Feminine Ideal," *Atlantic Monthly*, March 1910, p. 291; Charlotte Perkins Gilman, *The Man-Made World, or, Our Androcentric Culture* (New York: Charlton, 1911), p. 27.

12 *Historical Statistics of the United States* (Washington: Government Printing Office, 1961), pp. 23, 24, 180, 181; T. Roosevelt, *Foes*, p. 257.

13 *Messages and Papers of the Presidents* 16 (New York: Bureau of National Literature, n.d.): 6984; Theodore Roosevelt, "Race Decadence," *Outlook*, April 8, 1911, p. 765.

of women of foreign parentage is nearly twice as great as that of native American women." But significantly, the Immigration Commission reported another phenomenon: the average number of childern borne by the second generation immigrant woman "was invariably smaller than the average for the first generation." Clearly, then, the determinants of fertility were not solely ethnic; they apparently had a great deal to do with economic status and the amorphous notion of class.[14]

That perception added to ethnocentric fears the alarming prospect that not simply native Americans but in particular the upper classes, the highest products of evolution and natural selection, were failing to reproduce themselves. President Charles W. Eliot of Harvard confirmed the worst suspicions in 1902 when he reported that a typical group of Harvard graduates fell 28 percent short of replenishing its number. A later study revealed that only 75 percent of late nineteenth-century Harvard graduates married; of these, nearly a quarter had childless marriages, and the rest averaged scarcely two children per marriage. Yale graduates did little better. That was "gloomy enough," the report concluded, but it called the birthrate among college women "the most pathetic spectacle of all." In the average Wellesley class, for example, only one-half the graduates married, and those who did invariably had small families. A New York newspaper reporter in 1907 found only fifteen children in sixteen of the highest-rent residential blocks in New York. It seemed that the very class upon which many in the Progressive generation pinned their hopes for an orderly future was disappearing.[15]

Commentators cited a myriad of causes for the decline in the upper-class birthrate, ranging from the spread of venereal disease, to "physiological infertility" induced by "the high voltage of American civilization," to the inevitable consequences of spiritual degeneracy. But more disinterested observers recognized that the decline in the birthrate was voluntary. One writer noted that "outside our immigrant class, and a few native-born families scattered here and there, women have learned the art of preventing pregnancy." [16] Charles Knowlton's handbook of contraceptive techniques, *Fruits of Philosophy*, had only a small underground circulation in this country after its publication in 1832; but the declining birthrate indicated that the practices he described—probably vaginal douching in particular—were increasingly employed in certain social

[14] Theodore Roosevelt to Cecil Arthur Spring Rice, August 11, 1899, in *The Letters of Theodore Roosevelt*, Elting E. Morison, ed., 8 vols. (Cambridge: Harvard University Press, 1951–54), 2:1053; R. R. Kuczynski, "The Fecundity of the Native and Foreign Born Population in Massachusetts," *Quarterly Journal of Economics* 16 (1902): 141–86; U.S., Congress, Senate, *Report of the United States Immigration Commission*, 61st Cong., 2d sess. (Washington: Government Printing Office, 1911), 28:753, 749.

[15] *Annual Reports of the President and the Treasurer of Harvard College, 1901–02* (Cambridge: Harvard University, 1903), pp. 31–32; John C. Phillips, "A Study of the Birth-Rate in Harvard and Yale Graduates," *Harvard Graduates Magazine*, September, 1916, p. 25; Commander, *American Idea*, p. 198.

[16] Edward L. Thorndike, "The Decrease in the Size of American Families," *Popular Science Monthly* 63 (May 1903): 64–70.

classes. A doctor, as early as 1867, said that "there is scarcely a young lady in New England—and probably it is so throughout the land—whose marriage can be announced in the paper, without her being insulted within a week by receiving through the mail a printed circular, offering information and instrumentalities, and all needed facilities, by which the laws of heaven in regard to the increase of the human family may be thwarted." Anthony Comstock corroborated that statement in 1880 when he reported the confiscation, over the preceding seven years, of 64,094 "articles for immoral use, of rubber, etc.," and 700 pounds of "lead moulds for making Obscene Matter." Despite scanty official medical attention, by the late 1800s certain sections of the public were well supplied with contraceptive information and devices. There was "hardly a single middle-class family" among his clients, said a doctor in 1906, that did not expect him to implement their "desire to prevent conception." [17] As Lydia Commander said in 1907, among the upper classes some kind of contraceptive knowledge was "practically universal." [18]

But the availability of that knowledge did not in itself cause the general restriction in the size of native middle- and upper-class families. Many Americans manifested the modern consideration for the welfare of the child when they decided to limit their offspring to as many as could be "given the necessary education to fit them for the best in life." [19] But that idea, though pervasively "modern" in its concern for children, took firmest hold among the middle class; and in its emphasis on the "best in life" it reflected more than enlightened theories of child-rearing. It also revealed an increasing concern for social mobility and the development of a middle-class definition of an acceptable standard of living. The *Nation*, in 1903, noted the apparent paradox that in America, contrary to all Malthusian predictions, the population was beginning to shrink in the face of an increasing food supply. But the paradox was easily explained, said the *Nation*: Malthus "did not, perhaps, give sufficient weight to the fact that the means of subsistence is a relative term, varying from age to age, and having different meanings to different peoples." [20] Similarly, Lydia Commander argued that the instinct of reproduction was subordinate to the instinct of self-preservation, which had taken on a new meaning in America. "The full dinnerpail," she said, did not mark the limits of the American's ambition. "It is only the bare beginning of his needs." [21] An article in the *North American Review* in 1903, by "Pater-

---

[17] Arthur W. Calhoun, *Social History of the American Family*, 3:228, 239; Anthony Comstock, *Frauds Exposed* (New York: J. Howard Brown, 1880), p. 435. Anthony Comstock, by his own account, also confiscated 202,679 "obscene pictures and photos," 4,185 "boxes of pills, powders, etc., used by abortionists," and 26 "obscene pictures, framed on walls of saloons"; see also E. A. Ross, "Western Civilization and the Birth Rate," American Sociological Society, *Papers and Proceedings* 1 (1907): 29–54; and Hawkins, *Will the Home Survive?* p. 12.
[18] Commander, *American Idea*, pp. 89–92.
[19] Hawkins, *Will the Home Survive?* p. 12.
[20] "The Question of the Birth Rate," *Nation*, June 11, 1903, p. 469.
[21] Commander, *American Idea*, p. 96.

familias," frankly stated that the modern family limited its size in order to enjoy a certain "style of living." The author's "social position" was "very dear" to him, he said, and it would be threatened by additional children. Furthermore, more children would make a household drudge of his wife. Therefore he intended to have no more. "I presume," he said, "there are those who will think that this is an ignoble statement. But it is not only true, but it is true of about every family of which I have any personal acquaintance." [22]

The article by Paterfamilias elicited extensive comment in 1903, and though few disputed the accuracy of its thesis about the motives behind family limitation, many saw in those motives, as Theodore Roosevelt put it, "frightful and fundamental immorality." What Paterfamilias had defended as dedication to his "style of living," Roosevelt called submission "to coldness, to selfishness, to love of ease, to shrinking from risk, to an utter and pitiful failure in sense of perspective." [23]

Many observers agreed with Roosevelt that a new and destructive slavishness to the self was strangling the American family, but they went beyond his criticism when they branded the feminist movement as the principal vehicle of that egotism. In the simultaneous rise of the emancipated woman and decline of the family, they saw the fulfillment of a dark prophecy. Herbert Spencer had proclaimed in the mid-nineteenth century the iron biological law of antagonism between "Individuation and Genesis." Every higher degree of evolution, he said, was followed by a "lower degree of race-multiplication." As the New Woman, therefore, evolved to a greater individualism and self-sufficiency, she lost her capacity for reproduction. Specifically, Spencer said, "the overtaxing of their brains" through too much mental effort had "a serious reaction on the physique" of women and resulted in a "diminution of reproductive power." Spencer thus lent the prestige of evolutionary science to the argument that the women's movement bore a heavy responsibility for the shrinking family. In fact, Spencer provided only one of many points of contact between the criticisms of the modern family and the criticisms of the New Woman. From the time in the late nineteenth century when the condition of the family became a topic of general public discussion, it was rarely mentioned apart from the "woman question." [24]

Edward Alsworth Ross ascribed both the liberation of women and the transformation of the family to a "transition process in social evolu-

---

[22] Paterfamilias, " 'Race Suicide' and Common Sense," *North American Review* 176 (1903): 897. The phenomenon of lower fertility associated with social mobility and class standing was by no means peculiarly American. The French demographer Jacques Bertillon found that as the Frenchman advanced from "prolétaire" to "propriétaire," he limited the size of his family. Bertillon concluded that "l'aisance entrain la stérilité." *La Depopulation de la France* (Paris: Felix Alcan, 1911). See also J. A. Banks, *Prosperity and Parenthood* (London: Routledge and Kegan Paul, 1954).

[23] T. Roosevelt, "Race Decadence," p. 764.

[24] Herbert Spencer, *The Principles of Biology*, 2 vols. (New York: D. Appleton, 1898–99), 2:430, 512–13.

tion." At the heart of that process, said Ross, was a new sense of individuality which provided women with "a point of view of their own"
and replaced the patriarchal with the "democratic" family. Though the
process sometimes produced an "exaggerated self-will," Ross contended
that it was rare and not to be held responsible for divorce and smaller
families.[25]

But the individualism Ross thought salutary, conservative defenders
of the family continued to damn as rank selfishness. They especially indicted women. A symposium in the *North American Review* in 1889
blamed women's self-indulgent romanticism for the divorce rate. Twenty
years later Anna B. Rogers confidently explained "why American marriages fail": because women had become devoted to "the latter-day cult
of individualism; the worship of the brazen calf of Self." [26]

Feminists admitted their role in changing the family, but they had a
different explanation of their motives. In the feminists' view, the women's
movement was redressing an ancient historical grievance. Social scientists
such as Lewis Henry Morgan and Lester Ward, they said, had shown that
the original family was a matriarchal institution. Somewhere along the
line men had subverted that order and robbed women of their status and
independence. As Thorstein Veblen wrote, the masculine ideal of marriage was "in point of derivation, a predatory institution." It rested, said
Veblen, on the mechanisms of ownership, coercion, and control. More
than anything else, the feminists objected to the coercion to which they
said all married women were expected to submit. In that protest they but
shared a general antipathy to authority deeply seated in American traditions. Henry James, in 1870, touched on that tradition when he said
that marriage came into "dishonor" when it was not *freely* honored, or
honored exclusively for its own sake." Prevailing opinion, on the other
hand, regarded marriage as "properly honored when it is enforced by
some external sanction." That element of force, said James, had made
marriage "the hotbed of fraud, adultery, and cruelty." It could only become "holy" when it rested not on constraint but on the sentiments of
its members.[27]

The acrimony of the debate on the transformation of the family
and the role of women in that process often obscured the common assumptions from which both sides argued. Conservatives wished to preserve the sanctity of the home, while reformers wanted to restore it to an
ancient dignity. Practically everyone agreed on the paramount importance of the family in human life. Both advocates and adversaries of easier
divorce invoked the sacredness of the marital relation in support of their

[25] Ross, "Significance of Increasing Divorce," pp. 151–52.

[26] "Are Women to Blame?" *North American Review* 148 (1889): 622–42; Anna B.
Rogers, *Why American Marriages Fail* (Boston: Houghton Mifflin, 1909), p. 16.

[27] Lewis Henry Morgan, *Ancient Society* (Cambridge: Harvard University Press,
Belknap Press, 1964; first published, 1877); Lester Ward, *Pure Sociology* (New
York: Macmillan, 1914), Ch. 14; Thorstein Veblen, "The Barbarian Status of
Women," *American Journal of Sociology* 4 (1899): 503–14; Henry James, letter
to the editor, *Nation*, June 9, 1870, p. 366.

respective cases. Partisans of women's suffrage and education justified their causes with reference to the improvement of the home fully as often as their opponents warned of its destruction. There were really no radical opinions about the family. Even the Socialist critics of marriage wanted only those changes that would "make it possible for every mother to devote herself to the care of her children." [28] From that goal, virtually no one dissented. For all the noise surrounding the transformation of the family in the late Victorian era, in the end the process simply strengthened the three distinctive characteristics that had been developing for two centuries. Beneath the confrontation of conservative and reformist views lay an undeniable consensus that the family had greater emotional importance than ever. With that growing importance had come the increasing privacy of the home. And within the segregated emotional center of the family, the child had come to be its greatest concern.

The divorce and race suicide alarm preoccupied, for a time, the debate on the "woman question," but that debate was an ancient one, and long after the height of the panic over the condition of the family had passed, Americans continued to disagree over the proper status of women. Indeed, that debate goes on, unresolved, in the present day. In the late nineteenth century, however, the age-old discussion of woman's place was just beginning to take on its modern urgency. No longer could that discussion be academic, as it had been earlier in the century: the New Woman was appearing on the scene and demanding to be taken seriously. The New Woman was in fact two different ladies, the self-sufficient working girl and the dependent, restless "parasite woman," the idle wife in a middle class with growing wealth and leisure. But each of these women was new, and each, in her own way, repudiated the nineteenth-century ideal of femininity.

The feminine ideal which the nineteenth century made an article of faith grew up as part of a reaction against older convictions of the sinfulness and depravity of humanity. That ideal was not so much Puritanical as it was anti-Puritan when it made woman symbolize the possibilities of perfection and benevolence. Man saw in woman, as Henry James said, "a diviner self than his own," and James himself enshrined such American goddesses as Daisy Miller and Milly Theale in the national imagination. [29]

The idealized American woman was above all incorruptibly innocent. James made Daisy Miller's unreflecting innocence the quality that most puzzled Europeans. That innocence, said the biographer and muckraker Ida Tarbell, came easily to American girls who were "brought up

[28] Spargo, *Socialism and Motherhood*, p. 32.

[29] James, "Is Marriage Holy?" p. 364. For the development of the symbolic view of women, see Leslie Fiedler, *Love and Death in the American Novel* (New York: Criterion Books, 1960); William Wasserstrom, *Heiress of All the Ages: Sex and Sentiment in the Genteel Tradition* (Minneapolis: University of Minnesota Press, 1959); and Barbara Welter, "The Cult of True Womanhood," *American Quarterly* 18 (1966): 151–74.

as if wrongdoing were impossible to them." [30] Susan B. Anthony's mother had such a deeply bred fealty to the ideal of innocence that "before the birth of every child she was overwhelmed with embarrassment and humiliation, secluded herself from the outside world and would not speak of the expected little one." [31] High-minded men protected their wives and daughters from the outside world by making the home a citadel against threatening influences. Single-minded devotion to domestic duties, men preached, to "marriage and motherhood . . . the highest, indeed the only successful career for woman," was more than woman's duty; it was the only sure protection against the forces of corruption.[32]

A second characteristic of the feminine ideal was helplessness. In 1908 H. L. Mencken protested the "absurd" but nevertheless ubiquitous idea "that the civilization of a people is to be measured by the degree of dependence of its women." The idea of helplessness Veblen again traced to the predatory origins of marriage. But most Americans probably agreed with Theodore Roosevelt that "the woman has a harder time than the man, and must have, from the mere fact that she must bear and largely rear her children." Her dependence, in that view, proceeded from the "laws of nature," and it demanded of men, said Roosevelt, that they treat women with special respect, as they would treat "anything good and helpless." [33]

In a special way, the ideal American girl also embodied and symbolized goodness. Again, Henry James created the fictional archetype of the absolutely good woman in Milly Theale, the heroine of *The Wings of the Dove*. In Milly's unflinching purity of motive and action, James sought expression for an important part of the myth of the American woman. Milly's European acquaintances at first found her simply naïve; later, the terrible consistency of her conscience affected them all profoundly. "We shall never again be as we were," concluded Kate Croy after Milly's death, and she echoed James's own thoughts on the death of his cousin, Mary Temple. That death, he wrote, marked "the end of our youth." Somehow, James and other American men expressed their sense of lost youthful innocence, dependence, and goodness by creating an idealized picture of the American woman.[34]

Bronson Alcott pointed to another large component of the goodness the American woman was supposed to possess when he described his

30 Ida M. Tarbell, *The Business of Being a Woman* (New York: Macmillan, 1912), p. 179.
31 Ida Husted Harper, *The Life and Work of Susan B. Anthony* (Indianapolis: Bowen-Merrill, 1899), pp. 12–13.
32 Mary Roberts Coolidge, *Why Women Are So* (New York: Henry Holt, 1912), pp. 44–45.
33 H. L. Mencken, *The Philosophy of Friedrich Nietzsche* (Boston: Luce, 1908), p. 189; Veblen, "Barbarian Status of Women," pp. 504–07; Morison, *Letters of Theodore Roosevelt*, 2:904 (Roosevelt to Helen Kendrick Johnson, January 10, 1899), 3:520 (Roosevelt to Hamlin Garland, July 19, 1903).
34 Henry James, *Wings of the Dove* (New York: Dell, 1963), p. 512; Henry James, *Notes of a Son and Brother* (London: Macmillan, 1914), p. 47. See also Fiedler, *Love and Death in the American Novel*, and Wasserstrom, *Heiress of All the Ages*.

daughter as "duty's faithful child." [35] Louisa May Alcott earned that paternal praise by eschewing marriage and personal happiness and tending her father without complaint until his dying day. To pious believers in the feminine ideal, Miss Alcott revealed her true womanhood by that self-abnegating devotion to the service of another. So central was the belief in the generosity of the idealized woman that Americans found any contrary suggestion blasphemous or incomprehensible. When Henrik Ibsen's *Doll's House* opened in Boston in 1889, a reviewer remarked that the "ending can never be liked by American audiences, who will be loath to believe that a woman owes a higher duty to the development of her own nature than to the young children she has brought into the world." In New York, a reviewer confessed to "the difficulty an average audience experiences to see what the playwright means—what he is driving at." Another observer noted that when Americans came across a (rare) woman like Nora Helmer, who resolved to "do her duty to herself," they had "a dull trick of suspecting mental disease." [36] The nineteenth-century woman, said Mary Roberts Coolidge, a perceptive and sympathetic critic of the feminist movement, was raised to please men, not herself. Woman's personality had come to resemble that of an actor, who, "like the woman," Mrs. Coolidge wrote, "makes his place in life chiefly by the cultivation of manner and appearance. He, like her, depends for success upon pleasing rather than being admirable. The 'matinee idol' is an extreme example of character—or, rather, perversion of character—by the social necessity of being charming and of trading in assumed emotions." [37] Though "other-direction" has been called a characteristically twentieth-century component of personality, American women obviously knew its meaning well before 1900. So too, it could be argued, the "individualism" so highly valued in the nineteenth century and ever since regarded as a distinctive quality of American life in that epoch was apparently for men only.

By the end of the century, however, feminists had mounted an active revolt against the burden of assumed emotions. The picture of the idealized woman, they said, was false; and certainly that picture of American women—as innocent, dependent, good, and selfless—had always fitted masculine wishes better than it had the facts.

What men cherished as "innocence" was purchased at the price of often disastrous ignorance. Charlotte Perkins Gilman indicted the belief that innocence was a woman's chief charm. "What good does it do her?" she asked. "Her whole life's success is made to depend on her marrying; her health and happiness depends [*sic*] on her marrying the right man. The more 'innocent' she is, the less she knows, the easier it is for the wrong man to get her." Mary Roberts Coolidge noted ironically that though marriage and motherhood constituted a woman's only permitted

[35] Thomas Beer, *The Mauve Decade* (Garden City, N.Y.: Garden City Publishing, 1926), pp. 19–21.

[36] *New York Daily Tribune*, October 31, 1889, p. 6; *New York Times*, December 22, 1889, p. 11; *Belford's Magazine*, April 1890, p. 772.

[37] Coolidge, *Why Women Are So*, p. 101.

career, "yet, nothing in her training had any direct relation to it, and the conventional standard of modesty required her to be wholly ignorant of its physical aspects." Certainly Susan B. Anthony learned little about the "physical aspects" of married life from a mother who took her confinement literally. An anonymous feminist in 1906 said that the average nineteenth-century girl "contemplated the sexual relation with the bitterest reluctance," because she had been "sedulously guarded from knowledge of the fundamental reasons of her being, cast suddenly and unprepared into marriage." Robert Latou Dickinson, probably America's most prominent gynecologist, corroborated those women's observations when he reported that his clinical practice had shown that "no single cause of mental strain in married women is as widespread as sex fears and maladjustments." He blamed the prevalence of those fears on the enforced sexual ignorance of women.[38]

The pathologic effects of the regimen of sheltered domesticity were not all psychological. The helplessness of the American woman—especially in the urban East and the upper-class South—owed at least as much to real physiological weakness as it did to compliance with a rigid moral ideal. "An American sculptor unhampered by the models of the past," said a woman writer in 1873, "would represent the Three Graces as lolling on sofa-cushions, with a bottle of salts in one hand and a fan in the other." To be ladylike, she said, was to be "lifeless, inane, and dawdling," and another woman later recalled a nineteenth-century rhyme which told that "the bride, *of course*, fainted, for, being acquainted with manners, she knew what was right." Robert Latou Dickinson insisted in the 1890s that the neurasthenic female was more than a caricature and that the causes of her condition were plain: lack of exercise and ridiculous standards of dress. "It is supposed to be sufficient exercise for the sister," he wrote, "to wave her handkerchief from the grand stand." Dickinson also suggested that the alleged "sexlessness" of American women owed at least in part to the relatively primitive state of gynecological medicine. Low-grade vaginal infections, later remedied routinely, could in the nineteenth century be an enduring and debilitating discomfort. And scores of other medical writers joined Dickinson in pointing out the harmful effects of the steel-ribbed corsets women wore to shrink their waists and expand their busts. The rigid "health waists" were especially damaging to working girls who leaned forward all day over a typewriter or a sewing machine. Still, in spite of almost daily evidence of the injury done to women by overdomestication and overdressing, the American male—whose house women kept and for whose eye they attired themselves—continued to pride himself on the manly protection he offered his delicate, dependent charges.[39]

38 Gilman, *Man-Made World*, p. 167; Coolidge, pp. 44–45. Elizabeth B. Wetmore, *The Secret Life* (New York: John Lane, 1906), p. 93; Robert Latou Dickinson, "Marital Maladjustment—The Business of Preventive Gynecology," *Long Island Medical Journal* 2 (1908)1: 1–5.
39 Woolson, *Woman in American Society*, p. 192; Deland, "Change in the Feminine Ideal," p. 293; R. L. Dickinson, "Simple and Practical Methods in Dress Reform,"

Similarly, the myth of the ideal woman sanctified her generosity and selflessness by piously glorifying the sacrifices she was expected cheerfully to make. Men impressed upon women, said Lydia Commander, the authoress of one of the most popular contemporary books on the family and feminism, "that it was a religious duty to suffer," especially to suffer the pains of childbirth and the exasperations of child-rearing. The duties of the American woman, said Theodore Roosevelt, exceeded those of the American fighting man and should receive far more adulation. Because of biology, he said, the woman "has a harder time than the man." A woman writer in 1916 perceived that in the nineteenth-century feminine ideal "the element of sacrifice is so obvious that it is even seized upon and treated as a virtue, an added glory for the crown of the wife and mother." [40]

Finally, the myth of the idealized American woman preserved her innocence and her goodness by denying her sexuality. In nineteenth-century fiction, said Thomas Beer, "the female principal is risen above romance and becomes an opalescent cloud, dripping odours which had nothing to do with the process of childbearing at all." The myth, therefore, not only kept women ignorant of what it simultaneously glorified as their chief honor and duty. It also insulated them from all passion and erotic desire. As Viola Klein has observed, in the whole Western world "during the nineteenth and at the beginning of the twentieth century it would have been not only scandalous to admit the existence of a strong sex urge in women, but it would have been contrary to all observation." H. L. Mencken called it a "good old sub-Potomac" idea that a woman "who loses her virtue is, *ipso facto,* a victim and not a criminal or *particeps criminis,* and that a 'lady,' by virtue of being a 'lady,' is necessarily a reluctant and helpless quarry in the hunt of love." But the idea held with nearly unassailable force above the Potomac as well. No genuinely passionate woman appeared in American fiction at least from the time of the Civil War to the naturalist outburst at the turn of the century. As late as 1908, Robert Latou Dickinson was urging the medical profession to tell nervous women patients there was no cause for alarm if they enjoyed sexual intercourse. And even such an otherwise perceptive man as E. A. Ross asserted confidently in 1906 that it was a "physiological fact that the sexual instinct is not only very much weaker in most women, but is altogether absent in a growing number of them." [41]

Gynecological Transactions 18 (1893): 411; R. L. Dickinson, "Bicycling for Women from the Standpoint of the Gynecologist," *American Journal of Obstetrics* 31 (1895): 25. See also Mark Sullivan, *Our Times,* vol. 1, *The Turn of the Century* (New York: Charles Scribner's Sons, 1926), pp. 385–95.

[40] Commander, *American Idea,* p. 235; Morison, *Letters of Theodore Roosevelt,* 3:520–21 (Roosevelt to Hamlin Garland, July 19, 1903); Jessie Taft, *The Woman Movement from the Point of View of Social Consciousness* (Chicago: University of Chicago Press, 1916), p. 55.

[41] Beer, *Mauve Decade,* p. 54; Viola Klein, *The Feminine Character* (New York: International Universities Press, 1949), p. 85; Mencken, *Philosophy of Friedrich Nietzsche,* p. 186; Dickinson, "Marital Maladjustment"; Ross, "Western Civilization and the Birth Rate," p. 51. See Steven Marcus, *The Other Victorians: A Study*

Feminists reacted against both the myth and the facts it so sancti-moniously concealed but could not change. By the end of the nineteenth century women were telling men that they wanted neither innocence nor ignorance, dependence or disease, self-abnegation or sacrifice, good-ness nor sexlessness. The New Woman, Leslie Fiedler has said, refused to accept her prescribed function of "redemptive suffering," and with that refusal she "threatened to upset the whole Sentimental Love Reli-gion" in which the myth of the ideal woman was enshrined. Independence became the religion of the New Woman, and Henrik Ibsen was one of its chief prophets. Ibsen showed, said one of his American admirers in 1890, "the necessity of a new life . . . a life divested of the conventional ideas of what is Woman's duty." In contrast to early feminist reformers who had sought to restructure legal forms in order to give women con-trol over their own property and persons, by the late nineteenth century feminists more or less consciously sought to restructure the feminine personality itself.[42]

Lydia Commander, describing the New Woman in 1907, noted the "radical alteration in her personality. Under the old regime," she said, "humility, self-sacrifice, and obedience were assiduously cultivated as the highest of womanly virtues." But now, she concluded, "self-sacrifice . . . is no longer in favor. Self-development is rapidly taking its place." For many American feminists in the last quarter of the century, an encounter with European ideas—in Ibsen, Friedrich Nietzsche, Henri Bergson, or George Bernard Shaw—finally broke the long-standing tension of trying to live up to the duties of the feminine ideal. After more than two gen-erations of strictly legal progress, the women's movement began to turn inward to search for a definition of a new feminine personality. Later, the movement would again turn at least partly outward and justify itself with claims of the benefits it could bestow on society. But for a season its paramount concern was the development of a new sense of self. And in that development, society, and society's expectations, could only be enemies.[43]

The idea of antagonism between the feminine self and society coin-cided strikingly with a notion that underlay the very feminine ideal against which the reformers protested: the idea of woman's victimization. Men constantly regarded the innocent woman as a potential victim of sin-ister forces. They even sentimentalized the obviously corrupted woman, as H. L. Mencken noted, as an unwitting gull of evil persons. When the white slave panic reached its height around 1910, the image of the hapless prostitute as a victim of poverty or lechery found ready acceptance and

---

of Sexuality and Pornography in Mid-Nineteenth Century England (New York: Basic Books, 1964), pp. 28–32, for a most interesting discussion of a similar de-sexualizing of women in nineteenth-century England; for more on the phenome-non in the United States, see Fiedler, *Love and Death in the American Novel*, and Joseph Wood Krutch, *The Modern Temper* (New York: Harcourt, Brace, 1929).

42 Fiedler, p. 221; Annie Nathan Meyer, letter to the editor, *Critic*, March 22, 1890, p. 148.

43 Commander, *American Idea*, pp. 144–45.

frequent expression. And behind Theodore Roosevelt's idea that the woman achieved nobility by sacrifice stood the premise that biology— regrettably, but unavoidably—victimized women far more than it did men. A woman writer noted that society displayed its recognition of that victimization when it attempted to translate the experiences of women in marriage and motherhood "into a sort of fetish . . . exalted to the point where they are assumed to be a sufficient compensation for any and all sacrifices." [44]

But though the New Woman was not to be so easily compensated, she herself nevertheless appealed to society's sense of her victimization when she did demand compensation in the shape of legal, economic, and social reforms. When the suffragists first shifted from a "natural rights" to an "expediency" argument for the vote, says Aileen Kraditor, they insisted "that women needed the ballot for self-protection." In other words, they asked for political power to combat the forces that victimized them. Similarly, protective labor legislation first came into being "in the name of defenseless women and children." And Christopher Lasch has noted perceptively that "it was not the image of women as equals that inspired the reform of the divorce laws, but the image of women as victims." In her search for equality, says Lasch, by appealing to the idea of victimization, "woman depended on a sentimentalization of womanhood which eroded the idea of equality as easily as it promoted it." [45]

Both feminists and antifeminists spoke of woman's victimization in terms of her sex. As Aileen Kraditor notes, "the antis regarded each woman's vocation as determined not by her individual capacities or wishes but by her sex. Men were expected to have a variety of ambitions and capabilities, but all women were destined from birth to be full-time wives and mothers. To dispute this eternal truth was to challenge theology, biology, or sociology." [46] Feminists flirted occasionally with the idea that their distinctive sexual characteristics made them superior. That idea proceeded logically from the feminine myth which told women they were purer, more generous, and morally better than men. But more often women, in their quest for a new definition of self, resented what Elsie Clews Parsons, a prominent woman sociologist, called "the domination of personality by sex." When the feminists talked about sex, they did not intend the word as it is usually understood today. Today, "sex" has an erotic meaning. It generally connotes instinct, passion, emotion, stimulation, pleasure, often intercourse itself. But the nineteenth-century feminists used "sex" almost exclusively to denote gender. For them, "sex" indicated all the special feminine characteristics men used to differentiate and, said the feminists, to subjugate women. Charlotte Perkins Gilman

---

[44] Taft, *The Woman Movement*, p. 55. See also Illinois, General Assembly, Senate, Vice Committee, *Report* (Chicago: State of Illinois, 1916); and Prince A. Morrow, *Social Diseases and Marriage* (New York: Lea Brothers, 1904).

[45] Aileen Kraditor, *The Ideas of the Woman Suffrage Movement, 1890–1920* (New York: Columbia University Press, 1965), p. 54; Smuts, *Women and Work in America*, p. 107; Lasch, "Divorce and the Family," p. 59.

[46] Kraditor, p. 15.

repeatedly condemned what she called masculine oversexualization of the world; she was speaking not of pornography or lechery but of a caste system which kept women in their place. Men saw "nothing in the world *but* sex, either male or female," she argued, and in such an atmosphere neither men nor women could develop the truly human qualities common to each. "Our distinctions of sex," she said, "are carried to such a degree as to be disadvantageous to our progress as individuals and as a race." For women like Mrs. Gilman and Mrs. Parsons, the new feminine personality could only emerge when sex became "a factor, not an obsession." Then "relations between men and women will be primarily personal relations, secondarily sexual." That was the dominant feminist position, though some other feminist sympathizers, such as Ellen Key, and even, in his own way, Theodore Roosevelt, promoted the alternative view that women had a separate sexual identity but were nevertheless the equals of men. In any case, all the theories about the relation of feminine sex characteristics to personality manifested a conscious effort to define, or to redefine, woman's role.[47]

The redefinition of woman's role encountered entrenched but confused opposition. Antifeminists argued on the one hand that woman's God-given, natural role was so immutable that the suggestion of change was ludicrous, and on the other that her sacred maternal and connubial functions were so susceptible to corruption that she must be protected from the forces of change. But the antifeminists' confusion did not temper the strenuousness of their objections. Indeed, the strength of the objections indicated anxieties that only indirectly touched the question of economic and educational equality for women. Those anxieties primarily concerned the male's own social role and his sexual identity.

"The study of the changes in sexual attitudes is the very first step, the *sine qua non*, of all coherent historical research," writes Gordon Rattray Taylor, because sex lies at the heart of personality. Though Taylor somewhat overstates his case the fact nevertheless remains, as Phillipe Ariés has said, that "society's consciousness of its behaviour in relation to age and sex" is still an "unexplored subject," and the historical imagination is poorer for the lack.[48] While it is undoubtedly difficult to trace events in the innermost lives of men, it is more difficult to imagine that the developments that moved nineteenth-century American life worked no changes on sexuality. And at no time did the effects of those changes come closer to the surface than when the nineteenth-century man confronted the New Woman.

Sex has always been central to the human condition, but Steven Marcus has found that only in the nineteenth century "did there emerge

---

47 Elsie Clews Parsons, *Social Freedom* (New York: G. P. Putnam's Sons, 1915), pp. 29, 36; Gilman, *Man-Made World*, p. 154; Charlotte Perkins Gilman, *Women and Economics* (New York: Harper and Row, 1966; first published, 1898), p. 33.

48 G. Rattray Taylor, *Sex in History* (New York: Vanguard Press, 1954), p. 3; Ariés, *Centuries of Childhood*, p. 58.

as part of the general educated consciousness the formulation that it might in fact be problematical—it is an idea that forms part of our inheritance." Nineteenth-century Americans first met the modern problem of sex by officially denying sexuality. In their minds, as William Wasserstrom has said, "manliness signified a state of the soul which negated the claims of the body; womanliness resulted when the body was eliminated." Lester Ward complained that antagonism to the idea of sexuality was so pervasive that his fellow ethnologists even covered up the sex lives of former ages in an attempt "to palliate the supposed humiliation involved in such a state of things." [49]

In *Three Contributions to the Theory of Sex*, Freud noted that "the most pronounced difference between the love life of antiquity and ours lies in the fact that the ancients placed the emphasis on the impulse itself, while we put it on the object. The ancients extolled the impulse and were ready to ennoble through it even an inferior object, while we disparage the activity of the impulse as such and only countenance it on account of the merits of the object." [50] Only in that context did the oft-noted nineteenth-century ideal of sexlessness have meaning. The Victorian man honored the ideal of sexlessness when he disparaged and even feared his own sexual instinct and denied the existence of the instinct in women. But, as the feminists often complained, he exaggerated sex—in the meaning of gender—when he emphasized and glorified the distinctly feminine qualities of his sexual object.

On the occasion of a sex murder in New York in 1870, Henry James and the editors of the *Nation* debated the nature of the problematic sexual instinct and its relation to marriage. Only in marriage, said James, could men's "baser nature"—their sexuality—be adequately contained. The purpose of wedlock, he said, "is to educate us out of our animal beginnings." The *Nation*, though more extreme, agreed. Sex, it said, was an "animal, brute passion, through which God, apparently in ignorance of the laws of 'moral progress,' has provided for the perpetuation of the species." But since "moral progress" was so desirable, some means had to be devised to regulate sex, and that means, adopted in the infancy of the race, was marriage. "The first object of marriage," said the *Nation*, "still is to regulate [sex]." If the abstract entity, society, could somehow enunciate that Pauline doctrine, the *Nation* went on, it would say: "To keep down within [man] the animal love of change and attach him to his home, I excite in his mind extravagant notions of his authority and of the strength of the tie which unites his wife to him, and I confess that from this *some* women do suffer a great deal; but I am sure the whole female sex profits by it." In the *Nation*'s view, marriage, whatever its cost to the individual, was essential to the social order. Henry James hoped for a more spontaneous, humanitarian basis for marriage. But though James and the *Nation* disagreed over the proper sources of marital

---

[49] Marcus, *The Other Victorians*, p. 2; Wasserstrom, *Heiress of All the Ages*, p. vii; Ward, *Pure Sociology*, p. 340.

[50] Sigmund Freud, *Three Contributions to the Theory of Sex* (New York: Nervous and Mental Disease Monographs, 1948), p. 14 n.

stability, they nevertheless shared a common appraisal of male sexuality as a bestial, egocentric, antisocial instinct that must somehow be regulated. And the *Nation*'s idea of marriage as the proper regulatory mechanism came closer than James's to the current popular view.[51]

Just as women were sentimentally venerated partly as compensation for their victimization, men, the *Nation* implied, were granted all the prerogatives of the patriarchal family to compensate for the difficulty with which they held their sexual instinct in check. In both cases, the denial of sexuality, in its modern sense of instinct, was closely tied to the nineteenth-century idea of sexual role. And in both cases, for themselves and for women, men defined the proper roles. Men saw themselves as patriarchal and authoritarian because they suppressed a sexual nature that was aggressive, even potentially brutal. And they saw woman as innocent, dependent, good, and generous because she was—ideally—sexless.

By the end of the nineteenth century, it was becoming increasingly difficult to contain real women within the myth of the feminine ideal. The emergence of the New Woman necessitated adjustments in man's role, and, less demonstrably but no less importantly, in his sexuality. Women entered the work force by the hundreds of thousands. Men showed their sensitivity to role when, often without economic logic, they allowed many newly emerging forms of employment to become exclusively women's. While women felt free to attempt almost any traditionally male job, men usually abandoned any occupation that became identified with women. G. Stanley Hall, the psychologist who brought Freud to Clark University, touched on that phenomenon in 1906 when he reported that several "independent statistical studies" showed that girls often held masculine "ideals," but that "boys almost never choose feminine ideals." In the transvaluation of sexual roles, the movement seemed to be all in one direction. Women took on traditionally masculine functions with apparently little stress; men, by contrast, feared the impairment of the very masculinity they had previously characterized as nearly beyond restraint. The "feminization" of education, Hall complained, rather than producing a desirable refinement in boys, instead unnaturally stifled their most virile traits—their "brutish elements." The fault with the women's movement, said Hall, lay in its exaggerated notion of sexual equality. The time had come, he insisted, for a "new movement . . . based upon sexual differences, not identities." He urged that course— which was in fact reactionary—not, as conservatives had previously done, for the sake of preserving a delicate femininity, but in defense of a beleaguered masculinity.[52]

Steven Marcus found in investigating the sex life of Victorian England that masculine fear of sexuality was ambivalent—men feared both impotence and potency, impulse and loss, attraction and repulsion. So too in America; ambivalence was built in. The furor over the changes

---

51 James, "Is Marriage Holy?" p. 364; "Society and Marriage," *Nation*, May 26, 1870, pp. 332–33.
52 G. Stanley Hall, "The Question of Co-Education," *Munsey's Magazine*, February 1906, pp. 588–92.

in men's and women's roles showed that while he had made the feminine principle symbolize goodness, the prospect of his "feminization" evoked profound anxieties in the nineteenth-century American man. And though he invested his sexual object with qualities which, according to Freud, should have justified the gratification of a supposedly despicable instinct, he often found that the glorified object, instead of elevating the instinct, precluded it. The figure of woman in American fiction, as Leslie Fiedler has said, became "refined to the point where copulation with her seems blasphemous." Further, however much the American man had denigrated his latent bestiality and bemoaned the difficulty of keeping it in check, that view of his sexual nature had lain at the heart of his self-image. By the 1890s it appeared that his purportedly primeval, almost irrepressible instinct was in fact propped up by an elaborate but fragile system of role definition based on exaggerated sexual differentiation. When women rebelled against that system, the illusion of man's aggressiveness—which seemed so indispensable to his sexual identity—grew more difficult to maintain. And in such laments as G. Stanley Hall's for the stifling of the "brutish elements," it became clear that the American man had feared more than the unleashing of his aggressive sexual instinct; he had also feared its loss.[53]

Male sexual ambivalence had underlain the notorious "double standard" against which feminists and moralists railed. "As a result of this double standard," said Dr. Prince Morrow, "society practically separates its women into two classes: from the one it demands chastity, the other is set apart for the gratification of the sexual caprices of its men. It thus proclaims the doctrine, immoral as it is unhygienic, that debauchery is a necessity for its men." [54] In either case, men made objects of women. Both the Fair Maiden and the Dark Lady served man's needs—one the needs of his conscience, the other the needs of his body. But the New Woman who came to self-consciousness toward the end of the century was no longer content to serve as a mere object. In a few years the double standard, and with it the traditional nineteenth-century idea of masculine sexuality, was under severe attack. It drew its heaviest fire in the hysteria about prostitution during the Progressive period.

The new form of male sexuality that began to emerge in the late nineteenth century was forced to abandon "full aggressive potency, demonic genitality," as Steven Marcus has said, because such a definition of personality was "permanently at odds with that elaborately developed life of the emotions which is our civilized heritage—and our burden." [55] That heritage proceeded primarily from the romantic movement of the late eighteenth and early nineteenth centuries. The feminists—indeed nearly all Progressives—spoke often about the "social consciousness" they wished to inaugurate. Under that regime, they thought, the self would no longer be the first referent for experience but would "appear and develop as the

[53] Marcus, *The Other Victorians*, p. 29; Fiedler, *Love and Death in the American Novel*, p. 276.
[54] Morrow, *Social Diseases and Marriage*, p. 342.
[55] Marcus, *The Other Victorians*, p. 180.

result of its relation to other selves." The new, socially conscious self would be the basic building unit in a society founded on cooperation and harmony rather than the pursuit of self-interest. That vision looked forward to the character style later called "other-directed." It also looked backward to the romantic philosophers' notion that sympathy should form the basis of all moral decision and human interaction.[56] Lester Ward considered it one of the nineteenth century's greatest tragedies that it had submerged the romantic heritage and allowed the "rational faculty" to outstrip the "moral sentiments." Even Spencer, he said, had recognized "that the abuse of women by men is due in the main to the feeble development of sympathy." But by the early twentieth century, said Elsie Clews Parsons, "sympathy and insight [were] called upon in measure undreamed of by the antique moralist whose sole anxiety is to preserve his reassuring social categories intact." And with the growth of the sympathetic faculty, men grew less able to objectify women. That did not mean that they afforded women full equality. But with sympathy the touchstone for sexual relationships, men no longer could entrap women so easily in myths and ignore their individual personalities.[57]

The romantic influence also modified that ambivalent fear of the emotions so evident in the nineteenth century. "There has been an increasing tendency," said Mary Roberts Coolidge, "to believe that imagination and intuition were effecting quite as much progress as the logical understanding." And, she implied, the system of masculine values was becoming "feminized" in a subtle way not usually perceived by the antifeminists: modern psychologists were "placing higher value upon the very mental quality [intuition] which was not long ago held to establish woman's inferiority." In America, William James contributed much to the development of a new regard for sensibility and the validity of emotional experience. And the increasing emphasis on the emotions sanctioned a new sense of subjectivism. That subjectivism harked back to Emerson, but it grew especially strong in the late nineteenth century because it went hand in hand with the relativism engendered by new researches in the biological and social sciences. And with the liberation of women, the transformation of masculine sexuality, the destruction of the double standard, the sanctioning of emotional experience, and the encouragement of a new sense of subjectivism, the nineteenth century had set the scene for the revolution in morals of the twentieth.[58]

The new notion of morality shared the endemic contempt for formalism characteristic of the early twentieth century. The old morality, as exemplified by Theodore Roosevelt, had been founded on the concept of duty; and as Roosevelt said, "The doing of duty generally means pain,

[56] Taft, *The Woman Movement*, pp. 37–49.

[57] Ward, *Pure Sociology*, pp. 346–47; Parsons, *Social Freedom*, p. 32.

[58] Coolidge, *Why Women Are So*, p. 299; see also Henry May, *The End of American Innocence* (Chicago: Quadrangle Books, 1964); and for a good account of the elements of romanticism, see Walter Jackson Bate, *From Classic to Romantic: Premises of Taste in Eighteenth Century England* (New York: Harper and Row, 1961), especially Chs. 4 and 5.

hardship, self-mastery, self-denial." [59] But as the emotions grew less fear-some, they no longer needed to be so strenuously mastered and denied. As a sociologist said in 1908, "Virtue no longer consists in literal obedience to arbitrary standards set by community or church but rather in conduct consistent with the demands of a growing personality." [60] The new moral-ity no less than the old sprang from a sense of inwardness common to the Puritans, the proper Victorians, and the romantics; but the romantic ap-praisal of the inner self was by far the most sanguine. That optimistic view of the self, for example, revolutionized the function of the school, which had been one of the principal agencies of moral indoctrination. In the new view the school should no longer mold the child to make his behavior conform with rigid social rules. The popularity of the ideas of Maria Montessori and John Dewey reflected a new confidence in the goodness of the unfettered personality. Education should not discipline; it should liberate. And in its emphasis on the liberation of the individual personality, the new morality legitimized subjectiveness. Just as the family grew more and more private as it became increasingly an emotional center, so too did the new approval of emotionalism and subjectivism in the life of the individual reinforce the view that his conduct was his private concern.

The romantic ideas of sympathy, emotion, and subjectivism took more than one hundred years noticeably to affect sexual relationships. Nevertheless, by the early twentieth century the influence of those ideas could not be doubted. Then came Sigmund Freud. Freud did not so much start a revolution as rechannel one already in progress. William James and others in the nineteenth century had identified the inner self with the emotions. Freud superimposed on that view the idea that all emotion—indeed all psychic life—sprang from sexuality, and therefore that the self was defined by sexuality. Freud also provided the discussion of sex with a new, scientific vocabulary.

Unquestionably, Freud did much to further the liberation of sexual behavior, but in many ways Freud's influence was reactionary. For the old belief that woman was victimized by biology or by selfish men, Freud substituted the view that penis envy and a peculiar Oedipal situation made women the victims of their own psychic natures. The maternal impulse, according to the Freudians, proceeded not so much from biological and evolutionary laws as from inner psychological needs. That new thesis was scarcely less deterministic than the old. Thus Freud furnished scientific support for the old Victorian view that Nature victimized women and that they should seek compensation in wifehood and maternity. More-over, just as sympathy was beginning at last to inform sexual relation-ships, Freud reemphasized sexual differences and reinstated, in a new form, the old notion of necessary sexual inequality. For Freud, the essence of masculinity was action; of femininity, passiveness. The only currency of sexual interaction, therefore, must consist of power and domination.

[59] Morison, *Letters of Theodore Roosevelt*, 3:521 (Roosevelt to Hamlin Garland, July 19, 1903).
[60] American Sociological Society, *Papers and Proceedings* 3 (1908):171.

Finally, Freud's insistence that the primary component of the emotional life was sexual, irrational, and morally uncommitted both undermined the romantic confidence in the goodness of the emotions and made them seem more important than ever. Freud diverted a romantic revolution, or emotional revolution, at its very beginning and made it a sexual revolution. The sexual revolution, though carried forward under the banner of Freudian science, would continue to show its romantic beginnings. And the women's movement, with which the revolution, by whatever name, was intimately bound up, found in Freud a false liberation. Freudian ideas proved a diversion and an obstacle which women have not yet overcome.[61]

[61] See R. V. Sampson, *Equality and Power* (London: Heinemann Educational Books, 1965) and Hendrik M. Ruitenbeek, *Freud and America* (New York: Macmillan, 1966) for the influence of Freudian ideas.

Slavic Immigrants
in the Steel Mills

DAVID BRODY

Because of their high visibility and strange ways, the wave of new immigrants seemed to present a real threat to traditional American institutions. The theory of race suicide that was propounded at this time was a manifestation of the fear that the new immigration created in the existing population. Both the basis of this fear and the reality of the threat can be appraised through an investigation of the immigration statistics covering this period.

That there was a tidal wave of exotic immigrants is unquestionable. Between 1900 and 1915, nine and one-half million persons emigrated to the United States from Southern and Eastern Europe. This is almost equal to the total number of emigrants from the United Kingdom for the more than one hundred years previously. Most of the new immigrants poured into the country through the seaports of the Northeast, and most of them never left the cities of the Eastern seaboard. Their presence in massive numbers in these cities gave them a greater visibility than would have occurred had they been more evenly dispersed among the general population. In spite of the vast number of immigrants during this period, however, a study carried out in the 1920s showed that 51 percent of the American people were descended from families who had lived here during colonial times. Further studies have also demonstrated that in 1880 about 12 percent of the population was foreign born and that, while the figure for the foreign born rose to 15 percent at the height of the new immigration, by 1930 the percentage had receded to twelve. It seems, then, that the fears of being overwhelmed by an alien horde were based more on the customary American xenophobia (fear of strangers) than on the reality. As far as race suicide is concerned, studies have indicated that between 1890 and 1930 the total number of children born to native whites more than doubled, while the number of children born of foreign or mixed parentage did not quite double. So "the race" did not die out but continued to dominate the country's life and institutions.

In the revival of ethnic consciousness that began in the late 1960s, the major role in New York City has been played by Jews and Italo-Americans; in the rest of the nation, particularly in the centers of heavy industry and mining, Slavic peoples—for example, Poles, Czechs, Slovaks—have taken the lead. Perhaps the clearest and bitterest statement of the resentment on which this ethnic revival is based can be found in **The Rise of the Unmeltable Ethnics** by Michael Novak, a theologian-philosopher of Slovak parentage. He angrily maintains that the Slavic population of the United States has been passed by in the recent attempts to establish nondiscriminatory patterns in American life, which have been directed more often toward the non-

white minorities than toward other traditionally deprived groups of
the population, notably the Slavs.

The conditions under which the Slavic immigrants made their
way into American life are described in the selection reprinted below.
David Brody, of the University of California at Davis, has written ex-
tensively on the steel industry and in his work has carefully explored
the role played by the Slavic immigrants. Brody argues that the massive infusion of immigrant labor with its conservative, peasant background, constrained the unions in their attempts to organize the steel
industry. His primary concern in this selection, however, is the working conditions and living situations of the newcomers. Elsewhere in
his work he dwells on the conflict between the Slavs and the native
American workers, a conflict that gave rise to the "strong back, weak
mind" stereotype that has been so hard for the Slavic workers to dis-
pel and about which Novak complains so bitterly.

Before 1880, "English-speaking" workmen had manned America's iron
and steel plants. Then immigrants from South and East Europe began to
arrive in increasing numbers. More than 30,000 were steelworkers by 1900.
The newcomers soon filled the unskilled jobs in the Northern mills, forcing
the natives and earlier immigrants upward or out of the industry. In the
Carnegie plants of Allegheny County in March 1907, 11,694 of the 14,359
common laborers were Eastern Europeans.[1] The recent arrivals dominated
the bottom ranks of the steel industry.

The Slavic influx shaped the labor stability at the unskilled level. A
lowly job in the mills, however ill-paid and unpleasant, was endurable if
it enabled the immigrant to leave in a few years with funds enough to re-
sume his accustomed place in his native village. That was his original purpose. The majority, who in time decided to stay in America, usually had
by then risen into higher paid jobs. In either event, the acceptance of the
hard terms of common labor was the necessary prelude to a better life.
Immigrant mobility was at the center of the peaceable adjustment of the
unskilled steelworkers.

"The Sources of Stability: The Immigrants" (Editor's title: "Slavic Immigrants in the
Steel Mills"). Reprinted by permission of the publishers from *Steelworkers in Amer-
ica: The Nonunion Era* by David Brody (Cambridge, Mass.: Harvard University
Press, 1960), pp. 96–111. Copyright © 1960 by the President and Fellows of Harvard
College.

[1] *Stanley Hearings* [Kennedy, U.S. House, Committee on the Investigation of the
United States Steel Corporation, *Hearings*, 62 Cong., 2nd Sess. (1911–12), referred
to hereafter as Stanley Hearings], IV, 2889–2893. For the general movement of
Eastern Europeans into the industry, see second chapters in all the sections of *Report on Immigration* [U.S. Immigration Commission, *Reports: Immigrants in In-
dustries, Iron and Steel Manufacturing*. Washington, 1911], VIII, XI.

Fixed for centuries, by 1900 the peasant society of Eastern Europe had begun to disintegrate. The abolition of serfdom gave the peasant the right to mortgage and sell his land, and, later, to subdivide it. The falling death rate upset the ancient balance between population and acreage, leaving sons unprovided for or with insufficient land. Manufactured goods destroyed the peasant's self-sufficiency, raised his living standards and costs, and emphasized the inefficiency of his farming methods. When misfortune struck — a destructive storm, a drought, an outbreak of phylloxyra in the vineyards or disease in the livestock — he fell into debt, or, already mortgaged, lost his farm.

The peasant was linked to a chain of family inheritance and tradition. He had a name, a reputation, and a posterity. His self-esteem went with property, independence, and an assured social position. All this rested on his land, located in a certain village and held by his family from the immemorial past. The peasant with mortgage payments he could not meet faced an intolerable decline into the dependent, propertyless servant class. Rooted to the land, he saw his salvation only in emigration to a country from which men returned with money.

Inhabitants of the Western provinces of Austria-Hungary had long been accustomed to migrate seasonally to Germany for the harvests. To supplement meager farm incomes, Slovaks had peddled goods or followed wandering trades as wiremakers, pot-menders, and glaziers. From the peasant viewpoint the longer move to America differed from seasonal migration only in degree. Men went to Germany to add to a slender livelihood. In America they would save enough to pay off the mortgage or to buy the land that would restore their social position. A Polish immigrant expected to "remain for some years and return with something to our country, so that later we might not be obliged to earn [as hired laborers.]" [2] The Atlantic crossing meant a heavy investment, a long absence, unaccustomed work in mill or mine; but the essential purpose did not differ from seasonal migration. The immigrant hoped to earn a stake and return to his village. With this end Slovaks, Poles, Croats, Serbs, Magyars, and Italians made the passage to America, and many found their way into the steel mills.

They entered the mills under the lure of wages. Earnings of $1.50 or $2.00 a day, it was true, would not support a wife and children. In the Pittsburgh district, where a family required $15 a week, two-thirds of the recent immigrants in the steel plants made less than $12.50, and one-third less than $10. The Pittsburgh Associated Charities in 1910 found that, if a steel laborer worked twelve hours every day in the year, he could not provide a family of five with the barest necessities. Every steel center had large numbers who earned much below the minimum for family existence.

---

[2] Raczkowski Series, April 8, 1907, W. I. Thomas and F. Znaniecki, *The Polish Peasants in Europe and America* (2 vols., New York, 1927), I, 771, as well as similar statements in other series, I, 454, 1023, 1041, and letters to the Emigrants Protective Society in Warsaw, II, 1504–1509. The immigrants' quotations in this chapter come from the collections of letters in these volumes, unless otherwise stated in the footnotes, and will not be individually cited.

But the immigrant steelworkers had not expected to support families in America. The vast majority came alone. One-third of those surveyed by the Immigration Commission were single, and roughly three-quarters of the married men who had been in the country under five years reported their wives abroad.[3] The minority with families supplemented its income by lodging the others.

A "boarding-boss system" developed, benefiting all except perhaps the overburdened women. The workmen paid the "boss" $2.50 or $3.00 a month for lodging, including cooking and washing. The wife, or occasionally a hired housekeeper, bought the food for the household, and at the end of each month the total bill was divided among the adult males. There were variations. The boss might charge a flat monthly rate, or provide only a specified amount of food. In Granite City, Illinois, the Bulgarians economized by doing their own housework. But the system was essentially the same. A boarder could live for about $15 a month, and even after spending another $10 on clothing and trifles, could put aside $15. The boarding boss increased his income usually by more than half his mill earnings, and, in addition, was likely to be made a foreman.

The immigrants, moreover, counted the value of their hoards in terms of the increased buying power in their native villages. Mentally converting dollars into roubles, they estimated carefully that a few years of steady work would bring enough to buy a piece of land. "If I don't earn $1.50 a day," figured a prospective immigrant, "it would not be worth thinking about America." He could surely get that much in a steel mill. The large sums deposited in banks or sent home during prosperous years like 1907 verified the calculations. America, a Polish workman wrote home, "is a golden land as long as there is work." The wages in steel mills appeared to enable the peasant to achieve his purpose.[4]

The newcomers harbored no illusions about America. "There in Pittsburgh, people say, the dear sun never shines brightly, the air is saturated with stench and gas," parents in Galicia wrote their children. A workman in the South Works warned a prospective immigrant: "if he wants to come, he is not to complain about [reproach] me for in America there are neither Sundays nor holidays; he must go and work." Letters emphasized that "here in America one must work for three horses." "There are different kinds of work, heavy and light," explained another, "but a man from our country cannot get the light." An Hungarian churchman inspecting Pittsburgh steel mills exclaimed bitterly: "Wherever the heat is most

---

[3] *Report on Immigration*, VIII, 139–151, also, III, 47, for numbers of males and females coming to the United States, 1899–1910. The bulk of the statistical data in this chapter comes from vols. VIII and IX of the invaluable *Reports* of the Immigration Commission, covering the iron and steel industry, and will hereafter not be specifically cited in the footnotes.

[4] In 1907 immigrants in Johnstown and Steelton sent abroad $1,400,000. In September 1907 one bank on the South Side of Pittsburgh had on deposit $609,000 in immigrant accounts. See Emil Lengyel, *Americans from Hungary* (Philadelphia, 1948), pp. 182–185, for functioning of Transatlantic Trust Company set up by the Hungarian Postal Savings Bank.

insupportable, the flames most scorching, the smoke and soot most chok-
ing, there we are certain to find compatriots bent and wasted with toil." [5]
Returned men, it was said, were worn out by their years in America.

Knowing about the taxing labor awaiting them, only the hardier men
immigrated. Letters cautioned, "let him not risk coming, for he is still too
young," or "too weak for America." The need to borrow for the trip
tended to limit the opportunity to those who expected to make "big
money." [6] This selectivity gave the steel mills the best of Europe's peasant
population.

Accustomed to village life, the adjustment to the new world of the
steel mills was often painful. An Austrian Jew recalled his first day in a
plant.

> The man put me in a section where there was [sic] terrible
> noises, shooting, thundering and lightning. I wanted to run away
> but there was a big train in front of me. I looked up and a big train
> carrying a big vessel with fire was making towards me. I stood
> numb, afraid to move, until a man came to me and led me out of
> the mill.[7]

Most weathered the first terror, the bewildering surroundings, the shouts
in an unknown tongue. Appearing passive and unflinching, they grew used
to the tumult and became skillful in their simple tasks.

A fat pay envelope overshadowed heavy labor and long hours; a few
years' hardship was a cheap enough price for the precious savings. "I
should like to have piecework, for work is never too hard," wrote a Polish
peasant. "The work is very heavy, but I don't mind it," a brick factory
worker informed his wife, "let it be heavy, but may it last without inter-
ruption." Russian steel laborers in Pittsburgh told an investigator they
were glad to work extra days. A majority voluntarily reported on Sundays
in 1907 to clear the yards and repair equipment.[8] An immigrant characterized his twelve-hour position: "A good job, save money, work all time,
go home, sleep, no spend." [9] Thus did the immigrant's purpose match the
policies of the employers.

The hazards of the mill alone troubled the workmen. Dangerous to
experienced men, steelmaking was doubly so to untutored peasants. The
accident rate for non-English-speaking employees at the South Works
from 1906 to 1910 was twice the average of the rest of the labor force. Almost one-quarter of the recent immigrants in the works each year — 3,273
in the five years — were injured or killed. In one year 127 Eastern Euro-

---

[5] Peter Vay de Vaya und zu Luskod, *Inner Life in North America*, reprinted in
Oscar Handlin, *This Was America* (Cambridge, Mass., 1949), p. 410.

[6] Emily G. Balch, *Our Slavic Fellow Citizens* (New York, 1910), p. 186.

[7] Saposs Interviews [David Saposs, Personal Interviews with Steel Workers during
the summer of 1920, Saposs Papers, University of Wisconsin Library], anonymous.

[8] [Paul U. Kellogg (ed.),] *Pittsburgh Survey*. [6 vols. New York, 1909–1914.] VI, 39–
44.

[9] Walker, *Steel*, p. 28.

peans died in the steel mills of Allegheny County.[10] Letters told, sometimes in gory detail, the sudden end of friend or relative. The debilitating effects of industrial life took their quieter toll on the health of the immigrants.

In misfortune, the peasant had depended on his kin and parish, whose obligations to assist were defined and certain. He left this secure web of mutual help when he came to America. A Pole explained to his wife the hard lot of an immigrant.

> As long as he is well then he always works like a mule, and therefore he has something, but if he becomes sick then it is a trouble, because everybody is looking only for money in order to get some of it, and during the sickness the most will be spent.

Illness meant expenditure without income; a lengthy convalescence drained his savings and completely frustrated his ends.

Accidents were equally catastrophic. Illiterate, ignorant of the law, unable to speak the language, the immigrant had small likelihood of successfully presenting his compensation claim. If he was killed, the chances of his dependents were even more dubious. The Pennsylvania courts had ruled that the liability statute did not extend to nonresident aliens. Whatever the company's negligence, the victim's family in Europe was helpless. More than one-fourth of the men killed in Allegheny County in the year ending July 1907 had left their dependents in Europe, and the families of a score more departed soon after the funeral. Destitution awaited them. Friends learned from letters that "the widow begs, and the children are in rags," that the woman "works in the fields" or has "gone out to service," or that the family returned to the grandparents "who are old and have nothing." [11]

Very early, the immigrants sought to ease the heavy individual risks. As soon as a number gathered in a mill town, they set up an informal mutual help society obligating each member to assist at sickness or death. These became local insurance associations, in time affiliating with national benefit societies which were able to provide better and cheaper coverage. For example, the National Slavonic Society for monthly dues of 60 cents paid a death benefit of $1,000 and a sick benefit of $5.00 for the first thirteen weeks and $2.50 for another thirteen weeks. Immigrant steelworkers joined in large numbers. The Polish National Alliance had thirty locals in Pittsburgh in 1908. In Homestead 421 men belonged to the Greek Catholic Union, 363 to the National Slavonic Society, 460 to the First Catholic Slovak Union, 130 to the National Croatian Society.[12] In much the same way

[10] [Crystal] Eastman, *Work-Accidents [and the Law*. Vol. II of Pittsburgh Survey], p. 14.

[11] Eastman, pp. 132, 185; *Pittsburgh Survey*, VI, 44.

[12] [Margaret F.] Byington [*Homestead: The Households of a Mill Town*. Vol. IV of *Pittsburgh Survey*], p. 162; Thomas and Znaniecki, II, 1517–1521, 1570, 1577 ff. See also "The Slovaks in America," *Charities and the Commons*, Dec. 3, 1904, p. 242, on the history and functioning of the National Slavonic Society. Also, A. A. Marchbin, "Hungarian Activities in Western Pennsylvania," *Western Pennsylvania Historical Magazine*, XXIII (Sept. 1940), 163–174.

as the native steelworkers, the immigrants partially coped with the hazards
of the new world.

Bleak prospects faced the newcomers outside the mill. They settled
on the low ground never far from the smoke and clamor of the plant, but
also within easy walking distance to work. At Lackawanna they occupied
the marshy land surrounding the works, living in houses on "made ground"
surrounded by stagnant, filthy pools. In the older mill towns they pushed
the inhabitants of the dreariest streets into better neighborhoods. They
huddled apart in enclaves often called Hunkeyvilles — in Gary, the Patch;
in Granite City, Hungary Hollow; in Vandergrift, Rising Sun.[13]

Flimsy, dilapidated structures lacking the most elementary sanitary
facilities sheltered the immigrants. The Pittsburgh Bureau of Health reported after its 1907 inspection of tenement houses:

> The privy vaults were often found to be foul and full to the
> surface, sinks without trap or vent, the rain conductor serving to
> carry off waste water; damp, dark, and ill-smelling cellars used for
> sleeping purposes; cellars filthy; leaky roofs causing the walls and
> ceilings to become watersoaked, rendering the rooms damp and
> unhealthy; broken and worn floors; broken stair railings . . . plas-
> ter broken and paper torn and dirty.[14]

Conditions were little better outside urban centers. Croatian workmen in
Johnstown occupied frame houses edging a courtyard. A low four-room
closet serving over fifty groups stood in the center directly over an exposed
cesspool. The houses were dark, poorly ventilated, and in bad repair. Similarly, families depended on outside hydrants in the dismal immigrant courts
of Homestead's Second Ward.

The inadequate dwellings were greatly overcrowded. The boarding
boss and his family slept in one downstairs room in the standard four-room
frame house. The kitchen was set aside for eating and living purposes, although it, too, often served as a bedroom. Upstairs the boss crammed
double beds which were in use night and day when the mill was running
full. Investigators came upon many cases of extreme crowding. Thirty-
three Serbians and their boarding boss lived in a five-room house in Steelton. In Sharpsburg, Pennsylvania, an Italian family and nine boarders existed
without running water or toilet in four rooms on the third floor of a
ramshackle tenement. According to the Immigration Commission report,
the number per sleeping room in immigrant households averaged around
three; a sizable portion had four; and a small number six or more.

Ignorance compounded the living problems. Country people, the
immigrants could not fathom the ways of urban life. Before the Pittsburgh
filtration plant went into operation in 1908, many contracted typhoid
fever. Doctors complained of the refusal to boil water. Despite warnings,

[13] Map of Johnstown showing immigrant settlements in *Report on Immigration*, VIII,
329; map of Steelton in *ibid.*, p. 659, and description of settlement process, *ibid.*,
pp. 659–660; *ibid.*, p. 767, on Lackawanna; *ibid.*, IX, 44–45, on Granite City.
[14] *Pittsburgh Survey*, V, 90 ff.

men persisted in going to the river to quench their thirst as they had at home. Nor did they easily adjust to crowded, indoor life. Investigators found their rooms filthy, windows shut tight, sanitary facilities neglected and clogged. The occasional indoor bathrooms were left unused or served as storerooms.

The landlords, for their part, considered the immigrants fair game. When the newcomers invaded neighborhoods, property depreciated and frequently passed into new hands. The speculators ignored housing regulations, made no repairs or improvements, and in the continuing housing shortage and animus against immigrants, charged exorbitant rents. In some instances they received an extra dollar a month for each boarder. For much inferior accommodations, immigrant steelworkers paid an average 20 per cent more per room than did English-speaking tenants.

The local courts also fleeced the immigrants. The "squires" of the aldermanic courts in Pennsylvania received no salary, but were entitled to the fees incident to minor criminal and civil cases. Untutored in the law, they were usually brokers or real estate agents who regarded their office as a source of easy profit. And their prey were the foreigners, ignorant, inarticulate, and frightened. On pay nights the aldermen reaped handsomely from the workmen corralled into their dingy "shops" on dubious charges. An investigation of two aldermen revealed that only a small part of their criminal cases justified indictment. A Ruthenian boarding boss who had been fined $50 for disorderly conduct commented scornfully:

> Huh! The police are busy enough all right stopping disorder when the men have got money. But when there's hard times, like there is now, a man can make all the noise he pleases. . . . It ain't law they think about. It's money.

Indiana, Ohio, and Illinois justice was equally corrupt.[15]

Harsh as life in the mill towns was, room still remained for a happier side. The newcomers went usually to friends and relatives, and worked with men from their own villages. The benefit societies were convivial, and from them sprang other social organizations. Priests arrived as soon as there were people enough to support a church. The parish emerged to unite the activities of the ethnic, religious group into a coherent community. The later arrival in steel towns found his social needs relatively well satisfied.

There were other means of consolation. Intemperance, particularly during pay nights and marriage and birth celebrations, dismayed social workers. The immigrants had ready money, beer and whiskey cost little, and saloons served as social centers. Investigators counted 30 saloons in Duquesne, 65 in Braddock, 69 in McKeesport. Gary had one saloon for less than every hundred inhabitants; barrooms lined solidly the immigrant end of the main thoroughfare, known locally as Whiskey Row.

[15] *Pittsburgh Survey*, V, 139–152, VI, 72, 378–379; E. A. Steiner, *The Immigrant Tide* (New York, 1909), pp. 250–251.

But the main consolation was the knowledge that the hard life was temporary, a few years' sacrifice in exchange for a competence at home.

The one essential was not wages, working conditions, or living standards, but employment itself. "When there is none," wrote one Polish laborer, America "is worth nothing." Prospective immigrants wanted to know only "whether work is good and whether it is worth while to go to America." Favorable reports emptied the villages. "An awful multitude of people are going from here to America," a Polish peasant informed his brother during the high prosperity of early 1907. The peak years of American industry — 1892, 1903, 1907, 1910 — matched the heights of immigration.

The newcomer's stay depended directly on his employment. "I have had no work for four months now," a workman wrote his brother in February 1904. "If conditions don't improve by Easter, we will go back to our country, and if they improve and I get work, I will immediately send a ship ticket and you will come." In depressed years immigration dropped sharply; one Polish woman reported in 1908 "whole throngs of people coming back from America." More Austro-Hungarians and Italians departed than arrived that year.

The effects of trade fluctuations were, if anything, exaggerated in the unstable steel industry. And the immigrants were the first to be let go. Non-English-speaking men constituted 48 per cent of the South Works labor force in 1907, 37 per cent in 1908.[16] Thirty per cent of the immigrant steelworkers surveyed by the Immigration Commission in 1908 worked less than six months, almost two-thirds under nine months. Approximately 2,425 recent immigrants left Steelton, where only half the normal work force had employment. By the end of the depression, nine-tenths of the Bulgarians, the chief unskilled labor of Granite City, had departed.

Unemployment frustrated the immigrant's aims in much the same way as illness or injury. If the depression was prolonged, he might be reduced to real want. Granite City's Hungary Hollow came with reason to be called Hungry Hollow during 1908. But the boarding boss system mitigated the worst of extreme hardship; the fortunate boarders shared with the others, and the boss rarely forced a penniless workman to leave. In every case, nevertheless, the lost job meant the collapse of the immigrant's plan. Not only did his savings stop, but his accumulation quickly drained out. Unemployment, impossible to accommodate within the immigrant's purpose, alone disturbed the unskilled labor pattern. Otherwise, the Slavic steelworker found entirely acceptable the terms of work imposed by the system of economy.

The immigrants intended to return to their villages, and many did. From 1908 to 1910 (including a bad, middling, and prosperous year) forty-four South and East Europeans departed for every hundred that arrived; altogether, 590,000 left in the three years. But more remained.

[16] *Labor Conditions* [U.S. Bureau of Labor, *Report on Conditions of Employment in the Iron and Steel Industry.* (4 vols., Washington, 1911–13.)] IV, 108, 166.

Many forces turned the immigrant away from his homeland. He saw little enough of the new country, but he was nevertheless influenced by it. He at once discarded his peasant garb, and he sensed, despite the hard life and the hostility of Americans, the disappearance of clear lines of class and status. Nothing revealed more of the American influence than the complaints of the gentry that immigrants, when they returned, were disrespectful.

Migration weakened the familial solidarity of peasant society, clouded the purposes and inherited values of the immigrant, and, particularly after the wife arrived, dimmed the image of the home village. Moreover, the presence of friends and relatives and the developing social institutions began to meet the needs of the immigrants. They in time regarded their jobs, not as temporary chances, but as their careers, and their goal became promotion rather than property at home.

The crucial fact was that in the steel mills immigrants did rise. Thomas Huras, for example, came to America in October 1910 and the following February found a job in the open-hearth department of the Gary Works. He transferred to the merchant mill, where there was more opportunity, gradually rose, and in 1918 was a catcher in the ten-inch mill. Walter Stalmaszck, at fifteen going to work on a blast furnace in the South Works, eventually became a straightener on No. 1 rail mill. When in 1914 the Joliet Works picked out men to serve as safety supervisors for their sections, many immigrant workmen received their first chance to advance.[17]

Statistics showed the process. At one large Pittsburgh mill in 1910 none of the recent immigrants with under two years' service had skilled jobs, 56 were semiskilled, 314 unskilled; between two and five years, 17 were skilled, 243 semiskilled, 544 unskilled; between five and ten years, 79 were skilled, 441 semiskilled, 475 unskilled; and over ten years, 184 were skilled, 398 semiskilled, 439 unskilled.[18] The income of immigrant steelworkers increased steadily. Less than one-tenth of any ethnic group resident less than five years earned over fifteen dollars a week; between 13 and 25 per cent resident from five to ten years; and 20 to 33 per cent resident over ten years. Altogether, 13 per cent of the recent immigrants in the industry held skilled jobs, another 42 per cent semiskilled.[19]

The pattern of life changed with lengthening residence and rising earnings. The immigrant steelworker sent for his family; two-thirds in America under five years reported wives abroad, one-third from five to nine years, and one-seventh after nine years. His living standards rose; more money went for food, clothing, and luxuries. He was willing to pay

---

[17] *Gary Works Circle*, October 1918; *South Works Review*, June 1918, also, February 1918; *Joliet Works Mixer*, July 15, 1914. For example, Samuel Starkovitch, employed for five years in the yard now was promoted to safety man in the yard department. Many other issues give squibs on such safety workers, almost invariably immigrants.

[18] *Labor Conditions*, III, appendix C, 480 ff.; *Stanley Hearings*, IV, 2889–2893. See also *Report on Immigration*, VIII, 395–399, for figures on Cambria Works.

[19] *Report on Immigration*, VIII, 54–55. Lowering the figure to $12.50 a week added 25 per cent to each group.

higher rent for better lodging, frequently moved his family out of the densest immigrant sections, and abandoned the boarding boss system. Habitually saving, he often bought his house. One-sixth of 1,674 immigrant steelworkers in the Immigration Commission survey owned their homes. In time he learned to speak English with fair fluency. Steve Augustinovitch, a Croat who immigrated at the age of eighteen, was typical. Foreman of a repair crew at the Gary Works at twenty-eight, he owned his house, had savings, a large family, and his first citizenship papers.[20]

In short, he merged with other skilled steelworkers. Distinguishable ethnically and perhaps socially, within the plant he moved in the same orbit of dependence and repression. If anything, the immigrants were more susceptible to the employer's strategy, for the peasant mentality sharply distinguished between independent farming and hired labor. The immigrant felt less secure in his job than the native steelworkers, whose experience encompassed only hired employment, and he therefore became a more docile, loyal employee.[21]

The stability in the unskilled ranks thus rested on mobility. The newcomers either moved up into the skilled force; or they moved out at the first depression or with a satisfactory accumulation. Despite the harsh terms of work, therefore, steel companies enjoyed peaceful relations with their common laborers.

The employer's part in maintaining the pattern was essentially passive. He was generally ignorant of the reasons why the immigrants came to America. But he recognized them as a "floating supply of labor." [22] That simple, crucial fact governed his decisions.

Hiring and firing policies assumed the mobility of common labor. Employment officials did not investigate the immigrants, kept no detailed records, and observed individual capacity only for physical strength. When labor was plentiful, foremen usually picked likely men out of the jobless crowds that gathered before the mill gates at the changing of the shift.

To insure a steady supply, companies reached understandings with immigrant leaders. The employment manager, said the labor supervisor of the South Works,

> . . . must not only be aware of the location of all the groups of foreign settlement in the community, but he must become personally acquainted with the individual boarding bosses, steamship agents, clergymen, and other influential agents. . . . These are his supply depots, and only by perpetual, personal reconnoitering can he remain familiar with the quality and quantity of available applicants.[23]

[20] *Gary Works Circle,* February 1918.
[21] See, for example, Saposs Interviews, Mike Stephan in McKeesport, July 29, 1920; Julius Danko, McKeesport; and blast furnace labor foreman in McKeesport, August 2, 1920.
[22] *IA,* October 30, 1913, p. 987.
[23] A. H. Young, "Employing Men for a Steel Mill," *IA,* November 16, 1916, p. 1108.

The steel plants in Granite City, for instance, had an agreement to employ all the applicants of a Bulgarian leader. Boarding bosses, when they were gang foremen, could hire as well as lodge workmen. Before the immigrant channels to mill towns developed, steel companies had sent agents to New York City docks or employed labor agencies. That was rarely necessary in later years except during serious shortages.

Welfare efforts, designed to attach workmen to the company, did not extend to common labor. "The problem of maintaining a force of skilled workmen is realized by every employer" and "much attention has been given to" their welfare, observed the *Iron Age,* "but the unskilled employee of shop or foundry gets little attention." [24] The difference could be seen most clearly in housing programs. One company in the Eastern district provided excellent facilities at low cost for its higher paid men. For unskilled labor, the firm offered "shanties," an appropriate designation. Ten by fourteen feet, these were constructed of ordinary rough pine boards weatherstripped on the outside. Four men ate, washed, and slept in each shanty. Four "barracks," built like the shanties, housed twenty men each. All the structures were primitively furnished, and damp and cold in winter. According to the federal Bureau of Labor estimate, the rent amounted each year to more than 200 per cent of the company's original investment.[25] In less isolated areas employers generally ignored the housing problems of the immigrants.

The few efforts at improvement proved dismal failures. Lackawanna erected a village of monotonous but substantial houses around its new plant for low paid employees. And the Steel Corporation put up fifty dwellings — "double dry goods boxes" — for its laborers at Gary. But the men did not understand the need for sanitation and objected to the lack of amusements in the vicinity. The Gary houses were filthy, used as boarding houses, and greatly overcrowded. Within a few years the Corporation evicted the inhabitants of the notorious Hunkeyville and razed the houses.[26] The experiment was admittedly unsuccessful.

> The housing provided by the Corporation is perhaps better suited to the needs of the skilled workmen than to the wages of the unskilled laborers [who are] largely foreigners without families. . . . These men earn low wages, out of which they seek to save the utmost amount possible.[27]

The Steel Corporation thereupon left the immigrant steelworkers to their own devices, erecting housing designed only for the higher ranks. Other measures to reduce labor turnover — pensions, profit sharing, stock purchase — likewise bypassed the unskilled.

[24] *IA,* February 19, 1914, p. 504.
[25] *Labor Conditions,* III, 420–426.
[26] G. R. Taylor, "Creating the Newest Steel City," *Survey,* April 3, 1909, pp. 20–36; J. A. Fitch, "Lackawanna," *Survey,* October 7, 1911, pp. 929–945; Gary *Post-Tribune,* May 23, 1923.
[27] U.S. Steel Corporation, Bureau of Safety, Sanitation, and Welfare, *Bulletin,* No. 5, p. 56.

The steel manufacturers had ready answers for the criticisms of reformers. The immigrants, they said, were eager to work the long hours
for the greater earnings. They received wages higher than for similar work
in Europe. Their living conditions were worse than the skilled workers'
not because of smaller income, but because their wages were dissipated in
"debauch." However bad their life appeared, said a Pittsburgh employer,
it "is probably somewhat better than that to which such foreign workmen
were accustomed in their own countries." [28]

It was not that steel manufacturers undervalued the immigrants. Although claiming natives to be superior workmen, employers understood
very well their good fortune. They dealt with the immigrant steelworkers
as they did because nothing else was necessary. Developing without any
effort on their part, the unskilled labor pattern of mobility fitted perfectly
into the scheme of economical steel manufacture. The steelmakers were
content.

[28] *IA*, March 24, 1910, pp. 670–671 (a series of short statements by Pittsburgh employers in reply to charges by the Federal Council of Churches).

Konklave in Kokomo

ROBERT COUGHLAN

Americans have always been enamored of secret societies. Since before the War of American Independence such organizations have been available for those seeking them. Most of these organizations were relatively harmless gatherings of men seeking to practice private peccadilloes as in the Hell Fire Club, or to escape humdrum religious belief as in the Rosicrucian and Freemason societies.

In the middle of the nineteenth century, however, the growing agitation against "foreign" influence in American life, primarily Roman Catholicism, led to a more ominous development. Indeed, a political party, the Know Nothings, grew out of a secret organization known as the Order of the Star Spangled Banner and had as its purpose the banning of foreigners from American political life.

During Reconstruction, the most famous of the secret societies was organized—the Ku Klux Klan. After a harmless beginning, the Klan took as its purpose the elimination of blacks and their white supporters and allies from political participation in the post-bellum South. Reconstruction and the first Klan died at about the same time. There was, in fact, no need for the Klan in the post-Reconstruction South because legal segregation forced the blacks into a subordinate caste system from which they only began to emerge after the Second World War.

That did not mean, however, that all threats to traditional society had been defeated. The new immigrants from Southern and Eastern Europe provided an even greater threat to "the American way of life" than did the blacks. After all, the new threat was from white men (albeit often swarthy in complexion) who followed alien dogmas. One medium for dealing with this problem proved to be the reborn Klan—whose white knights had become a legend that had grown through fiction and in fancy and had been fixed in celluloid with the production of D. W. Griffith's film classic "The Birth of a Nation."

A major factor in the growth of the second Klan was the social dislocation that came as a result of the First World War. The new Klan gave disgruntled native Americans a voice and an organization with which to try to turn back the clock. Interestingly, the new Klan had its greatest success, not in its old homeland, but in the transitional areas in the Border States and in the new industrial cities of the North and Midwest.

In the selection reprinted below, Robert Coughlan, magazine writer and editor, describes what the Klan meant in his home town of Kokomo, Indiana. Rather than discussing the violence and excesses of the Klan that have been adequately described elsewhere, Coughlan concentrates on the banality and unintentional humor of Klan ritual and practice. All the marks of the secret society are there: private language, secret signs, elaborate costume (the plain bed sheet was only for the rank and file), and complicated ritual. The author portrays the way in which charismatic leaders preyed on the simple prejudices of ordinary people in order to bind them together in a political movement that proved to be remarkably potent in the mid-1920s. Fortunately for American society, the new Klan fell apart in disillusionment with the revelation of immoral activities by the leadership. Having based the power of the Klan on the simple pieties and moralities of ordinary people, the leadership could not survive the moral revulsion of its members. Thus the second Klan died.

This does not mean that the sentiments expressed in the Ku Klux Klan have passed from the American scene. As a matter of fact, many private organizations today continue to bemoan the existence of alien elements in American life and spend a great deal of time espousing what is now usually called "one hundred percent Americanism." These organizations, along with many of the churches, formed the backbone of the anti-Communist hysteria of the post–Second World War era, and many of them continue to issue anti-Semitic, anti-Catholic, and, of course, anti-black propaganda.

1

On a hot July day in central Indiana—the kind of day when the heat shimmers off the tall green corn and even the bobwhites seek shade in the brush—a great crowd of oddly dressed people clustered around an open meadow. They were waiting for something; their faces, framed in white hoods, were expectant, and their eyes searched the bright blue sky. Suddenly they began to cheer. They had seen it: a speck that came from the south and grew into an airplane. As it came closer it glistened in the sunlight, and they could see that it was gilded all over. It circled the field slowly and seesawed in for a bumpy landing. A bulky man in a robe and hood of purple silk hoisted himself up from the rear cockpit. As he climbed to the ground, a new surge of applause filled the country air. White-robed figures bobbed up and down; parents hoisted their children up for a view. A small delegation of dignitaries filed out toward the airplane, stopping at a respectful distance.

The man in purple stepped forward.

"Kigy," he said.

"Itsub," they replied solemnly.

With the newcomer in the lead the column recrossed the field, pro-

"Konklave in Kokomo," by Robert Coughlan. From *The Aspirin Age*, edited by Isabel Leighton, pp. 105–29. Copyright © 1949 by Simon & Schuster, Inc. Reprinted by permission of the publisher.

ceeded along a lane carved through the multitude, and reached a platform decked out with flags and bunting. The man in purple mounted
the steps, walked forward to the rostrum, and held up his right hand to
hush the excited crowd.

"My worthy subjects, citizens of the Invisible Empire, Klansmen all,
greetings!

"It grieves me to be late. The President of the United States kept me
unduly long counseling upon vital matters of state. Only my plea that
this is the time and place of my coronation obtained for me surcease
from his prayers for guidance." The crowd buzzed.

"Here in this uplifted hand, where all can see, I bear an official document addressed to the Grand Dragon, Hydras, Great Titans, Furies,
Giants, Kleagles, King Kleagles, Exalted Cyclops, Terrors, and All Citizens of the Invisible Empire of the Realm of Indiana. . . .

"It is signed by His Lordship, Hiram Wesley Evans, Imperial Wizard, and duly attested.

"It continues me officially in my exalted capacity as Grand Dragon
of the Invisible Empire for the Realm of Indiana. It so proclaims me by
Virtue of God's Unchanging Grace. So be it."

The Grand Dragon paused, inviting the cheers that thundered around
him. Then he launched into a speech. He urged his audience to fight
for "one hundred per cent Americanism" and to thwart "foreign elements" that he said were trying to control the country. As he finished
and stepped back, a coin came spinning through the air. Someone threw
another. Soon people were throwing rings, money, watch charms, anything bright and valuable. At last, when the tribute slackened, he motioned to his retainers to sweep up the treasure. Then he strode off to
a near-by pavilion to consult with his attendant Kleagles, Cyclopses, and
Titans.

2

That day, July 4, 1923, was a high-water mark in the extraordinary
career of David C. Stephenson, the object of these hysterics; and it was
certainly one of the greatest days in the history of that extraordinary
organization the Knights of the Ku Klux Klan. The occasion was a tri-
state Konklave of Klan members from Illinois, Ohio, and Indiana. The
place was Melfalfa Park, the meeting place, or Klavern, of the Klan chapter of Kokomo, Indiana, the host city. Actually, although planned as
a tri-state convention, it turned out to be the nearest thing to a rank-
and-file national convention the Klan ever had. Cars showed up from
almost every part of the country. The Klan's official estimate, which
probably was not far wrong in this case, was that two hundred thousand
members were there. Kokomo then had a population of about thirty
thousand, and naturally every facility of the town was swamped.

The Konklave was an important day in my life. I was nine years old,
with a small boy's interest in masquerades and brass bands. But I was
also a Catholic, the son of a Catholic who taught in the public schools

and who consequently was the object of a good deal of Klan agitation. If anything worse was to come, the Konklave probably would bring it. Every week or so the papers had been reporting Klan atrocities in other parts of the country—whippings, lynchings, tar-and-feather parties—and my father and his family were logical game in our locality.

Nevertheless, in a spirit of curiosity and bravado, my father suggested after our holiday lunch that we drive out to Melfalfa Park, which lies west of the town, to see what was happening. My mother's nervous objections were overcome, and we all got into the family Chevrolet and set out for West Sycamore Road. We saw white-sheeted Klansmen everywhere. They were driving along the streets, walking about with their hoods thrown back, eating in restaurants—they had taken the town over. But it was not until we were well out toward Melfalfa Park that we could realize the size of the demonstration. The road was a creeping mass of cars. They were draped with flags and bunting, and some carried homemade signs with Klan slogans such as "America for the Americans," or "The Pope will sit in the White House when Hell freezes over." There were Klan traffic officials every few yards, on foot, on motorcycles, or on horseback, but they were having a hard time keeping the two lanes of cars untangled and moving, and the air was full of the noise of their police whistles and shouts. The traffic would congeal, grind ahead, stop again, while the Klan families sat steaming and fanning themselves in their cars. Most of them seemed to have made it a real family expedition: the cars were loaded with luggage, camping equipment, and children. Quite a few of the latter—even those too young to belong to the junior order of the Klan—were dressed in little Klan outfits, which did not save them from being smacked when their restiveness annoyed their hot and harassed parents. The less ardent or more philosophical Klansmen had given up and had established themselves, with their picnic baskets and souvenir pillows, in shady spots all along the road and far into the adjoining fields and woods. From his gilded airplane, D. C. Stephenson must have seen a landscape dappled for miles around with little knots of white.

Since there was no way of turning back we stayed with the procession, feeling increasingly conspicuous. Finally we came to the cross road whose left branch led past the entrance to Melfalfa. We turned right and started home.

So we missed seeing the Konklave close up. But the newspapers were full of it, and people who were there have been able to fill in the details for me. The program gave a good indication of what the Klan was all about, or thought it was about. The Konklave started in midmorning with an address by a minister, the Reverend Mr. Kern of Covington, Indiana. The Reverend Kern spent most of his time warning against the machinations of Catholics and foreigners in the United States. When he finished, a fifty-piece boys' band from Alliance, Ohio, played "America" and the crowd sang. Then a band from New Castle, Indiana, played the "Star-Spangled Banner" and the Reverend Everett Nixon of Kokomo gave the invocation. These preliminaries led up to a speech by Dr. Hiram

Wesley Evans, the national leader of the Klan, who had come all the way from headquarters at Atlanta, Georgia. Dr. Evans commented gracefully on the fact that the center of Klan activities seemed to have shifted from Atlanta to Kokomo, and then talked on "Back to the Constitution." In his view, the Constitution was in peril from foreigners and "foreign influences," and he urged his audience to vote for Congressmen who would legislate "to the end that the nation may be rehabilitated by letting Americans be born into the American heritage." By the time Dr. Evans finished it was lunch time, and the Klan families spread their picnic cloths through the leafy acres of Melfalfa Park. Block-long cafeteria tables lined the banks of Wildcat Creek. From these, the women's auxiliary of the Klan dispensed five thousand cases of pop and near-beer, fifty-five thousand buns, twenty-five hundred pies, six tons of beef, and supplementary refreshments on the same scale.

It was after lunch, at about 2 P.M., when the crowd was full of food and patriotic ecstasy, that D. C. Stephenson made his dramatic descent from the sky.

The rest of the day, after Stephenson's speech, was given over to sports, band concerts, and general holiday frolic. That night there was a parade down Main Street in Kokomo. And while an outside observer might have found a good deal to be amused at in the antics of the Klan during the day, no one could have seen the parade that night without feelings of solemnity. There were thirty bands; but as usual in Klan parades there was no music, only the sound of drums. They rolled the slow, heavy tempo of the march from the far north end of town to Foster Park, a low meadow bordering Wildcat Creek where the Klan had put up a twenty-five-foot "fiery cross." There were three hundred mounted Klansmen interspersed in companies among the fifty thousand hooded men, women, and children on foot. The marchers moved in good order, and the measured tread of their feet, timed to the rumbling of the drums and accented by the off-beat clatter of the horses' hoofs, filled the night with an overpowering sound. Many of the marchers carried flaming torches, whose light threw grotesque shadows up and down Main Street. Flag bearers preceded every Den, or local Klan chapter. Usually they carried two Klan flags flanking an American flag, and the word would ripple down the rows of spectators lining the curbs, "Here comes the flag! Hats off for the flag!" Near the place where I was standing with my parents one man was slow with his hat and had it knocked off his head. He started to protest, thought better of it, and held his hat in his hand during the rest of the parade.

Finally the biggest flag I have ever seen came by. It must have been at least thirty feet long, since it took a dozen or more men on each side to support it, and it stretched almost from curb to curb. It sagged in the center under a great weight of coins and bills. As it passed us the bearers called out, "Throw in! Give to the hospital!" and most of the spectators did. This was a collection for the new "Klan hospital" that was to relieve white Protestant Kokomoans of the indignity of being born, being sick, and dying under the care of nuns, a necessity then since the Catholics supported the only hospital in town. It was announced afterward that the huge flag had collected fifty thousand dollars.

When the last of the marchers had filed into Foster Park the "fiery cross" was touched off. The Klansmen sang "The Old Rugged Cross," the Klan anthem, heard a few more speeches, and then dispersed, the hardier ones to drive back to Melfalfa Park to see a fireworks exhibition. Many of them were too spent, however, emotionally and physically, to make the trip. As we sat on our front porch after watching the parade, we could see the Klansmen of our neighborhood trickling home. Some still wore their regalia, too tired to bother with taking it off before they came into sight. Others carried little bundles of white: they were the ones who still made some pretense of secrecy about being members. One of the last to come down the street was old Mrs. Crousore, who lived a few doors away. Her white robe clung damply, and her hood was pushed back. As she climbed her steps and sank solidly into a rocking chair on her porch, we could hear her groan, "Oh, my God, my feet hurt!"

Mrs. Crousore spoke with such feeling that her words seemed to summarize the whole day. My parents adopted her comment as a family joke. July 4, 1923, became for us the day when Mrs. Crousore's feet hurt. But it was clear to me when I grew a little older that my parents needed the joke as much as Mrs. Crousore needed her rocking chair. There were wild rumors in the town in the months that followed: Father Pratt, the pastor at St. Patrick's Church, was on the list for tar-and-feathering; the church was going to be burned; the Klan was going to "call" on the Jewish merchants; it was going to "get" my father and Miss Kinney, another Catholic who taught in the public schools. Considering all the violent acts committed by the Klan elsewhere in the country, it seemed quite possible that any or all of these notions might mature into action.

As it turned out, none of them did. Six years later, in 1929, when the Klan was almost dead, vandals broke into St. Patrick's and defaced some of the statuary. Perhaps they were remnants of the Klan; perhaps they were only ordinary cranks. As for my family, nothing worse happened than that a few days after the Konklave I found a small cross painted in tar on one of our front steps—an ominous sign with no aftermath. I know of no explanation for the lack of violence, for Kokomo was one of the most "Klannish" towns in the United States. Perhaps the answer lay in the dead level typicalness of the town: a population overwhelmingly white Protestant, with small, well-assimilated numbers of Catholics, Jews, foreigners, and Negroes, and an economy nicely balanced between farming and industry. There were few genuine tensions in Kokomo in 1923, and hence little occasion for misdirected hate to flame into personal violence.

It may be asked why, then, did the town take so whole-heartedly to the Klan, which made a program of misdirected hate? And the answer to that may be, paradoxically enough, that the Klan supplied artificial tensions. Though artificial, and perhaps never quite really believed in, they were satisfying. They filled a need—a need for Kokomo and all the big and little towns that resembled it during the early 1920's.

3

In 1923, Kokomo, like the rest of the United States, was in a state of arrested emotion. It had gone whole-hog for war in 1917–18. My own earliest memories are mostly of parading soldiers, brass bands, peach pits thrown into collection stations on Main Street to be used "for gas masks," Liberty Bonds, jam-packed troop trains, the Kaiser hung in effigy, grotesque drawings of Huns in the old *Life*. But it was mostly a make-believe war, as it turned out, and by the time it was well started it was all over.

The emotions it had whipped up, however, were not over. As Charles W. Furgeson says in *Confusion of Tongues*: "We had indulged in wild and lascivious dreams. We had imagined ourselves in the act of intercourse with the Whore of the World. Then suddenly the war was over and the Whore vanished for a time and we were in a condition of *coitus interruptus*." To pursue the imagery, consummation was necessary. With the real enemy gone, a fresh one had to be found. Find an enemy: Catholics, Jews, Negroes, foreigners—but especially Catholics.

This seemingly strange transmutation was not really strange, considering the heritage of the times. Anti-foreignism has been a lively issue in American history since before the Republic. It became a major issue from the 1830's on, as mass migrations took place from Ireland, Germany, Scandinavia, Italy, Poland, Russia, and the Far East. Before immigration was finally curbed by the quota laws, many old-stock Americans in the South and Central West had been roused to an alarmed conviction that they were in danger of being overrun. The "foreigners" with their different ways and ideas were "ruining the country"; and hence anything "foreign" was "un-American" and a menace.

Another main stream in American history was anti-Catholicism, for the good and sufficient reason that a great many of the founding fathers had come to this continent to escape Catholic persecutions. This stream ran deep; and periodically it would emerge at the surface, as in the Know Nothing Party of the 1850's and the American Protective Association of the 1890's. It was submerged but still strong as this century began, and it came to a violent confluence in the 1920's with the parallel stream of anti-foreignism. The conscious or unconscious syllogism was: (1) foreigners are a menace, as demonstrated by the war, (2) the Catholic Church is run by a foreign Pope in a foreign city, (3) therefore the Catholic Church is a menace. Here was a suitable enemy—powerful, mysterious, international, aggressive.

To some extent, of course, the violence with which the jaws of this syllogism snapped shut was a result of parallel thinking in Washington. Wilson had been repudiated, and with him the League and the World Court, and internationalism had become a bad word. The great debates accompanying these events had stirred the country as it had not been stirred since the days preceding the Civil War, and things said then by the isolationists had been enough to frighten even normally sensible people. The exact sequence is a conundrum like that of the chicken and egg: whether the isolationist politicians led the people or whether the people drove the isolationist politicians. The postwar dis-illusionment that swept all ranks, including the new generation of authors, would seem to indicate the latter. Great men might have controlled the tide, but they were not to be found in the administrations of Harding and Coolidge.

There were other factors too: the deadly tedium of small-town life, where any change was a relief; the nature of current Protestant theology, rooted in Fundamentalism and hot with bigotry; and, not least, a native American moralistic blood lust that is half historical determinism, and half Freud. The Puritan morality that inspired *The Scarlet Letter* and the hanging of witches spread across the country not far behind the moving frontier; it gained new strength, in fact, in the revulsion against the ex-cesses of frontier life. But Puritanism defies human nature, and human nature, repressed, emerges in disguise. The fleshly appetites of the small townsman, when confronted by the rigid moral standards of his social environment, may be transformed into a fanatic persecution of those very appetites. The Klan, which sanctified chastity and "clean living" and brought violent punishment to sinners, was a perfect outlet for these repressions. It is significant that the favored Klan method of dealing with sexual transgressors was to strip them naked and whip them, an act of sadism.

This sexual symbolism could, with not too much effort, be made to dovetail with anti-foreignism and anti-Catholicism. Foreigners were notoriously immoral, as proven by the stories the soldiers brought back from wicked Paris. The Catholic Church, the "foreign church," must condone such things; and besides, who knew *what* went on among the priests and nuns! A staple in pornographic literature for at least one hundred years had been the "revelations" of alleged ex-priests. The Klan made use of these and other fables, such as the old and ever popular one about the mummified bodies of newborn infants found under the floor when a nunnery was torn down. Unhappily, Klan propagandists could also find real ammunition by looking back far enough in history. The Borgias were an endless mine of material, and their exploits came to be as familiar to readers of the Klan press as the lives of soap-opera characters are to modern housewives. Constant readers must, after a time, have begun to think of them as The Typical Catholic Family of the Renaissance.

Thus the Catholic Church very easily assumed, in the minds of the ignorant majority, the proportions of a vast, immoral, foreign conspiracy against Protestant America, with no less a design than to put the Pope in the White House. The Knights of Columbus were in reality a secret army pledged to this aim. They kept their guns in the basements of Catholic churches—which usually had high steeples and often were located on the highest ground in town, so that guns fired from the belfries could dom-inate the streets. Not all Catholics were in on the plot: for example, the Catholics you knew. These were well-meaning dupes whom one might hope to save from their blindness. My parents were generally considered to be among them. My mother's friend, Mrs. Wilson, would come often and, in a high-strung and urgent manner, try to argue the thing out. Against my mother's gentle insistences to the contrary, she would usually end up by declaring, "Now I want to tell *you*, honey! As sure as you're born, the Pope is coming over here with his shirttail aflyin'!"

Mrs. Wilson was not a completely reliable witness, since she had also once had a vision of Jesus standing on the steps of the Baptist church. But the mass acceptance of this idea was shown one day at the little town of North Manchester, Indiana, when the rumor spread that the Pope was finally pulling into town on the south-bound from Chicago to take over. A mob formed and stormed the train. To their mixed disappointment and relief, all they found on the lone day coach was a traveling salesman who was able to give satisfactory evidence that he was not the Pope in disguise.

Kokomo first began to hear about the Klan in 1920. In 1921 the local Nathan Hale Den was established, and within two years the town had become so Klannish as to be given the honor of being host city for the tri-state Konklave. (Of course its name helped: the Klan loved alliterative K's.) Literally half the town belonged to the Klan when I was a boy. At its peak, which was from 1923 through 1925, the Nathan Hale Den had about five thousand members, out of an able-bodied adult population of ten thousand. With this strength, the Klan was able to dominate local politics. In 1924 it elected the mayor, a dapper character named Silcott E. "Silk" Spurgeon, a former clothing salesman, and swept the lists for city councilmen. It packed the police and fire departments with its own people, with the result that on parade nights the traffic patrolmen disappeared, and traffic control was taken over by sheeted figures whose size and shape resembled those of the vanished patrolmen. It ran the town openly and insolently.

As in most of the thousands of other towns where the Klan thrived, there was a strong undercurrent of opposition. But as in most towns, few men were brave enough to state their disapproval openly. The Klan first appealed to the ignorant, the slightly unbalanced, and the venal; but by the time the enlightened elements realized the danger, it was already on top of them. Once organized in strength, the Klan had an irresistible weapon in economic boycott. The anti-Klan merchant saw his trade fade away to the Klan store across the street, where the store window carried a "TWK" (Trade with Klansmen) sign. The non-Klan insurance salesman hadn't a chance against the fraternal advantage of one who doubled in the evenings as a Kladd, Nighthawk, or Fury. It takes great courage to sacrifice a life's work for a principle.

It also takes moral conviction—and it is difficult to arrive at such conviction when the pastor of one's own church openly or tacitly takes an opposite stand. Kokomo's ministers, like her merchants and insurance men, swung with the tide. Most of them, in fact, took little or no swinging, since they saw in the Klan what it professed to be: the militant arm of evangelical Protestantism. There were a few holdouts, but they remained silent; and their silence was filled by the loud exhortations of others such as the Reverend Everett Nixon, Klan chaplain and Klan-sponsored city councilman, and the Reverend P. E. Greenwalt, of the South Main Street Methodist Church, who whipped a homemade Klan flag from his pocket as he reached the climax of his baccalaureate sermon at the high-school graduation exercises. Other ministers, while less fanatic, were perhaps no less sure that the Klan was doing God's work. They found that it stimulated church attendance, with a consequent and agreeable rise in collections. They found their churches visited in rotation by a Klan "team" which would appear at the door unexpectedly, stride up the aisle with Klan and American flags flying, deposit a money offering at the foot of the pulpit, and silently depart. Generally, while this was going on, the ministers would find it in their consciences to ask the choir to sing "Onward, Christian Soldiers."

And so it went in Kokomo and in its equivalents all over the Middle West and South. The Klan made less headway in the big cities, with their strong foreign, Catholic, Negro, and Jewish populations, but from the middle-sized cities down to the country villages it soon had partial or full control of politics and commerce. Indianapolis, with a population of some two hundred thousand, was dominated almost as completely as Kokomo. D. C. Stephenson, the Grand Dragon, had his headquarters there, in a suite of offices in a downtown business building, and from there he ran the state government. "I am the law in Indiana," he said, and there was no doubt about it. He owned the legislature; he owned the Governor, a political hack named Ed Jackson; he owned most of the Representatives and both United States Senators. The Junior Senator was Arthur Robinson, a dark, thin-faced man with the eyes of a zealot and the instincts of a Torquemada. The Senior Senator was genial Jim Watson, who had his own powerful machine within the Republican party. Watson was the arch type of the cartoon politician: big, paunchy, profane, and opportunistic. He thought that he could control the Klan for his own ends, joined up, and shortly found himself swallowed by the new machine.

4

Stephenson in turn took his orders, after a fashion, from Atlanta, Georgia, where Dr. Evans presided over the Invisible Empire from a sumptuous Imperial Palace on fashionable Peachtree Road. Dr. Evans was a dentist by trade and an Imperial Wizard by usurpation. He had unhorsed the previous Wizard and founder, "Colonel" William Joseph Simmons, several months before the Kokomo Konklave. It was in Kokomo, incidentally, that Evans made his first Imperial appearance before a really large Klan audience, thus giving that event an extra significance for history, since it was during his Reign that the Klan was to have its greatest triumphs and sink finally almost to its nadir.

However, in understanding the place of the Klan in American life, Dr. Evans' significance is less than "Colonel" Simmons'. Evans was shrewd, aggressive, and a good administrator, but he stepped into a going concern. The concern existed because of Simmons. And it was going not through the efforts of either Evans or Simmons but those of an obscure couple named Edward Young Clark and Mrs. Elizabeth Tyler.

The tangled story of the Klan's twentieth-century rebirth opens officially in 1915, but stems back to a day in 1901 when Simmons was sitting
on a bench outside his home. The future Emperor at that time was a
preacher, but wasn't doing very well at it. As he sat gazing into the sky,
watching the wind drive masses of cumulus clouds along, he noticed an
interesting formation. As he watched, it split into two billowy lengths,
and these in turn broke up into smaller clouds that followed one another
in a procession across the sky. Simmons took the phenomenon as a sign
from God, and fell to his knees with a prayer.

A devotee of Southern history, Simmons was even more familiar
than most Southerners with the legends of the old Ku Klux Klan.
Founded in 1866 in Pulaski, Tennessee, by a group of young Confederate
troopers home from the war and with time heavy on their hands, it had
started out simply as a social club—a device, significantly enough, to re-
capture some of the lost wartime excitement and comradeship. The
young ex-soldiers picked their name from *Kuklos*, the Greek word for
"circle," which they transformed to Ku Klux, and framed a fantastic
ritual and nomenclature for their own amusement. The idea spread, and
as it spread it found a serious purpose in restoring the South to home rule.
Eventually the best manhood (and much of the worst) of the South took
part, with General Nathan Bedford Forrest as Imperial Wizard. Finally
it degenerated into mere terrorism, and General Forrest disbanded it in
1869, but not until the Carpetbaggers had been dispersed and the Klan
had become immortalized in Southern memory. It was the old Klan that
the convulsed mind of Reverend Simmons saw in the clouds.

Since he had been a boy, he later recalled, he had been dreaming of
organizing real Americans into an army of salvation. His cloudy vision
told him what form it should take. But it was not until 1915 that he felt
prepared for the great task. Meantime he carried on as a preacher, as
an instructor in history at Lanier University, a dubious little enterprise
that later became the official Klan university, and latterly as an itinerant
organizer for the Modern Woodmen of the World. Then, on Thanksgiving night, 1915, he led a troupe of sixteen followers up Stone Mountain near Atlanta and there, "on the top of a mountain at the midnight
hour while men braved the surging blasts of wild wintry mountain
winds and endured temperatures far below freezing [The temperature
was forty-five degrees.—R. C.], bathed in the sacred glow of the fiery
cross, the Invisible Empire was called from its slumber of half a century."

What Simmons called forth was not the old Klan, however, but a
greatly distorted image of it. For all its excesses, the original Klan had
some constructive purposes. Its prescript shows that it was devoted to
restoring Constitutional rights to white Southerners, to the protection
of Southern womanhood, and to the re-establishment of home rule. It
operated in secrecy for the good reason that its members would have been
shot or imprisoned by federal troops had they been found out.

The new Klan adopted the costume, the secrecy, and much of the
ritual of the old, but very little of the substance. Its purposes are indicated
in the Kloran, or book of rules and rituals:

1. Is the motive prompting your ambition to be a Klansman serious and unselfish?

2. Are you a native born, white, gentile American?

3. Are you absolutely opposed to and free of any allegiance of any nature to any cause, government, people, sect, or ruler that is foreign to the United States of America?

4. Do you believe in the tenets of the Christian religion?

5. Do you esteem the United States of America and its institutions above all other government, civil, political, or ecclesiastical, in the whole world?

6. Will you, without mental reservation, take a solemn oath to defend, preserve, and enforce same?

7. Do you believe in clannishness, and will you faithfully practice same toward Klansmen?

8. Do you believe in and will you faithfully strive for the eternal maintenance of white supremacy?

9. Will you faithfully obey our constitution and laws, and conform willingly to all our usages, requirements, and regulations?

10. Can you always be depended on?

Only in "white supremacy" did the aims of the old and new Klans coincide, aside from the banalities about unselfishness, patriotism, and dependability. By questions 2 and 3 Simmons excluded foreigners, Jews, and Catholics, all of whom had been accepted into the original Klan, and thereby set his course in an altogether new direction.

While appropriating much of the ritual of the original, Simmons also added some mumbo-jumbo of his own. The old plus the new enveloped his converts in a weird and unintelligible system of ceremonies, signs, signals, and words. The Klan had its own calendar, so that July 4, 1923, for example, became "The Dismal Day of the Weeping Week of the Hideous Month of the year of the Klan LVII." The local "dens" were governed by an "Exalted Cyclops," a "Klaliff," "Klokard," "Kludd," "Kligrapp," "Klabee," "Kladd," "Klagaro," "Klexter," "Klokann," and "Nighthawk," corresponding respectively to president, vice-president, lecturer, chaplain, secretary, treasurer, conductor, inner guard, outer guard, investigating committee, and proctor in charge of candidates. The Klansmen sang "klodes," held "klonvocations," swore blood oaths, burned crosses, muttered passwords ("Kotop," to which the reply was "Potok," both meaning nothing), and carried on "klonversations." The latter were an exchange of code words formed from the first letters of sentences.

Ayak	Are you a Klansman?
Akia	A Klansman I am.
Capowe	Countersign and password or written evidence.
Cygnar	Can you give number and realm?
No. 1 Atga	Number one Klan of Atlanta, Georgia.
Kigy	Klansman, I greet you.
Itsub	In the sacred, unfailing bond.

They would then *Klasp* left hands (Klan loyalty a Sacred Principle). If a known non-member approached at this fraternal moment, the one who spied him first would break off the klonversation with a warning, "*Sanbog.*" (Strangers are near. Be on guard!)

Non-members were "aliens," and remained so until they were "baptized" as "citizens of the Invisible Empire," whereupon they received the "Mioak," or Mystical Insignia of a Klansman, a little red celluloid button bearing the inscrutable words "Kotop" and "Potok." Having taken the sacred oath, the new member was reminded by the Exalted Cyclops that "Mortal man cannot assume a more binding oath; character and courage alone will enable you to keep it. Always remember that to keep this oath means to you honor, happiness, and life; but to violate it means disgrace, dishonor, and *death*. May happiness, honor, and life be yours." The member's subsequent duties included absolute obedience to the Imperial Wizard, who was described in the Kloran as "The Emperor of the Invisible Empire, a wise man, a wonder worker, having power to charm and control."

Thus equipped, the Reverend Simmons set about creating his Empire. It was uphill work, however. Five years later he had enrolled only a few thousand subjects. The times, perhaps, were not quite right, but in addition the Emperor himself lacked two mundane qualities—executive ability and calculating greed. Both of these lacks were supplied in the spring of 1920, when he met Mr. Clark and Mrs. Tyler.

This couple were professional fund raisers and publicity agents whose accounts had included the Anti-Saloon League, Near East Relief, the Roosevelt Memorial Fund, and others of similar scope. Simmons' Ku Klux Klan was almost too small to be worth their attention, but they decided that it had possibilities. As Southerners, they saw in the anti-foreign, Catholic, Jewish, Negro provisions the raw material with which to appeal to four deep prejudices among other Southerners. After they took the project on Clark became King Kleagle, or second in command, and head of the promotion department, and Mrs. Tyler became his chief assistant. Simmons was left in the misty heights as Imperial Wizard and Emperor, where he was happy. Thereafter, between them, Clark and Mrs. Tyler systematized the appeals to racial and religious hatred and organized the sale of Klan memberships on a businesslike basis.

They divided the country into eight "domains," each headed by a Grand Goblin, and subdivided it into "realms," or states, each in charge of a Grand Dragon, such as Stephenson. The initiation fee was $10, of which $4 went to the Kleagle, or local solicitor, when he signed up a recruit, $1 to the King Kleagle, the state sales manager, 50 cents to the Grand Goblin, and $4.50 to Atlanta. Robes, which were made by the affiliated Gate City Manufacturing Company at a cost of $3.28, were sold for $6.50. Newspapers, magazines, Klorans, and other Klan printed matter was turned out at a substantial profit by the Searchlight Publishing Company, another Klan enterprise, and miscellaneous real estate was handled by the Clark Realty Company. The local Klaverns were supported by dues of a dollar a month, part of which was sent to the state organization. It was somewhat like a chain letter; almost everyone seemed guaranteed to make money.

Within a year and a half, this system had netted more than a hundred thousand members. It had also, according to the New York *World*, caused four killings, one mutilation, one branding with acid, forty-one floggings, twenty-seven tar-and-feather parties, five kidnapings, and forty-three threats and warnings to leave town. The *World's* exposé pricked Congress into an investigation in October, 1921. Emperor Simmons was called, but proved to be a slippery witness. The atrocities ascribed to the Klan were, he said, the work of imposters. The Klan did not permit violence, he assured the Congressmen, and cited instances wherein he had rebuked dens which disobeyed this rule by withdrawing their charters. The Klan was "purely a fraternal organization," dedicated to patriotism, brotherhood, and maintenance of law and order. Although circumstantial evidence was strong, the investigators could find no legal evidence that the Klan's national organization had caused the outrages or even approved of them, and the inquiry petered out.

However, the *World's* detective work did have one notable result. Shortly before the Congressional investigation got under way, the paper printed an account of how, two years before, Clark and Mrs. Tyler had been "arrested at midnight in their sleeping garments, in a notorious underworld resort at 185 South Pryor Street, Atlanta, run by Mrs. Tyler," and hauled off to jail, to be charged with "disorderly conduct" and possession of liquor. In the resultant furor Clark submitted his resignation to Simmons, which inspired Mrs. Tyler to issue a statement calling him "a weak-kneed quitter" and repudiating him. Simmons, who was well aware of what the couple had accomplished for the Klan, refused to take action against them. Instead, the propaganda department began to grind out denials, the *World* was branded as a "cowardly and infamous instrument of murder . . . against fair woman!" and the scandal was smoothed over.

But it left a scar. As the moral custodians of their communities, the rank-and-file Klansmen were deeply shocked by the story. Some of them were not convinced by the denials. Along with the evidence presented during the Congressional hearing, it gradually fermented into a basis for an insurgent movement within the ranks. This faction grew under the loving eye of Dr. Evans, who had deserted dentistry to become Grand Dragon of the Realm of Texas, and who had ambitions to the throne. In May, 1922, he became Kligrapp, or secretary, of the national organization, and from that vantage point accomplished a *coup d'état* the following Thanksgiving. With twelve of the fourteen members of the board of directors joining the cabal, he detached the Wizardship and all the real power from Simmons and took them himself, leaving Simmons only the cold comfort of a thousand dollars a month salary and a simple Emperorship. Simmons fought back energetically, and as a consequence, the following year, lost even this sop. "He Who Traversed the Realm of the Unknown, Wrested the Solemn Secret from the Grasp of Night, and Became the Sovereign Imperial Master of the Great Lost Mystery"—was out.

"I was in Gethsemane," Simmons wrote later, "and the gloom of its dense darkness entombed me; the cup which I drank surpassed bitterest gall, and my sweat was the sweat of blood; the hour of my crucifixion was at hand." He beckoned after his seduced flock: "Come unto ME all you who yearn and labor after Klankraft and I will give you rest. Take my program upon you and learn of me, for I am unselfish and true at heart. . . . I am the one custodian and sole Master of the sublime Mystery." But it was no use. Foxy Dr. Evans had stolen the show, and the ex-Emperor had to be content with a final cash settlement of ninety thousand dollars. He set about organizing a rival enterprise called the "Knights of the Flaming Sword," but was unsuccessful. In the mid-thirties he tried again with "The White Band," also a revival of a post-Civil War vigilante group, but had no better luck. He died in May, 1945, poor and disillusioned.

In spite of the shock of the Clark-Tyler case, the *World's* disclosures, and the Congressional investigation, the Klan continued to grow. It filled urgent needs in the contemporary psyche, and it was manifestly a good thing commercially. By the time Dr. Evans took over, it was adding thirty-five hundred members a day, and the national treasury was taking in forty-five thousand dollars a day. Within a year Evans could boast, probably with fair accuracy, of a membership of five million. Being in possession of that many adult voters, he and his henchmen naturally turned their thoughts to politics. Principles, they announced, were important to the Klan, not party labels; and accordingly the state and local organizations adopted whichever of the two major parties was stronger in its region. In the South, the Klan was Democratic, in the North, Republican. But since the Republicans were dominant nationally, both the arithmetic of membership and the ends of expediency dictated a stronger drive within that party. But 1924 was a poor year to interfere in Republican affairs. Calvin Coolidge was not only an extremely popular President, but represented in his person many of the parochial virtues that the Klan endorsed, and there was no point in contesting or even trying to bargain over his nomination. The Democratic convention was much more promising. The strongest candidate was Alfred E. Smith, Catholic, Tammany, wet, and a big-city product—in short, a symbol of everything the Klan was against. The Klan came out fighting for William Gibbs McAdoo and managed to split and stalemate the whole proceedings. It finally lost, but it also prevented Smith's nomination; and after many angry hours and smoke-filled meetings John W. Davis, a J. P. Morgan lawyer, was served up as a compromise. The Harding scandals were fresh in the minds of everyone, and 1924 logically should have been a Democratic year, but Davis lost. Considering later events, it is easy to speculate that the Klan's battle in the 1924 Democratic convention was a decisive event in United States and world history.

For Dr. Evans and his Goblins and Dragons it was an encouraging show of strength, despite their failure to nominate their man. They looked forward to 1928. Then, suddenly, there was a disaster. D. C. Stephenson, the Grandest Dragon of the Empire, made a mistake.

5

"Steve"—as he was usually known—kept a bust of Napoleon on his desk. And like Napoleon, he knew what he wanted. He wanted money and women and power, and later on he wanted to be President of the United States. He got plenty of the first three, and he might have got the fourth. He was a prodigy; he was at the height of his career when he was thirty-three years old. But he looked ten years older, and he encouraged his followers to refer to him as "the old man." He had a fleshy, handsome face, with blond hair, thin eyebrows, a small mouth, and small, shrewd eyes. He could be as hearty as a country drummer, and as cold as a hangman. He preached righteousness, but he was oversexed and he drank too much. He was vain, but beyond vanity he had certainty. He could command; his orders were obeyed; he exuded power. He understood the average man.

Not much is known about his early life. He was born in 1891, evidently in Texas, and spent part of his youth in Oklahoma. He was a second lieutenant in World War I but saw no service overseas. He was married twice, but had divorced or abandoned both women by the time he moved to Evansville, Indiana, shortly after the war. There he began organizing veterans, and this took him into politics. In 1920 he entered the Democratic Congressional primary as a wet. Defeated by the Anti-Saloon League, he promptly became a dry Republican and at the same time joined the newly rising Ku Klux Klan. He became an organizer for the Klan. By 1922 he had succeeded so well that he was made organizer for the State of Indiana, and shortly afterward for twenty other states, mostly Midwestern. After a short period in Columbus, Ohio, he moved his offices to Indianapolis, and on July 4, 1923, at Kokomo he officially added the Grand Dragonship of Indiana to his portfolio. By that time he was well on his way to his first million dollars.

Within a year or so he had passed far beyond that goal. He branched out into the coal and gravel business, the tailoring business, and various other sidelines. He imported Florida real-estate salesmen and other high-pressure operators to carry Klankraft into the towns and up and down the country roads, and arranged a split with these sub-salesmen. In one eighteen-month period his personal income is estimated to have been between two and five millions. He owned one of the showplace homes of suburban Irvington, maintained a suite of rooms at a big hotel, kept a fleet of automobiles, a covey of bodyguards, and a yacht in Lake Michigan. He knew many women, and had a way with most of them.

One of the women he knew, but not very well, was Madge Oberholzer. She had a small job at the State House in the office of the State Superintendent of Public Instruction. She was not particularly attractive. Unmarried at twenty-eight, which in Indiana means ripe spinsterhood, she was a buxom 145 pounds, had a rather long nose, and wore her hair in an exaggerated upsweep that hung over her forehead. But for some reason Steve, whose taste usually ran to ripe beauties, was interested in Madge. He took her to several parties, and once, when the legislature was considering a bill that would have abolished her state job, he gallantly killed it for her.

On the night of March 15, 1925, Madge came home about ten o'clock from a date with another man. Steve had been telephoning, and when she called him back he told her he was going to Chicago and wanted her to come and see him on an important matter before he left. He would send Earl Gentry, one of his bodyguards, to escort her.

She found Steve drinking when she arrived at his home, and according to her later testimony he "forced" her to drink with him. Three drinks later he asked her to go along to Chicago. When she refused, Steve motioned to Gentry and Earl Klenck, another bodyguard, who produced guns; the three men then led her outside and into Steve's waiting car. They drove to the railroad station and boarded the midnight train to Chicago. Steve, Gentry, and Madge went into a drawing room. Gentry climbed into an upper berth and Steve shoved Madge into the lower. "After the train started," her testimony says, "Stephenson got in with me and attacked me. He held me so I could not move. I . . . do not remember all that happened. . . . He . . . mutilated me. . . ."

The next day in Hammond, Indiana, where Steve had the presence of mind to get off the train to avoid the Mann Act, Madge managed on a pretext to get hold of some bichloride-of-mercury tablets. She swallowed six of them. By the time Steve discovered what she had done she was deathly ill. Steve tried to get her to a hospital, then offered to marry her, and finally drove her back to Indianapolis. He kept her in a loft above his garage with the threat that she would stay there until she agreed to marriage. She still refused and finally he had her taken to her home, where she died several weeks later. Before her death she dictated the full story to the prosecuting attorney, William H. Remy, who was one of the few officials of Marion County that Steve did not control.

The case caused an unimaginable uproar. Steve, who had said, "I am the law," was calm and confident, but he took the precaution of having the trial venued to the little town of Noblesville. A quarrel with Evans had created factionalism in his Indianapolis stronghold, and he was afraid of being double-crossed there. But to his shock and dismay, the Noblesville jury found him guilty of murder in the second degree, and the judge sentenced him to life imprisonment.

To his further shock, Governor Ed Jackson refused to pardon him. The case had created such a bad smell that not only Jackson but nearly all of Steve's other political allies abandoned him. Steve threatened to bring out the "little black box" containing his records; when finally produced, the box's contents sent a Congressman, the Mayor of Indianapolis, the Sheriff of Marion County, and various other officials to jail. Jackson was indicted for bribery but was saved by the statute of limitations. But although Steve got his revenge, he did not get his liberty. He tried every kind of threat and legal dodge, but every one failed. Years later, when he had served enough time with good behavior to come up for parole, public feeling against him was still so strong that no governor would take the responsibility of releasing him. He stayed in prison, in effect a political prisoner.

Steve's crude mistake was a disaster for the Klan not only in Indiana but everywhere. His trial was a national sensation, and his conviction was a national indictment of the organization. It became too absurd and ironic for any Goblin or Dragon to proselytize in the name of morality. The Bible Belt might dismiss the Clark-Tyler episode as malicious gossip, but it could hardly dismiss the legal conviction of one who was probably the Klan's most powerful local leader. The Klan began to break up rapidly, leaving political chaos in its wake. In Indiana, the Democratic boss, Frank P. Baker, said, "We don't want the poisonous animal to crawl into our yard and die." The Republicans earnestly disclaimed any relationship with the Klan.

The Klan tried just as eagerly to disassociate itself from Stephenson. It had nominal grounds for doing so, since Steve's differences with Evans had caused him to be read out of the organization some months before. In reply, however, Steve had merely declared his independence of Atlanta and had carried on in his own Realm with no diminution of power. The general public knew and cared little about this internal squabble. The label of "Stephensonism" was applied to the Klan as a whole, and it stuck.

The Klan died hard, however. It took a new grip on life in 1927–28, with the nomination of Al Smith again in prospect, and the old cries of "Keep the Pope out of the White House!" were heard again. Although it could not prevent Smith's nomination this time, the new wave of religious prejudice it stirred up, and the backwash of intolerance it had created in the years before, were important factors in defeating Smith for the Presidency. Thereafter it subsided again, and by the end of the decade it had only a tiny fraction of its former strength. Here and there, during the next years, one heard of it: a whipping, a castration, a cross burning. The propaganda line changed with the times. During the thirties, emphasis switched from Catholics, Negroes, Jews, and foreigners to Communism and "labor agitators." It was an unrewarding strategy, for although it may have gained contributions from employers, especially in the South, it won back few members.

The crowning irony came in 1935 when the Imperial Palace, after passing through the hands of ten owners, was finally bought for $32,500 by the Savannah-Atlanta diocese of the Catholic Church as the site for a new cathedral. Two years later at the cathedral's consecration Dr. Evans, as a token of the spirit of tolerance of the "new Klan," posed in a friendly attitude with the Bishop G. P. A. O'Hara. This was too much for the remaining brothers. In 1939 there was another revolution from below, and Evans was disposed of in favor of Dr. James A. Colescott, a former veterinarian of Terre Haute, Indiana, and latterly Grand Dragon of the Realm of Ohio. In 1944, Dr. Colescott voluntarily returned to doctoring animals, which give him a better living, and the Klan was disbanded as a national organization. It survives under a system of state autonomy, but has no appreciable strength in any state with the possible exceptions of Georgia and Florida. There may be a few thousand members in the entire country.

6

And today, in Kokomo, the Klan is only an old memory. The Reverend Everett Nixon carried on for years as Secretary of the Melfalfa Park Association, trying to hold together the property and few believers. But he failed, and now the park is overgrown with brush, deserted and decayed, its sagging pavilion a meeting place for bats and owls. Steve, who had his greatest moment there, is still in the state penitentiary at Michigan City, still hoping. Not long ago he made his fortieth unsuccessful petition for freedom. The accounts of his triumphs and his trial are embalmed in the brittle files of the Kokomo *Tribune* and *Dispatch*, along with the Nell Brinkley Girl and ads for the Apperson Jackrabbit. It all seems a long time ago.

Yet it was only a generation ago—time for the children who marched in the big parade, and who were held on their fathers' shoulders to see Steve's dramatic landing near Melfalfa Park, to grow up and have small children of their own. Like its population, the town seems substantially changed, with its new store fronts, its better paving, and its night-time neon glow. But in many, deeper ways, both the people and the town are much the same. And 1949 is not unlike 1920.

In his book, *The Ku Klux Klan,* James Moffatt Mecklin observes:

> What impresses the student of the Klan movement at every stage is the lack, on the part of the average American, of any real insight into its significance. Not man's innate depravity, not overt criminal acts, nor yet wicked attempts to subvert American institutions, but rather plain old-fashioned ignorance is the real enemy of the huge giant, the public, who is still the fumbling physician of our social ills.

When a new bogey appears on Main Street to take the place of the Pope, and a new organization arises to take the place of the Klan, one can only hope that the generation will turn out to be less ignorant than the old.

Training the Young

ROBERT S. LYND AND HELEN M. LYND

Americans take the existence of compulsory public schooling for granted. Probably no other institution in American life receives as much support from the general population. Even those who choose not to send their children to the public schools rarely criticize or challenge the system. Many in fact, particularly the parochial school parents, want to become part of the system, at least financially, by having public monies allocated for the support of their children's schools. The policy of providing ten to twelve years of free education for all is one of the mainstays of American institutional life.

It was not always this way, of course. Except for the colonial New England experience, and that more in theory than in practice, the public schools that existed before the Civil War were voluntary, and their very existence was controversial. Education was viewed as the responsibility of the family, and the middle and upper classes sent their children to private schools or taught them at home. The strongest impulse for the creation of a universal system of public education in the United States came in the middle and late nineteenth century as a response to the increasing immigration of non-Protestant, non-Anglo-Saxon peoples who did not fit neatly into the official culture of the nation.

Recent scholarship has demonstrated that public schools functioned, not so much as a route to upward mobility for immigrant populations, but as a form of social control. The immigrants found the public schools to be, in effect, Protestant parochial schools in which the dominant values of the society were the substance of the curriculum. This curriculum, with its inclusion not only of Protestant values but also of the myths of American history, had the intention of training a devout and loyal citizenry that would acquiesce in the dominant values and follow the leadership of the traditional elite. In struggling against this cultural chauvinism, Roman Catholics and others established competing school systems in an attempt to create and sustain their own particular loyalties.

What public education did exist in the nineteenth century consisted mainly of grammar schools that rarely were compulsory in attendance. After the Civil War, compulsory schooling became a controversial issue in many communities as parents saw in the compulsion an intrusion of the state into the management of children, which generally had been recognized by law as an almost exclusively parental function. By the turn of the century, however, even such establishment stalwarts as Theodore Roosevelt recognized that the state could serve as an "overparent" capable of providing services, including education, that an urban population found it increasingly difficult to manage for itself.

During the twentieth century, acceptance of education as a function of government has led to an increased desire for secondary schooling until, today, a high-school education has become the minimum educational goal sought by most American parents for their children. Colleges and junior colleges, particularly public institutions with open enrollment policies, are today in a comparable position in terms of growth and function as were the secondary schools early in this century.

The selection reprinted below from Robert and Helen Merrill Lynd's classic study of Muncie, Indiana, describes and evaluates the educational system found there in the 1920s. After the passing of a compulsory schooling law in Indiana in 1897, the school population of Muncie increased dramatically. An even more dramatic increase occurred in the number of high-school students. Between 1890 and 1924, high-school enrollment increased from 8 percent to 25 percent of total school enrollment. As the selection indicates, much of the high-school growth was in the area of vocational training. But more importantly, neither the students nor the townspeople saw the school as performing a basically educational function. Social and athletic activities as well as general socialization functions seemed more significant to all concerned.

Many of the Lynds' criticisms of the Muncie public schools are being echoed by critics of the schools today. Small but increasing numbers of parents and children are seeking alternate forms of schooling, including community control of schools in racial ghettos, in order to circumvent the political and social indoctrination encountered in the public schools. There is no doubt, however, that for the foreseeable future the traditional public school will be the dominant institution, more dominant even than the family, in the life of America's young.

WHO GO TO SCHOOL?

In an institutional world as seemingly elaborate and complex as that of Middletown, the orientation of the child presents an acute problem. Living goes on all about him at a brisk pace, speeded up at every point by the utilization of complex shorthand devices—ranging all the way from the alphabet to daily market quotations and automatic machinery—through which vast quantities of intricate social capital are made to serve the needs of the commonest member of the group. As already noted, the home operates as an important transfer point of civilization, mediating this surrounding institutional world to the uninitiated newcomer. Religious agencies take a limited part in the child's training at the option of his parents. *True Story* on the news-stand, *Flaming Youth* on the screen, books from the public library, the daily friction of life with playmates— all these make their casual though not insignificant contributions. But it is by yet another agency, the school, that the most formal and systematic training is imparted.

When the child is six the community for the first time concerns itself with his training, and his systematic, high-pressure orientation to life begins. He continues to live at home under the nominal supervision of his parents, but for four to six hours a day,[1] five days a week, nine months of the year, his life becomes almost as definitely routinized as his father's in shop or office, and even more so than his mother's at home; he "goes to school."

Prior to 1897 when the first state "compulsory education" law was passed, the child's orientation to life might continue throughout as casually as in the first six years. Even after the coming of compulsory schooling only twelve consecutive weeks' attendance each year between the ages of eight and fourteen was at first required. During the last thirty years, however, the tendency has been not only to require more constant attendance during each year,[2] but to extend the years that must be devoted to this formal, group-directed training both upward and downward. Today, no person may stop attending school until he is fourteen,[3] while by taking over and expanding in 1924 the kindergartens, hitherto private semi-charitable organizations, the community is now allowing children of five and even of four, if room permits, to receive training at public expense.

This solicitude on the part of Middletown that its young have "an education" is reflected in the fact that no less than 45 per cent of all money expended by the city in 1925 was devoted to its school. The fourteen school plants are valued at $1,600,000—nearly nine times the value of the school equipment in 1890.[4] During 1923–24 nearly seven out of ten of all those in the city between the ages of six and twenty-one were going regu-

---

[1] Ranging from three hours and fifty minutes, exclusive of recess periods, in the first and second years, to five hours and fifty minutes in every year above the seventh. In 1890 it was five hours daily for all years.

[2] The average daily attendance in the two school years 1889–91 was 66 per cent. of the school enrollment as against 83 per cent. for the two school years 1922–24.

[3] Children of fourteen who have completed the eighth grade in school may be given a certificate allowing them to start getting a living, provided they can prove that money is needed for the support of their families and that they attend school in special part-time classes at least five hours a week; children who have not finished the eighth grade may start getting a living at sixteen; the community supervises the conditions under which they shall work until they are eighteen. Until 1924 the upper age limit for required school attendance was fourteen. The state law allows a city to require the minimum school attendance (five hours a week) for all children up to eighteen, but Middletown does not do this.

[4] The annual expenditures of the state for elementary and secondary education, meanwhile, increased from $5,245,218 in 1890 to $63,358,807 in 1922.

larly to day school, while many others of all ages were attending night classes.

No records are kept in the Middletown schools of the ages and grades at which children withdraw from school. The lengthening average number of years during which each child remains in school today can only be inferred from the heavier attendance in high school and college. While the city's population has increased but three-and-one-half-fold since 1890, enrollment in the four grades of the high school has mounted nearly elevenfold, and the number of those graduating has increased nineteenfold. In 1889–90 there were 170 pupils in the high school, one for every sixty-seven persons in the city, and the high school enrollment was only 8 per cent. of the total school enrollment, whereas in 1923–24 there were 1,849 pupils in high school, one for every twenty-one persons in the city, and the high school enrollment was 25 per cent. of the total school enrollment. In other words, most of Middletown's children now extend their education past the elementary school into grades nine to twelve. In 1882, five graduated from high school, one for each 1,110 persons in the community;[5] in 1890 fourteen graduated, one for each 810 persons; in 1899 thirty-four graduated, "one of the largest graduating classes the city ever had," making one for each 588 persons;[6] in 1920, 114 graduated, or one for each 320 persons; and in 1924, 236 graduated, or one for each 161.[7]

Equally striking is the pressure for training even beyond high school. Of those who continue their training for twelve years, long enough to graduate from high school, over a third prolong it still further in college or normal work. Two of the fourteen members of the high school graduating class of 1890 and nine of the thirty-two graduates of 1894 eventually entered a college or normal school, while by the middle of the October following graduation, a check of 153 of the 236 members of the class of 1924 revealed eighty as already in college, thirty-six of them in colleges other than the local college and forty-four taking either the four-year college course or normal training at the local college.[8] Between 1890 and 1924, while the population of the state increased only approximately 25 per cent., the number of students enrolled in the State University increased

[5] Population estimated at 5,550.

[6] Population estimated at 20,000.

[7] The 1920 Federal Census showed 76 per cent. of the city's population aged fourteen and fifteen and 30 per cent. of the group aged sixteen and seventeen as in attendance at school; the doubling of the high school graduating class between 1920 and 1924 suggests a substantial increase today over these 1920 percentages. According to the State Department of Public Instruction, high school attendance throughout the state increased 56 per cent. during the five years 1920 to 1924.

The high school in Middletown is used by the township, but the number of pupils from outside the city is small and the population of Middletown has therefore been used above as the basis in figuring.

[8] The 1924 data are from published lists in the high school paper and are not a sample, but probably include the majority of those who went to college. In addition to the eighty accounted for above, seven more were in business college, one in art school at the state capitol, and three were taking post-graduate courses in high school.

nearly 700 per cent., and the number of those graduating nearly 800 per cent. During the same period the number of students enrolled in the state engineering and agricultural college increased 600 per cent., and the number of those graduating over 1,000 per cent.

Even among those who do not go on to college or do not finish high school the same leaven is working; there were, in the spring of 1925, 1,890 enrollments in evening courses in the local schools—719 of them in trade and industry courses,[9] 175 in commercial courses, and 996 in home-making courses.[10]

In addition to other forms of training, fifty to one hundred people of both sexes take correspondence courses annually in the city. The Middletown Business College has an annual enrollment of about 300 students, roughly half of them coming from Middletown.

So general is the drive towards education in Middletown today that, instead of explaining why those who continue in high school or even go on to college do so, as would have been appropriate a generation ago, it is simpler today to ask why those who do not continue their education fail to do so. Answers to this question were obtained from forty-two mothers who had a total of sixty-seven children, thirty-seven girls and thirty boys, who had left high school. Fourteen girls and six boys had left because their financial help was needed at home; three girls and twelve boys because they "wanted to work"; six girls because of "poor health," and one boy because of bad eyes; seven girls and six boys because they "didn't like high school"; three of each left to go to business college and one girl to study music; one girl and two boys "had to take so many things of no use"; one girl was married; and one stayed home to help during her mother's illness.

Obviously such answers are superficial explanations, masking in most cases a cluster of underlying factors. The matter of mental endowment is, naturally, not mentioned, although, according to Terman, "The pupils who drop out [of high school] are in the main pupils of inferior mental ability." [11] And yet, important though this consideration undoubtedly is, it must not too easily be regarded as the prepotent factor in the case of many of those who drop out of high school and in that of perhaps most of those

---

[9] Machine shop practice, carpentry, blue printing, drafting, pattern making, lathe and cabinet work, shop mathematics, chemistry.

[10] Sewing, dressmaking, millinery, applied design, basketry, planning and serving meals.

    In general, attendance at evening courses of all kinds tends to be larger in "bad times." The director of this work attributes this to two factors: (1) people out of work have more time on their hands; (2) when competition for jobs is severe, workers realize the desirability of having education in addition to mere trade skill. A third factor, touching women only, is the increase in home sewing and the making of one's own hats when times are bad and the family pocket-book empty; these women may join a course to make one hat or dress and then drop out.

    In 1923–24 the modal group among the men students were in their early twenties, while the modal group of women were in their thirties.

[11] [Lewis M.] Terman, *The Intelligence of School Children* (Boston: Houghton Mifflin, 1919), pp. 87–90.

who complete high school but do not go on to college;[12] standards are relatively low both in the high school and in a number of near-by colleges. The formal, remote nature of much school work probably plays a larger rôle in discouraging children from continuing in school than the reference above to having "to take so many things of no use" indicates; save in the case of certain vocational courses, a Middletown boy or girl must take the immediate relevancy and value of the high school curriculum largely on faith.

Potent among the determining factors in this matter of continuance in school is the economic status of a child's family; here again, as in the case of the size of the house a given family occupies and in other significant accompaniments of living, we observe this extraneous pecuniary consideration dictating the course of the individual's life. The emphasis upon this financial consideration in the answers of the Middletown mothers cited above probably underestimates the importance of money. A number of mothers who said that a child had left school because he "didn't like it" finally explained with great reluctance, "We couldn't dress him like we'd ought to and he felt out of it," or, "The two boys and the oldest girl all quit because they hated Central High School. They all loved the Junior High School [13] down here, but up there they're so snobbish. If you don't dress right you haven't any friends." "My two girls and oldest boy have all stopped school," said another mother. "My oldest girl stopped because we couldn't give her no money for the right kind of clothes. The boy begged and begged to go on through high school, but his father wouldn't give him no help. Now the youngest girl has left 10B this year. She was doing just fine, but she was too proud to to go to school unless she could have clothes like the other girls." The marked hesitation of mothers in mentioning these distasteful social distinctions only emphasizes the likelihood that the reasons for their children's leaving school summarized above understate the real situation in this respect.

This influential position of the family's financial status emerges again in the answers of the women interviewed regarding their plans for their children's future, although these answers cannot be satisfactorily tabulated as they tended to be vague in families where children were still below high school age. Every business class mother among the group of

[12] In Middletown as in the rest of the state there seems to be little direct relation between the ability of high school seniors and the selection of those who go to college. Book says of the state, "Almost as many students possessing E and F grades of intelligence are going to college as merit a ranking of A-plus or A.

"Many of the brightest students graduating from our high schools are not planning to go to college at all. Of those rated A-plus, 22 per cent. stated that they never expected to attend a college or university. Of those rated A, 24 per cent. did not intend to continue their education beyond the high school. . . . Of those ranking D and E, 64 and 62 per cent. respectively stated they would attend college next year." (*Op. cit.*, pp. 39–40.)

[13] Working class children go to the Junior High School on the South Side until they have finished the ninth grade. For the last three years of the high school—tenth, eleventh, and twelfth grades—all children of the city go to the Central High School on the North Side.

forty interviewed was planning to send her children through high school, and all but three of the forty were definitely planning to send their children to college; of these three, two were planning a musical education for their children after high school, and the third had children under eight. Eight of those planning to send their children to college added, "If we can afford it." Three were planning graduate work in addition to college. Two others said that musical study might be an alternative to college.

The answers of the working class wives were in terms of "hope to" or "want to"; in almost every case plans were contingent upon "if we can afford it." Forty of these 124 working class families had no plans for their children's education, eighteen of the forty having children in high school; the attitude of some of these mothers is expressed by the mother of nine children who said wearily, "I don't know; we want them all to go as far as they can." Of those who had plans for their children's future, three were planning definitely to have their children stop school at sixteen, the legal age limit of compulsory attendance. Thirty-eight were planning if possible to have their children continue through high school. Five planned on the local Business College in addition to one or more years at high school; four on the local Normal School; twenty-eight on college following high school; one on musical training in addition to high school; five on music without high school; and one on Business College without high school.[14] The answer of one mother conveys the mood of many other families: "Our oldest boy is doing fine in high school and his father says he'd like to send him to some nice college. The others will go through high school anyhow. If children don't have a good education they'll never know anything except hard work. Their father wants them to have just as much schooling as he can afford." Over and over again one sees both parents working to keep their children in college. "I don't know how we're going to get the children through college, but we're *going* to. A boy without an education today just ain't *anywhere!*" was the emphatic assertion of one father.

If education is oftentimes taken for granted by the business class, it is no exaggeration to say that it evokes the fervor of a religion, a means of salvation, among a large section of the working class. Add to this the further fact, pointed out below, that the high school has become the hub of the social life of the young of Middletown, and it is not surprising that high school attendance is almost as common today as it was rare a generation ago.

THE THINGS CHILDREN LEARN

The school, like the factory, is a thoroughly regimented world. Immovable seats in orderly rows fix the sphere of activity of each child. For all, from the timid six-year-old entering for the first time to the most as-

---

[14] These figures are given in terms of families, not children. In some cases the plans given apply to only one or two children in a family when the parents have no plans for the others.

sured high school senior, the general routine is much the same. Bells divide the day into periods. For the six-year-olds the periods are short (fifteen to twenty-five minutes) and varied; in some they leave their seats, play games, and act out make-believe stories, although in "recitation periods" all movement is prohibited. As they grow older the taboo upon physical activity becomes stricter, until by the third or fourth year practically all movement is forbidden except the marching from one set of seats to another between periods, a brief interval of prescribed exercise daily, and periods of manual training or home economics once or twice a week. There are "study-periods" in which children learn "lessons" from "text-books" prescribed by the state and "recitation-periods" in which they tell an adult teacher what the book has said; one hears children reciting the battles of the Civil War in one recitation period, the rivers of Africa in another, the "parts of speech" in a third; the method is much the same. With high school come some differences; more "vocational" and "laboratory" work varies the periods. But here again the lesson-textbook-recitation method is the chief characteristic of education. For nearly an hour a teacher asks questions and pupils answer, then a bell rings, on the instant books bang, powder and mirrors come out, there is a buzz of talk and laughter as all the urgent business of living resumes momentarily for the children, notes and "dates" are exchanged, five minutes pass, another bell, gradual sliding into seats, a final giggle, a last vanity case snapped shut. "In our last lesson we had just finished"—and another class is begun.

All this ordered industry of imparting and learning facts and skills represents an effort on the part of this matter-of-fact community immersed in its daily activities to endow its young with certain essential supplements to the training received in the home. A quick epitome of the things adult Middletown has come to think it important for its children to learn in school, as well as some indication of regions of pressure and change, is afforded by the following summary of the work in Grades I and VII in 1890 and in 1924:

1890	1924
GRADE I	
Reading	Reading
Writing	Writing
Arithmetic	Arithmetic
Language	Language
Spelling	Spelling
Drawing	Drawing
Object Lessons (Science)	Geography
Music	Music
	Civic Training
	History and Civics
	Hygiene and Health
	Physical Education

1890   1924
GRADE VII

1890	1924
Reading	Reading
Writing	Writing
Arithmetic	Arithmetic
Language	Language
Spelling	Spelling
Drawing	Drawing
Music	Music
Geography	Geography
Object Lessons (Science)	Civic Training
Compositions and Declamation	History and Civics
	Manual Arts (Boys)
	Home Economics (Girls)
	Physical Education

In the culture of thirty-five years ago it was deemed sufficient to teach during the first seven years of this extra-home training the following skills and facts, in rough order of importance:[15]

>   *a.* The various uses of language. (Overwhelmingly first in importance.)
>   *b.* The accurate manipulation of numerical symbols.
>   *c.* Familiarity with the physical surroundings of peoples.
>   *d.* A miscellaneous group of facts about familiar physical objects about the child—trees, sun, ice, food, and so on.
>   *e.* The leisure-time skills of singing and drawing.

Today the things for which all children are sent to school fall into the following rough order:

>   *a.* The same uses of language.
>   *b.* The same uses of numerical figures.
>   *c.* Training in patriotic citizenship.
>   *d.* The same familiarity with the physical surroundings of peoples.
>   *e.* Facts about how to keep well and some physical exercise.
>   *f.* The same leisure-time skills of singing and drawing.
>   *g.* Knowledge and skills useful in sewing, cooking and using

[15] The state law of 1865 upon which the public school system rests provided for instruction in "orthography, reading, writing, arithmetic, English, grammar, and good behavior," and the minutes of the Middletown School Board for 1882 (the only minutes for a decade on either side of 1890 which describe the course of study in detail) affirm that "reading, writing, and arithmetic are the three principal studies of the public schools, and if nothing more is possible, pupils should be taught to read the newspapers, write a letter, and perform the ordinary operations of arithmetic."

tools about the home for the girls, and, for the boys, an introductory acquaintance with some of the manual skills by which the working class members get their living.

Both in its optional, non-compulsory character and also in its more limited scope the school training of a generation ago appears to have been a more causal adjunct of the main business of "bringing up" that went on day by day in the home. Today, however, the school is relied upon to carry a more direct, if at most points still vaguely defined, responsibility. This has in turn reacted upon the content of the teaching and encouraged a more utilitarian approach at certain points. A slow trend toward utilizing material more directly instrumental to the day-by-day urgencies of living appears clearly in such a course as that in hygiene and health, epitomized in the text-books used a generation ago and today, Jenkins' *Advanced Lessons in Human Physiology* in the one case and Emerson and Betts' *Physiology and Hygiene* in the other. The earlier book devoted twenty-one chapters, 287 of its 296 pages, to the structure and function of the body—"The Skeleton," "The Skin and the Kidneys," "The Anatomy of the Nervous System," and so on, and a final chapter, eight and one-quarter pages, to "the laws of health"; a three-page appendix on "Poisons and Antidotes" gave the various remedies to be used to induce vomiting after poisoning by aconite, arsenic, and so on, as well as rules for treating asphyxia. The current book, on the other hand, is primarily concerned throughout with the care of the body, and its structure is treated incidentally. Examination questions in the two periods show the same shift. Characteristic questions of 1890 such as "Describe each of the two kinds of matter of the nervous system" and "Tell weight and shape of brain. Tell names of membranes around it" are being replaced by "Write a paragraph describing exactly the kind of shoe you should wear, stating all the good points and the reasons for them," and "What is the law of muscles and bones (regarding posture)? How should it guide you in your daily life?"

Geography, likewise, according to the printed courses of study for the two periods, is less concerned today with memorizing "at least one important fact about each city located" and more with the "presence of storm and sunshine and song of bird," "interests of the child"; but classes visited are preoccupied with learning of facts, and 1890 and 1924 examination questions are interchangeable. Reading, spelling, and arithmetic, also, exhibit at certain points less emphasis upon elaboration of symbols and formal drill and more on the "practical application" of these skills; thus in reading, somewhat less attention is being paid to "clear and distinct enunciation" and "proper emphasis and expression" and more to "silent reading," which stresses content. But, in general, these subjects which are "the backbone of the curriculum" show less flexibility than do the subjects on the periphery or the newcomers. Most of these changes are indeed relatively slight; the social values represented by an "elementary education" are changing slowly in Middletown.

When we approach the high school, however, the matter-of-fact tendency of the city to commandeer education as an aid in dealing with its own concerns becomes more apparent. Caught less firmly than the elementary school in the wake of tradition and now forced to train children from a group not heretofore reached by it, the high school has been more adaptable than the lower school. Here group training no longer means the same set of facts learned on the same days by all children of a given grade. The freshman entering high school may plan to spend his four years following any one of twelve different "courses of study";[16] he may choose the sixteen different yearly courses which will make up his four years of training from a total of 102.[17] All this is something new, for the 170 students who were going to high school in the "bursting days of boom" of 1889–90 had to choose, as Middletown high school students had done for thirty years, between two four-year courses, the Latin and the English courses, the sole difference between them being whether one did or did not take "the language." The number of separate year courses open to them totaled but twenty.

The facts and skills constituting the present-day high school curriculum present a combination of the traditional learning reputed to be essential to an "educated" man or woman and newer applied information or skills constantly being inserted into the curriculum to meet current immanent concerns. Here, too, English, the successor in its varied forms of the language work in the grades, far outdistances all competitors for student time, consuming 22 per cent. of all student hours. It is no longer com-

---

[16]

1. General Course	7. Applied Electricity Course
2. College Preparatory Course	8. Mechanical Drafting Course
3. Music Course	9. Printing Course
4. Art Course	10. Machine Shop Course
5. Shorthand Course	11. Manual Arts Course
6. Bookkeeping Course	12. Home Economics Course

Courses Three to Twelve inclusive have a uniform first-year group of required and elective subjects. Four subjects are taken each half of each year, of which two or three are required and the rest selected from among a list offering from two to nine electives, according to the course and the year. The indispensables of secondary education required of every high school student are:

Four years of English for those taking Courses One through Six.
Three years of English for those taking Courses Seven through Twelve.
One year of algebra.
One year of general history.
One year of American history.
One-half year of civics.
One-half year of sociology.
One year of science.
One-half year of music.
One-half year of gymnasium.

This constitutes a total of ten required and six elective one-year courses or their equivalents during the four years for the academic department (Courses One through Six) and nine required and seven elective courses for those in the vocational department (Courses Seven through Twelve).

[17] The year unit rather than the term or semester unit is taken here as the measure of the number of courses, since it furnishes the only basis of comparison with 1890. When different subjects make up one year's course they are almost invariably related, e.g., civics and sociology, zoölogy and botany.

pulsory throughout the entire four years as it was a generation ago; instead, it is required of all students for the first two years, and thereafter the earlier literary emphasis disappears in seven of the twelve courses, being replaced in the third year by commercial English, while in the fourth year it disappears entirely in five courses save as an optional subject. Both teaching and learning appear at times to be ordeals from which teachers and pupils alike would apparently gladly escape: "Thank goodness, we've finished Chaucer's *Prologue!*" exclaimed one high school English teacher. "I am thankful and the children are, too. They think of it almost as if it were in a foreign language, and they *hate* it."

Latin, likewise, though still regarded by some parents of the business class as a vaguely significant earmark of the educated man or woman, is being rapidly attenuated in the training given the young. It is not required of any student for even one year, though in one of the twelve courses it or French is required for two years. Gone is the required course of the nineties taken by over half of the high school students for the entire four years and enticingly set forth in the course of study of the period as "Latin, Grammar, Harkness: Begun-Completed. Latin, Reader, Harkness: Begun-Completed. Latin, Caesar, Harkness: Begun-Completed. Latin, Virgil, Harkness: Begun-Completed." The "Virgil Club's" annual banquet and the "Latin Wedding" are, however, prominent high school social events today, and more than one pupil confessed that the lure of these in the senior year helped to keep him through four years of Latin. Although Latin is deader than last summer's straw hat to the men joshing each other about Middletown's Rotary luncheon table, tradition, the pressure of college entrance requirements, and such incidental social considerations as those just mentioned still manage to hold Latin to a place of prominence in the curriculum: 10 per cent. of all student hours are devoted to Latin, as against but 2 per cent. each to French and Spanish;[18] only English, the combined vocational courses, mathematics, and history consume more student hours.

The most pronounced region of movement appears in the rush of courses that depart from the traditional dignified conception of what constitutes education and seek to train for specific tool and skill activities in factory, office, and home. A generation ago a solitary optional senior course in bookkeeping was the thin entering wedge of the trend that today controls eight of the twelve courses of the high school and claimed 17 per cent. of the total student hours during the first semester of 1923–24 and 21 per cent. during the second.[19] At no point has the training prescribed for the preparation of children for effective adulthood approached more

[18] Since the World War German has not been taught in Middletown.

[19] . . . In the case of English, the only subject or group of subjects to exceed the time spent on these non-academic courses, it should be borne in mind that in seven of the twelve courses of study offered by the high school one-third of the total English work required is a new vocational kind of English called commercial English, reflecting the workaday emphasis rather than the older academic emphasis in the curriculum.

It should also be recalled that, in addition to this high school work, manual arts is compulsory for all boys in Grades VI to VIII of the elementary school, and home economics is also compulsory for girls in Grades VII and VIII.

nearly actual preparation for the dominant concerns in the daily lives of the people of Middletown. This pragmatic commandeering of education is frankly stated by the president of the School Board: "For a long time all boys were trained to be President. Then for a while we trained them all to be professional men. Now we are training boys to get jobs."

Unlike Latin, English, and mathematics in that they have no independent, honorific traditions of their own, these vocational courses have frankly adopted the canons of office and machine shop: they must change in step with the coming of new physical equipment in machine shops and offices, or become ineffective.[20] A recently organized radio class shows the possibility of quick adaptability to new developments. More than any other part of the school training, these vocational courses consist in learning *how* rather than learning *about*. Actual conditions of work in the city's factories are imported into the school shops; boys bring repair work from their homes; they study auto mechanics by working on an old Ford car; they design, draft, and make patterns for lathes and drill presses, the actual casting being done by a Middletown foundry; they have designed and constructed a house, doing all the architectural, carpentry, wiring, metal work, and painting. A plan for providing work in a local machine shop, alternating two weeks of this with two weeks of study throughout the year, is under discussion.

Under the circumstances, it is not surprising that this vocational work for boys is the darling of Middletown's eye—if we except a group of teachers and of parents of the business class who protest that the city's preoccupation with vocational work tends to drag down standards in academic studies and to divert the future college student's attention from his preparatory courses.[21] Like the enthusiastically supported high school basket-ball

[20] This conformity to existing conditions is accentuated by the necessity of bidding for union support and falling in with current trade union practices. The attitude of the unions toward this school training varies all the way from that of the carpenters whose president attends the evening classes and who start a high school trained boy with a journeyman's card and corresponding wages to that of the bricklayers and plasterers who start a high school vocational graduate at exactly the same wage as an untrained boy.

[21] Many Middletown people maintain that the coming of vocational work to the high school has tended greatly to lower its standing as a college preparatory school. More than one mother shook her head over the fact that her daughter never does any studying at home and is out every evening but gets A's in all her work. It is generally recognized that a boy or girl graduating from the high school can scarcely enter an Eastern college without a year of additional preparatory work elsewhere.

Leading nationally known universities in neighboring states gave the following reports of the work of graduates of the Middletown high school: In one, of eleven Middletown students over a period of fifteen years, one graduated, none of the others made good records, four were asked to withdraw because of poor scholarship; of the four in residence in 1924, two were on probation, one was on the warned list, and one was doing fair work. In another, of five Middletown students in the last five years, one did excellent work, one fair, two did very poor work and dropped out after the first term, one had a record below requirement at the time of withdrawal. In a third, of eight Middletown students in the last five

team, these vocational courses have caught the imagination of the mass of male tax-payers; ask your neighbor at Rotary what kind of schools Middletown has and he will begin to tell you about these "live" courses. It is not without significance that vocational supervisors are more highly paid than any other teachers in the school system.

Much of what has been said of the strictly vocational courses applies also to work in bookkeeping and stenography and in home economics. The last-named, entirely new since 1890, is devised to meet the functional needs of the major group of the girls, who will be home-makers. Beginning in the seventh and eighth years with the study of food, clothing, and house-planning, it continues as an optional course through the high school with work in dressmaking, millinery, hygiene and home nursing, household management, and selection of food and clothing. As in the boys' vocational work, these courses center in the more obvious, accepted group practices; much more of the work in home economics, for example, centers in the traditional household productive skills such as canning, baking, and sewing, than in the rapidly growing battery of skills involved in effective buying of ready-made articles. The optional half-year course for the future business girl in selection of food and clothing, equipping a girl "to be an intelligent consumer," marks, however, an emergent recognition of a need for training in effective consumption, as does also the class visiting of local stores to inspect and discuss various kinds of household articles. In 1925 a new course in child care and nutrition was offered in one of the grade schools; while it consists almost entirely in the study of child feeding rather than of the wider aspects of child care, it is highly significant as being the first and sole effort on the part of the community to train women for this fundamental child-rearing function. Standard women's magazines are resorted to in these courses for girls as freely as technical journals are employed in the courses for boys.

Second only in importance to the rise of these courses addressed to practical vocational activities is the new emphasis upon courses in history and civics. These represent yet another point at which Middletown is bending its schools to the immediate service of its institutions—in this case, bolstering community solidarity against sundry divisive tendencies. A generation ago a course in American history was given to those who survived until the eighth grade, a course in general history, "covering everything from the Creation to the present in one little book of a hundred or so pages," followed in the second year of the high school, and one in civil government in the third year. Today, separate courses in civic training and in history and civics begin with the first grade for all children and continue throughout the elementary school, while in high school the third-year course in American history and the fourth-year course in civics and sociology are, with the exception of the second-year English course, the only courses required of all students afer the completion of the first year. Sixteen per cent. of the total student hours in the high school are

---

years, one was an excellent student, four were fair, and three were on probation. The single Middletown student in a fourth university attended for only a year and was on probation the entire time.

devoted to these social studies—history, sociology, and civics—a total surpassed only by those of English and the combined cluster of vocational,
domestic science, manual arts, and commercial courses.

Evidently Middletown has become concerned that no child shall be
without this pattern of the group.[22] Precisely what this stamp is appears
clearly in instructions to teachers:[23]

> "The most fundamental impression a study of history should
> leave on the youth of the land when they have reached the period
> of citizenship," begins the section on history and civics of the Mid-
> dletown Course of Study of the Elementary Schools, "is that they
> are their government's keepers as well as their brothers' keepers
> in a very true sense. This study should lead us to feel and will that
> sacrifice and service for our neighbor are the best fruits of life;
> that reverence for law, which means, also, reverence for God, is
> fundamental to citizenship; that private property, in the strictest
> sense, is a trust imposed upon us to be administered for the public
> good; that no man can safely live unto himself. . . ."

> "History furnishes no parallel of national growth, national
> prosperity and national achievement like ours," asserts the State
> Manual for Secondary Schools for 1923. "Practically all of this has

[22] "Good citizenship as an aim in life is nothing new. . . . But good citizenship as a
dominant aim of the American public school is something new. . . . For the first
time in history, as I see it, a social democracy is attempting to shape the opinions
and bias the judgment of oncoming generations." From the *Annual Report* of
Dean James E. Russell of Teachers College for the year ending June, 1925.

In view of the manifest concern in Middletown to dictate the social attitudes
of its young citizens, the concentration of college attendance of local high school
graduates in local or near-by institutions is significant. As noted in the preceding
chapter, forty-four of the eighty members of the high school class of 1924 who
were attending college were enrolled in the small local college; twelve more were
in the two state universities, ten more in other small colleges within the state, nine
were in small colleges in adjoining states, two in nationally known state universities in adjoining states, two in prominent eastern colleges, and one in an eastern
school giving specialized training—a total of sixty-six within the city or state,
eleven in immediately adjoining states, and three in distant states. This when
coupled with the tendency already pointed out for from one-third to one-half of
each high school graduating class, including almost certainly many of the most
enterprising and original members, to migrate to other communities, and the further tendency of Middletown to favor teachers trained within the state, presents
some interesting implications for the process of social change in Middletown.

[23] Descriptions of courses and instructions to teachers as set forth by the School
Board or State Department of Education sometimes bear little relation to what
children are actually being taught in the classroom. But they do show what those
directing the training of the young think *ought* to be taught and what they believe the public thinks ought to be taught. As indicating major characteristics of
this culture, therefore, they are, in one sense, even more significant than the things
that actually go on in the class-room. And by and large they do, of course, indicate trends in teaching.

been accomplished since we adopted our present form of government, and we are justified in believing that our political philosophy
is right, and that those who are today assailing it are wrong. To
properly grasp the philosophy of this government of ours, requires
a correct knowledge of its history."

The State Manual for Elementary Schools for 1921 instructs
that "a sense of the greatness of their state and a pride in its history should be developed in the minds of children," and quotes as
part of its directions to teachers of history: "The right of revolution does not exist in America. We had a revolution 140 years ago
which made it unnecessary to have any other revolution in this
country. . . . One of the many meanings of democracy is that it
,is a form of government in which the right of revolution has been
lost. . . . No man can be a sound and sterling American who believes that force is necessary to effectuate the popular will. . . .
Americanism . . . emphatically means . . . that we have repudiated old European methods of settling domestic questions, and have
evolved for ourselves machinery by which revolution as a method
of changing our life is outgrown, abandoned, outlawed."

The president of the Board of Education, addressing a meeting of Middletown parents in 1923, said that "many educators have
failed to face the big problem of teaching patriotism. . . . We
need to teach American children about American heroes and American ideals."

The other social studies resemble history in their announced aims:
civic training, with its emphasis upon respect for private property, respect
for public property, respect for law, respect for the home, appreciation of
services of good men and women, and so on; economics, with its stressing
of "common and fundamental principles," "the fundamental institutions
of society: private property, guaranteed privileges, contracts, personal liberty, right to establish private enterprises"; and sociology.

Nearly thirty-five years ago the first high school annual summarized
the fruits of four years of high school training as follows: "Many facts
have been presented to us and thus more knowledge has been attained."
Such a summary would be nearly as applicable today, and nowhere more
so than in these social studies. Teaching varies from teacher to teacher, but
with a few outstanding exceptions the social studies are taught with close
reliance upon textbooks prescribed by the state and in large measure embodying its avowed aims. A leading teacher of history and civics in the
high school explained:

"In class discussion I try to bring out minor points, two ways
of looking at a thing and all that, but in examinations I try to
emphasize important principles and group the main facts that they
have to remember around them. I always ask simple fact questions
in examinations. They get all mixed up and confused if we ask
questions where they have to think, and write all over the place."

In the case of history, facts presented in the textbooks are, as in 1890, predominantly military and political, although military affairs occupy relatively less space than in the nineties. Facts concerning economic and industrial development receive more emphasis than in the earlier texts, although political development is still the core. Recent events as compared with the colonial period in colonial history are somewhat more prominent today.[24] Examination questions of the two periods indicate so little change in method and emphasis in teaching that it is almost impossible simply by reading a history examination to tell whether it is of 1890 or 1924 vintage.

It may be a commentary upon the vitality of this early and persistent teaching of American history that when pictures like the Yale Press historical series are brought to Middletown the children say they get enough history in school, the adults say they are too grown up for such things, and the attendance is so poor that the exhibitor says, "Never again!"

Further insight into the stamp of the group with which Middletown children complete their social studies courses is gained through the following summary of answers of 241 boys and 315 girls, comprising the social science classes of the last two years of the high school, to a questionnaire:[25]

Statement	Percentage answering "True"		Percentage answering "False"		Percentage answering "Uncertain"		Percentage not answering	
	Boys	Girls	Boys	Girls	Boys	Girls	Boys	Girls
The white race is the best race on earth	66	75	19	17	14	6	1	2
The United States is unquestionably the best country in the world ...	77	88	10	6	11	5	2	1
Every good citizen should act according to the following statement: "My country—right or wrong!"	47	56	40	29	9	10	4	5
A citizen of the United States should be allowed to say anything he								

[24] See W. C. Bagley and H. O. Rugg, *The Content of American History as Taught in the Seventh and Eighth Grades* (University of Illinois School of Education Bulletin No. 16, Vol. XIII, 1916), comparing textbooks from 1865 to 1911, with a supplementary study by Earle Rugg of *Eight Current Histories,* and Snyder's *An Analysis of the Content of Elementary High School History Texts* (University of Chicago Doctor's Dissertation, 1919). Montgomery's *The Leading Facts of American History,* used in the Middletown schools in the nineties, and Woodburn and Moran's *American History and Government,* used in 1924, were included in the Rugg-Bagley study. Fite's *History of the United States,* used in the Middletown schools in 1924, was included in Snyder's study.

[25] Students were requested to write "true," "false," or "uncertain" after each statement. No answers of Negroes are included in this summary. The greater conservatism of the girls in their answers to some of the questions is noteworthy.

Statement	Percentage answering "True"		Percentage answering "False"		Percentage answering "Uncertain"		Percentage not answering	
	Boys	Girls	Boys	Girls	Boys	Girls	Boys	Girls
pleases, even to advocate violent revolution, if he does no violent act himself	20	16	70	75	7	7	3	2
The recent labor government in England was a misfortune for England	16	15	38	20	38	57	8	8
The United States was entirely right and England was entirely wrong in the American Revolution	30	33	55	40	13	25	2	2
The Allied Governments in the World War were fighting for a wholly righteous cause	65	75	22	8	11	14	2	3
Germany and Austria were the only nations responsible for causing the World War	22	25	62	42	15	31	1	2
The Russian Bolshevist government should be recognized by the United States Government	8	5	73	67	17	24	2	4
A pacifist in war time is a "slacker" and should be prosecuted by the government	40	36	34	28	22	28	4	8
The fact that some men have so much more money than others shows that there is an unjust condition in this country which ought to be changed	25	31	70	62	4	5	1	2

Other new emphases in the training given the young may be noted briefly. Natural sciences, taught in 1890 virtually without a laboratory[26] by

[26] Says the high school annual in 1804: "The laboratory is situated in what is known as the south office—a room six by four feet. On the east side of the room are a few shelves containing a half dozen bottles of chemicals. This is the extent of the chemical 'laboratory.' The physical laboratory will be found (with the aid of a microscope) in the closet adjoining the south office. Here will be found the remnants of an old electric outfit, and a few worn-out pieces of apparatus to illustrate the principles of natural philosophy."

a teacher trained in English and mathematics and by the high school principal who also taught all other junior and senior subjects, is today taught in well-equipped student laboratories by specially trained teachers. In the first and second semesters of 1923–24, 7 per cent. and 8 per cent. respectively of the student hours were devoted to the natural sciences.

Although art and music appear to occupy a lesser place in the spontaneous leisure-time life of Middletown than they did a generation ago, both are more prominent in the training given the young. In 1890 both were unknown in the high school except for the informal high school choir; a lone music teacher taught three hours a day in the grades; and "drawing" was taught "as an aid to muscular coördination" on alternate days with writing. Today art is taught in all eight years of the grades, while in high school a student may center his four years' work in either art or music, two of the twelve courses being built around these subjects. The high school art courses consist in creative work, art history, and art appreciation, while art exhibits and art contests reach far beyond formal class-room work.[27] Over and above the work in ear training and sight reading throughout the grades, there are today sixteen high school music courses in addition to classes in instrumental work. They include not only instruction in harmony, history of music, and music appreciation, but a chorus, four Glee Clubs, three orchestras, and two bands. Victrolas, now a necessary part of the equipment of all schools, and an annual music memory contest in the schools, further help to bring music within the reach of all children.[28]

Another innovation today is the more explicit recognition that education concerns bodies as well as minds. Gymnasium work, required of all students during the last year of the elementary school and the first year of the high school, replaces the earlier brief periods of "setting-up exercises" and seems likely to spread much more widely.

Abundant evidence has appeared throughout this chapter of the emphasis upon values and "right" attitudes in this business of passing along the lore of the elders to the young of Middletown. Since the religious attitudes and values are nominally held in this culture to overshadow all others, no account of the things taught in the schools would be adequate without a discussion of the relation of the schools to the religious beliefs and practices of the city. Getting a living, as we have observed, goes for-

[27] The class work itself reaches all groups of students. A barber commented proudly on the interest of his daughter, a high school junior, in her art work: "We have some friends that made fun of her for taking art—they thought it meant painting big pictures. My wife heard her talking art to some people the other day and says she could hold up her end with the best of 'em. I'm all for it. Now it has practical applications. When it comes to fixing up a house she'll know what things go good together."

[28] Neither this music work nor the art work in the schools appears to be as rooted in the present-day local life as the emphasis upon vocational education and the social studies. In fact, they represent a tradition less strong in the everyday life of the city today than a generation ago. Whether they will tend to increase spontaneous and active participation in music and art, as opposed to the passive enjoyment of them that predominates in this culture today, is problematical.

ward without any accompanying religious ceremonies or without any formal relation to the religious life of the city save that it "keeps the Sabbath day." Religion permeates the home at many points: marriage, birth, and death are usually accompanied or followed by religious rites, the eating of food is frequently preceded by its brief verbal blessing, most children are taught to say their prayers before retiring at night, a Bible is found in nearly every home, and the entire family traditionally prays together daily, though this last, as noted elsewhere, is becoming rare; the family itself is regarded as a sacred institution, though being secularized at many points. Leisure-time practices are less often today opened by prayer or hymns; though they have traditionally "observed the Sabbath," abundant testimony appears throughout this study of the attenuation of such observance of the "Lord's Day" by young and old. The common group affairs of the city, likewise, are increasingly carried on, like getting a living, without direct recourse to religious ceremonies and beliefs. In the midst of the medley of secularized and non-secularized ways of living in the city, education steers a devious course. One religious group, the Catholics, trains its children in a special school building under teachers who are professional religious devotees and wear a religious garb; this school adjoins the church and the children attend a church service as part of their day's schooling. For the great mass of children, however, separate Sunday Schools, in no way controlled by the secular schools, teach the accepted religious beliefs to those who choose to attend. The Y.M.C.A. and Y.W.C.A. serve as a liaison between church and school, teaching Bible classes in all elementary schools, for the most part on school time, and giving work in the high school for which credit is granted towards graduation. But while the public schools themselves do not teach the group's religious beliefs directly, these beliefs tacitly underlie much that goes on in the class-room, more particularly those classes concerned not with the manipulation of material tools but with the teaching of ideas, concepts, attitudes. The first paragraph in the "Course of Study of the Elementary Schools" enjoins upon the teachers that "all your children should join in opening the day with some exercise which will prepare them with thankful hearts and open minds for the work of the day. . . . The Bible should be heard and some sacred song sung." The School Board further instructs its teachers that geography should teach "the spirit of reverence and appreciation for the works of God—that these things have been created for [man's] joy and elevation . . . that the earth in its shape and movements, its mountains and valleys, its drought and flood, and in all things that grow upon it, is well planned for man in working out his destiny"; that history should teach "the earth as the field of man's spiritual existence"; that hygiene create interest in the care of the body "as a fit temple for the spirit"; finally that "the schools should lead the children, through their insight into the things of nature that they study, to appreciate the power, wisdom, and goodness of the Author of these things. They should see in the good things that have come out of man's struggle for a better life a guiding hand stronger than his own. . . . The pupils should learn to appreciate the Bible as a fountain of truth and beauty through the lessons to be gotten from it. . . ."

This emphasis was if anything even stronger in 1890. At the Teachers' Institute in 1890 botany was discussed as a subject in which "by the study of nature we are enabled to see the perfection of creation," and a resolution was passed that "the moral qualifications of the teachers should be of such a nature as to make them fit representatives to instruct for both time and eternity." "In morals, show the importance of building upon principles. Encourage the pupil to do right because it is right," said the School Board instructions for 1882. One gains a distinct impression that the religious basis of all education was more taken for granted if less talked about thirty-five years ago, when high school "chapel" was a religio-inspirational service with a "choir" instead of the "pep session" which it tends to become today.

Some inkling of the degree of dominance of religious ways of thinking at the end of ten or twelve years of education is afforded by the answers of the 241 boys and 315 girls in the social science classes of the last two years of the high school appraising the statement: "The theory of evolution offers a more accurate account of the origin and history of mankind than that offered by a literal interpretation of the first chapters of the Bible": 19 per cent. of them marked it "true," 48 per cent. "false," 26 per cent. were "uncertain," and 7 per cent. did not answer.

SCHOOL "LIFE"

Accompanying the formal training afforded by courses of study is another and informal kind of training, particularly during the high school years. The high school, with its athletics, clubs, sororities and fraternities, dances and parties, and other "extracurricular activities," is a fairly complete social cosmos in itself, and about this city within a city the social life of the intermediate generation centers. Here the social sifting devices of their elders—money, clothes, personal attractiveness, male physical prowess, exclusive clubs, election to positions of leadership—are all for the first time set going with a population as yet largely undifferentiated save as regards their business class and working class parents. This informal training is not a preparation for a vague future that must be taken on trust, as is the case with so much of the academic work; to many of the boys and girls in high school this is "the life," the thing they personally like best about going to school.

The school is taking over more and more of the child's waking life. Both high school and grades have departed from the attitude of fifty years ago, when the Board directed:

> "Pupils shall not be permitted to remain on the school grounds after dismissal. The teachers shall often remind the pupils that the first duty when dismissed is to proceed quietly and directly home to render all needed assistance to their parents."

Today the school is becoming not a place to which children go from their homes for a few hours daily but a place from which they go home to eat and sleep.[29]

An index to this widening of the school's function appears in a comparison of the 1924 high school annual with the first annual, published thirty years before, though even this comparison does not reflect the full extent of the shift since 1890, for innovations had been so numerous in the years just preceding 1894 as to dwarf the extent of the 1890–1924 contrast. Next in importance to the pictures of the senior class and other class data in the earlier book, as measured by the percentage of space occupied, were the pages devoted to the faculty and the courses taught by them, while in the current book athletics shares the position of honor with the class data, and a faculty twelve times as large occupies relatively only half as much space. Interest in small selective group "activities" has increased at the expense of the earlier total class activities.[30] But such a numerical comparison can only faintly suggest the difference in tone of the two books. The description of academic work in the early annual beginning, "Among the various changes that have been effected in grade work are . . ." and ending, "regular monthly teachers' meetings have been inaugurated," seems as foreign to the present high school as does the early class motto "Deo Duce"; equally far from 1890 is the present dedication, "To the Bearcats."

This whole spontaneous life of the intermediate generation that clusters about the formal nucleus of school studies becomes focused, articulate, and even rendered important in the eyes of adults through the medium of the school athletic teams—the "Bearcats." [31] The business man may "lay down the law" to his adolescent son or daughter at home and patronize their friends, but in the basket-ball grandstand he is if anything a little less important than these youngsters of his who actually mingle daily with those five boys who wear the colors of "Magic Middletown." There were no high school teams in 1890. Today, during the height of the basket-ball season when all the cities and towns of the state are fighting for the state championship amidst the delirious backing of the rival citizens, the dominance of this sport is as all-pervasive as football in a college like Dartmouth

---

[29] This condition is deplored by some as indicative of the "break-up of the American home." Others welcome it as freeing the child earlier from the domination of parents and accustoming him to face adjustments upon the success of which adult behavior depends. In any event, the trend appears to be in the direction of an extension of the present tendency increasingly into the grades.

[30] The following shows the percentage of the pages of the annual occupied by the chief items in 1894 and 1924, the earlier year being in each case given first: Class data—39 per cent., 19 per cent.; faculty—16 per cent., 8 per cent. (brief biographies and pictures in 1894, list of names only and picture of principal in 1924); athletics —5 per cent., 19 per cent.; courses of study—6 per cent., 0.0 per cent.; class poems —13 per cent., 0.0 per cent.; activities other than athletics—5 per cent. (one literary society), 13 per cent. (thirteen *kinds* of clubs); jokes—5 per cent., 17 per cent.; advertisements and miscellaneous—11 per cent., 24 per cent.

[31] In the elementary grades athletics are still a minor interest, though a school base-ball and basket-ball league have been formed of recent years and the pressure of inter-school leagues and games is being felt increasingly.

or Princeton the week of the "big game." At other times dances, dramatics, and other interests may bulk larger, but it is the "Bearcats," particularly the basket-ball team, that dominate the life of the school. Says the prologue to the high school annual:

> "The Bearcat spirit has permeated our high school in the last few years and pushed it into the prominence that it now holds. The '24 *Magician* has endeavored to catch, reflect and record this spirit because it has been so evident this year. We hope that after you have glanced at this book for the first time, this spirit will be evident to you.
>
> "However, most of all, we hope that in perhaps twenty years, if you become tired of this old world, you will pick up this book and it will restore to you the spirit, pep, and enthusiasm of the old 'Bearcat Days' and will inspire in you better things."

Every issue of the high school weekly bears proudly the following "Platform":

> "1. To support live school organizations.
> "2. To recognize worth-while individual student achievements.
> "3. Above all to foster the real 'Bearcat' spirit in all of Central High School."

Curricular and social interests tend to conform. Friday nights throughout the season are preëmpted for games; the Mothers' Council, recognizing that every Saturday night had its own social event, urged that other dances be held on Friday nights instead of school nights, but every request was met with the rejoinder that "Friday is basket-ball night."

This activity, so enthusiastically supported, is largely vicarious. The press complains that only about forty boys are prominent enough in athletics to win varsity sweaters. In the case of the girls it is almost 100 per cent. vicarious. Girls play some informal basket-ball and there is a Girls' Athletic Club which has a monogram and social meetings. But the interest of the girls in athletics is an interest in the activities of the young males. "My daughter plans to go to the University of ———— " said one mother, "because she says, 'Mother, I just *couldn't* go to a college whose athletics I couldn't be proud of!' " The highest honor a senior boy can have is captaincy of the football or basket-ball team, although, as one senior girl explained, "Every member is almost as much admired."

Less spectacular than athletics but bulking even larger in time demands is the network of organizations that serve to break the nearly two thousand individuals composing the high school microcosm into the more intimate groups human beings demand. These groups are mainly of three kinds: the purely social clubs, in the main a stepping down of the social system of adults; a long distance behind in point of prestige, clubs formed around curriculum activities; and, even farther behind, a few groups sponsored by the religious systems of the adults.

In 1894 the high school boasted one club, the "Turemethian Literary Society." According to the early school yearbook:

> "The Turemethian Society makes every individual feel that practically he is free to choose between good and evil; that he is not a mere straw thrown upon the water to mark the direction of the current, but that he has within himself the power of a strong swimmer and is capable of striking out for himself, of buffeting the waves, and directing, to a certain extent, his own independent course. Socrates said, 'Let him who would move the world move first himself.' . . . A paper called the Zetetic is prepared and read at each meeting. . . . Debates have created . . . a friendly rivalry. . . . Another very interesting feature of the Turemethian Society is the lectures delivered to us. . . . All of these lectures help to make our High School one of the first of its kind in the land. The Turemethian Society has slowly progressed in the last year. What the future has in store for it we can not tell, but must say as Mary Riley Smith said, 'God's plans, like lilies pure and white, unfold; we must not tear the close-shut leaves apart; time will reveal the calyxes of gold.' "

Six years later, at the turn of the century, clubs had increased to the point of arousing protest in a press editorial entitled "Barriers to Intellectual Progress." Today clubs and other extracurricular activities are more numerous than ever. Not only is the camel's head inside the tent but his hump as well; the first period of the school day, often running over into the next hour, has recently, at the request of the Mothers' Council, been set aside as a "convocation hour" dedicated to club and committee meetings.

The backbone of the purely social clubs is the series of unofficial branches of former high school fraternities and sororities; Middletown boasts four Alpha chapters. For a number of years a state law has banned these high school organizations, but the interest of active graduate chapters keeps them alive. The high school clubs have harmless names such as the Glendale Club; a boy is given a long, impressive initiation into his club but is not nominally a member of the fraternity of which his club is the undergraduate section until after he graduates, when it is said that by the uttering of a few hitherto unspoken words he comes into his heritage. Under this ambiguous status dances have been given with the club name on the front of the program and the fraternity name on the back. Two girls' clubs and two boys' clubs which every one wants to make are the leaders. Trailing down from them are a long list of lesser clubs. Informal meetings are usually in homes of members but the formal fall, spring, and Christmas functions are always elaborate hotel affairs.

Extracurricular clubs have canons not dictated by academic standards of the world of teachers and textbooks. Since the adult world upon which the world of this intermediate generation is modeled tends to be dominated primarily by getting a living and "getting on" socially rather than by learning and "the things of the mind," the bifurcation of high school life is not surprising.

"When do you study?" some one asked a clever high school Senior who had just finished recounting her week of club meetings, committee meetings, and dances, ending with three parties the night before. "Oh, in civics I know more or less about politics, so it's easy to talk and I don't have to study that. In English we're reading plays and I can just look at the end of the play and know about that. Typewriting and chemistry I don't have to study outside anyway. Virgil is worst, but I've stuck out Latin four years for the Virgil banquet; I just sit next to ——— and get it from her. Mother jumps on me for never studying, but I get A's all the time, so she can't say anything."

The relative status of academic excellence and other qualities is fairly revealed in the candid rejoinder of one of the keenest and most popular girls in the school to the question, "What makes a girl eligible for a leading high school club?"

> "The chief thing is if the boys like you and you can get them for the dances," she replied. "Then, if your mother belongs to a graduate chapter that's pretty sure to get you in. Good looks and clothes don't necessarily get you in, and being good in your studies doesn't necessarily keep you out unless you're a 'grind.' Same way with the boys—the big thing there is being on the basket-ball or football team. A fellow who's just a good student rates pretty low. Being good-looking, a good dancer, and your family owning a car will help."

The clubs allied to curricular activities today include the Dramatic Club—plays by sophomore, junior, and senior classes in a single spring have replaced the "programs of recitations, selections, declamations, and essays" of the old days; the Daubers, meeting weekly in school hours to sketch and in evening meetings with graduate members for special talks on art; the Science Club with its weekly talks by members and occasional lectures by well-known scientists; the Pickwick Club, open to members of English classes, meeting weekly for book reviews and one-act plays, with occasional social meetings; the Penmanship Club; and the Virgil Club, carrying with it some social prestige. Interest in the work of these clubs is keen among some students. All have their "pledges," making their rituals conform roughly to those of the more popular fraternities and sororities.

On the periphery of this high school activity are the church and Y.M.C.A. and Y.W.C.A. clubs. All these organizations frankly admit that the fifteen to twenty-one-year [old] person is their hardest problem. The Hi-Y club appears to be most successful. The Y.M.C.A. controls the extra-curricular activities of the grade school boys more than any other single agency, but it maintains itself with only moderate success in the form of this Hi-Y club among the older boys. A Hi-Y medal is awarded each commencement to the boy in the graduating class who shows the best all-round record, both in point of scholarship and of character. The Y.W.C.A. likewise maintains clubs in the grades but has rough sledding when it comes to the busy, popular, influential group in high school. According to one representative senior girl:

> "High School girls pay little attention to the Y.W. and the Girl Reserves. The boys go to the Y.M. and Hi-Y club because it has a supper meeting once a month, and that is one excuse for getting away from home evenings. There aren't any supper meetings for the girls at the Y.W. It's not much good to belong to a Y.W. club; *any one* can belong to them."

All manner of other clubs, such as the Hiking Club and the Boys' and Girls' Booster Club and the Boys' and Girls' Pep Club hover at the fringes or even occasionally take the center of the stage. Says the school paper:

> "Pep Clubs are being organized in Central High School with a motive that wins recognition. Before, there has been a Pep Club in school, but this year we are more than fortunate in having two. Their business-like start this year predicts a good future. Let's support them!"

Pep week during the basket-ball season, engineered by these Pep Clubs, included:

> "*Monday:* Speakers in each of the four assemblies. . . .
> "*Tuesday:* Poster Day.
> "*Wednesday:* Reverend Mr. ——— in chapel. Booster pins and pep tags.
> "*Thursday:* Practice on yells and songs.
> "*Friday:* Final Chapel. Mr. ——— speaks. Yells and songs.
> "Pep chapel [32] for all students will be held in the auditorium the ninth period. Professor ——— and his noisy cohorts will furnish the music for the occasion. Immediately following the chapel the students will parade through the business district."

With the growth of smaller competitive groups, class organization has also increased, reaching a crescendo of importance in the junior and senior years. In a community with such a strong political tradition it is not surprising that there should be an elaborate ritual in connection with the election of senior and other class officers. The senior officers are nominated early in the school year, after much wire-pulling by all parties. "The diplomatic agents of the candidates have been working for weeks on this election," commented the school paper. The election comes a week later so as to allow plenty of electioneering; the evening before election an "enthusiasm dinner" is held in the school cafeteria at which nominees and their "campaign managers" vie with each other in distributing attractive

---

[32] The evolution of the chapel to anything from a "Pep chapel" to a class rally is an interesting example of the change of custom while the label persists.

favors (menus, printed paper napkins, and so on), and each candidate states his platform.

Amid the round of athletics, clubs, committees, and class meetings there is always some contest or other to compete for the time of the pupils. Principals complain that hardly a week passes that they do not have to take time from class work in preparation for a contest, the special concern of some organization. In 1923–24 these included art and music memory contests, better speech and commercial department contests, a Latin contest, a contest on the Constitution, essays on meat eating, tobacco, poster making, home lighting, and highways.

In this bustle of activity young Middletown swims along in a world as real and perhaps even more zestful than that in which its parents move. Small wonder that a local paper comments editorially, "It is a revelation to old-timers to learn that a genuine boy of the most boyish type nowadays likes to go to school." "Oh, yes, they have a much better time," rejoined the energetic father of a high school boy to a question asked informally of a tableful of men at a Kiwanis luncheon as to whether boys really have a better time in school than they did thirty-five years ago or whether they simply have more things. "No doubt about it!" added another. "When I graduated early in the nineties there weren't many boys—only two in our class, and a dozen girls. All our studies seemed very far away from real life, but today—they've got shop work and athletics, and it's all nearer what a boy's interested in."

The relative disregard of most people in Middletown for teachers and for the content of books, on the one hand, and the exalted position of the social and athletic activities of the schools, on the other, offer an interesting commentary on Middletown's attitude toward education. And yet Middletown places large faith in going to school. The heated opposition to compulsory education in the nineties[33] has virtually disappeared; only three of

[33] The following, from editorials in the leading daily in 1891, reflect the virulence with which compulsory education was fought by many, and incidentally exhibit a pattern of opposition to social change that bobs up from time to time today as innovations appear:

"Taxpayers of this county are upset by the state and county teachers' resolutions favoring compulsory education. . . . The teachers in our schools are not well versed in political economy. The most of them are young, and have had little time to study anything other than textbooks and their reports and programs. The idea of compulsion is detestable to the average American citizen. Men do not become good under compulsion. Two classes of men are clamoring for compulsory education: those who are depending upon school work for a living and for place and power, and those who are afraid of the Catholic Church. . . . The school system has not done what was expected of it. Immorality and crime are actually on the increase. . . . The states that have the greatest percentage of illiteracy have the smallest percentage of crime. . . . Compulsory education has failed wherever tried on American soil."

"The danger to the country today is through too many educated scoundrels. Boys and girls learn to cheat and defraud in copying papers for graduation essays. . . . A law compelling a child seven years of age to sit in a poorly ventilated school room and inhale the nauseous exhalations from the bodies of his mates for

the 124 working class families interviewed voiced even the mildest impatience at it. Parents insist upon more and more education as part of their children's birthright; editors and lecturers point to education as a solution for every kind of social ill; the local press proclaims, "Public Schools of [Middletown] Are the City's Pride"; woman's club papers speak of the home, the church, and the school as the "foundations" of Middletown's culture. Education is a faith, a religion, to Middletown. And yet when one looks more closely at this dominant belief in the magic of formal schooling, it appears that it is not what actually goes on in the schoolroom that these many voices laud. Literacy, yes, they want their children to be able to "read the newspapers, write a letter, and perform the ordinary operations of arithmetic," but, beyond that, many of them are little interested in what the schools teach. This thing, education, appears to be desired frequently not for its specific content but as a symbol—by the working class as an open sesame that will mysteriously admit their children to a world closed to them, and by the business class as a heavily sanctioned aid in getting on further economically or socially in the world.

Rarely does one hear a talk addressed to school children by a Middletown citizen that does not contain in some form the idea, "Of course, you won't remember much of the history or other things they teach you here. Why, I haven't thought of Latin or algebra in thirty years! But . . ." And here the speaker goes on to enumerate what *are* to his mind the enduring values of education which every child should seize as his great opportunity: "habits of industry," "friendships formed," "the great ideals of our nation." Almost never is the essential of education defined in terms of the subjects taught in the class-room. One member of Rotary spoke with pitying sympathy of his son who "even brought along a history book to read on the train when he came home for his Christmas vacation—the poor overworked kid!"

Furthermore, in Middletown's traditional philosophy it is not primarily learning, or even intelligence, as much as character and good will which are exalted. Says Edgar Guest, whose daily message in Middletown's leading paper is widely read and much quoted:

> "God won't ask you if you were clever,
> For I think he'll little care,
> When your toil is done forever
> He may question: 'Were you square?' "

---

six hours a day for three or four months at a time, is a wicked and inhuman law. . . . Children forced into schools are morally tainted—and neutralize the virtues of well-bred children. It is a great mistake for the state to undertake to carry forward the evolution of the race from such bad material when there is so much good material at hand. Every movement that tends to relieve the father or mother of the moral responsibility of developing, training and directing the moral and intellectual forces of their own children, tends to reduce marriage and the home to a mere institution for the propagation of our species."

The press of 1900 noted that "the problem of securing boy labor is still worrying [state] manufacturers. The truancy law, they say, is detrimental to their business."

"You know the smarter the man the more dissatisfied he is," says Will Rogers in a Middletown paper, "so cheer up, let us be happy in our ignorance." "I wanted my son to go to a different school in the East," said a business class mother, "because it's more cultured. But then I think you can have too much culture. It's all right if you're living in the East—or even in California—but it unfits you for living in the Middle West." Every one lauds education in general, but relatively few people in Middletown seem to be sure just how they have ever used their own education beyond such commonplaces as the three R's and an occasional odd fact, or to value greatly its specific outcome in others.

Some clew to these anomalies of the universal lauding of education but the disparagement of many of the particular things taught, and of the universal praise of the schools but the almost equally general apathy towards the people entrusted with the teaching, may be found in the disparity that exists at many points between the daily activities of Middletown adults and the things taught in the schools. Square root, algebra, French, the battles of the Civil War, the presidents of the United States before Grover Cleveland, the boundaries of the state of Arizona, whether Rangoon is on the Yangtze or Ganges or neither, the nature or location of the Japan Current, the ability to write compositions or to use semicolons, sonnets, free verse, and the Victorian novel—all these and many other things that constitute the core of education simply do not operate in life as Middletown adults live it. And yet, the world says education is important; and certainly educated men seem to have something that brings them to the top—just look at the way the college boys walked off with the commissions during the war. The upshot is, with Middletown reasoning thus, that a phenomenon common in human culture has appeared: a value divorced from current, tangible existence in the world all about men and largely without commerce with these concrete existential realities has become an ideal to which independent existence is attributed. Hence the anomaly of Middletown's regard for the symbol of education and its disregard for the concrete procedure of the school-room.

But the pressure and accidents of local life are prompting Middletown to lay hands upon its schools at certain points, as we have observed, and to use them instrumentally to foster patriotism, teach hand skills, and serve its needs in other ways. This change, again characteristically, is taking place not so much through the direct challenging of the old as through the setting up of new alternate procedures, e.g., the adding to the traditional high school, offering only a Latin and an English course in 1890, of ten complete alternate courses ranging all the way from shorthand to home economics and mechanical drafting. The indications seem to be that the optional newcomers may in time displace more and more of the traditional education and thus the training given the young will approach more nearly the methodically practical concerns of the group.

Lest this trend of education overtaking the life of Middletown appear too simple, however, it should be borne in mind that even while Middletown prides itself on its "up-to-date" schools with their vocational training, the local institutional life is creating fresh strains and maladjustments heretofore unknown: the city boasts of the fact that only 2.5 per cent. of its population ten years of age or older cannot read and write, and meanwhile the massed weight of advertising and professional publicity are creating, as pointed out above, new forms of social illiteracy, and the invention of the motion picture is introducing the city's population, young and old, week after week, into types of vivid experience which they come to take for granted as parts of their lives, yet have no training to handle. Another type of social illiteracy is being bred by the stifling of self-appraisal and self-criticism under the heavily diffused habit of local solidarity in which the schools coöperate. An organized, professional type of city-boosting, even more forceful than the largely spontaneous, amateur enthusiasm of the gas boom days, has grown up in the shelter of national propaganda during the war. Fostered particularly by the civic clubs, backed by the Chamber of Commerce and business interests, as noted elsewhere, it insists that the city must be kept to the fore and its shortcomings blanketed under the din of local boosting—or new business will not come to town. The result of this is the muzzling of self-criticism by hurling the term "knocker" at the head of a critic and the drowning of incipient social problems under a public mood of everything being "fine and dandy." Thus, while education slowly pushes its tents closer to the practical concerns of the local life, the latter are forever striking camp and removing deeper into the forest.

Suggestions for Further Reading

The classic description of American life in this period is Mark Sullivan, *Our Times, 1900–1925*, 6 vols. (New York, 1926–35). Other general treatments that consider various periods of the early twentieth century are Henry May, *The End of American Innocence: A Study of the First Years of Our Time, 1912–1917** (New York, 1959); Walter Lord, *The Good Years** (New York, 1960); and Gilman Ostrander, *American Civilization in the First Machine Age, 1890–1940** (New York, 1970). The standard popular treatment of the 1920s is Frederick Lewis Allen, *Only Yesterday** (New York, 1931). Two recent works that challenge Allen's interpretations are Paul Carter, *The Twenties in America** (New York, 1968), and John Braeman, Robert H. Bremner, and David Brody, eds., *Change and Continuity in Twentieth-Century America: The 1920's* (Columbus, Ohio, 1968). The novelist John Dos Passos' classic trilogy, *U.S.A.** (Boston, 1937) contains much valuable material on this period.

Two recent collections of historical essays that enable readers to see the newly developing methodologies in the field of family history are Michael Gordon, ed., *The American Family in Social-Historical Perspective** (New York, 1973), and Theodore K. Rabb and Robert Rotberg, eds., *The Family in History: Interdisciplinary Essays** (New York, 1974), a volume that was originally printed as an issue of the *Journal of Interdisciplinary History*. There is a great deal of useful material in the long-standard but seriously flawed Arthur W. Calhoun, *A Social History of the American Family*, 3 vols. (Cleveland, Ohio, 1919). Interesting but controversial insights are found in Philippe Ariés, *Centuries of Childhood** (New York, 1962). On feminism and the new role of women, see two works by William O'Neill, *Divorce in the Progressive Era** (New Haven, Conn., 1967) and *Everyone Was Brave: The Rise and Fall of Feminism in America** (Chicago, 1969), and Jane Sochen, *The New Woman: Feminism in Greenwich Village, 1910–1920** (New York, 1972). A good history of the feminist movement is Eleanor Flexner, *Century of Struggle: The Woman's Rights Movement in the United States** (Cambridge, Mass., 1959). Works by two important feminists are Charlotte Perkins Gilman, *Women and Economics** (Boston, 1898) and *The Home: Its Work and Its Influence** (New York, 1903), and Emma Goldman's autobiography, *Living My Life** (New York, 1931), available in a two-volume paperback edition. See also Richard Drinnon, *Rebel in Paradise: A Biography of Emma Goldman* (Chicago, 1961). The controversy over Margaret Sanger and the birth control movement in a single

---

* Available in paperback edition.

New England town is described by Kenneth Underwood in *Protestant and Catholic* (Boston, 1957). One approach to the race-suicide problem is found in Mark H. Holler, *Eugenics: Hereditarian Attitudes in American Thought* (New Brunswick, N.J., 1963).

An excellent recent article on the immigrant working class is Herbert Gutman, "Work, Culture and Society in Industrializing America, 1815–1919," *American Historical Review* 78 (June 1973): 531–88. For further information on the steelworkers, see David Brody, *Labor in Crisis: The Steel Strike of 1919** (Philadelphia, 1965). The classic study of Polish immigration is found in W. I. Thomas and Florian Znaniecki, *The Polish Peasant in Europe and America*, 2 vols. (New York, 1927). A fictional treatment of Slavic immigrants at work can be found in Upton Sinclair, *The Jungle** (New York, 1906), a novel about the meatpacking industry in Chicago. For background on Italian immigrants and their descendants, see Alexander De Conde, *Half Bitter, Half Sweet: An Excursion into Italian-American History* (New York, 1971); Humbert S. Nelli, *The Italian in Chicago, 1880–1930: A Study in Ethnic Mobility** (New York, 1970); Virginia Yans McLaughlin, "Patterns of Work and Family Organization: Buffalo's Italians," *Journal of Interdisciplinary History* 2 (Autumn 1971): 299–314; and Herbert J. Gans, *The Urban Villagers: Group and Class in the Life of Italian Americans** (New York, 1962). Apart from Michael Novak, perhaps the most persistent advocate of the new ethnicity is Andrew Greeley, an Irish-American priest-sociologist. For a sample of his work, see *Why Can't They Be Like Us? Facts and Fallacies about Ethnic Differences and Group Consciousness in America** (New York, 1969).

The best book on the first Ku Klux Klan is Allen W. Trelease, *White Terror: The Ku Klux Klan Conspiracy and Southern Reconstruction** (New York, 1971). For information on the second Klan, see Kenneth Jackson, *The Ku Klux Klan in the City, 1915–1930** (New York, 1968), and Stanley Cohen, "The Failure of the Melting Pot," in *The Great Fear: Race in the Mind of America,** edited by Gary B. Nash and Richard Weiss (New York, 1970). John Higham describes the long tradition of anti-foreign agitation in *Strangers in the Land: Patterns of American Nativism, 1860–1925** (New Brunswick, N.J., 1955). Conservative Protestantism played an important role in the shaping of attitudes in this period. Two excellent books by William McLoughlin that give some insight into these attitudes are *Modern Revivalism: Charles Grandison Finney to Billy Graham* (New York, 1959) and *Billy Sunday Was His Real Name* (Chicago, 1955). See also Norman F. Furniss, *The Fundamentalist Controversy, 1918–1931* (New Haven, Conn., 1954). For the most significant religious confrontation of the period, see Ray Ginger, *Six Days or Forever: Tennessee v. John Scopes** (Boston, 1958).

Very little outstanding work has been produced on the history of education in the twentieth century. Most of what has been done concerns intellectual history rather than institutional history. See, for example, the excellent work by Lawrence Cremin, *The Transformation of the School: Progressivism in American Education, 1876–1957** (New York, 1961). Richard Hofstadter deals with many of the same ideas in the last section of *Anti-Intellectualism in American Life** (New York, 1963). To appreciate the difficulties of writing education history, see Ellwood P. Cubberley, *Public Education in the United States* (New York, 1934), which must be read in conjunction with Lawrence Cremin, *The Wonderful World of Ellwood Patterson Cubberley: An Essay on the Historiography of American Education** (New York, 1965). Cremin has also contributed an essay on secondary education during this period, "The Revolution in American Secondary Education. 1893–1918," *Teachers College Record* 56 (1955): 295–308. For public education in the nineteenth century, see Rush Welter, *Popular Education and Democratic Thought in America** (New York, 1962), and Michael B. Katz, *The Irony of Early School Reforms: Educational Innovation in Mid-Nineteenth Century Massachusetts** (Cambridge, Mass., 1968). For recent criticisms of the public schools in the United States, see the writings of Charles Silberman, Jonathan Kozol, Herbert Kohl, and John Holt. Perhaps no better description of the modern high school exists than Frederick Wiseman's documentary film, *High School*. An unusual collection of extremely provocative source material is found in Robert H. Bremner et al., eds., *Children and Youth in America: A Documentary History*, 3 vols. (Cambridge, Mass., 1970–74).

1930–1952
Depression and War

What the Depression Did
to People

EDWARD ROBB ELLIS

After a period of relative affluence and optimism in the 1920s, the American economy crashed in a shambles in late 1929. Although the Great Depression of the 1930s is usually dated from the stock market crash of October 1929, prudent men might have foreseen the dangers as the rate of real investment began to drop and speculation increased. The widely noted Wall Street collapse and the subsequent failure of apparently stable economic institutions brought to the attention of the nation and the world that the affluence and optimism of the 1920s had been increasingly composed of hope (that is, speculation) and promises rather than of stable economic growth.

The economic downturn led to loss of hope and, so it seemed to some, a failure of nerve. It has been explained that loss of confidence in the business system was a major contributing factor in the spread of the depression. Whatever the causes—and these are still being debated—the bubble burst, and the country plunged into poverty and despair.

In writing the history of the 1930s, scholars have tended to concentrate on political developments. The election of Franklin Delano Roosevelt to the presidency and the advent of what he called the New Deal have captured the imagination of the historians of the period and have led to an overemphasis on the importance of the Roosevelt administration. While it is true that several important innovations in public welfare were adopted by the New Deal, these were applied only half-heartedly. And they did not end the depression, although they did ease its effects for some of the population. The end of the depression was brought about by the Second World War and the full employment that resulted from the United States establishing itself as the "arsenal of democracy."

What has often been slighted in the historical writing, then, is the impact of the depression on the lives of ordinary people. The best descriptions of the period have come from the pens of the creative writers of the decade; no later work is likely to surpass John Steinbeck's **The Grapes of Wrath** or James Agee and Walker Evans' **Let Us Now Praise Famous Men** as portraits of the despair of the 1930s. Today, however, there is a rising interest in the human cost of the depression, and many recent articles and books attempt to describe the suffering that afflicted so many during that decade.

One reason for the new interest in the depression is the advent of a new generation of historians who were very young or were not yet born in the 1930s and, therefore, have no memories of the period. The searing experiences of the older generation, who could recall the hunger and frustration of the times, led them to try to forget, not remember.

One who has tried to remember is Edward Robb Ellis, a former newspaperman and popular historian, who is the author of **A Nation in Torment,** a chapter of which is reprinted below. Ellis, who entered college in 1929, found that the crash wiped out the savings he had laid away for his education. After working his way through journalism school, he became that college graduate described in the selection below who took a job as a newspaper reporter for exactly nothing in salary.

Writing anecdotally and relying on a diary he kept in those years as well as memoirs of others like himself, Ellis describes the costs in human suffering paid by people across the United States. He juxtaposes the arrogant and stupid attitudes of the rich against the despair and hunger of the poor. There is an overriding sense of desperation in many of the statements found in this selection, and one wonders at the lack of success of alternative political movements that might have led to an easing of the burden of the depression for many.

The runaway economic consumerism of the post–Second World War era may have its source in the contrast between the affluence of the 1920s and the poverty of the 1930s. Many middle-class and would-be middle-class Americans were not able, because of the depression, to enjoy the fruits of the consumer society that had developed in the 1920s. As the economy took off again during the Second World War, these potential consumers took off with it, and it often seems as though they are attempting to ward off future terrors by surrounding themselves with as many material objects as possible.

The Depression smashed into the nation with such fury that men groped for superlatives to express its impact and meaning.

Edmund Wilson compared it to an earthquake. It was "like the explosion of a bomb dropped in the midst of society," according to the Social Science Research Council Committee on Studies in Social Aspects of the Depression.

Alfred E. Smith said the Depression was equivalent to war, while Supreme Court Justice Louis D. Brandeis and Bernard Baruch declared that it was worse than war. Philip La Follette, the governor of Wisconsin, said: "We are in the midst of the greatest domestic crisis since the Civil War." Governor Roosevelt agreed in these words: "Not since the dark days of the Sixties have the people of this state and nation faced problems as grave, situations as difficult, suffering as severe." A jobless textile worker told Louis Adamic: "I wish there would be war again." In a war against a foreign enemy all Americans might at least have felt united by a common purpose, and production would have boomed.

Poor and rich alike felt anxious and helpless.

Steel magnate Charles M. Schwab, despite his millions and the security of his Manhattan palace, freely confessed: "I'm afraid. Every man is afraid." J. David Stern, a wealthy newspaper publisher, became so terrified that he later wrote in his autobiography: "I sat in my back office, trying to figure out what to do. To be explicit, I sat in my private bathroom. My bowels were loose from fear." Calvin Coolidge dolorously told a friend: "I can see nothing to give ground for hope."

Herbert C. Pell, a rich man with a country estate near Governor Roosevelt's, said the country was doomed unless it could free itself from the rich, who have "shown no realization that what you call free enterprise means anything but greed." Marriner Eccles, a banker and economist who had *not* lost his fortune, wrote that "I awoke to find myself at the bottom of a pit without any known means of scaling its sheer sides." According to Dwight W. Morrow, a Morgan associate, diplomat and Senator: "Most of my friends think the world is coming to an end— that is, the world as we know it." Reinhold Niebuhr, the learned and liberal clergyman, said that rich "men and women speculated in drawing-rooms on the best kind of poison as a means to oblivion from the horrors of revolution."

In Youngstown, Ohio, a friend of Mayor Joseph L. Heffernan stood beside the mayor's desk and said: "My wife is frantic. After working at the steel mill for twenty-five years I've lost my job and I'm too old to get other work. If you can't do something for me, I'm going to kill myself." Governor Gifford Pinchot of Pennsylvania got a letter from a jobless man who said: "I cannot stand it any longer." Gan Kolski, an unemployed Polish artist from Greenwich Village, leaped to his death from the George Washington Bridge, leaving this note: "To All: If you cannot hear the cry of starving millions, listen to the dead, brothers. Your economic system is dead."

An architect, Hugh Ferriss, stood on the parapet of a tall building in Manhattan and thought to himself that the nearby skyscrapers seemed like monuments to the rugged individualism of the past. Thomas Wolfe wrote: "I believe that we are lost here in America, but I believe we shall be found." Democratic Senator Thomas Gore of Oklahoma called the Depression an economic disease. Henry Ford, on the other hand, said the Depression was "a wholesome thing in general."

*   *   *

Obviously, the essence of a depression is widespread unemployment. In one of the most fatuous remarks on record, Calvin Coolidge said: "The final solution of unemployment is work." He might have added that water is wet. Senator Robert Wagner of New York called unemployment inexcusable.

A decade before the Crash the British statesman David Lloyd George had said: "Unemployment, with its injustice for the man who seeks and thirsts for employment, who begs for labour, and cannot get it, and who is punished for failure he is not responsible for by the starvation of his children—that torture is something that private enterprise ought to remedy for its own sake." Winston Churchill now used the same key word, "torture," in a similar comment: "This problem of unemployment is the most torturing that can be presented to a civilized society."

Before Roosevelt became President and named Frances Perkins his secretary of labor, she was so pessimistic that she said publicly it might take a quarter century to solve the unemployment problem. A Pennsylvania commission studied 31,159 workless men and then reported that the typical unemployed man was thirty-six years old, native-born, physically fit and with a good previous work record. This finding contradicted Henry Ford's belief that the unemployed did not want to work.

However, the Pennsylvania study was *not* typical of the unemployed across the entire nation. Negroes and aliens were the last hired and the first fired. Young men and women were graduated from high schools and colleges into a world without jobs. Mississippi's demagogic governor and sometime senator, Theodore G. Bilbo, vowed the unemployment problem could be solved by shipping 12,000,000 American blacks to Africa. The United Spanish War Veterans, for their part, urged the deportation of 10,000,000 aliens—or nearly 6,000,000 more than the actual number of aliens in the United States. Some noncitizens, unable to find work here, voluntarily returned to their homelands. With the deepening of the Depression, immigration dropped until something strange happened in the Year 1932: More than three times as many persons left this country as entered it. No longer was America the Promised Land.

*   *   *

The Depression changed people's values and thus changed society.

The Chamber of Commerce syndrome of the Twenties became a mockery in the Thirties. Business leaders lost their prestige, for now it had become apparent to all Americans that these big shots did not know what they were talking about when they said again and again and again that everything would be all right if it were just left to them. Worship of big business was succeeded by greater concern for human values. The optimism of the speculative decade was replaced by the pessimism of the hungry decade, by anguished interest in the problem of having enough food on the table.

People eager to make a big killing in the stock market had paid scant attention to politics, but now they wondered about their elected representatives and the kind of political system that could permit such a catastrophe to happen. Indifference gave way to political and social consciousness. Dorothy Parker, the sophisticate and wit, cried: "There is no longer I. There is WE. The day of the individual is dead." Quentin N. Burdick, who became a Senator from North Dakota, said long after the Depression: "I guess I acquired a social conscience during those bad days, and ever since I've had the desire to work toward bettering the living conditions of the people." Sylvia Porter, who developed into a financial columnist, said that while at Hunter College she switched from English to economics because of "an overwhelming curiosity to know why everything was crashing around me and why people were losing their jobs."

People lost their houses and apartments.

Franklin D. Roosevelt said: "One of the major disasters of the continued depression was the loss of hundreds of thousands of homes each year from foreclosure. The annual average loss of urban homes by foreclosure in the United States in normal times was 78,000. By 1932 this had increased to 273,000. By the middle of 1933, foreclosures had advanced to more than 1,000 a day."

In New York City, which had more apartments than private houses, there were almost 200,000 evictions in the year 1931. During the first three weeks of the following year there were more than 60,000 other evictions. One judge handled, or tried to handle, 425 eviction cases in a single day! On February 2, 1932, the New York *Times* described the eviction of three families in the Bronx:

> Probably because of the cold, the crowd numbered only about 1,000, although in unruliness it equalled the throng of 4,000 that stormed the police in the first disorder of a similar nature on January 22. On Thursday a dozen more families are to be evicted unless they pay back rents.
>
> Inspector Joseph Leonary deployed a force of fifty detectives and mounted and foot patrolmen through the street as Marshal Louis Novick led ten furniture movers into the building. Their appearance was the signal for a great clamor. Women shrieked from the windows, the different sections of the crowd hissed and booed and shouted invectives. Fighting began simultaneously in the house and in the street. The marshal's men were rushed on the stairs and only got to work after the policemen had driven the tenants back into their apartments.

In that part of New York City known as Sunnyside, Queens, many homeowners were unable to meet mortgage payments and were soon ordered to vacate. Eviction notices were met with collective action, the residents barricading their doors with sandbags and barbed wire, flinging pepper and flour at sheriffs who tried to force their way inside. However, it was a losing battle; more than 60 percent of Sunnyside's householders lost their homes through foreclosure.

Harlem Negroes invented a new way to get enough money to pay their rent. This, as it came to be called, was the house-rent party. A family would announce that on Saturday night or Thursday night they would welcome anyone and everyone to their home for an evening of fun. Sometimes they would print and distribute cards such as this: "There'll be plenty of pig feet/And lots of gin;/Jus' ring the bell/An' come on in." Saturday night, of course, is the usual time for partying, while Thursday was chosen because this was the only free night for sleep-in black domestics who worked for white people. Admission to a house-rent party cost 15 cents, but more money could be spent inside. A festive mood was es-

tablished by placing a red bulb in a light socket, by serving food con-
sisting of chitterlings and pigs' feet and by setting out a jug of corn liquor.
These parties often went on until daybreak, and the next day the landlord got his rent. The innovation spread to black ghettos in other big
cities across the land, and some white people began imitating the Negroes.

In Chicago a crowd of Negroes gathered in front of the door of a
tenement house to prevent the landlord's agent from evicting a neighborhood family, and they continued to stand there hour after hour, singing
hymns. A Chicago municipal employee named James D. O'Reilly saw his
home auctioned off because he had failed to pay $34 in city taxes at the
very time the city owed him $850 in unpaid salary.

A social worker described one pathetic event: "Mrs. Green left her
five small children alone one morning while she went to have her grocery
order filled. While she was away the constable arrived and padlocked her
house with the children inside. When she came back she heard the six-
weeks-old baby crying. She did not dare to touch the padlock for fear
of being arrested, but she found a window open and climbed in and
nursed the baby and then climbed out and appealed to the police to let
her children out."

In widespread areas of Philadelphia no rent was paid at all. In this
City of Brotherly Love evictions were exceedingly common—as many as
1,300 a month. Children, who saw their parents' distress, made a game of
evictions. In a day-care center they piled all the doll furniture in first one
corner and then another. One tot explained to a teacher: "We ain't got
no money for the rent, so we's moved into a new house. Then we got the
constable on us, so we's movin' again."

In millions of apartments, tension mounted and tempers flared toward
the end of each month, when the rent was due. Robert Bendiner, in his
book *Just Around the Corner*, wrote about conditions in New York City:

> Evictions and frequent moves to take advantage of the apart-
> ment market were as common in middle-income Washington
> Heights as in the poor areas of town, and apartment hopping be-
> came rather a way of life. My own family moved six times in
> seven years. . . . Crises occurred monthly, and several times we
> were saved from eviction by pawning leftover valuables or by my
> mother's rich talent for cajoling landlords. On one more than rou-
> tinely desperate occasion she resorted to the extreme device of
> having one of us enlarge a hole in the bathroom ceiling and then
> irately demanding repairs before another dollar of rent should be
> forthcoming.

In moving from one place to another, some families left their furniture behind because it had been bought on the installment plan and they
were unable to meet further payments. Time-payment furniture firms
owned warehouses that became crammed with tables and chairs and other
items reclaimed from families without money. Whenever a marshal, sheriff or constable evicted a family from a house or apartment, the landlord
would simply dump the furniture on the sidewalk. If the installment com-

pany failed to pick it up, each article would soon be carried away by needy neighbors.

What happened to people after they were dispossessed? Many doubled up with relatives—or even tripled up, until ten or twelve people were crammed into three or four rooms. Human beings are like porcupines: they like to huddle close enough to feel one another's warmth, but they dislike getting so close that the quills begin pricking. Now, in teeming proximity to one another, the quills pricked, and relatives quarreled bitterly.

*   *   *

The Depression strained the family structure and sometimes shattered it. Well-integrated families closed ranks in the face of this common danger and became ever more monolithic. Loosely knit families, on the other hand, fell apart when the pressures on them became too great.

After a man lost his job, he would trudge from factory to factory, office to office, seeking other employment, but after weeks of repeated rejections he would lose heart, mutely denounce himself as a poor provider, shed his self-respect and stay at home. Here he found himself unwelcome and underfoot, the target of puzzled glances from his children and hostile looks from his wife. In the early part of the Depression some women simply could not understand that jobs were unavailable; instead, they felt there was something wrong with their men. In Philadelphia one unemployed man begged a social worker: "Have you anybody you can send around to tell my wife you have no job to give me? She thinks I don't want to work."

The idle man found himself a displaced person in the household, which is woman's domain, and in nameless guilt he crept about uneasily, always finding himself in the way. He got on his wife's nerves and she on his, until tension broke in endless wrangles. If the man tried to help by washing dishes and making beds, he lost status in the eyes of the rest of the family.

The Depression castrated some men by dethroning them from their position as the breadwinner and the head of the family. Ashamed, confused and resentful, they became sexually impotent. In Western culture a man tends to think of himself in terms of the work he does, this self-identity being what Jung calls his persona. Man does. Woman is. To rob a man of his work was to rob him of his idea of himself, leaving him empty and without much reason for living. The displacement of the man as the head of the family and the way some women moved in to fill this vacuum were described sensitively by John Steinbeck in his novel *The Grapes of Wrath*. This great book tells the story of the flight of the Joad family from the dust bowl of Oklahoma to the green valleys of California:

> "We got nothin', now," Pa said. "Comin' a long time—no work, no crops. What we gonna do then? How we gonna git stuff to eat? . . . Git so I hate to think. Go diggin' back to a ol' time to keep from thinkin'. Seems like our life's over an' done."

"No, it ain't," Ma smiled. "It ain't, Pa. An' that's one more thing a woman knows. I noticed that. Man, he lives in jerks—baby born an' a man dies, an' that's a jerk—gets a farm an' loses his farm, an' that's a jerk. Woman, it's all one flow, like a stream, little eddies, little waterfalls, but the river, it goes right on. Woman looks at it like that. We ain't gonna die out. People is goin' on—changin' a little maybe, but goin' right on."

Some adolescent girls felt their fathers' agony and tried to comfort them with lavish expressions of love, much to the embarrassment of the man and the uneasiness of his wife. This did emotional damage to father, mother and the young girl, whose fixation on her father retarded her normal interest in boys her own age.

Strife between parents, together with the realization that it cost money to marry and have babies, resulted in a decision by many young people to postpone their weddings. One young man joined the Communist Party and swore he never would marry or have children under "the present system." Unable to repress their human needs, however, young men and women made love secretly and guiltily, regarding pregnancy as a disaster. Despite an increase in the sale of contraceptives, the abortion rate rose, and so did venereal disease. The birthrate dropped.

It has been estimated that the Depression postponed 800,000 marriages that would have occurred sooner if it had not been for hard times. Margaret Mead, the noted anthropologist, argued that there was nothing wrong about letting girls support their lovers so they could marry sooner. Surprisingly, there even was a decline in marriage among members of the *Social Register*. Liberals and feminists pointed out that half of all births were in families on relief or with incomes of less than $1,000 a year; they strongly advocated birth control. Who could afford babies when a sixty-one-piece layette cost all of $7.70? Gasps of horror arose when it was reported in Illinois that a sixteenth child had been born to a family on relief.

Housewives suffered as acutely as their husbands. Many had to send their kids to live with relatives or friends. Others took part-time jobs, while a few wives actually became temporary whores to earn enough money to keep the family going. Lacking money for streetcars and buses, without the means to buy clothes to keep them looking attractive, they remained cooped up in their homes until their nerves screamed and they had nervous breakdowns.

All too often their men simply deserted them. A California woman said: "My husband went north about three months ago to try his luck. The first month he wrote pretty regularly. . . . For five weeks we have had no word from him. . . . Don't know where he is or what he is up to."

A young man who lived in the French Quarter of New Orleans was solicited by five prostitutes during a ten-block stroll, each woman asking only 50 cents. In Houston a relief worker, curious about how the people were getting along, was approached by one girl after another. For the benefit of an insistent streetwalker, the man turned his pockets inside out to prove that he had no money. Looking at him ruefully, she said: "It doesn't cost much—only a dime!"

The close relationship between poverty and morals shocked Franklin D. Roosevelt, who told reporters about an investigator who went to southeastern Kentucky: "She got into one of those mining towns," Roosevelt said, "and started to walk up the alley. There was a group of miners sitting in front of the shacks, and they pulled down their caps over their faces. As soon as she caught sight of that she walked up and said, 'What are you pulling your caps down for?' They said, 'Oh, it is all right.' 'Why pull your caps down?' They said, 'It is sort of a custom because so many of the women have not got enough clothes to cover them.'"

*   *   *

The Depression made changes in the country's physical appearance.

Fewer pedestrians were to be seen on the streets since many men did not go to work and women shopped less frequently; for lack of warm clothing and fuel, many people stayed in bed most of the day during winter. The air became cleaner over industrial cities, for there was less smoke from factory chimneys. The downtown business districts of most cities had long rows of empty shops and offices. Trains were shorter, and only rarely did one see a Pullman car. However, gas stations multiplied because millions of Americans drove their battered family cars here and there in endless quest of work. In conflicting attempts to solve their problems, farmers moved into town while city folks moved into the country to build their own houses and grow their own food. More and more blacks were seen in northern cities as desperate Negroes fled from the hopeless South. Telephones were taken out of homes, and mail deliveries were lighter. Houses and stores, parks and fences sagged and lapsed into unpainted, flaked ugliness for want of money to make repairs.

In his novel called *You Can't Go Home Again*, Thomas Wolfe described a comfort station in front of New York City Hall:

> . . . One descended to this place down a steep flight of stairs from the street, and on bitter nights he would find the place crowded with homeless men who had sought refuge there. Some were those shambling hulks that one sees everywhere, in Paris as well as in New York. . . . But most of them were just flotsam of the general ruin of the time—honest, decent, middle-aged men with faces seamed by toil and want, and young men, many of them mere boys in their teens, with thick, unkempt hair. These were the wanderers from town to town, the riders of freight trains, the thumbers of rides on highways, the uprooted, unwanted male population of America. They drifted across the land and gathered in the big cities when winter came, hungry, defeated, empty, hopeless, restless, driven by they knew not what, always on the move, looking everywhere for work, for the bare crumbs to support their miserable lives, and finding neither work nor crumbs. Here in New

York, to this obscene meeting place, these derelicts came, drawn into a common stew of rest and warmth and a little surcease from their desperation.

Heywood Broun devoted a column to a description of a slum in San Antonio, Texas:

. . . The Church of Guadalupe stands upon the fringe of what had been described to me as the most fearsome slum in all America. It covers four square miles. At first I thought that the extreme description might have been dictated by local pride. It was my notion to protest and say, "Why, we in New York City know worse than that." But after we had gone up the third back alley I had to confess defeat gracefully.

You can see shacks as bad as these in several States, but I do not know of any place where they have been so ingeniously huddled together. This is flat, sprawling country, and there is much of it, and so it seems devilish that one crazy combination of old lumber and stray tin should be set as a flap upon the side of another equally discreditable. I did not quite comprehend the character of the alley until I discovered that what I took to be a toolhouse was a residence for a family of eleven people.

And these are not squatter dwellings. People pay rent for them, just as if a few rickety boards and a leaky roof constituted a house. They even have evictions and go through the solemn and obscene farce of removing a bed and a frying pan as indication that the landlord's two-dollars-and-a-half rent has not been forthcoming. . . .

Back at the Church of Guadalupe, the priest said, "I have other letters from those who fight federal housing because they like their rents." He tossed over an anonymous message, which read, "I could start a story that there is a priest who writes love letters to young girls and gives jewels to women of his congregation."

"Doesn't this worry you?" one of us asked.

"No," said the priest. "Last month we buried thirty-nine persons, mostly children, from this little church alone.

"I am worried," he said, "about people starving to death."

Louis Adamic and his wife were living with her mother in New York City in January, 1932. Born in Yugoslavia, now a naturalized American, he was a writer, a tall young man with a look of eager curiosity in his eyes. One cold morning at seven forty-five the doorbell rang, and Adamic, thinking it was the postman, opened the front door. In his book called *My America*, he told what happened next.

There stood a girl of ten and a boy of eight. They had schoolbooks in their arms, and their clothing was patched and clean, but hardly warm enough for winter weather. In a voice strangely old for her age, the girl said: "Excuse me, mister, but we have no eats in our house and my mother she said I should take my brother before we go to school and ring a doorbell in some house"—she swallowed heavily and took a deep breath—"and ask you to give us . . . something . . . to eat."

"Come in," Adamic said. A strange sensation swept over him. He had heard that kids were ringing doorbells and asking for food in the Bronx, in Harlem and in Brooklyn, but he had not really believed it.

His wife and her mother gave the children some food. The girl ate slowly. Her brother bolted his portion, quickly and greedily.

"He ate a banana yesterday afternoon," said his sister, "but it wasn't ripe enough or somethin', and it made him sick and he didn't eat anything since. He's always like this when he's hungry and we gotta ring door-bells."

"Do you often ring doorbells?"

"When we have no eats at home."

"What made you ring our bell?"

"I don't know," the girl answered. "I just did."

Her name was Mary, and her brother's name was Jimmie. They lived in a poor neighborhood five blocks away.

Mary said: "We used to live on the fourth floor upstairs and we had three rooms and a kitchen and bath, but now we have only one room downstairs. In back."

"Why did you move downstairs?"

The boy winced.

"My father," said the girl. "He lost his job when the panic came. That was two years ago. I was eight and Jimmie was six. My father he tried to get work, but he couldn't, the depression was so bad. But he called it the panic."

Adamic and the two women were astonished at her vocabulary: "panic" . . . "depression."

"What kind of work did your father do?"

"Painter and paperhanger. Before things got so bad, he always had jobs when his work was in season, and he was good to us—my mother says so, too. Then, after he couldn't get any more jobs, he got mean and he yelled at my mother. He couldn't sleep nights and he walked up and down and talked, and sometimes he hollered and we couldn't sleep, either."

"Was he a union man?"

"No, he didn't belong to no union."

"What did your father holler about?"

"He called my mother bad names."

At this point in the conversation, Adamic wrote, the little girl hesitated, and her brother winced again. Then she continued: "Uh . . . he was angry because my mother, before she married him, she was in love with another man and almost married him. But my mother says it wasn't my father's fault he acted mean like he did. He was mean because he had no job and we had no money."

"Where's your father now?"

"We don't know. He went away four months ago, right after Labor Day, and he never came back, so we had to move downstairs. The landlord didn't want to throw us out, so he told my mother to move in down-stairs."

Between sips of milk the girl said her mother did household work whenever she could find a job, but earned very little money this way. A charity organization had been giving her $2.85 a week, but lately it had stopped. Mary did not know why. Her mother had applied for home relief, but had not yet received anything from that source.

The boy stopped eating, turned to his sister and muttered: "You talk too much! I told you not to talk!"

The girl fell silent.

Adamic said: "It's really our fault, Jimmie. We're asking too many questions."

The little boy glared and said: "Yeah!"

*   *   *

In Detroit someone gave another little girl a nickel, which seemed like such a fortune to her that she agonized three full days about how best to spend it.

In Erie, Pennsylvania, a seven-year-old boy named Tom received a tiny yellow chick as an Easter present. Using some old chicken wire, he built a coop for his pet beneath the back step to the house and fed and tended it carefully. His father was an unemployed molder, and the family often ate nothing but beans. Time passed. Now the little chick had grown into a full-sized chicken. One day Tom's father announced that the boy's pet would have to be killed and served for Sunday dinner, since every-one was hungry. Tom screamed in horrified protest but was unable to prevent his father from taking his chicken into the backyard and chop-ping off its head. Later that day the family sat around the table feasting on fowl, while the boy hunched in his chair, sobbing.

There was another boy who never forgot a scene from his childhood days during the Depression. He lived in a small town in Iowa. Every so often a train would stop there for a few minutes, and a man would get out carrying bags of buttons. He would distribute these buttons to wait-ing farmers and their wives, collect the cards to which they had sewn other buttons, pay them a meager sum for their labor, get back into the train and depart. This trivial piecework provided them with the only income they could get.

*   *   *

President Hoover was foolish enough to let himself be photographed on the White House lawn feeding his dog. This picture did not sit well with Americans who were hungry, suffering from malnutrition or even starving to death. Several times Hoover denied that there was widespread undernourishment in the nation, but he depended on unreliable statistics. Comedian Groucho Marx, who was closer to the people, said he knew things were bad when "the pigeons started feeding the people in Central Park." However, it was no laughing matter.

In Oklahoma City a newspaper reporter was assigned to cover state relief headquarters. Walking into the building one morning, he ran into a young man he had met through his landlady. This fellow offered the reporter some candy. The reporter did not want the candy but accepted it lest he hurt the other's feelings. As they stood and chewed, a social worker approached them.

"We don't allow any eating in here," she said.

The reporter, who thought she was jesting, made a wisecrack.

"We don't allow any eating in here," she repeated sternly. "Some of these applicants haven't had any breakfast. We make it a rule among ourselves never to eat or to drink Cokes in front of them."

Ashamed of himself, the reporter mumbled an apology and slunk behind a beaver-board wall. He wanted to throw away the morsel of candy remaining in his hand but felt that this would be even more sinful with hungry people so near.

Arthur Brisbane, the rich columnist and editor, walked into a Manhattan restaurant and ordered two lamb chops. When he had finished the first one, he looked longingly at the second but was too full to eat it, too. After much thought he summoned a waiter.

"What happens if I don't eat this chop?" Brisbane asked. "Will you take it back?"

"No, sir. We can't do that, sir."

"But what will you do with it? Will it be thrown away?"

"Not at all, sir. We give the leftovers to poor people."

Brisbane sighed in relief, nodded approvingly, paid his check and left.

In 1933 the Children's Bureau reported that one out of every five children in the nation was not getting enough of the right things to eat. A teacher in a coal-mining town asked a little girl in her classroom whether she was ill. The child said: "No. I'm all right. I'm just hungry." The teacher urged her to go home and eat something. The girl said: "I can't. This is my sister's day to eat." In the House of Representatives, during a debate about appropriations for Indians living on reservations, a Congressman said that eleven cents a day was enough to feed an Indian child. A Senate subcommittee learned that the president of a textile firm had told his workers they should be able to live on six cents a day.

AFL President William Green said: "I warn the people who are exploiting the workers that they can only drive them so far before they will turn on them and destroy them. They are taking no account of the history of nations in which governments have been overturned. Revolutions grow out of the depths of hunger."

Sidney Hillman, president of the Amalgamated Clothing Workers of America, appeared at a Senate hearing in 1932 and was told that it was not yet time to give federal relief. Angrily, he cried: "I would ask by what standards are we to gauge that time! Must we have hundreds of thousands of people actually dead and dying from starvation? Must we have bread riots? What is necessary to convince them that there is a need for federal and speedy relief?"

The Communists took up the slogan: "Starve or fight!"

At the University of Pennsylvania a prim audience was shocked to hear Daniel Willard, president of the B & O Railroad, say: "While I do not like to say so, I would be less than candid if I did not say that in such circumstances I would steal before I would starve."

Obviously, less fortunate Americans agreed. Petty thievery soared. Children hung around grocery stores begging for food. Customers emerging from groceries had bundles snatched from their arms by hungry kids, who ran home with the food or ducked into alleys to gobble it as fast as they could. Small retail stores had their windows smashed and their display goods stolen. Grown men, in groups of two and three, walked into chain store markets, ordered all the food they could carry and then quietly walked out without paying for it. Chain store managers did not always report these incidents to the police for fear that publicity would encourage this sort of intimidation. For the same reason the newspapers engaged in a tacit conspiracy of silence.

However, newspapers did not mind reporting that in Manhattan a debutante supper for 600 guests at the Ritz-Carlton cost $4,750. On nearby Park Avenue, beggars were so numerous that a well-dressed man might be asked for money four or five times in a ten-block stroll. President Hoover not only denied that anyone was starving, but said: "The hoboes, for example, are better fed than they ever have been. One hobo in New York got ten meals in one day."

People of means thought up ways to protect themselves from panhandlers and from begging letters. Boston's mayor, James M. Curley, had a male secretary named Stan Wilcox, who was adept at brushing off approaches. Whenever a beggar asked if he had a quarter, Wilcox would reply: "Heavens, no! I wouldn't dream of taking a drink at this hour!" Alfred E. Smith received the following letter from Milwaukee: "This is unusual, but I am in need. Would you send me $2,500, as this is the amount I am in need of. I will give you as collateral my word of honor that I will repay you if possible. If not, let the good Lord repay you and he will also pay better interest."

Governor Gifford Pinchot of Pennsylvania flatly declared that starvation was widespread. Among the many pathetic letters he received was this one: "There are nine of us in the family. My father is out of work for a couple of months and we haven't got a thing eat [*sic*] in the house. Mother is getting $12 a month of the county. If mother don't get more help we will have to starve to death. I am a little girl 10 years old. I go to school every day. My other sister hain't got any shoes or clothes to wear to go to school. My mother goes in her bare feet and she crys every night that we don't have the help. I guess that is all, hoping to hear from you."

Bernard Baruch, who felt burdened by the thought of his wealth, got a desperate letter from his cousin, Fay Allen Des Portes, who lived in his home state of South Carolina. "The horrible part of the whole situation," she wrote to him, "is these poor starving people here in our midst. The banks can't let anyone have money, the merchants are all broke; the farmers can't let the poor Negroes on the farm have anything to eat. I don't know what is going to happen. I have about four hundred Negroes that are as absolutely dependent upon me as my two little boys, but I can't help them any more and God knows what is going to happen to them."

John L. Lewis, president of the United Mine Workers, once said to a group of mine operators: "Gentlemen, I speak to you for my people. I speak to you for the miners' families in the broad Ohio valley, the Pennsylvania mountains and the black West Virginia hills. There, the shanties lean over as if intoxicated by the smoke fumes of the mine dumps. But the more pretentious ones boast a porch, with the banisters broken here and there, presenting the aspect of a snaggle-toothed child. Some of the windows are wide open to flies, which can feast nearby on garbage and answer the family dinner call in double-quick time. But there is no dinner call. The little children are gathered around a bare table without anything to eat. Their mothers are saying, 'We want bread.' "

A writer named Jonathan Norton Leonard described the plight of Pennsylvania miners who had been put out of company villages after losing a strike: "Reporters from the more liberal metropolitan papers found thousands of them huddled on the mountainsides, crowded three or four families together in one-room shacks, living on dandelion and wild weed-roots. Half of them were sick, but no local doctor would care for the evicted strikers. All of them were hungry and many were dying of those providential diseases which enable welfare workers to claim that no one has starved."

In 1931 four New York City hospitals reported 95 deaths from starvation. Two years later the New York City Welfare Council said that 29 persons had died from starvation, more than 50 others had been treated for starvation, while an additional 110 individuals—most of them children—had perished of malnutrition. In one routine report the council gave this picture of the plight of one family in the Brownsville section of Brooklyn: "Family reported starving by neighbors. Investigator found five small children at home while mother was out looking for vegetables under pushcarts. Family had moved into one room. Father sleeping at Municipal Lodging House because he could get more to eat there than at home and frequently brought food home from there in pockets for children and wife. Only other food they had for weeks came from pushcarts."

A family of fourteen was on relief in Kewanee, Illinois, the hog-raising center of the Midwest. The family was given $3 worth of groceries a week, and of course this food soon ran out. After giving the last crumbs to the children, the adults would exist on nothing but hot water until they received their next grocery allotment.

In Chicago a committee investigated city garbage dumps and then reported: "Around the truck which was unloading garbage and other refuse were about 35 men, women and children. As soon as the truck pulled away from the pile all of them started digging with sticks, some with their hands, grabbing bits of food and vegetables."

Edmund Wilson described another Chicago scene: "A private incinerator at Thirty-fifth and La Salle Streets which disposes of garbage from restaurants and hotels, has been regularly visited by people, in groups of as many as twenty at a time, who pounce upon anything that looks edible before it is thrown into the furnace. The women complained to investigators that the men took unfair advantage by jumping on the truck before it was unloaded; but a code was eventually established which provided that different sets of people should come at different times every day, so that everybody would be given a chance."

A ballad called "Starvation Blues" was sung by some of the poor people of America during the Depression.

Prentice Murphy, director of the Children's Bureau of Philadelphia, told a Senate committee: "If the modern state is to rest upon a firm foundation, its citizens must not be allowed to starve. Some of them do. They do not die quickly. You can starve for a long time without dying."

Scientists agree that a person can starve a long time without dying, but this is what it is like to starve to death: After a few days without food the stomach cramps and bloats up. Later it shrinks in size. At first a starving child will cry and eat anything to ease hunger pains—stuffing his mouth with rags, clay, chalk, straw, twigs, berries and even poisonous weeds. Then, as the child weakens, his cries change to whimpers. He feels nauseated. All the fat is being burned from his body. This burning produces acidosis. The fruity odor of acetone can be smelled on the breath, and it also appears in the urine. When starvation reaches this point, nature becomes kinder. The child grows listless and sleepy. The bulging eyes are sad and dull. Now body proteins have been depleted, while the water and electrolyte balance has been destroyed. Degeneration of the vital organs, such as the liver and kidneys, proceeds in earnest. By this time the child lacks all resistance to diseases and may be killed by some infection.

*   *   *

John Steinbeck has told how he survived the early part of the Depression before he became a famous author. "I had two assets," he wrote. "My father owned a tiny three-room cottage in Pacific Grove in California, and he let me live in it without rent. That was the first safety. Pacific Grove is on the ocean. That was the second. People in inland cities or in the closed and shuttered industrial cemeteries had greater problems than I. Given the sea, a man must be very stupid to starve. That great reservoir is always available. I took a large part of my protein food from the ocean.

"Firewood to keep warm floated on the beach daily, needing only handsaw and ax. A small garden of black soil came with the cottage. In northern California you can raise vegetables of some kind all year long. I never peeled a potato without planting the skins. Kale, lettuce, chard, turnips, carrots and onions rotated in the little garden. In the tide pools of the bay, mussels were available and crabs and abalones and that shiny kelp called sea lettuce. With a line and pole, blue cod, rock cod, perch, sea trout, sculpin could be caught."

The sale of flower seeds shot up as Americans, tired of the ugliness of their lives, turned to the beauty of homegrown flowers. As might have been expected, there was widespread cultivation of vegetable gardens. Many did this on their own, while others received official encouragement. Big railroads rented garden plots for their workers. The United States Steel Corporation used social workers and faculty members of Indiana University to develop an extensive garden project for its workers in Gary, Indiana. In New York State, in the summer of 1933, jobless men and women were tending 65,000 gardens. The city of Detroit provided tools and seed for "thrift gardens" on empty lots, an idea which Mayor Frank Murphy said he had borrowed from Hazen S. Pingree. During the Panic of 1893 Pingree had been the mayor of Detroit, and confronted with a city of jobless men, he provided them with gardens to cultivate—"Pingree's Potato Patches"—receiving national attention.

Now, in the present emergency, Henry Ford ordered all his workmen to dig in vegetable gardens or be fired. Out of his imperious command there developed what the Scripps-Howard Washington *News* called 50,000 "shotgun gardens." Rough-grained Harry Bennett, chief of Ford's private police, supervised this vast project and kept a filing system on all Ford employees. If a man had no garden in his own backyard or on some neighborhood lot, he was assigned a patch of earth somewhere on Ford's 4,000 acres of farmland around Dearborn, Michigan. Each workman had to pay fifty cents to have his strip plowed.

More than one-third of the men employed in Ford's Dearborn plant lived 10 to 20 miles away, and some protested that since they did not own a car they would have to spend an extra two hours daily just traveling to and from their allotted patches. A Bennett henchman would snarl: "Why don't-cha buy a car? You're makin' 'em, ain't-cha?" Bone-weary workmen who simply couldn't muster the energy to toil on their garden plots soon were brought into line by Bennett's personal deputy, Norman Selby, the former boxer "Kid McCoy."

*   *   *

In the spring of 1932 the Community Council of Philadelphia ran out of private funds for the relief of needy families. Eleven days elapsed before this relief work could be resumed with public funds, and many families received no help during this interim. A study was made to find out what had happened when food orders stopped.

One woman borrowed 50 cents from a friend and bought stale bread at 3½ cents per loaf. Except for one or two meals, this was all she could serve her family throughout those eleven days.

A pregnant mother and her three children could afford only two meals a day. At eleven o'clock in the morning she would serve breakfast, which consisted of cocoa, bread and butter. This left everyone so hungry that the mother began advancing the time of their evening meal, which was just one can of soup.

Another woman scoured the docks, picking up vegetables that fell from produce wagons. Fish vendors sometimes gave her a fish at the end of the day. On two separate occasions her family went without food for a day and a half.

On the day the food orders stopped, one family ate nothing all day. At nine o'clock that night the mother went to a friend's house and begged for a loaf of bread. Later she got two days' work at 75 cents a day. With this pittance she bought a little meat. Then, adding vegetables picked up off the street, she made a stew which she cooked over and over again each day to prevent spoilage.

One family ate nothing but potatoes, rice, bread and coffee, and for one and a half days they were totally without food.

*   *   *

Hunting jackrabbits to feed the family became a way of life among farmers and ranchers. This gave birth to a Depression joke reported by John Steinbeck in *The Grapes of Wrath.* One man said to another: "Depression is over. I seen a jackrabbit, an' they wasn't nobody after him." The second man said: "That ain't the reason. Can't afford to kill jackrabbits no more. Catch'em and milk'em and turn'em loose. One you seen prob'ly gone dry."

Audie Murphy was born on a Texas farm five years before the Crash, the son of very poor parents. Almost as soon as he could walk, he began hunting game for the family. Since shells were expensive, every shot had to count. Aware of this, Audie Murphy developed into an expert marksman—so expert that when he was a GI during World War II, he killed 240 Nazis and emerged as the most decorated American soldier of the war.

Wheat growers, bankrupted by drought, talked about heading for Alaska to kill moose to fill their growling bellies. In the timberlands of the great Northwest some desperate men set forest fires so that they would be hired to extinguish them, while in big cities other men prayed for heavy snowfalls to provide them with shoveling jobs. When some Pittsburgh steel mills reopened briefly, the steelworkers called back to their jobs were too weak from hunger to be able to work.

At the age of eleven Cesar Chavez, who later won renown as a Mexican-American labor leader, fished and cut mustard greens to help keep his family from starving.

Charles H. Percy, who wound up a multimillionaire and a United States Senator, never forgot what it was like to be a poor boy in Chicago during the Depression: "I remember a great feeling of shame when the welfare truck pulled up to our house. And you talk about cheating! Once they delivered us 100 pounds of sugar by mistake. My father wanted to return it, but my mother said, 'God willed us to have it,' and she wouldn't give it up." She swapped some of the sugar for flour and helped tide the family over by baking cookies that little Chuck Percy peddled door to door.

Americans under the stress of the Depression behaved with a dignity that varied in terms of their religious backgrounds, their mental images of themselves and their rigidity or flexibility. Brittle people snapped, while the pliant bent and survived.

In Georgia a blind Negro refused all relief, harnessed himself to a plow like a mule and tilled the fields, day after day. In Pittsburgh a father with starving children stole a loaf of bread from a neighbor, was caught, hanged himself in shame. In Youngstown, Ohio, a father, mother and their four sons preferred to starve rather than accept charity. Before they died, their condition was discovered by a neighbor who happened to be a newspaper reporter. They were existing on fried flour and water.

Charles Wayne also lived in Youngstown. He had been a hot mill worker for the Republic Iron and Steel Company until he was laid off. For the next two years he was unable to get any kind of work. Now a fifty-seven-year-old man, workless, hopeless, unable to feed his wife and ten children, he climbed onto a bridge one morning. He took off his coat, folded it neatly, then jumped into the swirling Mahoning River below. Instinct caused him to swim a few strokes, but then he gave up and let himself drown. Later his wife sobbed to reporters: "We were about to lose our home and the gas and electric companies had threatened to shut off the service."

An elderly man receiving $15-a-week relief money for his large family went out each day, without being asked, to sweep the streets of his village. "I want to do something," he said, "in return for what I get." A graduate of the Harvard Law School, now old and almost deaf, gladly took a $15-a-week job as assistant caretaker at a small park.

Rather than accept charity, a New York dentist and his wife killed themselves with gas. He left this note: "The entire blame for this tragedy rests with the City of New York or whoever it is that allows free dental work in the hospital. We want to get out of the way before we are forced to accept relief money. The City of New York is not to touch our bodies. We have a horror of charity burial. We have put the last of our money in the hands of a friend who will turn it over to my brother."

John Steinbeck wrote: "Only illness frightened us. You have to have money to be sick—or did then. And dentistry also was out of the question, with the result that my teeth went badly to pieces. Without dough you couldn't have a tooth filled."

Shoes were a problem. Upon reaching home, poor people took off their shoes to save wear and tear. Middle-class people bought do-it-yourself shoe-repair kits. Those unable to afford the kits would resole their shoes with strips of rubber cut from old tires. Some wore ordinary rubbers over shoes with holes in their bottoms. A miner's son, Jack Conroy, told what a hole in a shoe could mean to a man walking the streets looking for work: "Maybe it starts with a little hole in the sole; and then the slush of the pavements oozes in, gumming sox and balling between your toes. Concrete whets Woolworth sox like a file, and if you turn the heel on top and tear a pasteboard inner sole, it won't help much. There are the tacks, too. You get to avoiding high places and curbstones because that jabs the point right into the heel. Soon the tack has calloused a furrowed hole, and you don't notice it unless you strike something unusually high or solid, or forget and walk flat-footed. You pass a thousand shoe-shops where a tack might be bent down, but you can't pull off a shoe and ask to have *that* done—for nothing."

Keeping clean was also a problem, since soap cost money. Steinbeck washed his linen with soap made from pork fat, wood ashes and salt, but it took a lot of sunning to get the smell out of sheets. As the sale of soap declined across the nation, its production was reduced. Procter & Gamble did not lay off its workers, as it might have done under the circumstances, but put them to work cutting grass, painting fences and repairing factories until soap production began to rise again.

Steinbeck wrote a short story called "Daughter" about a sharecropper who shot and killed his own daughter because he had no food to give her. This could not be shrugged off as mere fiction, for in Carlisle, Pennsylvania, a starving man named Elmo Noakes actually suffocated his three small daughters rather than see them starve.

*   *   *

The Depression scarred many young men and women who later became celebrities or who already were well known. Jack Dempsey, former heavyweight boxing champion of the world, became so strapped for money that at the age of thirty-six he got himself sufficiently back into shape to fight fifty-six exhibition bouts. Babe Ruth, always a big spender, tried to supplement his income by opening a haberdashery on Broadway but lost his own shirt after five months.

Clifford Odets wrote his first play while living on ten cents a day. Lillian Hellman, who later became a renowned playwright, earned $50 a week as a script reader for Metro-Goldwyn-Mayer. William Inge, who also won fame as a playwright, acted in tent shows during the Depression, long afterward recalling: "We actors considered ourselves fortunate if we earned five dollars a week. Sometimes the farmers of Kansas would bring in flour and meat as barter for admission to Saturday matinees."

Songwriter Frank Loesser learned from his parents that they had lost all their money. He took any job he could get, including screwing the tops on bottles of an insecticide. He also worked as a spotter for a chain of restaurants, getting seventy-five cents a day plus the cost of each meal for reporting on the food and service. Later he reminisced: "I used to eat twelve times a day. When you're poor, you're always hungry from walking around so much."

Danny Thomas performed in saloons, but finally even this kind of work came to an end. The chance of getting another job seemed so slim that he considered giving up show business. In desperation, he prayed to St. Jude, the patron saint of the hopeless, and the next day he landed a job in Chicago that proved to be the turning point of his career.

Ralph Bellamy almost starved to death in the basement of a Greenwich Village apartment. Cary Grant was working in Hollywood as an extra. Dana Andrews worked four years as a gas station attendant in Van Nuys, California. Robert Young was employed as a soda jerk, grease monkey and truck driver. Ray Milland, living on credit in Hollywood, was about to go to work in a garage when he landed a part in a movie called *Bolero*. In Chireno, Texas, a twelve-year-old girl named Lucille Ann Collier began dancing professionally to help the family finances; later she grew into a long-legged beauty and won fame under the name of Ann Miller. In the Bronx a four-year-old girl named Anna Maria Italiano sang for WPA men working on a nearby project; today she is known as Anne Bancroft.

Victor Mature set out for Hollywood in 1935 at the age of seventeen, with $40 in cash and a car loaded with candy and chewing gum. He drove for five days and slept in his automobile each night, and by the time he reached the film capital he was almost broke. To his father in Louisville he wired: ARRIVED HERE WITH 11 CENTS. His father, an Austrian scissors grinder who had taken up refrigerator selling, wired back: FORTY-THREE YEARS AGO I ARRIVED IN NEW YORK WITH FIVE CENTS. I COULD NOT EVEN SPEAK ENGLISH. YOU ARE SIX CENTS UP ON ME.

The effect of the Depression on Hollywood extras was told by Grover Jones to an amused courtroom in a trial concerning Metro-Goldwyn-Mayer. Jones, once an extra and then a scriptwriter, gave this entertaining testimony: "They wanted eighty Indians, and I got the job only because I knew how to put on what they called bolamania—burnt umber and raw umber mixed. But they made me a chief. That meant I didn't have to go naked. I could wear a suit, you see. And at that time I was convinced I was fairly smart. So there were now eighty-one Indians. I had never seen a camera during all those months, because I was always in the background, waiting over in back of the hill for the call to come over the hill on the horses to rescue the child. And I had never been on horses. So we sat on these horses, each confiding in the other, and none of them had ever been on horses, except we were all hungry. Finally the man said, 'Now look, when you hear shooting I want you all to come over the hills, and I want some of you to fall off the horses.' Well, in those days they paid three dollars extra for a man who would fall off a horse, because it is quite a stunt. So we waited until finally we got the call to come over the hill, and somebody shot a gun off—and eighty-one Indians fell off their horses."

*   *   *

There was nothing surprising about the fact that men would risk injury or death by falling off a horse to earn an extra $3 a day. People felt that if they could just live through the Depression, they could endure anything else life had to offer. To *endure* was the main thing. Many took pay cuts without a murmur. A young man just out of college with a Bachelor of Journalism degree accepted a job on a newspaper at exactly *nothing* per week; a month later he was grateful to be put on the payroll at $15. Graduate engineers worked as office boys. College graduates of various kinds ran elevators in department stores. Unemployed architects turned out jigsaw puzzles. One jobless draftsman, Alfred Butts, used his spare time to invent the game of Scrabble.

Young men who might have grown into greatness chose, instead, to seek the security of civil service jobs, becoming policemen, firemen, garbage collectors. Fewer sailors deserted from the Navy. Enlistments rose in all branches of the nation's military establishment. When Congress voted a 10 percent pay cut for all federal employees, President Hoover secretly asked the Senate to make an exception for soldiers and sailors, because he did not wish to rely on disgruntled troops in case of internal trouble.

Women and children toiled for almost nothing in the sweatshops of New York City, welfare workers reporting these grim examples:

• A woman crocheted hats for 40 cents a dozen and was able to make only two dozen per week.

• An apron girl, paid 2½ cents per apron, earned 20 cents a day.

• A slipper liner was paid 21 cents for every seventy-two pairs of slippers she lined, and if she turned out one slipper every forty-five seconds she could earn $1.05 in a nine-hour day.

• A girl got half a cent for each pair of pants she threaded and sponged, making $2.78 a week.

Connecticut's state commissioner of labor said that some sweatshops in that state paid girls between 60 cents and $1.10 for a fifty-five-hour week. In Pennsylvania men working in sawmills were paid 5 cents an hour, men in tile and brick manufacturing got 6 cents per hour, while construction workers earned 7½ cents an hour. In Detroit the Briggs Manufacturing Company paid men 10 cents and women 4 cents an hour, causing auto workers to chant: "If poison doesn't work, try Briggs!" Also in Detroit, the Hudson Motor Car Company called back a small-parts assembler and then kept her waiting three days for a half hour of work, forcing her to spend 60 cents in carfare to earn 28 cents.

Two Maine fishermen put out to sea at four o'clock one morning and did not return to port until five o'clock that afternoon. During this long day of toil they caught 200 pounds of hake and 80 pounds of haddock. They burned up eight gallons of gas at 19 cents a gallon and used 100 pounds of bait costing two cents a pound. For their catch they were paid one cent a pound for the hake and four cents a pound for the haddock. Thus they earned less than two cents an hour for their day's work.

Meantime, Henry Ford was declaring: "Many families were not so badly off as they thought; they needed guidance in the management of their resources and opportunities." Ford needed no guidance. He managed to transfer 41½ percent of stock in the Ford Motor Company to his son, Edsel, without paying a cent in inheritance or estate taxes.

*   *   *

Ford, who liked to boast that he always had to work, declared in 1930 that "the very poor are recruited almost solely from the people who refuse to think and therefore refuse to work diligently." Roger W. Babson, the statistician, pontificated two years later: "Better business will come when the unemployed change their attitude toward life." Most rich men were quick to moralize.

The concept of hard work was central to capitalism and the Protestant ethic. Americans had been raised on a diet of aphorisms praising work and self-reliance. Benjamin Franklin said: "God helps them that help themselves." The Bible insisted: "In the sweat of thy face shalt thou eat bread." Thomas Carlyle said: "All work, even cotton-spinning, is noble; work alone is noble." Elizabeth Barrett Browning wrote: "Whoever fears God, fears to sit at ease." It was either Bishop Richard Cumberland or George Whitefield (no one is sure) who first said: "Better to wear out than to rust out." Most Americans agreed, but now in these Depression times men did sit at home and rust, through no fault of their own, losing the fine edge of their skills.

Idle, dispirited, hungry, defeated, withdrawn, brooding—people began to feel that somehow they were to blame for everything, that somehow, somewhere, they had failed. Maybe the Depression was punishment for their sins. After all, Protestant Episcopal Bishop John P. Tyler attributed it to the lack of religion. Perhaps Christians, if they wished to be good Christians, should bow to fate by accepting Christ's words that "to everyone that hath shall be given; and from him that hath not, even that which he hath shall be taken from him." But some found it difficult to find comfort in a sermon preached by the Reverend William S. Blackshear, an Episcopalian clergyman, in the bleak year of 1932. Blackshear said in part: "Christ was happy to be at the banquets of the rich. It was at such a place that the woman broke the vial of costly ointment and anointed His feet. There were those who cried out for the improvident and rebuked the woman, saying that this should have been converted into cash and given to the poor. It was then that Christ spoke on the economic plan, 'The poor ye have always with you.' "

This kind of sermon, representing conservative Protestantism, offended liberal clergymen. Forced by the Depression to rethink their values, they began searching for a new theology. Some began with the premise that if the church were to serve any purpose or perform realistically, it had to divorce itself from economic and political values. This developing viewpoint was expressed with crystal clarity by H. Richard Niebuhr, a pastor and a brother of Reinhold Niebuhr. He wrote:

> The church is in bondage to capitalism. Capitalism in its contemporary form is more than a system of ownership and distribution of economic goods. It is a faith and a way of life. It is faith in wealth as the source of all life's blessings and as the savior of man from his deepest misery. It is the doctrine that man's most important activity is the production of economic goods and that all other things are dependent upon this. On the basis of this initial idolatry it develops a morality in which economic worth becomes the standard by which to measure all other values and the economic virtues take precedence over courage, temperance, wisdom and justice, over charity, humility and fidelity. Hence nature, love, life, truth, beauty and justice are exploited or made the servants of the high economic good. Everything, including the lives of workers, is made a utility, is desecrated and ultimately destroyed. . . .

Other dissenters noted the supremacy of capitalism over every other value in the fact that church property was exempt from taxation. State constitutions and special statutes declared that no real estate taxes could be levied on church-owned properties, such as the church building itself, parochial schools, parsonages, the parish house and cemeteries. Why? A Missouri Supreme Court decision said that "no argument is necessary to show that church purposes are public purposes."

But was this really true? The United States of America was a Christian nation nominally, but not legally. No single religion, sect or church was recognized as the established church. Although the phrase "separation of church and state" does not appear in the Constitution of the United States or in that of any state but Utah, the idea for which it stands is found in the constitutional provisions against religious tests and in the words of the First Amendment: "Congress shall make no law respecting an establishment of religion. . . ."

During the Depression some liberal Christians, agnostics, atheists and others fretted about the special status given churches and church property. A few scholars recalled that President Ulysses S. Grant had said: "I would suggest the taxation of all property equally, whether church or corporation, exempting only the last resting place of the dead, and possibly, with proper restrictions, church edifices." Dissenters objected on principle to the exemption of church property, regarded this as an indirect subsidy by the state to religion and pointed out that personal taxes might be less if churches bore their share of the tax burden.

They got nowhere. At the core of capitalism was the belief that God looked with favor on the rich. This idea had been expressed as long ago as 1732 by one of J. P. Morgan's ancestors, the Reverend Joseph Morgan, who sermonized: "Each man coveting to make himself rich, carries on the Publick Good: Thus God in His Wisdom and Mercy turns our wickedness to Publick Benefit. . . . A rich Man is a great friend of the Publick, while he aims at nothing but serving himself. God will have us live by helping one another; and since Love will not do it, Covetousness shall."

*   *   *

J. P. Morgan himself flatly told a Senate committee: "If you destroy the leisure class you destroy civilization." When reporters pressed for a definition of the leisure class, Morgan said it included all who could afford a maid. In 1931, according to *Fortune* magazine, there still were 1,000,000 families with servants. One wealthy family announced that it had solved its Depression problem by discharging fifteen of its twenty servants— although the family members showed no curiosity or concern about the fate of the unemployed fifteen.

John Jacob Astor came of age in 1933 and thereupon inherited about $4 million. Nonetheless, he dabbled at a job in a downtown Manhattan brokerage house. Before long he quit with the explanation: "I didn't finish until five o'clock and by the time I got uptown it was six. And then I had to get up early the next morning." At a later date Astor was employed briefly by a shipping firm, and when he quit this second job, he commented: "I have discovered that work interferes with leisure." He was a representative of that leisure class which Morgan felt must be maintained to save civilization.

When Dwight Morrow was running for governor of New Jersey, he said: "There is something about too much prosperity that ruins the fiber of the people. The men and women that built this country, that founded it, were people that were reared in adversity." Morrow made this statement and died before Adolf Hitler declared: "It was poverty that made me strong." Joseph P. Kennedy, a busy member of the leisure class, felt that the rich had to make some sacrifices. Writing about the Depression, Kennedy said: "I am not ashamed to record that in those days I felt and said I would be willing to part with half of what I had if I could be sure of keeping, under law and order, the other half."

One member of the enormously wealthy Du Pont family seems to have been out of touch with reality. An advertising agency wanted his company to sponsor a Sunday afternoon radio program, but this Du Pont rejected the idea, saying: "At three o'clock on Sunday afternoons everybody is playing polo."

Everybody except the millions of Americans gobbling the last morsel of food from their plates in the fear that it might be their last meal—a habit that persisted in some people down through the next three decades. As Sinclair Lewis commented in his novel *It Can't Happen Here*, people were so confused, insecure and frustrated that they hardly could do anything more permanent than shaving or eating breakfast. They were tortured with feelings of inadequacy and guilt.

A young Alabama school teacher with eight years of tenure was fired after the Wall Street Crash. Eager to work, willing to take any job however low in the social scale, she became a maid in a private home. However, upon learning that she would be expected to work seven days a week, getting room and board but no wages, she quit. Then she took a job in a convalescent home which paid her room and board and $3 a week, but soon the home closed for lack of funds. The gentle schoolteacher completely lost faith in herself, confessing to a caseworker: "If, with all the advantages I've had, I can't make a living, then I'm just no good, I guess!"

Forty experienced secretaries found work after being unemployed a year, but the first few days on the job they were unable to take dictation from their bosses without weeping from sheer nervousness. After seeking employment for a long time, a man finally landed a job and became so overwrought with joy that he died of excitement. A corporation executive was given the nasty chore of firing several hundred men. A kind and compassionate person, he insisted on talking to each of them personally and asking what plans each had for the future. In a few months the executive's hair had turned gray.

*   *   *

The Depression began to erode freedom.

Some Americans, a little more secure than others, asked harsh questions. How about fingerprinting everyone on relief? Was it proper for a man on relief to own a car—even if he needed it to try to find work? Wasn't it wrong to sell liquor to the head of a family on relief? Did anyone owning a life insurance policy deserve relief? Should reliefers be allowed to vote? Did they deserve citizenship?

In New Orleans a federal judge denied citizenship to four qualified persons because they were on relief and therefore, in the judge's words, "unable financially to contribute to the support of the government." In California another judge withheld citizenship from Jacob Hullen; in response to the judge's questions Hullen had said he believed in municipal or federal ownership of public utilities.

In New York City, one cold and rainy day, the police arrested 38 men who had taken shelter in the Pennsylvania Railroad's ferry terminal on Cortlandt Street. All were marched to the nearest police station. Fifteen of them, able to prove that they had a few nickels and dimes in their pockets, were released. The other 23 men, who did not have a cent on them, were led before a magistrate, who sentenced them to jail for vagrancy. Newspaper stories about this obvious injustice raised such a hullabaloo, however, that the 23 prisoners soon were freed.

Robert Morss Lovett, a professor of English literature at the University of Chicago, wrote in his autobiography:

> An example of the injustice meted out to foreign-born workers involved a Yugoslav named Perkovitch. When conditions were at their worst in 1932–33 the unemployed on the West Side [of Chicago] were in the habit of crossing the city to the South Side where food was sometimes available from bakeries, disposing of yesterday's bake, and where, at least, the garbage was more lavish.
>
> One morning these itinerants were picked up by the police and held at the station house on the absurd pretext that a revolution was planned. Perkovitch told me that he and about one hundred others were kept in the basement all day without food. Once a lieutenant with a bodyguard of patrolmen raged through the room, striking and kicking the men in an ecstasy of sadism. At six the prisoners were released with no charges.

Paul D. Peacher, the town marshal of Jonesboro, Arkansas, arrested a group of Negro men without cause and forced them to work on his farm. A federal grand jury indicted him under Title 18 of the Anti-Slavery Act of 1866 for "causing Negroes to be held as slaves" on a cotton plantation. This was the first case ever tried under the slavery statute. A county grand jury absolved Peacher, but the federal Department of Justice would not drop the case. Now the marshal was forced to stand trial—this time before a *federal* jury. Taking the witness chair in his own behalf, he denied that he had done anything wrong. However, the jury disagreed with him and found him guilty. Peacher was sentenced to two years in prison and fined $3,500. He appealed, lost his appeal, paid the fine and accepted a two-year probationary sentence.

Someone asked Eugene Talmadge, the governor of Georgia, what he would do about the millions of unemployed Americans. Talmadge snarled: "Let 'em starve!" It made him happy when the city fathers of Atlanta put unwanted nonresidents in chain gangs. When some textile workers went on strike in Georgia the governor had barbed-wire concentration camps built and threw pickets into them. Frank Hague, the mayor and ruthless boss of Jersey City, called for the erection in Alaska of a concentration camp for native "Reds."

Wise and temperate men worried about the growing loss of liberty in America, the land of the free and the home of the brave. George Boas, a professor of philosophy, sadly said: "It is taken for granted that democracy is bad and that it is dying." Will Durant, busy writing his many-volumed *Story of Civilization*, asked rhetorically: "Why is it that Democracy has fallen so rapidly from the high prestige which it had at the Armistice?"

Race Relations in
a Southern Town

HORTENSE POWDERMAKER

In the Southern United States prior to the end of the Civil War, the relationship between blacks, most of whom were slaves, and whites was carefully regulated by a complex of laws and customs based on the institution of slavery. After abolition, for a few years, race relations were in a relatively ambiguous state. C. Vann Woodward's **The Strange Career of Jim Crow,** revised for the third time in 1974, and the controversy this work has engendered have charted for us the formulation of a new pattern of Southern race relations that was substantially complete by the opening years of the twentieth century. The resulting system of segregation, or "Jim Crow," called for legally enforced separation of the races into a two-level caste system that permeated both public and private life in the South.

The public aspects of segregation, because of their basis in law and local ordinance, finally came under attack by the federal judiciary after years of litigation forced primarily by the National Association for the Advancement of Colored People. The decision of the United States Supreme Court in 1954 declaring school segregation unconstitutional rang the death knell for official racial discrimination in the public sphere. But it has been a long time dying. In the years after 1954, continued litigation brought many areas of segregation under public scrutiny, and as federal legislation was gradually enforced in the South and border regions, the long-standard structure of race relations began to crumble.

Less well known, but in many ways more dehumanizing, were the private patterns of racial discrimination throughout the South. Historians have been more interested in the larger, public institutions and their change over time. Sociologists, however, and particularly social and cultural anthropologists, have through the years been concerned with the more intimate relationships within communities and groups of all sorts. During the 1930s and 1940s, several excellent studies of black communities and race relations in the South were published. Perhaps the best of these is an anthropological study of Indianola, Mississippi, published in 1939 by Hortense Powdermaker, formerly of Queens College of the City University of New York. While the primary purpose of Powdermaker's work was to provide a social portrait of the black people in Indianola (called Cottonville in the study), she necessarily included a great deal of material on the relationship between the races. Few people who have not lived in the segregated South can understand the extent to which race relations formed a major topic of interest and concern for all involved, the dominant as well as the dominated. This same level of concern, however, is now being approached in urban centers, which have taken the place of the South as the major area of racial conflict.

It has often been said that the major difference between Northern and Southern white attitudes toward blacks in past times has
been that in the North black people were loved as a race and despised
as individuals, while in the South they were loved as individuals and
despised as a race. The practical application of this Southern attitude, however, was set within narrow limits. In the selection from
Powdermaker's book reprinted below, she explores these limitations
and delineates the ways in which the racial attitudes of whites work
themselves out in action. Her concern here is not with the segregation
of public institutions but with the refusal of whites to grant to blacks
the common respect of humanity. The constant interpersonal humiliation, and its ultimate form, lynching, rather than the better known
institutional discrimination is her subject in this section.

As the pattern of public segregation began to break down in recent years, a concomitant change often occurred in interpersonal relations. The "affection" based on hard and fast caste lines often was
lost as the caste lines became more permeable. But, at the same
time, a grudging acknowledgment of respect based on a common humanity began to develop. A major factor in the elimination of the kind
of discriminatory behavior described below has been the increasing
refusal of black Americans to accept such treatment. And, as far as
racial attitudes and patterns of racial relationships are concerned, the
nation now more nearly resembles the condition described by Malcolm
X: "The South begins at the Canadian border." For the first time in
American history, race relations now are being looked at from a national, rather than a regional, perspective.

W hat the white inhabitants of the Cottonville community think and
feel about the Negro finds expression whenever there is contact between
the two races. The more subtle manifestations of prevailing attitudes appear only after examination, but the cruder expressions are apparent to any
visitor who is not so familiar with them as to take them for granted. That
the local Whites do take them for granted so thoroughly as hardly to be
aware of them until they are commented upon or violated is an essential
feature of the social scene.

Any American visitor is prepared to find the well-known Jim Crow
arrangements of the railroad station with its separate waiting-rooms and
toilets. He will know that there are separate and inferior day coaches
reserved for the Negroes at the standard fares, and that they are not permitted to ride in Pullmans at any price. He will note that here, as in many

"Social Mechanisms Expressing White Attitudes" (Editor's title: "Race Relations in a
Southern Town"). From *After Freedom: A Cultural Study of the Deep South*, by
Hortense Powdermaker, pp. 43–55. Copyright 1939, © renewed 1967 by Hortense
Powdermaker. Reprinted by permission of The Viking Press, Inc.

places up north, Negroes are not allowed to eat in white restaurants, but may patronize two or three small eating places run by and for colored people. The balcony of the one moving picture theater is reserved for them. Seats here are cheaper than those downstairs, and they may not buy the more expensive seats. There are separate schools and churches for Negroes, in buildings removed from the white neighborhood—either Across the Tracks or in the country. These divisions are absolute. No white person would attend a Negro institution or sit in the places reserved for Negroes, though presumably he could if he would. No Negro would be admitted to the institutions or places reserved for Whites.

Hardly less rigid are the social mechanisms which express the conviction that the two races are distinct and that one of them is distinctly inferior, and which confirm the well-known fact that in this section of our democracy the accepted order is analogous to, though not identical with, a caste system. These social mechanisms are familiar enough to American readers so that brief mention of a few will suffice to indicate their nature and their relation to factors already discussed. They take the form of prohibitions, injunctions, usages; they may be chiefly "social," or may carry economic and even legal consequences. They vary also in the significance attached to them, which is not always in proportion to their apparent magnitude.

A social prohibition to which great weight is attached is that which forbids addressing a Negro as "Mr.," "Mrs.," or "Miss." Just what the white person withholds in avoiding the use of these titles is suggested by those he is willing to employ. Ordinarily, a Negro is simply called by his first name, regardless of his age, attainments, or wealth, and often by Whites who may be less endowed in any of these respects. "Doctor" and "Professor" are readily granted to professional people, however. A teacher who has charge of a small one-room country school, and who himself has never been to high school, is regularly called Professor. A medical man will be addressed as "Doctor" by Whites who could not conceivably bring themselves to call him "Mister." It may not seem entirely inappropriate that members of a race considered inferior should more easily be accorded an indication of status achieved by effort than one which stands for respect and social parity acquired by birth. It is to be remembered, however, that special titles are used more easily and with less significance in the South than in the North, and that the general American attitude toward members of the learned professions is somewhat ambiguous.

It is quite in order for Whites to address Negroes by terms which imply relationship or affection. Women are called "Aunty" and men "Uncle" even when they are younger than the person speaking to them. On the other hand, Whites often say "Boy" or "Girl" to Negroes who are much older than themselves.

> A moderately prosperous man in his late fifties is a highly respected member of the Negro group. As presiding elder in his church on Sunday, wearing gloves and a neatly pressed suit, he presents a most dignified appearance. On Monday, going to work, he is stopped by a young white woman who is having tire trouble.

Both have lived in the same town all their lives and she knows his name very well. She addresses him only as "Boy," repeating the word sharply as she orders his moves in rendering her this unpaid service.

The prohibition against courtesy titles extends to the telephone. If a Negro puts in a long-distance call for "Mr. Smith" in a town fifty miles away, the operator, who can tell where the call comes from, will ask: "Is he colored?" On being told that he is, she replies: "Don't you say 'Mister' to me. He ain't 'Mister' to me."

To violate this strong taboo is to arouse the resentment, suspicion, fear, which attends the breaking of taboos or customs in any culture. If a Melanesian is asked what difference it would make if he failed to provide a feast for his dead maternal uncle, or if he broke the rule of exogamy, his attitude is one of complete bewilderment and strong fear at the mere suggestion. If a member of his community should actually commit such a breach, he would resent it as an invitation to general disaster. The exogamy rule is felt, inarticulately, to be an inherent and indispensable part of the Melanesian *status quo*, one of the balances which keep the culture revolving in orderly fashion. The title taboo is sensed as equally essential to the *status quo* in Mississippi. To question either is to question the whole system; to violate either is to violate, weaken, endanger, the entire *status quo*. In either case this is merely the background to the immediate reaction, which is seldom reasoned, and may be intensified by the secondary meanings which become attached to any social pattern.

The rule for forms of address is concerned also with what the Negro calls the White. The white person's name is never to be mentioned without some title of respect. It may be the first or the last name, depending on the degree of acquaintance. Military titles, traditionally accorded to Whites, are less frequently heard today, and the old-time "Massa" has given way to "Boss." If no other title is used, the Negro says "Ma'am" or "Sir." Among Whites and among Negroes, this is a matter of courtesy; but when a Negro is speaking to a white person it is compulsory. If he mails a package at the post office he must be very careful to observe this usage toward the clerk who is serving him. He must be equally careful in addressing the telephone operator.

A man who had lived in a large city for several years forgot the injunction when he was putting in a long-distance call. The operator repeated his number several times, each time asking if it was correct, and each time receiving the answer: "Yes." Finally in an ominous tone she said: "You'll say 'Yes, Ma'am' to me." The Negro canceled his call. Since then a kind of secret warfare has gone on. Whenever he uses the phone the operator asks a question that would ordinarily be answered with a "Ma'am," and he extricates himself by saying: "That's it," "That is correct," or some phrase that evades the difficulty. The operator continues her campaign, undaunted.

There often appears to be a relation between the insistence of the White upon observance of such a usage, and his own adjustment within his group.

> A woman who was disliked and resented by both races tried to get the Negroes to call her Miss Sylvia instead of Mrs. T. The Negro who spoke of this said: "Miss Sylvia is more like slavery times," and added scornfully that she guessed Mrs. T. didn't know other people have been born since slavery.

Closely connected with the title taboo is the term used when Whites talk among themselves about Negroes. "Nigger" is the term used almost universally. Its emotional tone varies according to the context of the situation and the individual using it. It ranges from contempt to affection, and its use is so prevalent and so much a part of the *mores*, that it may not necessarily be deeply charged. "Darky" is sometimes substituted for "nigger," and then the tone is practically always one of affection. When a white person is talking to a Negro, and wishes to use the third person, "nigger" is the common term. There are occasional exceptions. A sensitive and "good White" may substitute "your people." State and county officials in addressing Negro groups use this term, or "colored people," or "Negroes." The latter is the one to which the Whites show the most resistance, and several linguistic variations have occurred as a result, such as "niggra."

Although all these terms occur in intra-Negro conversation, they always resent intensely "nigger" and "darky" when used by the Whites. "Negro" and "colored people" are the preferred terms. Among themselves, "darky" is heard rarely, but "nigger" is used frequently, and again its emotional tone varies. A colored person may call another "nigger" in either affection or anger, and the emotion connected with the term may be small or great. The term does not usually call forth resentment when used by a Negro, as it always does when used by a White.

The taboo against eating with a Negro is another which suggests analogies from different cultures. Eating with a person has strong symbolic value in many societies, and usually signifies social acceptance. White children may on special occasions eat with Negroes, but for colored and white adults to eat together under ordinary conditions is practically unheard of. If a white person in the country would for some reason ask for food at a Negro home, he would eat apart. Special circumstances may, however, constitute an exception to the rule: if a white man and a colored man went fishing, they might grill their fish over an open fire and eat together, in the open. Exceptions are extremely rare, and the taboo is extended to colored people who are not Negroes.

> A Chinese doctor who was participating in a public health study lived at one of the town's boarding houses. Several of the boarders objected to sitting at the same table with him. The woman who told about it added: "You know, we are so narrow down here."

The rule that a Negro should not enter the front door of a house is so taken for granted that many white people, when they go out for a short time, will lock the back door against thieves and leave the front door open. They assume that no colored person would go in the front way and, apparently, that no white person would steal. The visibility of the front entrance in the daytime lends a practical support to the assumption.

The front-door prohibition is far less important to some Whites than to others.

> "A poor-raised white person can work alongside of you," one Negro said, "and then if he gets a fortune, you can't come to the front door but have to go round to the back. But a rich-raised White don't care if you walk out of the front door."
>
> Two women, each of whom considers herself a typical Southerner, illustrate divergent attitudes. Both are members of the middle class, but they represent as much contrast as can be found within the limits of that comparatively homogeneous group. One belongs to the "best people" of the town; the other has recently acquired a small competence, after years of insecurity and strain. The son of the second woman happened to see the first woman's cook leave the house by the front door. "Do you allow your cook to go out that way?" he asked in surprise. His hostess replied that it didn't make any difference to her which door her cook used. The boy exclaimed that his mother would never allow anything like that; one day when their cook did try to go out the front way, his mother picked up a piece of wood from the fireplace and threw it at her.

Few cooks would attempt to leave by the front door, and still fewer mistresses would be indifferent to it. The amount of individual variation with regard to this prohibition, however, suggests that it is not one of those which carry the strongest symbolic force for the Whites.

In connection with shaking hands, it again appears that affection may be permissible where respect is denied. A colored mammy may kiss her charges, perhaps even on rare occasions after they have grown up. But colored people and white people do not as a rule shake hands in public. If a white educator addresses a group of Negro teachers, he might shake hands with them after his speech. On such occasions refreshments might also be served, but it would be lap service, with no question of sitting at the same table.

It is of course taken for granted that ordinary courtesies have no place between the two races. A white man thinks nothing of sitting while a colored woman stands, regardless of who she is. A highly educated woman who always stood in talking to the white man under whose direction she worked was frightened when on one occasion he invited her to sit.

Courtesies of the road are among those withheld. Negroes in Cottonville are very cautious drivers, and they have need to be, since white drivers customarily ignore the amenities toward a car driven by a colored person.

A white Northerner driving through the town with Negro passengers in the rumble seat of her car was startled to find other machines passing her without sounding their horns. It is simply assumed that the Negro will proceed with caution, keep to the side of the road, and not count on the right of way. The assumption is sound, since if there is an accident the Negro as a rule shoulders the penalty.

> A white lawyer driving at about fifty miles an hour came to a cross road. He saw another car coming but did not stop, figuring that the other would do so. He figured wrong, and there was a collision in which he was slightly bruised and his car was battered. A white bystander urged him to "just kill the nigger," since he couldn't collect any money for damages. "That's the only thing to do—just kill him." The lawyer said he would not kill him, but would take the case to court. When it came up, the Negro pleaded guilty and was fined $25, which he had to work out at the county work house, as he did not have the money. The white woman who told the story said it was good he pleaded guilty or "he'd have got worse." It might be unjust, she admitted, but "you have to treat the niggers that way; otherwise nobody knows what would happen." The lawyer received insurance for his car and nothing but satisfaction from the Negro's sentence.
>
> Exceptions happen to this rule also. One occurred when the mayor of the town happened to witness an accident in which the white man was unmistakably at fault. The white driver, not knowing this, had the Negro arraigned and brought before the mayor, who promptly dismissed the case. The Negroes' comment was that the mayor "is mighty fair for a southern man."

It is of course assumed that Negroes always wait until white people are served. In the case of an appointment, the Negro waits until all Whites have been taken care of, even if they come in after him. If someone comes in during an interview, he is expected to step aside and wait. He may also expect to be kept waiting even if nobody else is there. There are always and everywhere people ready to employ this popular device for putting others in their places and feeling that one is in his own place. Certain local Whites derive obvious satisfaction from being able to keep Negroes waiting as long as possible, and for no reason—especially the educated, prosperous, or "uppity" Negroes.

In the white stores, where Negroes do the bulk of their buying, they have to wait until the white clientele has been served. A Negro who has money for purchases is permitted to enter almost any store and buy, although certain ones cater to the colored trade and others do not. Even in the latter, however, the more distinguished individuals among the Negroes may expect to receive courteous treatment. The depression has wrought a definite change in the policy of most white shops toward the other race. Under stress of hard times, the shopkeepers made an effort to attract Negro trade as they had never done before. Negro customers were no longer kept waiting indefinitely for attention. In many cases they were permitted to try on garments rather than, as before, being required to buy shoes, gloves, hats, without first finding out whether they were the right size or shape. Once such concessions have been granted, they cannot easily be withdrawn.

The granting of the privilege of trying on garments before they are bought has an economic value for the Whites not directly involved in such a usage as, for example, the front-door prohibition. Economic implications are strong in several others among the mechanisms expressing white attitudes toward the Negro—notably the Jim Crow arrangements, which are also more official in their manner of enforcement. In the subtle gradation from social through economic to legal aspects, one comes finally to issues which seem of a different order, although they rest upon the same basis. The attitudes that prompt minor social taboos, prohibitions, injunctions, also underlie the disenfranchisement of the Negro, his exclusion from jury service, and his liability to lynching. These have been investigated throughout the deep South, and the reports and discussions published cover Mississipp. They will be touched upon here only in connection with the attitudes that surround them.

The device for withholding the franchise from Negroes in the community is very simple. In order to qualify as a voter, one must have paid one's taxes, including the two-dollar poll tax, and must be able to read and interpret a paragraph of the Constitution. This test is admittedly designed to prevent Negroes from voting; no white person in charge of it would admit that a Negro's interpretation was correct. Knowing this, the Negroes make no attempt to qualify. The Whites justify the prohibition on the ground that, since the Negroes are in the majority, the franchise would give them political control, which would spell disaster: a Negro might even be elected to office. It is assumed that the Negroes would all vote Republican, because that party freed the slaves. The Whites feel that any measure is justifiable that would prevent control by the Negroes or the Republicans, and that either eventuality might lead to the other. One reason for fearing the entrance of the Republican Party is the suspicion that it would give the Negro the vote in order to strengthen its following. The danger is not imminent, since the community is so strongly Democratic that no Republican primaries are held there.[1]

That no Negro should serve on a jury is as universally taken for granted by the Whites as that no Negro should vote. The two prohibitions are closely linked, and the fact that Negroes pay so small a percentage of the taxes is offered as partial justification for both.

Denial of legal rights guaranteed by the Constitution is more severe and more tangible in its effects than denial of social amenities. Most severe of all are the denials involved in lynching. Nevertheless, it too is a mode of behavior customary in certain situations, and is a direct product of the creed and attitudes which have been described. It differs from the other mechanisms in its spectacular nature, in the fact that it is a sporadic mani-

[1] The author's impression is that, if they had had the chance, most Negroes during the period of this survey would have voted the Democratic ticket because of their faith in the New Deal.

festation, and in the more limited and covert social sanction which supports it.

Very few white men except the Poor Whites would declare in favor of lynchings. Very few white men would actively try to halt one. There is a report from another community that a member of the aristocracy did once come out definitely against a lynching and succeeded in stopping it. A middle-class storekeeper, under rather special circumstances, did much the same thing in a case given earlier. The rarity of such an act is due chiefly to the danger of opposing a mob. In addition, many a White who deplores lynching yet feels it may serve a beneficent purpose. There are good and kind Christians who will explain that lynchings are terrible, but must happen once in a while in order to keep the Negro in his place.

It is generally assumed that lynching as a rule occurs because of an alleged sexual crime. This is not strictly true, but it is usually associated with the cry of rape. The alarm is calculated to set off a maximum of excitement. It awakens latent fears in connection with the Negro man and the white woman, against a background of guilt and fear related to the white man and the Negro woman. It brings out into the open the forbidden subject of sex. And in addition, it affords the Poor Whites their one opportunity to avenge themselves for the degradation and misery of their own position. A lynching is the one occasion when they can vent all their stored-up resentment without fear of the other Whites, but rather with their tacit consent.

Under proper stimulation, the consent becomes more than tacit. The following reports and editorials in a local paper concern an incident which took place in a near-by community during the course of this study.

> Crimes like the one that shocked this county last week call for the most severe and swift penalty that can be invoked. Our officers are doing their utmost to capture the guilty fiends, and when caught "may the Lord have mercy on their souls." The swiftest penalty that will be given them will be entirely too slow for the temper of the people at present.

> One of the most horrible crimes ever attempted in the county occurred about two miles west of M. Tuesday evening, when two negroes attempted to kill a young man . . . and after cutting his throat, stabbing him several times in the chest, and throwing him in the rear of the car, drove off toward a secluded place with the young lady. . . .

> After going some distance the young lady, with rare presence of mind, when they came near a house, told one of them to open the car door as she wanted to spit. When he opened the door she jerked the key out of the car and threw it away, and jumped out screaming. People who lived in the house came running and the negroes fled. When assistance came the wounded young man was taken . . . to the hospital . . . where his wounds were pronounced fatal, as his jugular vein was almost severed, besides the chest wounds.

The alarm was quickly sounded and posses rapidly assembled organized for the man hunt. . . . [The sheriff] was quickly on the scene with his deputies and hunted all Tuesday night but failed to capture them. The sheriff found out where they lived and arrested a brother of one of the fiends, who told all he knew of them. That they had come to his house with bloody clothes and changed the clothes and told him they had gotten into some trouble and had to run for it. They left and up to this time they have not been captured, although Sheriff L. is still on the trail. The bloody clothes were secured by the sheriff. It is a miracle that the young lady was unharmed and had the presence of mind to distract their attention while she threw the car key away.

We hope they will be speedily caught near the scene of their crime. We do not think the county jail has any room at present for such criminals, but we feel certain that the splendid citizens of C. and vicinity will properly place them should they get hold of them.

These newspaper accounts and comments were hardly calculated to act as a deterrent to the mob, made up mainly of Poor Whites. On the day after the attack, a group of these shabby men, their eyes burning, tramped up and down the road and through the woods, mingling their oaths with the barking of their dogs. The middle-class white men sitting in their offices or homes remarked that of course they did not approve of lynching, but that undoubtedly these Negroes would be lynched, and "what can you do when you have to deal with the primitive African type, the killer?" The Negroes in the neighborhood sat at home all day, afraid to go out. Those in a town thirty miles distant said that things must be getting better because a few years ago, if the mob had not found the men they wanted by this time, they would have lynched someone else.

The town in which the murder had been committed was quiet. The Negroes had escaped into another state. Nobody knew where they were. At last the mob broke up; the dogs were quiet. A few of the middle-class Whites murmured that perhaps the Negroes were after the man and not the girl; that maybe there was some real ground for their grudge against him. These were a few almost inaudible whispers. Most of the people said nothing. The eyes of the shabby men no longer gleamed with excitement. They had gone back to the dull routine of the sharecropper. The middle class sat back and reaffirmed that they did not believe in lynching.

Not all of them say so, however. A few openly condone it. Interestingly enough, of the group who answered the questionnaire, more young people than old said that lynching for rape is justifiable, and slightly more women than men. If any weight can be attached to this type of sampling, it must be assumed that, despite the more liberal and less emotional attitude of the younger generation in general, a "nigger-hunt" appeals to them more than to their parents. The vigor of youth may have something to do with this, and the type of imagery that would be evoked by the suggestion of a Negro raping a white woman. Perhaps also there is less interference by social and religious inhibitions. It is hardly to be supposed that when these Junior College students are middle-aged they will be more in favor of lynching than their parents are today. The differential between men and women could not be accepted as reliable in itself, but corresponds to the difference in attitudes generally expressed, and is not at odds with impressionistic evidence. It is to be remembered of course that none of the Whites who answered the questionnaire was of the class that takes an active part in this practice.

Of the social mechanisms described, lynching is the one that has the least consistent, the least whole-hearted, and certainly the least open sanction from the white group. It is also the one that has roused the most active protest from the North. If a Federal law is passed prohibiting it, change will be enforced from the outside. In any case, the pressure of outside opinion is a potent factor in its gradual decline. Furthermore, the attention drawn to the South by lynching tends to overflow onto mechanisms of racial discrimination that might otherwise be less noticed from the outside.

From the sketch of white attitudes and the social mechanisms that express them, it can readily be seen that the Negro carries a large load of the white man's prejudices and fears. All peoples in all cultures have both prejudice and fear; the forms they take are determined by the historical accidents that have shaped the culture and the way the culture impinges upon the individuals who participate in it. In a community such as this, where there are socially sanctioned channels for group fear and prejudice and a socially determined object for them, their effects become somewhat specialized. We shall be concerned chiefly with the effects on the Negroes, although it may be assumed that they are equally profound for the Whites, and would well repay investigation.

Repression of
Mexican-Americans
in Los Angeles

CAREY McWILLIAMS

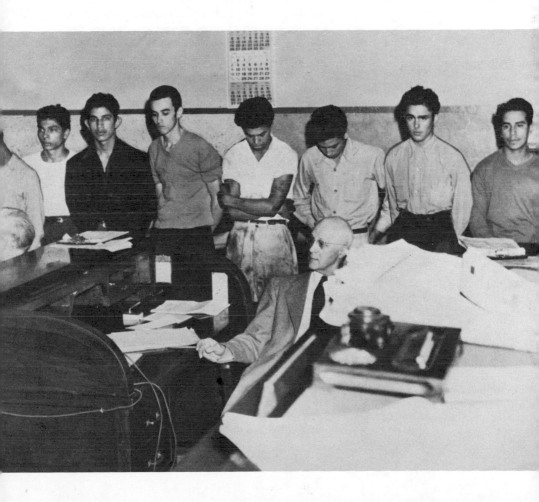

Race riots and outbreaks of other intergroup violence have taken place with some regularity in America since before the founding of the United States. Recently, a great deal of attention has been paid to the phenomenon of violence in American history. Much of this interest was generated by the civil disorders that took place in black ghettos in the mid-1960s. Presidential commissions as well as citizen groups have investigated the sources and causes of violent activity. These investigations disclosed that most of the disorders in the 1960s were a reaction by the ghetto population to activities of the police or other law enforcement personnel. It was pointed out that the police regularly harass ghetto residents, particularly young men—a tactic that is not restricted to black ghettos but is widespread in nonwhite communities.

Mexican-Americans are one group who have felt and reacted to the discriminatory practices of law enforcement officials. This type of harassment led to a major episode of racial violence during the Second World War years—the so-called "zoot suit" riot in Los Angeles involving Mexican-Americans and Anglos, particularly Anglo police and servicemen.

The selection reprinted below describes the background to this riot. The author, Carey McWilliams, formerly a writer and social activist in California and now editor of **The Nation,** included this report in his history of Mexican-Americans, **North from Mexico.**

Americans of Mexican ancestry occupy a special place in our history. Unlike blacks and American Indians, the Mexicans were neither brought here in chains nor conquered in battle; they became American by treaty. After the Mexican War (1846–48), the Treaty of Guadalupe Hidalgo transferred thousands of Mexicans and Indians from Mexican sovereignty to that of the United States. The terms of the treaty provided for protection of their rights and claims, but, as is so often the case in matters of this sort, they found themselves deprived of promised land and resources by the Anglo population.

In the twentieth century, many thousands of Mexicans have migrated to the United States to seek work. Most of the work they have found is temporary and low paying. Many immigrants, both legal and illegal, have become itinerant farm workers. Those who join the migrant stream, deprive themselves of any opportunity to become economically stable and culturally assimilable. At the same time, many other Mexicans who have joined the ranks of the urban working class live in segregated areas where, until recently, they met with widespread social segregation, particularly in the Southwest and California.

As is the case with other minority groups today, the Mexican-Americans are forming protest organizations and political parties. In

some areas of high concentration of Mexican population, political control has been wrested from the Anglos. Recently, Mexican-Americans
in New Mexico formed the **Alianza** movement in an attempt to force
the United States to comply with the terms of the Treaty of Guadalupe Hidalgo.

In the essay that follows we see the interaction between the
police and the Mexican-American youth of Los Angeles. The harassment by law enforcement officials and discriminatory treatment by
the courts and the media that has been so typical in nonwhite areas
rests on racist assumptions held by the dominant culture.   Only
with genuinely representative political power and the elimination of
racist thinking can this situation be changed. Although the events
described below took place in 1942, their equivalent can be found in
most parts of the United States today.

In March, 1942, the Japanese were excluded from the West Coast and the
remaining citizens found, rather to their surprise, that this drastic wartime
measure had not solved all their social and economic problems as the more
rampant West Coast newspapers had led them to believe. Problems which
had existed before the Japanese exclusion still existed, intensified by the
war activities which involved most of Southern California. In Los Angeles,
where fantasy is a way of life, it was a foregone conclusion that Mexicans
would be substituted as the major scapegoat group once the Japanese were
removed. Thus within a few days after the last Japanese had left, the Los
Angeles newspapers, led by the Hearst press, began to play up "Mexican"
crime and "Mexican" juvenile delinquency, as though the Mexican element
in crime and delinquency could be considered apart from the ordinary
crime experienced by a large, congested metropolitan area in wartime.

A number of minor incidents in the spring of 1942 enabled the newspapers and the police to build up, within the short period of six months,
sufficient anti-Mexican sentiment to prepare the community for a full-scale
offensive against the Mexican minority. Once prepared, of course, this
sentiment could be expected to assume violent expression with the first
major incident. A young Mexican who had been arrested and sentenced
to forty-five days in jail for having accosted a woman was, upon his re-
lease, taken before the Grand Jury and, if you please, reindicted for rape,
on the same offense, and promptly sentenced to prison for twelve years!
The case was quickly appealed and, of course, the conviction was reversed.
A short time late, a group of Mexican men, celebrating a wedding, were
arrested for playing a penny crap game, an offense usually ignored by the

"The Pattern of Violence" (Editor's title: "Repression of Mexican-Americans in Los
Angeles"). From *North from Mexico: The Spanish Speaking People of the United
States,* by Carey McWilliams (Philadelphia: J. B. Lippincott, 1949), pp. 227–43. Re-
printed with permission of Carey McWilliams, the copyright holder.

police as being inconsequential. But, in this instance, a "conspiracy" indictment was secured from the Grand Jury, thereby neatly converting a petty misdemeanor into a felony charge. On July 13, 1942, the press gave great prominence to a story involving a fight between two groups of Mexican boys, the Belvedere "gang" and the Palo Verde "gang." In all these preliminary "incidents" pointed mention was made of the "Mexican" character of the people involved. By these techniques, the groundwork was carefully prepared for the "big incident."

1. THE CASE OF SLEEPY LAGOON

On the afternoon of August 1, 1942, Henry Leyvas, a young Mexican-American, had taken his girl for a drive near a little pond in a gravel pit near what was called the Williams Ranch on the east side of Los Angeles. In lieu of other recreational facilities, this abandoned gravel pit had long been used by Mexican youngsters in the neighborhood as a swimming pool. Early that evening, a Saturday night, Leyvas and his girl had been set upon by members of a rival "gang" and a fight had occurred. (Leyvas himself was a member of a group known as the 38th Street "gang.")

Later, the same evening, Leyvas returned to the gravel pit with members of his own gang, in several cars, to look for the troublemakers. Some of the members of this sortie knew that Leyvas intended "to get even," but others merely went along for the ride and a swim and a general good time. Finding the gravel pit deserted, they discovered that a party was in progress at a nearby house belonging to the Delgadillo family and decided "to crash the gate." Some fighting and scuffling occurred at the Delgadillo home and the invaders, after a time, left the scene of the party.

Early on the morning of August second, the body of young José Díaz was picked up from a dirt road near the Delgadillo house and taken to the General Hospital where Díaz died without ever regaining consciousness. The autopsy showed that he had met his death as the result of a fracture at the base of the skull. He had apparently been in a fight, for his hands and face were bruised, but there were neither knife nor gun wounds on the body. The road where his body was found was well travelled and the autopsy showed that he was probably drunk at the time of his death. Díaz had left the Delgadillo home with two friends—presumably the last persons to have been with him prior to his death. *Never called as witnesses*, their version of what happened to Díaz is not known. The autopsy surgeon, it should be noted, testified that Díaz could have met his death by repeated hard falls on the rocky ground of the road and admitted that the injuries at the base of his skull were similar to those seen on the victims of automobile accidents. Such are the facts of the case.

With the prior background in mind, it is not surprising that the Los Angeles press welcomed the death of Díaz like manna from the skies. Around the essentially bare facts of the case, they promptly proceeded to weave an enormous web of melodramatic fancy. The old gravel pit was dubbed "The Sleepy Lagoon" by a bright young reporter and the whole case was given an air of sordid mystery. Quick to cooperate, the police rounded up twenty-four youngsters, all alleged to be members of the 38th Street "gang," and charged them with the murder of Díaz. Two of them had the wits to demand separate trials and the charges against them were later dropped. But to a fantastic orchestration of "crime" and "mystery" provided by the Los Angeles press, seventeen of the youngsters were convicted in what was, up to that time, the largest mass trial for murder ever held in the county.

In the process of "investigating" the case, the police severely beat up two of the boys. While testifying that he had been beaten by the police, one of the boys was shown a photograph by the prosecution. This photograph had been taken of him, purportedly, just prior to his entering the Grand Jury room, and indicated that, at that time, he was unmarked and unbeaten. The boy then pulled from his pocket a photograph which had been taken by a newspaper photographer just as he was leaving the Grand Jury room. This untouched photograph showed him with severe bruises about the head and face. Anna Zacsek, attorney for Leyvas, testified that she had walked into a room at the police station where her client, hand-cuffed to a chair, was being beaten by the police, and that she found him barely conscious, smeared with his own blood. Held incommunicado while they were being "worked over" by the police, the defendants were then marched, en masse, to the Grand Jury which proceeded to indict the lot of them for first-degree murder. When they appeared before the Grand Jury they were dirty, haggard, bruised—a thoroughly disreputable-appearing group of youngsters completely terrified by the treatment they had just received. Who were these "criminals,"—these hardened "gangsters"?

Henry Leyvas, twenty, worked on his father's ranch. Chepe Ruiz, eighteen, a fine amateur athlete, wanted to play big league baseball. In May, 1942, his head had been cracked open by the butt of a policeman's gun when he had been arrested on "suspicion of robbery," although he was later found not guilty of the charge. In San Quentin Prison, where he and the others were sent after their conviction in the Sleepy Lagoon case, Ruiz won the admiration of the warden, the prison staff, and the inmates when he continued on in a boxing match, after several of his ribs had been broken. Robert Telles, eighteen, was working in a defense plant at the time of his arrest. Like many Mexican youngsters on the east side, he had remarkable skill as a caricaturist and amused his co-defendants during the trial by drawing caricatures of the judge, the jury, and the prosecutor. Manuel Reyes, seventeen, had joined the navy in July, 1942, and was awaiting induction when arrested. Angel Padilla, one of the defendants most severely beaten by the police, was a furniture-worker. Henry Ynostrosa, eighteen, was married and the father of a year-old girl. He had supported his mother and two sisters since he was fifteen. Manuel Delgado, nineteen, also a woodworker, was married and the father of two children, one born on the day he entered San Quentin Prison. Gus Zamora, twenty-one, was also a furniture-worker. Victor Rodman Thompson, twenty-one, was an Anglo youngster who, by long association with the Mexican boys in his neighborhood, had become completely Mexicanized. Jack Melendez, twenty-one, had been sworn into the navy before he was arrested. When a dishonorable discharge came through after his conviction, he said it was "like kicking a guy when he's down." John Matuz, twenty, had worked in Alaska with the U.S. Engineers.

These, then, were the "criminals," the "baby gangsters," the "murderers" who provided Los Angeles with a Roman holiday of sensationalism, crime-mongering, and Mexican-baiting. From the very outset, a "gang" was on trial. For years, Mexicans had been pushed around by the Los Angeles police and given a very rough time in the courts, but the Sleepy Lagoon prosecution capped the climax. It took place before a biased and prejudiced judge (found to be such by an appellate court); it was conducted by a prosecutor who pointed to the clothes and the style of haircut of the defendants as evidence of guilt; and was staged in an atmosphere of intense community-wide prejudice which had been whipped up and artfully sustained by the entire press of Los Angeles.

From the beginning the proceedings savored more of a ceremonial lynching than a trial in a court of justice. The defendants were not allowed to sit with their counsel—there were seven defense attorneys—and were only permitted to communicate with them during recesses and after adjournment. For the first weeks of the trial, the defendants were not permitted to get haircuts and packages of clean clothes were intercepted by the jailer on orders of the prosecutor. As a consequence of this prejudicial order, the defendants came trouping into the courtroom every day looking like so many unkempt vagabonds. Following a trial that lasted several months and filled six thousand pages of transcript, they were convicted on January 13, 1943: nine were convicted of second-degree murder plus two counts of assault and were sentenced to San Quentin Prison; others were convicted of lesser offenses; and five were convicted of assault and sentenced to the county jail.

Following the conviction, the Sleepy Lagoon Defense Committee was formed which raised a large fund to provide new counsel and to appeal the case. I served as chairman of this committee and Harry Braverman, a member of the Grand Jury who had tried to stop the indictment, served as its treasurer. On October 4, 1944, the District Court of Appeals, in a unanimous decision, reversed the conviction of all the defendants and the case was later dismissed "for lack of evidence." In its decision, the court sustained all but two of the contentions which our defense committee had raised, castigated the trial judge for his conduct of the trial, and scored the methods by which the prosecution had secured a conviction. On October twenty-fourth, when the charges were finally dismissed after the defendants had served nearly two years in San Quentin Prison (we had been unable to provide bonds during the appeal), hundreds of Mexicans crowded the corridors of the Hall of Justice to greet the boys. "Hysterical screams and shrieks," reported the Los Angeles Times, "laughter and cries of jubilation welled from the crowd. The atmosphere was electric with excitement as the liberated men were besieged by well-wishers who enthusiastically pumped their hands and slapped their backs. Tears flowed unashamedly." For the first time in the history of Los Angeles, Mexicans had won an organized victory in the courts and, on this day, bailiffs and deputy sheriffs and court attachés were looking rather embarrassed in the presence of Mexicans.

The work of the Sleepy Lagoon Defense Committee received nation-wide attention and was hailed as an important contribution to the war effort by ex-President Cárdenas of Mexico and by the Mexican consul-general. In Mexico City, the magazine *Hoy* devoted a three-page spread in its issue of September 30, 1944, to the work of the defense committee. During the time the committee was in existence, we received hundreds of letters from GI's, from posts in Guam, New Guinea, Hawaii, the Fiji Islands, the Aleutians; in fact, from all over the world. Soldiers with names like Livenson, Hart, Shanahan, Hecht, Chavez, Scott, Bristol, Cavouti, and Burnham enclosed dimes, quarters, and dollars for the work of the committee. Marine Corps Captain M. A. Cavouti wrote us from New Guinea: "This war is being fought for the maintenance and broadening of our democratic beliefs and I am heartily in accord with any effort to apply these principles by assisting in obtaining a review of this case. Please accept my modest contribution." From Hawaii, Corporal Samuel J. Fore-man, a Negro, wrote: "I saw in the Pittsburgh *Courier* that you were lead-ing the fight for victims of aggression. We members of the colored race are sympathetic to your worthwhile and moral fight to free these Mexican boys." Dozens of letters came from Mexican-Americans in the service.

Everyone liked what we had done except, of course, the dominant cliques in Los Angeles. Since the initial suggestion for the formation of the committee had come from LaRue McCormick, a member of the Com-munist Party, we were systematically red-baited. The press accused us of "inciting racial prejudice," scoffed at the charge of bias during the trial, and lauded the trial judge and the prosecutor. Even the unanimous deci-sion of the District Court of Appeals, sustaining the charges we had made, failed to bring so much as a mumbled retraction of the accusations that had been made against the boys or so much as a grudging acknowledgment that we had been right.

While the case was pending on appeal, several members of the com-mittee, including myself, were subpoenaed by the Committee on Un-American Activities in California, headed by Senator Jack Tenney, and grilled at great length. Naturally these various grillings were reported in the press in a manner calculated to make it most difficult for us to raise money for the appeal. The assistant district attorney, who conducted the prosecution, threatened the First Unitarian Church of Los Angeles with the removal of its tax-exempt status if it permitted the committee to hold a meeting on its premises. In fact, permission to hold the meeting, was, at the last minute, revoked by the church in response to this pressure. That I had expressed opposition to segregation and had testified that I was op-posed on principle to miscegenation statutes was actually cited by the Tenney Committee on page 232 of its report as *proof* (!) of Communistic inclinations!

As a postscript to this section, I should add that not long after his re-lease from prison Henry Leyvas was convicted of a criminal offense after receiving a fair trial. So far as Leyvas was concerned, he had been con-victed of being a Mexican long years ago and the damage was done. Need-less to say, his general morale and attitude were not improved by his experiences in the Sleepy Lagoon case.

2. CAPTAIN AYRES: ANTHROPOLOGIST

To appreciate the social significance of the Sleepy Lagoon case, it is necessary to have a picture of the concurrent events. The Anti-Mexican press campaign which had been whipped up through the spring and early summer of 1942 finally brought recognition, from the officials, of the existence of an "awful" situation in reference to "Mexican juvenile delinquency." A special committee of the Grand Jury, shortly after the death of José Díaz, was appointed to investigate "the problem." It was before this committee, within two weeks after the arrest of the defendants in the Sleepy Lagoon case, that Captain E. Duran Ayres, chief of the "*Foreign* Relations Bureau" of the Los Angeles sheriff's office, presented a report presumably prepared under the instructions of his superiors.

"Mexicans as a whole, in this county," reads the report, "are restricted in the main only to certain kinds of labor, and that being the lowest paid. It must be admitted that they are discriminated against and have been heretofore practically barred from learning trades. . . . This has been very much in evidence in our defense plants, in spite of President Roosevelt's instructions to the contrary. . . . Discrimination and segregation, as evidenced by public signs and rules, such as appear in certain restaurants, public swimming plunges, public parks, theaters, and even in schools, cause resentment among the Mexican people. . . . There are certain parks in this state in which a Mexican may not appear, or else only on a certain day of the week. There are certain plunges where they are not allowed to swim, or else only on one day of the week, and it is made evident by signs reading to that effect, for instance, 'Tuesdays reserved for Negroes and Mexicans.' . . . Certain theaters in certain towns either do not allow Mexicans to enter, or else segregate them in a certain section. Some restaurants absolutely refuse to serve them a meal and so state by public signs. . . . All this applies to both the foreign and American-born Mexicans."

So far, in the report, Captain Ayres was simply drawing a true picture of conditions in Los Angeles County. But, since his real purpose was "to explain" the causes of Mexican juvenile delinquency, he soon began to draw some extraordinary conclusions. "The Caucasian," he went on to report, "especially the Anglo-Saxon, when engaged in fighting, particularly among youths, resort to fisticuffs and may at times kick each other, which is considered unsportive: but this Mexican element considers all that to be a sign of weakness, and all he knows and feels is a desire to use a knife or some lethal weapon. In other words, his desire is to kill, or at least let blood. That is why it is difficult for the Anglo-Saxon to understand the psychology of the Indian or even the Latin, and it is just as difficult for the Indian or the Latin to understand the psychology of the Anglo-Saxon or those from northern Europe. When there is added to *this inborn characteristic* that has come down through the ages, the use of liquor, then we certainly have crimes of violence." (Emphasis added.)

This passage should, perhaps, be compared with similar conclusions drawn by another amateur anthropologist. "Race," wrote Adolf Hitler, "does not lie in the language but exclusively in the blood. A man may change his language without any trouble but . . . his inner nature is not changed." The close agreement between these two experts was shown after the publication of the Ayres Report when Radio Berlin, Radio Tokyo, and Radio Madrid quoted passages from the report to show that Americans actually shared the same doctrines as those advocated by Hitler. The Los Angeles sheriff, who had previously made much fuss over his "Latin blood" and his "early California background," was sufficiently embarrassed by these broadcasts to suggest to a reporter from the New York *Daily News* that the Japanese, upon being evacuated, had incited the Mexican population of Los Angeles to violence. Thus the sheriff, who had always identified himself with the Mexican population on Cinco de Mayo and the Sixteenth of September, inferentially charged that the Mexicans, his own people, had become agents of the Japanese government!

In considering the subsequent pattern of events, it is important to remember that the Ayres Report had been formally presented to the Grand Jury by the sheriff and had presumably represented the official views, candidly expressed, of law enforcement officers in Los Angeles. Thus the chief law enforcement agency in the county had given voice to the view that the Mexican minority possessed an inborn tendency to criminal behavior and to crimes of violence. Being primarily men of action, the law enforcement officials proceeded to act in accordance with this belief. Essentially, therefore, there is nothing incredible about their subsequent behavior and conduct.

3. PLOTTING A RIOT

If one spreads out the span of one's right hand and puts the palm down on the center of a map of Los Angeles County with the thumb pointing north, at the tip of each finger will be found a community where the population is predominantly Mexican. In each of these neighborhoods, moreover, a majority of the juveniles living in the area will be found to be first-generation Mexican-Americans, sons and daughters of the Mexican immigrants who came to Southern California during the 1920's.

Now, if one believes that Mexicans have an inherent desire to commit crimes of violence, the logical first step, in a crime prevention program, is to arrest all the people living in these areas. Unfortunately for the practice of this cosy little theory, there are well over a hundred thousand people living in these areas who are of Mexican descent. The maximum capacity of the Los Angeles jails being somewhat under this figure, it therefore becomes necessary to proceed on a more selective basis. If one group of Mexicans, say, the young people, could be selected for token treatment, and if sufficient arrests could be made from this group, perhaps this would serve as an example to all Mexicans to restrain their inborn criminal desires. . . .

If this sounds a bit fantastic, consider the following letter which Captain Joseph Reed sent to his superior on August 12, 1942:

C. B. Horrall,
Chief of Police.
Sir:

The Los Angeles Police Department in conjunction with the Sheriff, California Highway Patrol, the Monterey, Montebello, and Alhambra Police Departments, conducted a drive on Mexican gangs throughout Los Angeles County on the nights of August 10th and 11th. All persons suspected of gang activities were stopped. Approximately 600 persons were brought in. There were approximately 175 arrested for having knives, guns, chains, dirks, daggers, or *any other implement that might have been used in assault* cases. . . .

Present plans call for drastic action. . . .

Respectfully,
JOSEPH F. REED
Administrative Assistant

(Emphasis added.)

On the nights in question, August 10 and 11, 1942, the police selected the neighborhoods which lay at our fingertips on the maps and then blockaded the main streets running through these neighborhoods. All cars containing Mexican occupants, entering or leaving the neighborhoods, were stopped. The occupants were then ordered to the sidewalks where they were searched. With the occupants removed, other officers searched the cars for weapons or other illicit goods.

On the face of it, the great raid was successful, for six hundred people were arrested. The charges? Suspicion of assault, suspicion of robbery, suspicion of auto thefts, suspicion of this, suspicion of that. Of the six hundred taken into custody, about 175 were held on various charges, principally for the possession of "knives, guns, chains, dirks, daggers, or any other implement that might have been used in assault cases." This is a broad statement, indeed, but it is thoroughly in keeping with the rest of this deadly serious farce. For these "other" implements consisted, of course, of hammers, tire irons, jack handles, wrenches, and other tools found in the cars. In fact, the arrests seem to have been predicated on the assumption that all law-abiding citizens belong to one or another of the various automobile clubs and, therefore, do not need to carry their own tools and accessories.

As for those arrested, taking the names in order, we have, among those first listed, Tovar, Marquez, Perez, Villegas, Tovar, Querrero, Holguín, Rochas, Aguilera, Ornelas, Atilano, Estrella, Saldana, and so on. Every name on the long list was obviously either Mexican or Spanish and therefore, according to the Ayres Report, the name of a potential criminal. The whole procedure, in fact, was entirely logical and consistent once the assumptions in the report were taken as true.

Harry Braverman, a member of the Grand Jury who had opposed returning the indictment in the Sleepy Lagoon case, was greatly disturbed by these mass dragnet raids and by the manner in which the Grand Jury was being used as a sounding board to air the curious views of Captain

Ayres. Accordingly, he arranged for an open Grand Jury hearing on October 8, 1942, at which some of the damage caused by the Ayres Report might, if possible, be corrected. At this hearing, Dr. Harry Hoijer of the University of California; Guy T. Nunn of the War Manpower Commission (who later wrote, on his return from a German prison camp, a fine novel about Mexican-Americans called *White Shadows*); Manuel Aguilar of the Mexican consulate; Oscar R. Fuss of the CIO; Walter H. Laves of the Office of the Coordinator of Inter-American Affairs and myself all endeavored to create in the minds of the Grand Jurors at least a doubt that everything that Captain Ayres had said was true. To appreciate the incomparable irony of this situation, suffice it to say that here we were having to defend "the biological character" of the Mexican people months after Mexico had declared war on Germany, Italy, and Japan on May 22, 1942; after the first shipment of 1,500 Mexican workers—the vanguard of an army of 100,000 workers that Mexico sent to this country during the war—had arrived in California on September 29, 1942; and after Henry Wallace, then vice-president of the United States, had declared to a great Sixteenth of September celebration in Los Angeles that "California has become a fusion ground for the two cultures of the Americas. . . ."

On the occasion of this hearing, representatives of the coordinator of Inter-American Affairs made the rounds of the newspapers, calling attention to the serious harm being done the war effort and the Good Neighbor Policy by the newspaper campaign against resident Mexicans. In the interest of winning the war, these officials had suggested, there might well be some abatement in this campaign: we were fighting the Germans and the Japanese, not the Mexicans. With stated reluctance, and obvious misgivings, the newspapers promised to behave and, from October to December, 1942, the great hue and cry either disappeared from the press or was conducted *sotto voce*. That the campaign had seriously interfered with the war effort, there can be no doubt. When the Sleepy Lagoon defendants were convicted, for example, the Axis radio beamed the following message in Spanish to the people of Latin America:

> In Los Angeles, California, the so-called City of the Angels, twelve Mexican boys were found guilty today of a single murder and five others were convicted of assault growing out of the same case. The 360,000 Mexicans of Los Angeles are reported up in arms over this Yankee persecution. The concentration camps of Los Angeles are said to be overflowing with members of this persecuted minority. This is justice for you, as practiced by the "Good Neighbor," Uncle Sam, a justice that demands seventeen victims for one crime. (Axis broadcast, January 13, 1943.)

The representatives of the Coordinator's Office urged the newspapers in particular to cease featuring the word "Mexican" in stories of crime. The press agreed, but, true to form, quickly devised a still better technique for baiting Mexicans. "Zoot-suit" and "Pachuco" began to appear in the newspapers with such regularity that, within a few months, they had completely replaced the word "Mexican." Any doubts the public may have harbored concerning the meaning and application of these terms were removed after January 13, 1943, for they were consistently applied, and only applied, to Mexicans. Every Mexican youngster arrested, no matter how trivial the offense and regardless of his ultimate guilt or innocence, was photographed with some such caption as "Pachuco Gangster" or "Zoot-suit Hoodlum." At the Grand Jury hearing on October 8, 1942, some of us had warned the community that, if this press campaign continued, it would ultimately lead to mass violence. But these warnings were ignored. After the jury had returned its verdict in the Sleepy Lagoon case and Mr. Rockefeller's emissaries had left Los Angeles, the campaign, once again, began to be stepped up.

On the eve of the zoot-suit riots in Los Angeles, therefore, the following elements were involved: first, the much-publicized "gangs," composed of youths of Mexican descent, rarely over eighteen years of age; second, the police, overwhelmingly non-Mexican in descent, acting in reliance on the theories of Captain Ayres; third, the newspapers, caught in a dull period when there was only a major war going on, hell-bent to find a local scapegoat, "an internal enemy," on which the accumulated frustrations of a population in wartime could be vented; fourth, the people of Los Angeles, Mexican and non-Mexican, largely unaware that they were sponsoring, by their credulity and indifference, a private war; and, fifth, the men of the armed services stationed in or about the city, strangers to Los Angeles, bored, getting the attitudes of the city from its flamboyant press. They entered the plot, however, only at the climax. Knowing already of the attitude of the police and of the press, let's examine the Mexican "gang."

4. THE ORIGIN OF "PACHUQUISMO"

In Los Angeles, in 1942, if a boy wished to become known as a "gangster" he had a choice of two methods. The first, and by far the more difficult, was to commit a crime and be convicted. The second method was easier, although it was largely restricted to a particular group. If you were born of Mexican parents financially unable to move out of certain specific slum areas, you could be a gangster from birth without having to go to all the trouble of committing a crime. For Los Angeles had revised the old saying that "boys will be boys" to read "boys, if Mexican, will be gangsters." The only reservation to be noted, of course, consists in the definition of a "gang."

Adolescent boys in the United States are among the most gregarious groups in our society. American boys traditionally "hang out with the gang." Their association is based, of course, on common interests. The boys in the "gang" may go to the same school, live in the same neighborhood or have the same hobbies. There is, however, a difference in the degree to which the members of various "gangs" feel a sense of solidarity. A boy who belongs to a club for those who make model airplanes may have little loyalty toward the club. It serves a particular interest and beyond this interest he must have other associations. But a "gang" of Mexican boys in Los Angeles is held together by a set of associations so strong that they outweigh, or often outweigh, such influences as the home, the school, and the church.

The various teen-age clubs in the better part of Los Angeles often get together and spend an evening dancing in Hollywood. But the respectable places of entertainment will often refuse to admit Mexicans. The boys and girls who belong to the "Y" often make up theater parties. But the "best" theaters in Los Angeles have been known to refuse admission to Mexicans. Many youngsters like to go rollerskating or iceskating; but the skating rink is likely to have a sign reading "Wednesdays reserved for Negroes and Mexicans." Wherever the Mexicans go, outside their own districts, there are signs, prohibitions, taboos, restrictions. Learning of this "iron curtain" is part of the education of every Mexican-American boy in Los Angeles. Naturally it hits them hardest at the time when they are trying to cope with the already tremendous problems of normal adolescence. The first chapters are learned almost on the day they enter school, and, as time passes and the world enlarges, they learn other chapters in this bitter and peremptory lesson.

Most of the boys are born and grow up in neighborhoods which are almost entirely Mexican in composition and so it is not until they reach school age that they become aware of the social status of Mexicans. Prior to entering school, they are aware, to a limited extent, of differences in background. They know that there are other groups who speak English and that they will some day have to learn it, too. But it is at school that they first learn the differences in social rank and discover that they are at the bottom of the scale. Teachers in the "Mexican" schools are often unhappy about their personal situation. They would much rather be teaching in the sacrosanct halls of some Beverly Hills or Hollywood school. Assignment to a school in a Mexican district is commonly regarded, in Los Angeles, as the equivalent of exile. Plagued by teachers who present "personality problems," school administrators have been known to "solve" the problem by assigning the teacher to "Siberia." Neither in personnel nor equipment are these schools what they should be, although a definite attempt to improve them is now under way.

Discovering that his status approximates the second-rate school has the effect of instilling in the Mexican boy a resentment directed against the school, and all it stands for. At the same time, it robs him of a desire to turn back to his home. For the home which he knew prior to entering school no longer exists. All of the attitudes he has learned at school now poison his attitude toward the home. Turning away from home and school, the Mexican boy has only one place where he can find security and status. This is the gang made up of boys exactly like himself, who live in the same neighborhood, and who are going through precisely the same distressing process at precisely the same time.

Such is the origin of the juvenile gangs about which the police and the press of Los Angeles were so frenetically concerned. Gangs of this character are familiar phenomena in any large city. In Los Angeles, twenty years ago, similar gangs were made up of the sons of Russian Molokan immigrants. They have existed in Los Angeles since the city really began to grow, around 1900, and they will continue to exist as long as society creates them. Thus "the genesis of pachuquismo," as Dr. George Sanchez has pointed out, "is an open book to those who care to look into the situations facing Spanish-speaking people" in the Southwest. In fact, they were pointed out over a decade ago in an article which Dr. Sanchez wrote for the *Journal of Applied Psychology*.[1]

The *pachuco* gang differs from some other city gangs only in the degree to which it constitutes a more tightly knit group. There is more to the *pachuco* gang than just having a good time together. The *pachucos* suffer discrimination together and nothing makes for cohesiveness more effectively than a commonly shared hostility. Knowing that both as individuals and as a group they are not welcome in many parts of the city, they create their own world and try to make it as self-sufficient as possible.

While the fancier "palladiums" have been known to refuse them, even when they have had the price of admission, there are other dance halls, not nearly so fancy, that make a business of catering to their needs. It should be noted, however, that Mexican boys have never willingly accepted these inferior accommodations and the inferior status they connote. Before they have visited the "joints" on Skid Row, they have first tried to pass through the palatial foyers on Sunset Boulevard. When they finally give up, they have few illusions left about their native land.

It should also be remembered that *pachuquismo* followed a decade of important social change for Mexicans in Los Angeles. During the depression years, thousands of Mexicans had been repatriated and those remaining began to adjust to a new mode of existence. The residence of those who had been migratory workers tended to become stabilized, for residence was a condition to obtaining relief. Thousands of Mexicans were replaced, during these same years, by so-called Okies and Arkies in the migratory labor movement. A greater stability of residence implied more regular schooling, better opportunities to explore the intricacies of urban life, and, above all, it created a situation in which the Mexican communities began to impinge on the larger Anglo-American community.

During the depression years, one could watch the gradual encroachment of Mexicans upon downtown Los Angeles. Stores and shops catering to Mexican trade crossed First Street, moving out from the old Plaza district and gradually infiltrated as far south as Third or Fourth streets. The motion picture theaters in this neighborhood, by far the oldest in the city, began to "go Mexican" as did the ten-cent stores, the shops, and the small retail stores. Nowadays the old Mason Opera House, in this district, has become a Mexican theater. Being strangers to an urban environment, the first generation had tended to respect the boundaries of the Mexican communities. But the second generation was lured far beyond these boundaries into the downtown shopping districts, to the beaches, and above all, to the "glamor" of Hollywood. It was this generation of Mexicans, the *pachuco* generation, that first came to the general notice and attention of the Anglo-American population.

[1] *See* comments by Dr. George Sanchez, *Common Ground*, Autumn, 1943, pp. 13–20.

Thus concurrently with the growth of the gangs there developed a new stereotype of the Mexican as the "*pachuco* gangster," the "zoot-suiter." Many theories have been advanced and reams of paper wasted in an attempt to define the origin of the word "*pachuco*." Some say that the expression originally came from Mexico and denoted resemblance to the gaily costumed people living in a town of this name; others have said that it was first applied to border bandits in the vicinity of El Paso. Regardless of the origin of the word, the *pachuco* stereotype was born in Los Angeles. It was essentially an easy task to fix this stereotype on Mexican youngsters. Their skin was enough darker to set them apart from the average *Angeleno*. Basically bilingual, they spoke both Spanish and English with an accent that could be mimicked by either or both groups. Also there was an age-old heritage of ill-will to be exploited and a social atmosphere in which Mexicans, as Mexicans, had long been stereotyped. The *pachuco* also had a uniform—the zoot-suit—which served to make him conspicuous.

Mexican-American boys never use the term "zoot-suit," preferring the word "drapes" in speaking of their clothes. "Drapes" began to appear in the late thirties and early forties. In general appearance, "drapes" resemble the zoot-suits worn by Negro youngsters in Harlem, although the initiated point out differences in detail and design. Called "drapes" or "zoot-suit," the costume is certainly one of the most functional ever designed. It is worn by boys who engage in a specific type of activity, namely, a style of dancing which means disaster to the average suit. The trouser cuffs are tight around the ankles in order not to catch on the heels of the boy's quickly moving feet. The shoulders of the coat are wide, giving plenty of room for strenuous arm movements; and the shoes are heavy, serving to anchor the boy to the dance floor as he spins his partner around. There is nothing esoteric about these "sharp" sartorial get-ups in underprivileged groups, quite apart from their functional aspect. They are often used as a badge of defiance by the rejected against the outside world and, at the same time, as a symbol of belonging to the inner group. It is at once a sign of rebellion and a mark of belonging. It carries prestige.[2]

For the boys, peg-topped pants with pleats, high waists up under the armpits, the long loose-backed coat, thick-soled bluchers, and the duck-tailed haircut; for the girls, black huaraches, short black skirt, long black stockings, sweater, and high pompadour. Many of the boys saved their money for months to buy one of these get-ups. The length of the coat and the width of the shoulders became as much a mark of prestige as the merit badges of the Boy Scout. But, it should be noted, that the zoot-suit was not universal among Mexican boys. Some never adopted it, while others never adopted it completely. There were all varieties of acceptance. The newspapers, of course, promptly seized upon the zoot-suit as "a badge of crime." But as one zoot-suited boy said to me, with infallible logic, "If I were a gangster, would I wear a zoot-suit so that everyone would know I was a

---

[2] *See* comments by Albert Deutsch, *PM*, June 14, 1943; *Racial Digest*, July, 1943, pp. 3–7; New York *Times*, June 11, 1943.

gangster? No, I'd maybe dress like a priest or like everyone else; but no zoot-suit."

With the backdrops all in place, the curtain now rolls up on an interesting tableau in Our City the Queen of the Angels which was founded in the year 1781 by Mexican *pobladores* under the direction of Spanish officers who wore costumes far more outlandish than those worn by the most flamboyant *pachucos*.

An American Sacred Ceremony

W. LLOYD WARNER

Throughout the early history of the United States, Protestantism was the dominant religion in both the private and public lives of most Americans. While it was true that less than half of the population were members of the church, most public ceremonies gave at least lip service to Protestant Christianity as an integrating factor in American life.

After the middle of the nineteenth century, however, a shift in popular belief took place. More and more of the immigrant population practiced non-Protestant forms of religion. Most of the new immigrants were Roman Catholic, with a significant sprinkling of Jews. The strains in the national life and ethos that resulted from the new immigration necessitated that positive steps be taken to prevent the disintegration of certain aspects of the national life. One way this was achieved was through the development of national symbols to which all Americans, regardless of religious belief, could give assent.

Some of these symbols already existed in the form of political heroes and patriotic holidays; others came into existence as a result of crises in the nation's life that tended to bring people of diverse backgrounds together in defense of their common life. As the following essay points out, in the past, war has served this function admirably. When war breaks out, the government calls on religious leaders to sanction the national cause, and the religious bodies throw their considerable influence into justifying the conflict and praying for victory.

Remembering these wars, then, becomes an exercise in national piety. All citizens, regardless of church or sect, come together in celebration of what Robert Bellah has called "civil religion." Civil religion uses the symbols and practices of organized religion in order to honor the nation. Involved in this effort, leaders of otherwise competing and contradictory religious bodies celebrate the common national life.

These practices led in the 1950s to considerable speculation among scholars as to whether a new religion had sprung up in America. This religion was called, among other things, "faith in faith," and "religion of the American way of life." What was happening, in fact, was a tremendous upsurge in membership in religious organizations that caused many to believe a new day had arrived in American religious belief and practice. The rise was probably connected with rapid suburbanization of the population and an almost desperate attempt to create normalcy in the aftermath of the tremendous dislocations of the Second World War. Today there seems to be a precipitous decline in membership in many of these same churches.

In the essay reprinted below, W. Lloyd Warner, a social anthropologist who has done an extensive community study of "Yankee

City" (Newburyport, Massachusetts), describes what he calls "an American sacred ceremony." What is in fact taking place is the celebration of a Memorial Day holiday, which leads Warner to comment on the development of unifying symbols for American life that take on religious overtones in such celebrations.

For young people reared in the divisive years of the American-Indochina War, this type of celebration may seem strange indeed, for this latest of America's wars did for the American people none of the things that Warner suggests wars do. However, his thesis remains valid for most of America's history, and one wonders whether there isn't some functional equivalent to war that could bring the people together, even symbolically.

MEMORIAL DAY AND SYMBOLIC BEHAVIOR

Every year in the springtime when the flowers are in bloom and the trees and shrubs are most beautiful, citizens of the Union celebrate Memorial Day. Over most of the United States it is a legal holiday. Being both sacred and secular, it is a holy day as well as a holiday and is accordingly celebrated.

For some it is part of a long holiday of pleasure, extended outings, and great athletic events; for others it is a sacred day when the dead are mourned and sacred ceremonies are held to express their sorrow; but for most Americans, especially in the smaller cities, it is both sacred and secular. They feel the sacred importance of the day when they, or members of their family, participate in the ceremonies; but they also enjoy going for an automobile trip or seeing or reading about some important athletic event staged on Memorial Day. This chapter will be devoted to the analysis and interpretation of Memorial Day to learn its meanings as an American sacred ceremony, a rite that evolved in this country and is native to it.

Memorial Day originated in the North shortly after the end of the Civil War as a sacred day to show respect for the Union soldiers who were killed in the War Between the States. Only since the last two wars has it become a day for all who died for their country. In the South only now are they beginning to use it to express southern respect and obligation to the nation's soldier dead.

Memorial Day is an important occasion in the American ceremonial calendar and as such is a unit of this larger ceremonial system of symbols. Close examination discloses that it, too, is a symbol system in its own right existing within the complexities of the larger one.

Symbols include such familiar things as written and spoken words,

"An American Sacred Ceremony." From *America: Dream and Reality* by W. Lloyd Warner (Chicago: University of Chicago Press, 1953), pp. 1–26. Copyright 1953 by The University of Chicago. All rights reserved.

religious beliefs and practices, including creeds and ceremonies, the several arts, such familiar signs as the cross and the flag, and countless other objects and acts which stand for something more than that which they are. The red, white, and blue cloth and the crossed sticks in themselves and as objects mean very little, but the sacred meanings which they evoke are of such deep significance to some that millions of men have sacrificed their lives for the first as the Stars and Stripes and for the second as the Christian Cross.

The ceremonial calendar of American society, this yearly round of holidays and holy days, partly sacred and partly secular, but more sacred than secular, is a symbol system used by all Americans. Christmas and Thanksgiving, Memorial Day and the Fourth of July, are days in our ceremonial calendar which allow Americans to express common sentiments about themselves and share their feelings with others on set days pre-established by the society for this very purpose. This calendar functions to draw all people together to emphasize their similarities and common heritage; to minimize their differences; and to contribute to their thinking, feeling, and acting alike. All societies, simple or complex, possess some form of ceremonial calendar, if it be no more than the seasonal alternation of secular and ceremonial periods, such as that used by the Australian aborigines in their yearly cycle.

The integration and smooth functioning of the social life of a modern community are very difficult because of its complexity. American communities are filled with churches, each claiming great authority and each with its separate sacred symbol system. Many of them are in conflict, and all of them in opposition to one another. Many associations, such as the Masons, the Odd Fellows, and the like, have sacred symbol systems which partly separate them from the whole community. The traditions of foreign-born groups contribute to the diversity of symbolic life. The evidence is clear for the conflict among these systems.

It is the thesis of this chapter that the Memorial Day ceremonies and subsidiary rites (such as those of Armistice Day) of today, yesterday, and tomorrow are rituals of a sacred symbol system which functions periodically to unify the whole community, with its conflicting symbols and its opposing, autonomous churches and associations. It is contended here that in the Memorial Day ceremonies the anxieties which man has about death are confronted with a system of sacred beliefs about death which gives the individuals involved and the collectivity of individuals a feeling of well-being. Further, the feeling of triumph over death by collective action in the Memorial Day parade is made possible by re-creating the feeling of well-being and the sense of group strength and individual strength in the group power, which is felt so intensely during the wars when the veterans' associations are created and when the feeling so necessary for the Memorial Day's symbol system is originally experienced.

Memorial Day is a cult of the dead which organizes and integrates the various faiths and national and class groups into a sacred unity. It is a cult of the dead organized around the community cemeteries. Its principal themes are those of the sacrifice of the soldier dead for the living and the obligation of the living to sacrifice their individual purposes for the good of the group, so that they, too, can perform their spiritual obligations.

MEMORIAL DAY CEREMONIES

We shall first examine the Memorial Day ceremony of an American town for evidence. The sacred symbolic behavior of Memorial Day, in which scores of the town's organizations are involved, is ordinarily divided into four periods. During the year separate rituals are held by many of the associations for their dead, and many of these activities are connected with later Memorial Day events. In the second phase, preparations are made during the last three or four weeks for the ceremony itself, and some of the associations perform public rituals. The third phase consists of the scores of rituals held in all the cemeteries, churches, and halls of the associations. These rituals consist of speeches and highly ceremonialized behavior. They last for two days and are climaxed by the fourth and last phase, in which all the separate celebrants gather in the center of the business district on the afternoon of Memorial Day. The separate organizations, with their members in uniform or with fitting insignia, march through the town, visit the shrines and monuments of the hero dead, and, finally, enter the cemetery. Here dozens of ceremonies are held, most of them highly symbolic and formalized. Let us examine the actual ritual behavior in these several phases of the ceremony.

The two or three weeks before the Memorial Day ceremonies are usually filled with elaborate preparations by each participating group. Meetings are held, and patriotic pronouncements are sent to the local paper by the various organizations which announce what part each organization is to play in the ceremony. Some of the associations have Memorial Day processions, memorial services are conducted, the schools have patriotic programs, and the cemeteries are cleaned and repaired. Graves are decorated by families and associations and new gravestones purchased and erected. The merchants put up flags before their establishments, and residents place flags above their houses.

All these events are recorded in the local paper, and most of them are discussed by the town. The preparation of public opinion for an awareness of the importance of Memorial Day and the rehearsal of what is expected from each section of the community are done fully and in great detail. The latent sentiments of each individual, each family, each church, school, and association for its own dead are thereby stimulated and related to the sentiments for the dead of the nation.

One of the important events observed in the preparatory phase in the community studied occurred several days before Memorial Day, when the man who had been the war mayor wrote an open letter to the commander of the American Legion. It was published in the local paper. He had a city-wide reputation for patriotism. He was an honorary member of the American Legion. The letter read: "Dear Commander: The approaching Poppy Day [when Legion supporters sold poppies in the town] brings to my mind a visit to the war zone in France on Memorial Day, 1925, reaching Belleau Wood at about 11 o'clock. On this sacred spot we left floral tributes in memory of our town's boys—Jonathan Dexter and John Smith, who here had made the supreme sacrifice, that the principle that 'might makes right' should not prevail."

Three days later the paper in a front-page editorial told its readers: "Next Saturday is the annual Poppy Day of the American Legion. Everybody should wear a poppy on Poppy Day. Think back to those terrible days when the red poppy on Flanders Field symbolized the blood of our boys slaughtered for democracy." The editor here explicitly states the symbolism involved.

Through the early preparatory period of the ceremony, through all its phases and in every rite, the emphasis in all communities is always on sacrifice—the sacrifice of the lives of the soldiers of the city, willingly given for democracy and for their country. The theme is always that the gift of their lives was voluntary; that it was freely given and therefore above selfishness or thoughts of self-preservation; and, finally, that the "sacrifice on the altars of their country" was done for everyone. The red poppy became a separate symbol from McCrae's poem "In Flanders Fields." The poem expressed and symbolized the sentiments experienced by the soldiers and people of the country who went through the first war. The editor makes the poppy refer directly to the "blood of the boys slaughtered." In ritual language he then recites the names of some of the city's "sacrificed dead," and "the altars" (battles) where they were killed. "Remember Dexter and Smith killed at Belleau Wood," he says. "Remember O'Flaherty killed near Château-Thierry, Stulavitz killed in the Bois d'Ormont, Kelley killed at Côte de Châtillon, Jones near the Bois de Montrebeaux, Kilnikap in the St-Mihiel offensive, and the other brave boys who died in camp or on stricken fields. Remember the living boys of the Legion on Saturday."

The names selected by the editor covered most of the ethnic and religious groups of the community. They included Polish, Russian, Irish, French-Canadian, and Yankee names. The use of such names in this context emphasized the fact that the voluntary sacrifice of a citizen's life was equalitarian. They covered the top, middle, and bottom of the several classes. The newspapers throughout the country each year print similar lists, and their editorials stress the equality of sacrifice by all classes and creeds.

The topic for the morning services of the churches on the Sunday before Memorial Day ordinarily is the meaning of Memorial Day to the town and to the people as Christians. All the churches participate. Because of space limitations, we shall quote from only a few sermons from one Memorial Day to show the main themes; but observations of Memorial Day behavior since the second World War show no difference in the principal themes expressed before and after the war started. Indeed, some of the words are almost interchangeable. The Rev. Hugh McKellar chose as his text, "Be thou faithful until death." He said:

"Memorial Day is a day of sentiment and when it loses that, it loses all its value. We are all conscious of the danger of losing that sentiment.

What we need today is more sacrifice, for there can be no achievement without sacrifice. There are too many out today preaching selfishness. Sacrifice is necessary to a noble living. In the words of our Lord, 'Whosoever shall save his life shall lose it and whosoever shall lose his life in My name shall save it.' It is only those who sacrifice personal gain and will to power and personal ambition who ever accomplish anything for their nation. Those who expect to save the nation will not get wealth and power for themselves.

"Memorial Day is a religious day. It is a day when we get a vision of the unbreakable brotherhood and unity of spirit which exists and still exists, no matter what race or creed or color, in the country where all men have equal rights."

The minister of the Congregational Church spoke with the voice of the Unknown Soldier to emphasize his message of sacrifice:

"If the spirit of the Unknown Soldier should speak, what would be his message? What would be the message of a youth I knew myself who might be one of the unknown dead? I believe he would speak as follows: 'It is well to remember us today, who gave our lives that democracy might live, we know something of sacrifice.' "

The two ministers in different language expressed the same theme of the sacrifice of the individual for national and democratic principles. One introduces divine sanction for this sacrificial belief and thereby succeeds in emphasizing the theme that the loss of an individual's life rewards him with life eternal. The other uses one of our greatest and most sacred symbols of democracy and the only very powerful one that came out of the first World War—the Unknown Soldier. The American Unknown Soldier is Everyman; he is the perfect symbol of equalitarianism.

There were many more Memorial Day sermons, most of which had this same theme. Many of them added the point that the Christian God had given his life for all. That afternoon during the same ceremony the cemeteries, memorial squares named for the town's dead, the lodge halls, and the churches had a large number of rituals. Among them was the "vacant chair." A row of chairs decorated with flags and wreaths, each with the name of a veteran who had died in the last year, was the center of this ceremony held in a church. Most of the institutions were represented in the ritual. We shall give only a small selection from the principal speech:

"Now we come to pay tribute to these men whose chairs are vacant, not because they were eminent men, as many soldiers were not, but the tribute we pay is to their attachment to the great cause. We are living in the most magnificent country on the face of the globe, a country planted and fertilized by a Great Power, a power not political or economic but religious and educational, especially in the North. In the South they had settlers who were there in pursuit of gold, in search of El Dorado, but the North was settled by people seeking religious principles and education."

In a large city park, before a tablet filled with the names of war dead, one of our field workers shortly after the vacant-chair rite heard a speaker in the memorial ritual eulogize the two great symbols of American unity —Washington and Lincoln. The orator said:

"No character except the Carpenter of Nazareth has ever been honored the way Washington and Lincoln have been in New England. Virtue, freedom from sin, and righteousness were qualities possessed by Washington and Lincoln, and in possessing these characteristics both were true Americans, and we would do well to emulate them. Let us first be true Americans. From these our friends beneath the sod we receive their message, 'Carry on.' Though your speaker will die, the fire and spark will carry on. Thou are not conqueror, death, and thy pale flag is not advancing."

In all the other services, the same themes were used in the speeches, most of which were in ritualized, oratorical language, or were expressed in the ceremonials themselves. Washington, the father of his country, first in war and peace, had devoted his life not to himself but to his country. Lincoln had given his own life, sacrificed on the altar of his country. Most of the speeches implied or explicitly stated that divine guidance was involved and that these mundane affairs had supernatural implications. They stated that the revered dead had given the last ounce of devotion in following the ideals of Washington and Lincoln and the Unknown Soldier and declared that these same principles must guide us, the living. The beliefs and values of which they spoke referred to a world beyond the natural. Their references were to the supernatural.

On Memorial Day morning the separate rituals, publicly performed, continued. The parade formed in the early afternoon in the business district. Hundreds of people, dressed in their best, gathered to watch the various uniformed groups march in the parade. Crowds collected along the entire route. The cemeteries, carefully prepared for the event, and the graves of kindred covered with flowers and flags and wreaths looked almost gay.

The parade marched through the town to the cemeteries. The various organizations spread throughout the several parts of the graveyards, and rites were performed. In the Greek quarter ceremonies were held; others were performed in the Polish and Russian sections; the Boy Scouts held a memorial rite for their departed; the Sons and Daughters of Union Veterans went through a ritual, as did the other men's and women's organizations. All this was part of the parade in which everyone from all parts of the community could and did participate.

Near the end of the day all the men's and women's organizations assembled about the roped-off grave of General Fredericks. The Legion band played. A minister uttered a prayer. The ceremonial speaker said:

"We meet to honor those who fought, but in so doing we honor ourselves. From them we learn a lesson of sacrifice and devotion and of accountability to God and honor. We have an inspiration for the future today—our character is strengthened—this day speaks of a better and greater devotion to our country and to all that our flag represents."

After the several ceremonies in the Elm Hill Cemetery, the parade reformed and started the march back to town, where it broke up. The firing squad of the American Legion fired three salutes, and a bugler sounded the "Last Post" at the cemetery entrance as they departed. This, they said, was a "general salute for all the dead in the cemetery."

Here we see people who are Protestant, Catholic, Jewish, and Greek Orthodox involved in a common ritual in a graveyard with their common dead. Their sense of separateness was present and expressed in the different ceremonies, but the parade and the unity gained by doing everything at one time emphasized the oneness of the total group. Each ritual also stressed the fact that the war was an experience where everyone sacrificed and some died, not as members of a separate group, but as citizens of a whole community.

The full significance of the unifying and integrative character of the Memorial Day ceremony—the increasing convergence of the multiple and diverse events through the several stages into a single unit in which the many become the one and all the living participants unite in the one community of the dead—is best seen in Figure 1. It will be noticed that the

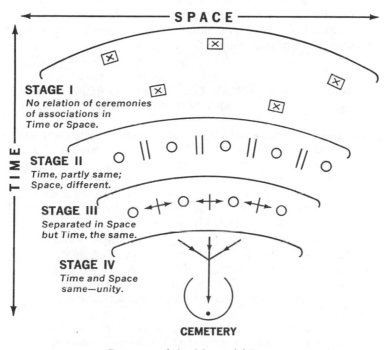

FIG. 1   Progress of the Memorial Day ceremony

horizontal extension at the top of the figure represents space; and the vertical dimension, time. The four stages of the ceremony are listed on the left-hand side, the arrows at the bottom converging and ending in the cemetery. The longer and wider area at the top with the several well-spread rectangles represents the time and space diversities of stage 1; the interconnected circles in stage 3 show the closer integration that has been achieved by this time.

During stage 1 it will be recalled that there is no synchronization of rituals. They occur in each association without any reference to one another. All are separate and diverse in time and space. The symbolic references of the ceremonies emphasize their separateness. In general, this stage is characterized by high diversity, and there is little unity in purpose, time, or space.

Although the ceremonies of the organizations in stage 2 are still separate, they are felt to be within the bounds of the general community organization. There is still the symbolic expression of diversity, but now diversity in a larger unity (see Fig. 1). In stage 3 there are still separate ceremonies but the time during which they are held is the same. Inspection of the chart will show that time and space have been greatly limited since the period of stage 1.

The ceremonies in stage 4 become one in time and one in space. The representatives of all groups are unified into one procession. Thereby, organizational diversity is symbolically integrated into a unified whole. This is not necessarily known to those who participate, but certainly it is felt by them. The chart is designed to symbolize the progressive integration and symbolic unification of the group.

LINCOLN—AN AMERICAN COLLECTIVE REPRESENTATION MADE BY AND FOR THE PEOPLE

Throughout the Memorial Day ceremony there were continual references to Lincoln and his Gettysburg Address. The symbol of Lincoln obviously was of deep significance in the various rituals and to the participants. He loomed over the memorial rituals like some great demigod over the rites of classical antiquity. What is the meaning of the myth of Lincoln to Americans? Why does his life and death as conceived in the myth of Lincoln play such a prominent part in Memorial Day?

Some of the answers are obvious. He was a great war president. He was the President of the United States and was assassinated during the Civil War. Memorial Day grew out of this war. A number of other facts about his life might be added; but for our present purposes the meaning of Lincoln the myth is more important to understand than the objective facts of his life-career.

Lincoln, product of the American prairies, sacred symbol of idealism in the United States, myth more real than the man himself, symbol and fact, was formed in the flow of events which composed the changing cultures of the Middle West. He is the symbolic culmination of America. To understand him is to know much of what America means.

In 1858, when Lincoln ran against Stephen Douglas for the United States Senate, he was Abraham Lincoln, the successful lawyer, the railroad attorney, who was noted throughout the state of Illinois as a man above common ability and of more than common importance. He was a former congressman. He was earning a substantial income. He had married a daughter of the superior classes from Kentucky. His friends were W. D. Green, the president of a railway, a man of wealth; David Davis, a representative of wealthy eastern investors in western property, who was on his way to becoming a millionaire; Jesse Fell, railway promoter; and other men of prominence and prestige in the state. Lincoln dressed like them; he had unlearned many of the habits acquired in childhood from his lowly placed parents and had learned most of the ways of those highly placed men who were now his friends. After the Lincoln-Douglas debates his place as a man of prestige and power was as high as anyone's in the whole state.

Yet in 1860, when he was nominated on the Republican ticket for the presidency of the United States, he suddenly became "Abe Lincoln, the rail splitter," "the rude man from the prairie and the river-bottoms." To this was soon added "Honest Abe," and finally, in death, "the martyred leader" who gave his life that "a nation dedicated to the proposition that all men are created equal" might long endure.

What can be the meaning of this strange transformation?

When Richard Oglesby arrived in the Republican convention in 1860, he cast about for a slogan that would bring his friend, Lincoln, favorable recognition from the shrewd politicians of New York, Pennsylvania, and Ohio. He heard from Jim Hanks, who had known Lincoln as a boy, that Lincoln had once split fence rails. Dick Oglesby, knowing what appeals are most potent in getting the support of the politicians and in bringing out a favorable vote, dubbed Lincoln "the rail splitter." Fence rails were prominently displayed at the convention, to symbolize Lincoln's lowly beginnings. Politicians, remembering the great popular appeal of "Old Hickory," "Tippecanoe and Tyler too," and "The Log Cabin and Cider Jug" of former elections, realized that this slogan would be enormously effective in a national election. Lincoln, the rail splitter, was reborn in Chicago in 1860; and the Lincoln who had become the successful lawyer, intimate of wealthy men, husband of a well-born wife, and man of status was conveniently forgotten.

Three dominant symbolic themes compose the Lincoln image. The first—the theme of the common man—was fashioned in a form pre-established by the equalitarian ideals of a new democracy; to common men there could be no argument about what kind of man a rail splitter is.

"From log cabin to the White House" succinctly symbolizes the second theme of the trilogy which composes Lincoln, the most powerful of American collective representations. This phrase epitomizes the American success story, the rags-to-riches *motif*, and the ideals of the ambitious. As the equal of all men, Lincoln was the representative of the Common Man, as both their spokesman and their kind; and, as the man who had gone "from the log cabin to the White House," he became the superior man, the one who had not inherited but had earned that superior status and thereby proved to everyone that all men could do as he had. Lincoln thereby symbolized the two great collective but opposed ideals of American democracy.

When Lincoln was assassinated, a third powerful theme of our Christian society was added to the symbol being created by Americans to strengthen and adorn the keystone of their national symbol structure. Lincoln's life lay sacrificed on the altar of unity, climaxing a deadly war which proved by its successful termination that the country was one and that all men are created equal. From the day of his death, thousands of sermons and speeches have demonstrated that Lincoln, like Christ, died that all men might live and be as one in the sight of God and man. Christ died that this might be true forever beyond the earth; Lincoln sacrificed his life that this might be true forever on this earth.

When Lincoln died, the imaginations of the people of the eastern seaboard cherished him as the man of the new West and translated him into their hopes for tomorrow, for to them the West was tomorrow. The defeated people of the South, during and after the reconstruction period, fitted him into their dark reveries of what might have been, had this man lived who loved all men. In their bright fantasies, the people of the West, young and believing only in the tomorrow they meant to create, knew Lincoln for what they wanted themselves to be. Lincoln, symbol of equalitarianism, of the social striving of men who live in a social hierarchy, the human leader sacrificed for all men, expresses all the basic values and beliefs of the Middle West and of the United States of America.

Lincoln, the superior man, above all men, yet equal to each, is a mystery beyond the logic of individual calculators. He belongs to the culture and to the social logics of the people for whom contradiction is unimportant and for whom the ultimate tests of truth are in the social structure in which, and for which, they live. Through the passing generations of our Christian culture the Man of the Prairies, formed in the mold of the God-man of Galilee and apotheosized into the man-god of the American people, each year less profane and more sacred, moves securely toward identification with deity and ultimate godhead. In him Americans realize themselves.

THE EFFECT OF WAR ON THE COMMUNITY

A problem of even greater difficulty confronts us on why war provides such an effective context for the creation of powerful national symbols, such as Lincoln, Washington, or Memorial Day. Durkheim gives us an important theoretical lead. He believed that the members of the group felt and became aware of their own group identity when they gathered periodically during times of plenty. For his test case, the Australian aborigines, a hunting and gathering tribe, this was the season when food was plentiful. It was then when social interaction was most intense and the feelings most stimulated.

In modern society interaction, social solidarity, and intensity of feelings ordinarily are greatest in times of war. It would seem likely that such periods might well produce new sacred forms, built, of course, on the foundations of old beliefs. Let us examine the life of American communities in wartime as a possible matrix for such developments.

The most casual survey supplies ample evidence that the effects of war are most varied and diverse as they are reflected in the life of American towns. The immediate effect of war is very great on some towns and very minor on others. During its existence it strengthens the social structure of some and greatly weakens the social systems of others. In some communi-

ties it appears to introduce very little that is new, while in others the
citizens are compelled by force of circumstances to incorporate whole new
experiences into their lives and into the social systems which control them.

In some communities during the second World War there was no decided increase or decrease in the population, and war did not change the
ordinary occupations of their people. Their citizens made but minor adjustments in their daily lives; no basic changes occurred in their institutions. For example, there were many small market towns servicing rural
areas about them where the round of events substantially repeated what
had occurred in all previous years from the time the towns grew to early
maturity. A few of their boys were drafted, possibly the market crops
were more remunerative, and it may be that the weekly paper had a few
more war stories. Changes there were, but they were few and minor in
their effect on the basic social system.

At the other extreme, most drastic and spectacular changes occurred
in the second World War. Small towns that had formerly existed disappeared entirely, and their former localities were occupied by industrial
cities born during the war and fathered by it. Sleepy rural villages were
supplanted by huge industrial populations recruited from every corner of
America. Towns of a few hundred people, traditionally quiet and well
composed, suddenly expanded into brawling young cities with no past and
no future. Market towns became industrial areas. The wives and mothers
in these towns left their homes and joined the newcomers on the assembly
line. The old people went into industry to take jobs they had to learn like
the youngest boy working beside them. This and that boy and some of
their friends left high school because they received tacit encouragement
from their elders and the school authorities to go to work to help in the
war effort. In some communities the whole system of control that had
formerly prevailed ceased to function or was superseded by outside authority. The influx of population was so great that the schools could teach
but a small portion of the children. The police force was inadequate. The
usual recreational life disappeared, to be supplanted by the "taxi dance
hall," "juke joint," "beer hall," and "gambling dive." Institutions such as
the church and lodge almost ceased to function. In some towns one could
drive through miles of trailer camps and small houses pressed against one
another, all recently assembled, where the inhabitants lived in squalid
anonymity with, but not of, the thousands around them. They were an
aggregate of individuals concentrated in one area, but they were not a
community.

We have described only the two extremes of the immediate influence
of war on the community. Soon, however, those communities which had
been little affected by the war felt some of its effects, and those which had
been disorganized developed habits of life which conformed to the ordinary pattern of American town life. The two extremes soon approached
the average.

But wars influence the average town quite differently. Changes take
place, the institutional life is modified, new experiences are felt by the
people, and the townsmen repeatedly modify their behavior to adapt to
new circumstances brought them by new events. These modifications do

not cause social breakdown. The contrary is true. The war activities strengthen the integration of many small communities. The people are more systematically organized into groups where everyone is involved and in which there is an intense awareness of oneness. The town's unity and feeling of autonomy are strengthened by competition in war activities with neighboring communities.

It is in time of war that the average American living in small cities and towns gets his deepest satisfactions as a member of his society. Despite the pessimistic events of 1917, the year when the United States entered the first World War, the people derived deep satisfaction from it, just as they did from the last war. It is a mistake to believe that the American people, particularly the small-towners, hate war to the extent that they derive no satisfaction from it. Verbally and superficially they disapprove of war, but at best this is only partly revealed in their deeper feelings. In simpler terms, their observed behavior reveals that most of them had more real satisfaction out of the second World War, just as they did in the previous one, than they had had in any other period of their lives. The various men's and women's organizations, instead of inventing things to do to keep busy, could choose among activities which they knew were vital and significant to them and to others.

The small-towner then had a sense of significance about himself, about those around him, and about the events which occurred, in a way that he had never felt before. The young man who quit high school during the depression to lounge on the street corner and who was known to be of no consequence to himself or to anyone else in the community became a seasoned veteran, fighting somewhere in the South Pacific—a man obviously with the qualities of a hero (it was believed), willing to give up his life for his country, since he was in its military forces. He and everyone else were playing, and they knew they were playing, a vital and significant role in the present crisis. Everyone was in it. There was a feeling of unconscious well-being, because everyone was doing something to help in the common desperate enterprise in a co-operative rather than in a private spirit. This feeling is often the unconscious equivalent of what people mean when they gather to celebrate and sing "Hail, hail, the gang's all here." It also has something of the deep significance that enters into people's lives only in moments of tragedy.

The strong belief that everyone must sacrifice to win a war greatly strengthens people's sense of their importance. Everyone gives up something for the common good—money, food, tires, scrap, automobiles, or blood for blood banks. All of it is contributed under the basic ideology of common sacrifice for the good of the country. These simple acts of giving by all individuals in the town, by all families, associations, schools, churches, and factories, are given strong additional emotional support by the common knowledge that some of the local young men are representing the town in the military forces of the country. It is known that some of them may be killed while serving their country. They are sacrificing their lives, it is believed, that their country may live. Therefore, all acts of individual giving to help win the war, no matter how small, are made socially significant and add to the strength of the social structure by being treated as sacrifices. The collective effect of these small renunciations, it is believed, is to lessen the number of those who must die on the altars of their country.

Another very strong integrative factor contributed by a war that strengthens the social structure of the small town and city is that petty internal antagonisms are drained out of the group onto the common enemy. The local antagonisms which customarily divide and separate people are largely suppressed. The feelings and psychic energies involved, normally expended in local feuds, are vented on the hated symbols of the enemy. Local groups which may have been excluded from participation in community affairs are given an honored place in the war effort, and the symbols of unity are stressed rather than the separating differences. The religious groups and the churches tend to emphasize the oneness of the common war effort rather than allow their differing theologies and competitive financing to keep them in opposing groups. The strongest pressure to compose their differences is placed against management and labor. (The small number of strikes is eloquent proof of the effectiveness of such pressure.) A common hate of a common enemy, when organized in community activities to express this basic emotion, provides the most powerful mechanism to energize the lives of the towns and to strengthen their feelings of unity. Those who believe that a war's hatreds can bring only evil to psychic life might well ponder the therapeutic and satisfying effects on the minds of people who turn their once private hatreds into social ones and join their townsmen and countrymen in the feeling of sharing this basic emotion in common symbols. Enemies as well as friends should be well chosen, for they must serve as objects for the expression of two emotions basic to man and his social system—hatred and love.

The American Legion and other patriotic organizations give form to the effort to capture the feelings of well-being when the society was most integrated and feelings of unity were most intense. The membership comes from every class, creed, and nationality, for the soldiers came from all of them.

Only a very few associations are sufficiently large and democratic in action to include in their membership men or women from all class levels, all religious faiths, and most, if not all, ethnic groups. Their number could be easily counted on the fingers of one hand. Most prominent among them are the patriotic associations, all of them structural developments from wars which involved the United States. The American Legion is a typical example of the patriotic type. Less than 6 per cent of several hundred associations which have been studied include members from all social classes. Of the remaining 94 per cent, approximately half have representatives from only three classes, or less than three, out of the six discussed in Chapter III. Although the associations which include members from all levels of the community are surprisingly few, those which stress in action as well as in words such other principles of democracy as the equality of races, nationalities, and religions are even fewer. Only 5 per cent of the associations are composed of members from the four principal religious faiths in America—Protestant, Catholic, Jewish, and Greek Orthodox— and most of their members come from the lower ranks of the society.

Lincoln and Washington and lesser ritual figures (and ceremonies such as Memorial Day) are the symbolic equivalent of such social institutions as the patriotic societies. They express the same values, satisfy the same social needs, and perform similar functions. All increase the social solidarity of a complex and heterogeneous society.

HOW SUCH CEREMONIES FUNCTION
IN THE COMMUNITY

Memorial Day and similar ceremonies are one of the several forms of collective representations which Durkheim so brilliantly defined and interpreted in *The Elementary Forms of the Religious Life*. He said: "Religious representations are collective representations which express collective realities." Religious collective representations are symbol systems which are composed of beliefs and rites which relate men to sacred beings. Beliefs are "states of opinion and consist in representations"; rites are "determined modes of action" which are expressions of, and refer to, religious belief. They are *visible* signs (symbols) of the invisible belief. The visible rite of baptism, for example, may express invisible beliefs about cleansing the newborn infant of sin and relating him to the Christian community.

Ceremonies, periodically held, serve to impress on men their social nature and make them aware of something beyond themselves which they feel and believe to be sacred. This intense feeling of belonging to something larger and more powerful than themselves and of having part of this within them as part of them is symbolized by the belief in sacred beings, which is given a visual symbol by use of designs which are the emblems of the sacred entities, e.g., the Cross of the Christian churches.

That which is beyond, yet part of, a person is no more than the awareness on the part of individuals and the collectivity of individuals of their participation in a social group. *The religious symbols, as well as the secular ones, must express the nature of the social structure of the group of which they are a part and which they represent.* The beliefs in the gods and the symbolic rites which celebrate their divinity are no more than men collectively worshiping their own images—their own, since they were made by themselves and fashioned from their experiences among themselves.

We said earlier that the Memorial Day rites of American towns are sacred collective representations and a modern cult of the dead. They are a cult because they consist of a system of sacred beliefs and dramatic rituals held by a group of people who, when they congregate, represent the whole community. They are sacred because they ritually relate the living to sacred things. They are a cult because the members have not been formally organized into an institutionalized church with a defined theology but depend on informal organization to bring into order their sacred activities. They are called a "cult" here, because this term most accurately places them in a class of social phenomena which can be clearly identified in the sacred behavior of non-European societies.

The cult system of sacred belief puts into the organized form of concepts those sentiments about death which are common to everyone in the

community. These sentiments are composed of fears of death, which conflict with the social reassurances that our culture provides us to combat
such anxieties. These assurances, usually acquired in childhood and thereby
carrying some of the authority of the adults who provided them, are a
composite of theology and folk belief. The deep anxieties to which we
refer include anticipation of our deaths, of the deaths or possible deaths
of loved ones, and, less powerfully, of the deaths or possible deaths of those
we know and of men in general.

Each man's church provides him and those of his faith with a set of
beliefs and a way of acting to face these problems; but his church and
those of other men do not equip him with a common set of social beliefs
and rituals which permit him to unite with all his fellows to confront this
common and most feared of all his enemies. The Memorial Day rite and
other subsidiary rituals connected with it form a cult which partially
satisfies this need for common action on a common problem. It dramatically expresses the sentiments of unity of all the living among themselves,
of all the living to all the dead, and of all the living and dead as a group
to the gods. The gods—Catholic, Protestant, and Jewish—lose their sec-
tarian definitions, limitations, and foreignness among themselves and become objects of worship for the whole group and the protectors of everyone.

The unifying and integrating symbols of this cult are the dead. The
graves of the dead are the most powerful of the visible emblems which
unify all the activities of the separate groups of the community. The cemetery and its graves become the objects of sacred rituals which permit opposing organizations, often in conflict, to subordinate their ordinary opposition and to co-operate in expressing jointly the larger unity of the total
community through the use of common rites for their collective dead. The
rites show extraordinary respect for all the dead, but they pay particular
honor to those who were killed in battle "fighting for their country." The
death of a soldier in battle is believed to be a "voluntary sacrifice" by him
on the altar of his country. To be understood, this belief in the sacrifice of
a man's life for his country must be judged first with our general scientific
knowledge of the nature of all forms of sacrifice. It must then be subjected to the principles which explain human sacrifice whenever and
wherever found. More particularly, this belief must be examined with the
realization that these sacrifices occur in a society whose deity was a man
who sacrificed his life for all men.

The principle of the gift is involved. In simple terms, when something
valuable is given, an equally valuable thing must be returned. The speaker
who quoted Scripture in his Memorial Day speech, "Whosoever shall save
his life shall lose it and whosoever shall lose his life in My name shall save
it," almost explicitly stated the feelings and principles involved. Finally, as
we interpret it, the belief in "the sacrifice of American citizens killed in
battle" is a social logic which states in ultimate terms the subordinate relation of the citizen to his country and its collective moral principles.

This discussion has shown that the Memorial Day ceremony consists of a series of separate rituals performed by autonomous groups which
culminate in a procession *of all of them as one group* to the consecrated

area set aside by the living for their dead. In such a place the dead are classed as individuals, for their graves are separate; as members of separate social situations, for they are found in family plots and formal ritual respect is paid them by church and association; and as a collectivity, since they are thought of as "our dead" in most of the ceremonies. The fences surrounding the cemetery place all the dead together and separate all the living from them.

The Memorial Day rite is a cult of the dead, but not just of the dead as such, since by symbolically elaborating sacrifice of human life for the country through, or identifying it with, the Christian church's sacred sacrifice of their god, the deaths of such men also become powerful sacred symbols which organize, direct, and constantly revive the collective ideals of the community and the nation.

Suggestions for Further Reading

Frederick Lewis Allen followed his work on the 1920s, *Only Yesterday*, with a work on the 1930s, *Since Yesterday** (New York, 1940). Two popular histories of the depression that consist partly of recollections are Carolyn Bird, *The Invisible Scar** (New York, 1966), and Robert Bendiner, *Just Around the Corner: A Highly Selective History of the Thirties** (New York, 1967). David A. Shannon has edited a collection of documents detailing the social impact of the depression in *The Great Depression** (Englewood Cliffs, N.J., 1960). See also Milton Meltzer, *Brother, Can You Spare a Dime? The Great Depression, 1929–1933** (New York, 1969). A view of the American workingman during this period is given in Irving Bernstein, *The Lean Years: A History of the American Worker, 1920–1933** (Boston, 1961) and *The Turbulent Years: A History of American Labor, 1933–1941** (Boston, 1970).

The impact of the depression is measured in the essays collected by Bernard Sternsher in *Hitting Home: The Depression in Town and Country** (Chicago, 1970) and *The Negro in Depression and War: Prelude to Revolution** (Chicago, 1970). The long-term impact on children raised during the 1930s is analyzed in a unique longitudinal study by Glen H. Elder, Jr., *The Children of the Great Depression: Social Change in Life Experience* (Chicago, 1974). Robert and Helen Merrill Lynd returned to Muncie, Indiana, to measure the changes wrought by the depression, which they describe in *Middletown in Transition** (New York, 1937). An important demographic shift is outlined by Walter J. Stein in *California and the Dust Bowl Migration** (Westport, Conn., 1973). The classic statement on this westward migration is found, of course, in John Steinbeck, *The Grapes of Wrath** (New York, 1939). For the effects of the depression on Appalachia, see Harry M. Caudill, *Night Comes to the Cumberlands: A Biography of a Depressed Area** (Boston, 1963). Recollections of the depression have been compiled by Studs Terkel in *Hard Times: An Oral History of the Great Depression** (New York, 1970), also available in a two-disc, long-playing record album. Woody Guthrie's autobiography, *Bound for Glory** (New York, 1943), contains a great deal of material on growing up in the dust bowl and bumming around the country in the 1930s.

W. J. Cash, *The Mind of the South** (New York, 1941) is an impressionistic and insightful study of Southern life and culture. Among the studies of race relations in the South, the following were produced in the period of the 1930s and 1940s: John Dollard, *Caste and Class in a Southern Town** (New Haven, Conn., 1937);

* Available in paperback edition.

Allison Davis, B. G. Gardner, and Mary R. Gardner, *Deep South: A Social Anthropological Study of Caste and Class** (Chicago, 1942); Allison Davis and John Dollard, *Children of Bondage** (Washington, 1940); Arthur F. Raper, *Preface to Peasantry** (Chapel Hill, N.C., 1934); and three works by Charles S. Johnson, *Shadow of the Plantation** (Chicago, 1934), *Growing Up in the Black Belt** (Washington, 1941), and *Patterns of Negro Segregation** (New York, 1943). A later community study is Hylan Lewis, *Blackways of Kent** (Chapel Hill, N.C., 1955). Sharecroppers are the subject of a recent study by Pete Daniel, *The Shadow of Slavery: Peonage in the South, 1901–1969** (Champaign-Urbana, Ill., 1972). Ernest J. Gaines' fictional *The Autobiography of Miss Jane Pittman** (New York, 1971), a narration of one woman's experiences, gives a sympathetic and brilliant portrait of black life from the end of the Civil War to the present. Autobiographical episodes about growing up in the depression South are found in Richard Wright, *Black Boy** (New York, 1945). Ralph Ellison, *Invisible Man** (New York, 1952), one of the best American novels of the century thus far, provides useful information about various facets of black life.

For the study of violence in American history, a good place to begin is with Hugh Davis Graham and Ted Robert Gurr, eds., *Violence in America: Historical and Comparative Perspectives,** 2 vols. (Washington, 1969), available in a one-volume paperback edition from Bantam and New American Library. The ghetto disorders of the 1960s are analyzed in David Boesel and Peter H. Rossi, eds., *Cities Under Siege: An Anatomy of Ghetto Riots* (New York, 1971); Robert M. Fogelson, *Violence As Protest: A Study of Riots and Ghettos** (Garden City, N.Y., 1971); and the *Report of the National Advisory Commission on Civil Disorders** (Washington, 1968). Manuel P. Servín has edited a useful set of readings in *The Mexican-Americans: An Awakening Minority** (Beverly Hills, Cal., 1970; rev. ed., 1974). The *Alianza* movement is explored in Peter Nabokov, *Tijerina and the Courthouse Raid** (Albuquerque, 1969). For expressions of the mood of the Mexican-American community, see Stan Steiner, *La Raza: The Mexican Americans** (New York, 1970).

The now-standard work on American religion is Sydney E. Ahlstrom's definitive study *A Religious History of the American People** (New Haven, Conn., 1972). A briefer general work is Martin E. Marty, *Righteous Empire: The Protestant Experience in America** (New York, 1970). Works exploring the interaction of religion and culture in the United States are Sidney Mead, *The Lively Experiment* (New York, 1963), and essays in James W. Smith and A. Leland Jamison, eds., *Religious Perspectives in American Culture** (Princeton, N.J., 1961). Ray H. Abrams, *Preachers Present Arms* (New York, 1933) is a fascinating study of the role ministers played in generating support for the First World War. Robert Bellah describes "civil religion" in his article "Civil Religion in America," *Daedalus* 96 (Winter 1967): 1–21. Works on religion in the 1950s include Will Herberg, *Protestant, Catholic, Jew: An Essay in American Religious Sociology** (Garden City, N.Y., 1956); Gibson Winter, *The Suburban Captivity of the Churches** (New York, 1962); and Gerhard Lenski, *The Religious Factor: A Sociological Study of Religion's Impact on Politics, Economics, and Family Life** (Garden City, N.Y., rev. ed., 1963).

1952–1975
Contemporary Society

The Quality of Suburban Life

HERBERT J. GANS

Although scholars have been writing for some time about the United States as an urban nation, as early as the 1920s, an important new demographic trend was noticed—the increasing growth of suburbs.

Before the advent of mass transportation facilities, the wealthy tended to live in the central city with the outlying areas being populated by the less wealthy and the poor. As the cities continued to grow, however, the older housing began to deteriorate, and the wealthy moved to newer, more fashionable urban neighborhoods, leaving the rundown areas to the working people and the poor. With the arrival of the first breakthrough in urban mass transit—the horse drawn streetcar—some of the more well-to-do citizens decided to abandon the older portions of the city altogether for new, culturally homogeneous settlements on the periphery called suburbs.

In the 1880s, a socialist critic had pointed out that "this modern fashionable suburbanism and exclusiveness is a real grievance to the working class. Had the rich continued to live among the masses, they would with their wealth and influence make our large towns pleasant places to live. . . ." What could not be seen at the time, of course, was the increased prosperity of the working classes that, along with the automobile, would make suburban living available to all except the poorest and most discriminated against among our citizens by the middle of the twentieth century.

By the 1920s, the rate of growth of the suburbs began to exceed that of the cities. The goal of almost every American family seemed to be the purchase of a single-family detached house in a suburban development. While many people moved to the suburbs to escape real or imagined perils in the city, most simply moved there because they found it a more congenial way of life.

Aided by federal legislation, suburban growth rocketed after the Second World War. Veterans Administration loans, Federal Housing Administration mortgage policy, and federally funded highway and road building all contributed to this development. In 1970, the census indicated that more people were living in suburbs—defined as the metropolitan area outside the central city—than in the cities themselves. By 1972, the number of jobs was about equal in both areas. Thus we are rapidly becoming, not an urban nation, but a suburban one.

In the late 1950s, social critics began to find in suburbia the source of many of the ills they saw plaguing American society. And what one sociologist called the myth of suburbia emerged. The fault, the myth ran, lay in the homogeneity of both the population and life-style in the typical suburb. This sameness led to a mass culture and the apparent ethic of conformity that so concerned the critics.

As serious scholarly studies of suburban communities began to appear, however, it became evident that, no matter how much the critics deplored the quality of life in the suburbs, the people who lived there liked it. Herbert J. Gans, of Columbia University, a sociologist who had previously studied an urban working-class community, decided to analyze suburban life firsthand. When the famous builder William Levitt began a new suburban development of lower-middle-class housing near Philadelphia, Gans moved into the community and remained there for two years. During that period, he explored the inhabitants' reasons for moving to the community and their attitudes after settling in. His book, **The Levittowners,** is a result of that study.

Gans' findings are most notable for their refutation of the suburban myth. With few exceptions, the people who moved to Levittown found there what they had expected to find, and consequently the level of satisfaction was quite high. In the selection from his book reprinted below, Gans discusses some of the questions raised by the critics about the relationship between suburban living and mass society. He describes the features of the life-style that have been scrutinized and found wanting by outsiders and reports that, rather than annoying the residents of the community, these very features make the community attractive. In closing, however, Gans notes that one segment of the population—the adolescent group—is generally dissatisfied with suburbia. He warns the residents of suburban communities that some steps should be taken to relieve teen-age discontent in order to prevent an increasingly dangerous generation gap, which might lead to undesirable consequences.

L eading with their assumption of homogeneity and conformity, many critics see the culture of communities like Levittown—those features transcending social life—as marked by sameness, dullness, and blandness. The image of sameness derives from the mass-produced housing, and also from the prevalence of a national and equally mass-produced culture of consumer goods which is extended to characterize the consumers themselves. Part of the critique is tinged with political fear that the national culture and the deleterious effects of conformity may sap the strength of local organizations, which will in turn break down the community social structures that act as barriers between the individual and the state. According to

"The Vitality of Community Culture" (Editor's title: "The Quality of Suburban Life"). From *The Levittowners,* by Herbert J. Gans, pp. 185–219. Copyright © 1967 by Herbert J. Gans. Reprinted by permission of Pantheon Books, a Division of Random House, Inc.

theorists of the mass society, the individual then becomes submissive and subject to demagoguery that can incite mass hysteria and mob action, destroying the checks and balances of a democratic society. This hypothesis, developed originally by Ortega y Gasset, the Spanish conservative philosopher who feared popular democracy, gained prominence during the 1930s when Hitler and Stalin systematically eliminated local organizations to forestall opposition to their plans. In America, this analysis has flowered with the increasing centralization of the federal government, but suburbia is considered particularly susceptible to the dangers of mass society because of the rootlessness and absence of community strength supposedly induced by the large number of Transients.[1] Other observers, less fearful of mass society, stress the blandness of suburban life, which, they fear, is producing dull and apathetic individuals.[2]

These charges are serious and, if accurate, would suggest that suburbia is a danger to American democracy and culture. Most of them, however, are either inaccurate or, when accurate, without the negative consequences attributed to them. Levittown is very much a local community; if anything, it neglects its ties to the larger society more than it should. It is not rootless, even with its Transients, and it is not dull, except to its teenagers. The critics' conclusions stem in part from the previously mentioned class and cultural differences between them and the suburbanites. What they see as blandness and apathy is really a result of the invisibility and home-centeredness of lower middle class culture, and what they consider dullness derives from their cosmopolitan standard for judging communities, which condemns those lacking urban facilities—ranging from museums to ethnic districts—that are favored by the upper middle class.

They also look at suburbia as outsiders, who approach the community with a "tourist" perspective. The tourist wants visual interest, cultural diversity, entertainment, esthetic pleasure, variety (preferably exotic), and emotional stimulation. The resident, on the other hand, wants a comfortable, convenient, and socially satisfying place to live—esthetically pleasing, to be sure, but first and foremost functional for his daily needs. Much of the critique of suburbia as community reflects the critics' disappointment that the new suburbs do not satisfy their particular tourist requirements; that they are not places for wandering, that they lack the charm of a medieval village, the excitement of a metropolis, or the architectural variety of an upper-income suburb. Even so, tourism cuts across all classes. A neighbor, returning from a trip to Niagara Falls, complained bitterly about commercialization, using much the same language as the critics do about suburbia. What he felt about the Falls, however, he did not feel about Levittown.

We are all tourists at one time or another, but most communities can serve both tourist and residential functions only with difficulty. For example, the crowding and nightlife that attract the tourist to Greenwich Village make it uncomfortable for the resident. Although the tourist perspec-

[1] See, e.g., Fromm, pp. 154–163; and Stein, Chaps. 9 and 12.
[2] This charge is made by Keats and, in more qualified and muted tones, by Riesman (1957).

tive is understandable, and even justifiable, it is not by itself a proper criterion for evaluating a community, especially a purely residential one like Levittown. It must be judged first by the quality of community life and culture it offers its residents; the needs of the tourist are secondary.

THE NATIONAL CULTURE AND THE COMMUNITY

To the outside observer, Levittown appears to be a community on which the national American culture has been imprinted so totally as to leave little room for local individuality. The houses express the current national residential style: pseudo-Colonial fronts borrowed from the eighteenth century glued on a variety of single-family house styles developed between the eighteenth and twentieth centuries, and hiding twentieth century interiors. Schools are contemporary, modular, one-story buildings that look like all other new schools. The shopping center is typical too, although the interior is more tastefully designed than most. It consists mainly of branches of large national chains, whose inventory is dominated by prepackaged national brands, and the small centers are no different. The old "Mom and Pop" grocery has been replaced by the "7 to 11" chain, which, as its name indicates, opens early and closes late, but sells only prepackaged goods so that each store can be serviced by a single cashier-clerk. Even the Jewish and Italian foods sold at the "delis" are cut from the loaf of a "pan-ethnic" culture that is now nationally distributed.

A large, partially preplanned residential development must almost inevitably depend on national organizations, since these are the only ones that can afford the initial capital investment and the unprofitable hiatus before the community is large enough to support them properly. This is as true of stores in a new shopping center—which sometimes wait years before they show a profit—as it is of churches and voluntary organizations. In addition, Levittown itself is in some ways a national brand, for the size of Levitt's operation in an industry of small entrepreneurs has made his communities a national symbol of low-price suburbia. This has helped to attract national organizations, as well as Transients who work for large national corporations. When they move into a new metropolitan area, they usually do not know where to find housing, and having heard of Levittown, are likely to look there first. The brand name "Levittown" makes the housing more trustworthy than a small subdivision constructed by an unknown local builder.

Although Levittown would thus seem to be, as much as any community in America, an example of Big Culture, this is only superficially true, for the quality of life in Levittown retains a strictly local and often antinational flavor, exploiting national bodies and resources for strictly local purposes whenever possible. To the visitor, the Levittown houses may look like all other pseudo-Colonial ones in South Jersey, but Levittowners can catalog the features that distinguish their houses from those in nearby subdivisions. The stores may be chains selling brand-name goods, but the managers become involved in local activities and enable local groups to hold bazaars and other fund-raising affairs, including bakesales which compete with store merchandise. The same patterns obtain in voluntary associations and churches. For example, the Boy Scouts are run by an intricate national bureaucracy which sets detailed rules for the activities of local troops. Since the organization must attract children, however, what actually goes on at troop meetings bears little resemblance to the rules, and the less the national office knows, the better for it and the troop leader.

The priority of local concerns is even more emphatic in government, for federal agencies and national party headquarters are viewed mainly as sources of funds and power to be used for local needs. A civil defense agency was set up in Levittown, not to satisfy national regulations, but because the county civil defense director was running for political office. The national program provided him an opportunity to distribute some funds to local communities, which in turn enhanced his political fortunes. Federal funds which came to Levittown for civil defense were used for local police and fire needs as much as possible within the limits of the law. Similarly, when the Township Committee in 1960 invited both Nixon and Kennedy to campaign in Levittown, its purpose was not to support the national candidates of the two parties but to gain publicity for Levittown.

Many Levittowners work in branch offices or factories of national corporations, and their reports about their work and their employers suggest that national directives are often viewed as outlandish and unreasonable, to be sabotaged in favor of local priorities. However much a national corporation may give the appearance of a well-run and thoroughly centralized monolith, in actual fact it is often a shaky aggregate of local baronies. The result is considerable skepticism among Levittowners about the effectiveness and power of national corporations, a skepticism easily extended to all national agencies.

Generally speaking, Levittowners do not take much interest in the national society, and rarely even see its influence on their lives. As long as they are employed, healthy, and able to achieve a reasonable proportion of their personal goals, they have no need for the federal government or any other national agency, and being locals, they do not concern themselves with the world outside their community. Indeed, they might better be described as *sublocals*, for they are home-oriented rather than community-oriented. Although the lower middle class is sometimes said to reject bigness, the Levittowners do not share this feeling. They do not scorn big supermarkets and national brands as do the critics, and although they do not see the big society very clearly, it appears to them as an inept octopus which can only cope with the community through force or bribery. It is opposed not because of its size, but because it is an outsider. When a national service club organized a branch in Levittown, one of the Levittowners said, "They are big and they can help us, but we don't have to follow national policy. . . . National headquarters is only a racket that takes your money." The cultural orientation toward localism is supported by more pressing sociological factors; if a local branch of a national association is to succeed, it must adapt itself to local priorities in order to attract members, and national headquarters must be opposed if it refuses to go along. The most disliked outsider is not the national society, however, but the cosmopolitan with his "Brookline values."

All this does not, of course, imply that the national society and culture are powerless in Levittown. When industrial giants set administered prices for consumer goods sold in the local shopping center, or when Detroit engineers the annual style change in its automobiles, the individual purchaser can only express his discontent by refusal to buy, and when it comes to necessities, he lacks even that choice. In Levittown, however, the discontent and the lack of choice are minimized, for most people have enough money to pay administered prices and enough freedom to choose among products. In fact, they find themselves well served by the corporations who sell them their housing, food, furnishings, and transportation. However, Levittowners are less concerned with "consumption" than the critics. They care less about the things they buy and are less interested in asserting individuality through consumer behavior, for they do not use consumption to express class values as much as the upper middle class does. They may not like mass-produced bread as well as the local bakery product they perhaps ate in childhood, but they do not make an issue of it, and do not feel themselves to be mass men simply because they buy a mass-produced item. Goods are just not important enough. Only when they become tourists are they "materialistic"—and traditional. One of my neighbors who was once stationed in Japan was not at all concerned about the national prepackaged brands sold in Levittown, but talked frequently about the commercialization of Japanese culture and the unattractive goods he found in the souvenir shops.

The Mass Media

For Levittowners, probably the most enduring—and certainly the most frequent—tie to the national culture is through the mass media. Yet even this is filtered through a variety of personal predispositions so that not many messages reach the receiver intact. Few people are dominated by the mass media; they provide escape from boredom, fill up brief intervals, and (perhaps most important) occupy the children while the adults go about their business.

The most frequently used mass medium is television, with newspapers, magazines, and paperback novels following in that order. In working class homes in Levittown as elsewhere, the TV set is likely to be on all the time, even when company comes, for as one Levittowner explained, "If conversation lags, people can watch or it gives you something to talk about." This statement suggests more the fears that working class people have about their social skills than their practice, for conversation does not often lag, at least among friends.

Middle class people, surer of their social skills, use television more selectively. The children watch when they have come in from play; after they are put to bed the adults may turn on the set, for television fills the hours between 9 P.M. and bedtime, when there is not enough of a block of time for other activities. A few favorite programs may get rapt attention, but I doubt that television supplanted conversation among either middle or working class Levittowners. There is no indication that television-viewing increased after people moved to Levittown, for no one mentioned it when interviewed about changes in spare-time activities. I suspect that viewing had actually decreased somewhat, at least during the time of my study, when gardening was still a time-consuming novelty for many people.

Television viewing is also a much less passive activity than the critics of the mass media suspect.[3] Routine serials and situation comedies evoke little response, although Levittowners are sensitive to anachronisms in the plots and skeptical of advertising claims.[4] Dramatic programs may provoke spirited—and quite personal—reactions. For example, one evening my neighbors and I watched an hour-long drama which depicted the tragic career of an introverted girl who wanted desperately to become a serious actress but was forced to work as a rock-and-roll dancer, and finally decided to give up show business. One neighbor missed the tragedy altogether, and thought the girl should have kept on trying to become an actress. The other neighbor fastened on—and approved of—the ending (in which the actress returned to her husband and to the family restaurant in which she had been "discovered") and wondered, rightly, whether it was possible to go back to a mundane life after the glamor of the entertainment world.

People do not necessarily know what they want from the media, but they know what they do not want and trust their ability to choose correctly. A discussion of television critics one night revealed that Levittowners read their judgments, but do not necessarily accept them. "The critics see so much that they cannot give us much advice," said one. "They are too different in their interests from the audience, and cannot be reviewers for it," said another.

Forty per cent of the people interviewed said they were reading new magazines since moving to Levittown; general-interest periodicals—*Life, Look, Reader's Digest, Time,* and the *Saturday Evening Post*—led the list. Only 9 of the 52 magazines were house-and-garden types such as *American Home* and *Better Homes and Gardens,* but then 88 per cent of the people were already reading these, at least in the year they moved to Levittown. Although not a single person said these magazines had helped in the decision to buy a home in Levittown, 57 per cent reported that they had gotten ideas from the magazines to try out in their houses, primarily on the use of space, furniture, and shrubbery arrangements, what to do about pictures and drapes, and how to build shelves and patios. The magazines provided help on functional rather than esthetic problems of fixing up the new house. People rarely copied something directly from the magazines, however. Most often, their reading gave them ideas which they then altered for their own use, sometimes after talking them over with the

---

[3] This cannot be surmised either from inferences about media content or from sociological surveys, but becomes quite evident when one watches TV with other people, as I did with my neighbors.

[4] I had observed the same reactions among the working class Bostonians I studied previously, although they were more interested in the performers than the Levittowners. Gans (1962a), Chap. 9.

neighbors. Similarly, people who adopted new furniture styles after moving to Levittown got their inspiration from their neighbors rather than from magazines, although all who changed styles (but only 53 per cent who did not) said they had obtained some hints for the house from the home and garden magazines.

The media also provide "ideas" for community activities, but these are altered by local considerations and priorities. For example, a few days after the Nixon-Kennedy television debates in 1960, candidates for township offices were asked to participate in a similar debate in Levittown. Everyone liked the idea, but after a few innocuous questions by out-of-town reporters, the debate turned into the traditional candidates' night, in which politicians from both parties baited their opponents from the audience with prepared questions. Sometimes, local organizations put on versions of TV quiz games, and honored retiring officers with a "This Is Your Life" presentation. A few clubs, especially Jewish ones, held "beatnik" parties, but since most Levittowners had never seen a beatnik, the inspiration for their costumes came from the mass media.

The impact of the media is most apparent among children; they are easily impressed by television commercials, and mothers must often fight off their demands on shopping trips. But the adults are seldom touched deeply; media content is always secondary to more personal experience. For example, people talked about articles on child-rearing they had seen in popular magazines, but treated them as topics of conversation rather than as possible guides for their own behavior. A neighbor who had read that "permissive" child-rearing was going out of style after thirty years had never even heard of it before, even though she had gone to college. I remember discussing Cuba with another neighbor, an Air Force officer, shortly after Castro confiscated American property there. Although he had been telling me endless and angry stories about being exploited by his superiors and about corruption among high-ranking officers, he could not see the similarity between his position and that of the Cuban peasant under Batista, and argued strenuously that Castro should be overthrown. His opinions reflected those of the media, but their content did not interest him enough to relate it to his own experiences. He did, however, feel that Castro had insulted the United States—and him personally—and the media helped him belong to the national society in this way. Indeed, the media are a message from that society, which, like all others, remains separate from the more immediate realities of self, family, home, and friends. These messages really touch only the people who feel isolated from local groups or who, like the cosmopolitans, pay close attention to the printed word and the screen image.

Levittown and the Mass Society

The Levittowners' local orientation will not prevent them from becoming submissive tools of totalitarian demagogues if, according to the critics of mass society, the community is too weak to defy the power of the state. Social scientists concerned about the danger of dictatorship have often claimed, with DeTocqueville, that the voluntary association is the prime bulwark against it. For example, Wilensky writes: "In the absence of effective mediating ties, of meaningful participation in voluntary associations, the population becomes vulnerable to mass behavior, more susceptible to personality appeals in politics, more ready for the demagogues who exploit fanatical faiths of nation and race." [5]

If Wilensky is correct, Levittowners should be invulnerable to mass behavior, for they have started about a hundred voluntary associations and 73 per cent of the two interview samples belong to at least one. Levittown should also be more immune than other communities, for about half of both interview samples reported more organizational participation than in the former residence.[6] The way they participate, however, has little consequence for their relation to the national society. The handful of leaders and really active people become familiar with the mechanics of organizational and municipal politics, but the rank-and-file members, coming to meetings mainly for social and service reasons, are rarely involved in these matters. Yet not even the active participants are exposed to national issues and questions, and they learn little about the ways of coping with the manipulatory techniques feared by the critics of mass society.

Nor does participation necessarily provide democratic experience. Organizations with active membership are likely to have democratic politics, but when the membership is passive, they are often run by an individual or a clique and there is little demand for democratic procedure. Nothing in the nature of the voluntary association would, however, preclude mob behavior and mass hysteria when the members demand it. The ad hoc groups that arose during the school budget fight and in the controversies over liquor, nonresident doctors, and fluoridation, often acted in near-hysterical ways. Admittedly, these were temporary organizations; permanent ones, conscious of their image, are more likely to refrain from such behavior and, like political parties, often avoid taking stands on controversial issues. They do inhibit mob action—or, rather, they refuse to be associated with it, forcing it into temporary organizations. Yet if the majority of a permanent group's membership is angry about an issue, it can act out that anger and even put its organizational strength behind hysteria. At the time of racial integration, a sizeable faction in one of the men's groups was contemplating quasi-violent protest, and was restrained as much by pressure from the churches, the builder, and some government officials as by cooler heads within the group.

Mob action and mass hysteria are usually produced by intense clashes of interest between citizens and government agencies, especially if government is not responsive to citizens' demands. If an issue is especially threatening and other avenues for coping with it are blocked, irrational action is often the only solution. Under such conditions, voluntary associations can do little to quell it, partly because they have no direct role in the government, but mainly because their impact on their membership is, in

[5] Wilensky, p. 237. See also Kornhauser, Chap. 3, and Lipset, pp. 66–67.
[6] Fifty-six per cent of the random sample and 44 per cent of the city sample reported more participation than previously.

Wilensky's terms, not meaningful enough to divert members from affiliating with violent protest groups. Even national officers of voluntary associations can rarely control irrational actions by local branches, especially since these rarely come to "national's" attention.

The other relationships of the individual Levittowners vis-à-vis the national society are so indirect that it would be hard to pinpoint where and how the two confront each other. It would be harder still to convince the average Levittowner, locally oriented as he is, to change his stance. Unlike the aristocrat or the intellectual, who was once able as an individual to influence the national society and still attempts to do so, the Levittowners come from a tradition—and from ancestors—too poor or too European even to conceive the possibility that they could affect their nation. And unlike the cosmopolitans of today, they have not yet learned that they ought to try. As a result, the Levittowner is not likely to act unless and until national issues impinge directly on his life. When this does happen, he is as frustrated as the cosmopolitan about how to be effective. All he can really do is voice his opinion at the ballot box, write letters to his congressman, or join protest groups. In times of crisis, none of these can change the situation quickly enough, and this of course exacerbates threat, hysteria, and the urge toward mob action or scapegoating.

The national society and the state have not impinged negatively on the average Levittowner, however; indeed, they have served him well, making him generally content with the status quo. The Congress is dominated by the localistic and other values of the white lower middle and working class population, and since the goods and services provided by the influential national corporations are designed largely for people like the Levittowners, they have little reason to question corporate behavior. The considerable similarity of interests between Levittowners and the nationally powerful agencies, private and public, makes it unnecessary for the Levittowners to concern themselves with the national society or to delude themselves about the sovereignty of the local community.[7]

What appears as apathy to the critics of suburban life is satisfaction with the way things are going, and what is interpreted as a "retreat" into localism and familism is just ahistorical thinking. Most lower middle and working class people have always been localistic and familistic; even during the Depression they joined unions only when personal economic difficulties gave them no other alternative, becoming inactive once these were resolved or when it was clear that political activity was fruitless.[8] Indeed, the alleged retreat is actually an advance, for the present generation, especially among working class people, is less isolated from the larger society than its parents, less suspicious, and more willing to believe

[7] In this respect, the Levittowners differed significantly from the residents of Springdale, a rural community in New York State, who developed a set of illusions to hide their dependence on state and national political and economic forces. See Vidich and Bensman.

[8] Part of the difficulty is that critics compare the present generation to the previous generation, that of the Depression, which was an unusual period in American history and no baseline for historical comparisons of any kind.

that it can participate in the community and the larger society. The belief is fragile and rarely exercised, but people like the Levittowners confront the national society more rationally than their ancestors did, and if the signs of progress are few, progress has nevertheless taken place. Whether there has been enough progress to prevent the emergence of dictatorship in a severe national crisis is hard to tell, but certainly the Levittowners and their community fit few of the prerequisites that would make them willing tools of totalitarian leaders today.

TRANSIENCE AND ROOTLESSNESS

Part of the fear of mass society theorists and suburban critics alike is the transience of the new suburban communities and the feelings of rootlessness that allegedly result. About 20 per cent of Levittown's first purchasers were Transients, who knew even when they came that their employers—national corporations or the armed services—would require them to move elsewhere some years hence. Their impermanency is reflected in residential turnover figures which showed that in 1964, 10 per cent of the houses were resold and another 5 per cent rented, and that annual turnover was likely to reach 20 per cent in the future.[9] Not all houses change hands that often, of course; a small proportion are sold and rented over and over again.[10] Much of the initial turnover resulted from job transfers—55 per cent in 1960, with another 10 per cent from job changes.[11]

Whether or not the 15 per cent turnover figure is "normal" is difficult to say. National estimates of mobility suggest that 20 per cent of the population moves annually, but this figure includes renters. Levittown's rate is probably high in comparison to older communities of home owners, fairly typical of newer ones, and low in comparison to apartment areas.[12]

[9] There is no secular trend in turnover, however, for between 1961 and 1964 the rate in the first neighborhood increased from 12 per cent to only 14 per cent, but the third and fourth neighborhoods both showed turnover rates of 19 per cent in 1964. Renting occurs primarily because the softness of the housing market makes it difficult for people to sell their houses without a considerable loss; they find it more profitable to rent them, with management turned over to the local realtors.

[10] According to a story in the October 21, 1957 issue of Long Island's *Newsday*, 27 per cent of the first 1800 families in Levittown, New York, were still living there ten year later.

[11] Another 10 per cent left because they were unhappy in the community; 7 per cent, for financial reasons; 5 per cent, because of an excessive journey to work; and 4 per cent, because of death, divorce, or other changes in the family. These figures were collected from real estate men and people selling their homes privately and may not be entirely reliable. Real estate men may not be told the real reasons for selling and private sellers may have been reluctant to mention financial problems. However, only about 1 per cent of the houses were foreclosed annually.

[12] In the mid-1950s, when Park Forest was seven years old, annual turnover of homes was 20 per cent. See Whyte (1956), p. 303. In Levittown, New York, a 1961 study reported an average annual rate of about 15 per cent. See Orzack and Sanders, p. 13. In Levittown, Pennsylvania, the rate varied from 12 to 15 per cent between 1952 and 1960. See Anderson and Settani. A study of a forty-year-old English new

Conventional standards of "normal" turnover are so old and communities like Levittown still so new on the American scene that it is impossible to determine a normal turnover rate. Indeed, the need to judge turnover stems from the assumption that it is undesirable; once there are sufficient data to test this assumption, the concept of normal turnover can perhaps be dismissed.

The crucial element in turnover is not its extent but the change in population composition and its consequences. If the departing Transients and Mobiles are replaced by Settlers, then turnover will of course be reduced. Early in the 1960s, the second buyers were, however, also Transients, who needed a house more quickly than the builder could supply it, as well as people of lower income (probably Settlers) who could not afford the down payment on a new house. If more of the latter come to Levittown over the years, the proportion of lower-status people in the community will increase, and there may be fears of status loss among those of higher status. Although such fears were rare during my time in the community, they existed on a few blocks and may account in part for the strong reactions to status-depriving governmental actions that I described earlier.

Despite the belief that Transients do not participate in community life, in Levittown they belonged to community organizations in considerably larger numbers than Settlers did, partly because of their higher status.[13] More of them also reported increased participation after moving to Levittown than did Settlers.[14] They were, however, likely to list fewer people with whom they visited frequently.[15] Their organizational activity is not surprising, for being used to transience, they are socially quite stable, usually gravitating to the same kinds of communities and joining the same kinds of organizations in them. In fact, their mobility has provided them with more organizational experience than other Levittowners have, enabling them to help found several groups in the community.

It has often been charged that modern transience and mobility deprive people of "roots." Because of the botanical analogy, the social conception of the word is difficult to define, but it generally refers to a variety of stable roles and relationships which are recognized by other residents.

---

town reported an annual rate of 10 per cent the first ten years, which has now dropped to 1 per cent. See Willmott (1963), p. 20. A study of 30,000 apartments in 519 buildings all over the country, conducted by the Institute of Real Estate Management and reported in the *New York Times* of November 10, 1963, showed an annual turnover of 28 per cent, and 35 per cent for garden apartments.

13 Eighty-four per cent of the Transients reported organizational membership at the time of the second interview, as compared to 86 per cent of the Mobiles and only 44 per cent of the Settlers. Sixty-two per cent of the Transients belonged to organizations other than the church, compared to only 25 per cent of the Settlers.

14 Seventy-five per cent of the Transients were more active than in their former residence, as compared to 60 per cent of the Settlers, and none of the Transients but 20 per cent of the Settlers said they were less active than before.

15 The mean number of couples named by Transients was 2.75; by Mobiles, 3.25; and by Settlers, 3.3. Nineteen per cent of the Transients said they had no friends in Levittown, as compared to 8 per cent of the Settlers.

Traditionally, these roles were often defined by one's ancestors as well. Such roots are hard to maintain today and few people can resist the temptation of social or occupational mobility that requires a physical move. This does not mean, however, that the feeling of rootedness has disappeared. One way in which Transients maintain it is to preserve the term "home" for the place in which they grew up. When Levittowners talk of "going home," they mean trips to visit parents. People whose parents have left the community in which they grew up may, however, feel homeless. I remember a discussion with a Levittowner who explained that he was going "home to Ohio" to visit his mother, and his wife said somewhat sadly, "My parents no longer live where I grew up, and I never lived with them where they live now. So I have only Sudberry Street in Levittown; I have no other home." Because they were Transients, she could not think of Levittown as home and, like many others, looked forward to the day when her husband's occupational transience would come to an end and they would settle down.

Such Transients obviously lack roots in an objective sense and may also have feelings of rootlessness. My impression is that these feelings are not intense or frequent. One way they are coped with is by moving to similar communities and putting down temporary roots; another, by joining organizations made up of fellow Transients.[16] Professionals who are transient often develop roots in their profession and its social groups. As Melvin Webber and others have argued, occupational or functional roots are replacing spatial roots for an ever increasing proportion of the population.[17] This kind of rootedness is easier for men to establish than for women, and wives, especially the wives of professionals, often suffer more from transience than their husbands. Some become attached to national voluntary associations—as men in nonprofessional occupations do—and develop roots within them. This is not entirely satisfactory, however, for it provides feelings of rootedness in only a single role, whereas spatial rootedness cuts across all roles, and rewards one for what one is rather than for what one does.

New communities like Levittown make it possible for residents, even Transients, to put down roots almost at once. People active in organizations become known quickly; thus they are able to feel part of the community. Despite Levittown's size, shopkeepers and local officials get to know people they see regularly, offering the feeling of being recognized to many. The ministers take special care to extend such recognition, and the churches appoint themselves to provide roots—and deliberately, for it attracts people to the church. Protestant denominations sought to define themselves as small-town churches with Colonial style buildings because these have been endowed with an image of rootedness.

Intergenerational rootedness is seldom found today in any suburban or urban community—or, for that matter, in most small towns—for it requires the kind of economic stability (and even stagnancy) characteristic only of depressed areas of the country. Moreover, the romanticizing of this type of rootedness ignores the fact that for many people it blocked

[16] Whyte (1956), p. 289.
[17] Webber.

progress, especially for low-status persons who were, by reason of residence and ancestry, permanently defined as "shiftless" or "good for nothing." Roots can strangle growth as well as encourage it.

Transience and mobility are something new in middle class American life, and like other innovations, they have been greeted by predictions of undesirable consequences, on family life, school performance, and mental health, for example. Interviews with school officials, doctors, and policemen indicated, however, that Transients appeared no more often as patients and police or school problems and delinquents than other Levittowners. Transience *can* create problems, but it has different effects for different people. For young men, a transfer usually includes a promotion or a raise; for older ones it may mean only another physical move or a transfer to a corporate "Siberia." If a Transient is attached to his home, but is asked to move by his company, he can say "no" only once or twice before being asked to resign or face relegation to the list of those who will not be promoted further. The move from one place to another is a pleasure for few families, but the emotional costs can easily be overestimated.[18] Because Transients move to and from similar types of communities, they have little difficulty adapting themselves to their new homes. In large corporations, they generally receive advice about where to look for housing, often going to areas already settled by colleagues who help them make the residential transition.

Frequent moving usually hurts other family members more than the breadwinner. Wives who had made good friends in Levittown were especially sad to go, and adolescents object strenuously to leaving their peers, so that parents generally try to settle down before their children enter high school. For wives and adolescents transience is essentially an involuntary move, which, like the forced relocation of slum dwellers under urban renewal, may result in depression and other deleterious effects.[19] Transience may also engender difficulties when problems of social mobility antedate or accompany it, as in the case of older corporate employees who must transfer without promotion, or suburbanites who move as a result of downward or extremely rapid upward social mobility.[20] Studies among children of Army personnel, who move more often than corporation Transients, have found that geographical mobility per se did not result in emotional disturbance,[21] except among children whose fathers had risen from working class origins to become officers.[22]

[18] Gutman, p. 180.

[19] See, e.g., Fried.

[20] Gordon, Gordon, and Gunther. This study did not distinguish between residential and social mobility, but its case studies of disturbed suburbanites suggest the deleterious effects of the latter.

[21] Pederson and Sullivan.

[22] This study—by Gabower—came to other conclusions, but a close reading of her data shows that the strains of the long and arduous climb required of an enlisted man in the Navy who becomes an officer were passed on to the children. Conversely, children from middle class homes, whose fathers had graduated from Annapolis, rarely suffered emotionally from geographical mobility. Teenagers of both groups suffered from moving, however.

These findings would suggest that transience has its most serious effects on people with identity problems. The individual who lacks a fairly firm sense of his identity will have difficulties in coping with the new experiences he encounters in moving. He will also suffer most severely from rootlessness, for he will be hindered in developing the relationships and reference groups that strengthen one's identity. This might explain why adolescents find moving so difficult. Transients without roots in their community of origin or their jobs must rely on their family members in moments of stress. Sometimes, the family becomes more cohesive as a result, but since stresses on one family member are likely to affect all others, the family is not always a reliable source of support. If identity problems are also present, the individual may have no place to turn, and then transience can produce the *anomie* that critics have found rampant in the suburbs. But such people are a small minority in Levittown.

THE VITALITY OF LEVITTOWN: THE ADULT VIEW

When the Levittowners were asked whether they considered their community dull, just 20 per cent of the random sample said yes, and of Philadelphians (who might have been expected to find it dull after living in a big city), only 14 per cent.[23] Many respondents were surprised at the very question, for they thought there was a great deal to do in the community, and all that was needed was a desire to participate. "It's up to you," was a common reaction. "If a person is not the friendly type or does not become active, it's their own fault." "I don't think it's dull here," explained another, "there are so many organizations to join." Some people noted that Levittown was short of urban amusements, but it did not bother them. A former Philadelphian pointed out: "If Levittown is compared to city living, there are no taverns or teenage hangout places. Then it is dull. But we never had any of this in our own neighborhood and it's even better here. . . . We are perfectly content here, I'm afraid. Social life is enough for us; we are becoming fuddy-duddy." Nostalgia for urban places was not common; most people felt like the one who said, "We like quiet things . . . visiting, sitting out front in summer, having people dropping by." And if Levittown seemed quiet to some, it did not to others. "This is the wildest place I've ever been. Every weekend a party, barbecues, picnics, and things like that. I really enjoy it." [24] The only people who thought Levittown was indeed dull were the socially isolated, and upper middle class people who had tasted the town's organizational life and found it wanting.

[23] The question read: "Some people have said that communities like Levittown are pretty dull, without any excitement or interesting things to do. How do you feel about that? Do you agree or disagree?"

[24] This respondent was describing the extremely active social life of the Jewish community. Even so, Jews (particularly the better educated) were more likely than non-Jews to agree that Levittown was dull. Jews also seem to be more interested in city amusements.

What Levittowners who enjoy their community are saying is that they find vitality in other people and organizational activities; the community is less important. That community may be dull by conventional standards (which define vitality by urban social mixture and cultural riches) but Levittowners reject these standards; they do not want or need that kind of vitality or excitement. Mothers get their share of it from the daily adventures of their children and the men get it at work. The threshold for excitement is low, and for many, excitement is identified with conflict, crisis, and deprivation. Most Levittowners grew up in the Depression, and remembering the hard times of their childhood, they want to protect themselves and their children from stress.

Another difference in values between critics and Levittowners is at play here. The Italians who lived in the center city working class neighborhood I studied before Levittown were bored by "the country"—in which they included the suburbs—and so are critics of suburbia, albeit for different reasons. Many working class city dwellers enjoy street life and urban eating or drinking places; upper middle class critics like crowds and cosmopolitanism. The lower middle class and the kinds of working class people that came to Levittown had no interest in either. Even previous urbanites had made little if any use of the cultural facilities valued by the cosmopolitan, and had no need for them in the suburbs. And as the struggles over the liquor issue suggest, they want none of the vitality sought by the working class urbanite, for they are just escaping corner bars and the disadvantages of aging urban areas. What they do want is a kind of interpersonal vitality along with privacy and peace and quiet.[25] Vicarious excitement is something else again. Television provides programmed and highly predictable excitement, but it can get boring. A fire or accident, a fight at a municipal or school board meeting, and marital strife or minor misbehavior among neighbors involve real people and known ones. The excitement they provide is also vicarious, but it is not programmed and is therefore more rewarding.

The Blandness of Lower Middle Class Culture

Levittown's criteria for vitality may spell dullness to the critic and the visitor, partly because much of community life is invisible. Lower middle class life does not take place either on the street or in meetings and

[25] Cosmopolitan friends often asked me if I did not find Levittown dull. As a participant-observer, I could not answer the question, for I was immersed in community life and strife and saw all of their vitality and excitement. Even the most routine event was interesting because I was trying to fit it into an overall picture of the community. As a resident, I enjoyed being with Levittowners, and the proportion of dull ones was certainly no higher than in academic or any other circles. Of course, Levittown lacked some of the urban facilities that I, as a city-lover, like to patronize. It was not dull, however—but then I would not make a public judgment about any community simply because it could not satisfy some of my personal preferences, particularly when the community seemed to satisfy the preferences of the majority of residents so well.

parties; it is home-centered and private. Once one penetrates behind the door, however, as does the participant-observer, people emerge as personalities and few are either dull or bland. But when all is said and done, something is different: less exuberance than is found in the working class, a more provincial outlook than in the upper middle class, and a somewhat greater concern with respectability than in either. In part, this is a function of religious background: being largely Protestant, the lower middle class is still affected by the Puritan ethos. It lacks the regular opportunity for confession that allows some Catholics to live somewhat more spiritedly, and has not adopted the sharp division into sacred and secular culture that reduces Jewish religiosity to observance of the High Holidays and permits Jews to express exuberance in their organizational, social, and cultural activities. But the difference is not entirely due to Puritanism, for "restrictive" lower middle class culture appears also among Catholics who have moved "up," especially German and Irish ones, and even among Italians and among some Jews who have risen from working class origins.

If "blandness" is the word for this quality, it stems from the transition in which the lower middle class finds itself between the familial life of the working class and the cosmopolitanism of the upper middle class. The working class person need conform only within the family circle and the peer group, but these are tolerant of his other activities. Believing that the outside world is unalterably hostile and that little is to be gained from its approval, he can indulge in boisterousness that provides catharsis from the tensions generated in the family and peer circles. The upper middle class person, on the other hand, is lodged firmly in the world outside the home. At times he may have trouble reconciling the demands of home and outside world, but he has a secure footing in both.

Lower middle class people seem to me to be caught in the middle. Those whose origins were in the working class are no longer tied so strongly to the extended family, but although they have gone out into the larger society, they are by no means at ease in it. They do not share the norms of the cosmopolitans, but, unlike the working class, they cannot ignore them. As a result, they find themselves in a situation in which every neighbor is a potential friend or enemy and every community issue a source of conflict, producing a restraining and even inhibiting influence on them. Others, lower middle class for generations, have had to move from a rural or small-town social structure. They too are caught in the middle, for now they must cope with a larger and more heterogeneous society, for which their cultural and religious traditions have not equipped them.

If left to themselves, lower middle class people do what they have always done: put their energies into home and family, seeking to make life as comfortable as possible, and supporting, broadening, and varying it with friends, neighbors, church, and a voluntary association. Because this way of life is much like that of the small-town society or the urban neighborhood in which they grew up, they are able to maintain their optimistic belief that Judeo-Christian morality is a reliable guide to behavior. This world view (if one can endow it with so philosophical a name) is best seen in the pictures that amateur painters exhibited at PTA meetings in Levittown: bright, cheerful landscapes, or portraits of children and pets painted in primary colors, reflecting the wish that the world be hopeful, humorous, and above all, simple. Most important, their paintings insisted that life can be happy.

Of course, life is not really like this, for almost everyone must live with some disappointment: an unruly child, a poor student, an unsatisfied husband, a bored wife, a bad job, a chronic illness, or financial worry. These realities are accepted because they cannot be avoided; it is the norms of the larger society which frustrate. Partly desired and partly rejected, they produce an ambivalence which appears to the outsider as the blandness of lower middle class life. This ambivalence can be illustrated by the way Levittown women reacted to my wife's paintings. Since her studio was at home, they had an opportunity to see her work and talk to her about being a painter. The working class Italians with whom we had lived in Boston previously knew, by and large, how to deal with her activity. Unacquainted with "art," they could shrug off her activity and her abstract expressionist style to admire colors they liked or forms that reminded them of something in their own experience. Not knowing what it all meant, and not having to know, they concluded that painting was a good thing because it kept her out of trouble, preventing boredom and potentially troublesome consequences such as drinking or extramarital affairs.

The lower middle class Levittowners could not cope with her paintings as easily. They did not like her abstract expressionist style any more than the working class women, but they knew it was "art" and so could not ignore it. They responded with anxiety, some hostility, and particularly with envy of her ability to be "creative." But even this response was overlaid with ambivalence. As teenagers they had learned that creativity was desirable, and many had had some cursory training in drawing, piano, or needlework. Once they had learned to be wives and mothers and had enough sociability, the urge for creativity returned—but not the opportunity.

For working class women, keeping the family together and the bills paid is a full-time job. Upper middle class women are convinced that life ought to be more than raising a family, but lower middle class ones are not that sure. They want to venture into nonfamilial roles, but not so intensively as to engender role conflict and anxiety. As a result, they search for easy creativity, activities that do not require, as Levittowners put it, "upsetting the family and household." Serious artistic activity is difficult under such conditions, yet a compromise solution such as needlework or painting-by-numbers is not entirely satisfactory either, because, however rewarding, people know it is not really art. One Levittowner I met expressed the ambivalence between the familial role and artistic aspirations in an especially tortured way. She explained that she was very sensitive to paintings, but confessed that whenever she visited museums, she would begin to think about her family. She resolved the ambivalence by rejecting paintings that made her "think too much about art." For most people, however, the ambivalence is less intense.

A similarly ambivalent pattern is evident in government involvement.

Many lower middle class people believe that the moral framework which governs their personal lives, the sort of relations they have with family members and friends, ought to govern organizational life and society as well. Any other type of behavior they call "politics," in and out of political life, and they try to avoid it as immoral. Working class people have the same perspective, but they are also realists and will exploit politics for their own ends, and upper middle class people believe in moral (reform) politics, but its norms are not borrowed from the family. Lower middle class citizens are once again caught between the standards of home and of the outside world, however, and the result is often political inaction. It is for them that politicians put on performances to show that their decisions are based on the standards of home and family and run election campaigns demonstrating the personal honesty of their candidates and the opposition candidates' immorality.

Of course, these are cultural propensities to act, and when personal interests are threatened, lower middle class people defend them as heartily as anyone else. Then, they identify their actions with morality—so much so that they lose sight of their self-interest and are easily hurt when others point out to them that they are selfishly motivated. Whereas working class people then become cynical, lower middle class people become hypocritical, often without being conscious of it. Blandness turns easily to bitterness, anger, and blind conflict—blind because every act of offense or self-defense is clothed in the terminology of personal morality.

What appears as blandness, then, to the outside observer is the outcome of conflict between self and society, and between what ought to be and what is. When and if a lower middle class person is secure, he appears bland, because he is not really willing to act within the larger society; when he is threatened, he is extremely angry, because his moral view of the world is upset. One target of his anger is the working class people who are less bothered by the moral dilemmas of the larger society; another is the upper middle class activists who keep pressuring him to translate morality into action and to take a stand on community issues.

Many of these cultural predispositions seem to occur more among lower middle class women than among their husbands. If the men are employed in a bureaucracy, as most are, their work involves them not only in the larger society but also in office or factory political struggles which leave them little time to think about the ambivalence between the standards of home and outside world. The women, however, caught in a role that keeps them at home, are forever trying to break out of its confines, only to confront ambivalent situations. They respond with inhibiting blandness; it is they who are most concerned with respectability. Indeed, living with neighbors employed in large bureaucracies, I was struck over and over again by the feeling that if the men were "organization men," they were so only by necessity, not by inclination, and that if they were left alone, they would gravitate toward untrammeled creativity and individualism. Their wives, on the other hand, defended what Whyte called the Social Ethic, rejecting extreme actions and skeptical opinions, and tried to get their men to toe the line of lower middle class morality. If anything, their inclinations drove them toward being "organization women." But then, they had the job of maintaining the family's status image on the block, and they spent their days in the near-anarchy created by small children. Perhaps they were simply escaping *into* the order of lower middle class norms, while the men were escaping *from* the order imposed by their bureaucratic work.

LEVITTOWN IS "ENDSVILLE": THE ADOLESCENT VIEW

The adult conception of Levittown's vitality is not shared by its adolescents. Many consider it a dull place to which they have been brought involuntarily by their parents. Often there is no place to go and nothing to do after school. Although most adolescents have no trouble in their student role, many are bored after school and some are angry, expressing that anger through thinly veiled hostility to adults and vandalism against adult property. Their relationship to the adults is fraught with tension, which discourages community attempts to solve what is defined as their recreational problem.

Essays which students in grades 6–12 wrote for me early in 1961 suggest that most children are satisfied with Levittown until adolescence.[26] Sixty-eight per cent of the sixth-graders liked Levittown, but only 45 per cent of the eighth-graders, 37 per cent of the tenth-graders, and 39 per cent of the twelfth-graders did. In comparison, 85 per cent of the adults responded positively to a similar question.[27] Likes and dislikes reflect the state of recreational and social opportunities. Girls make little use of recreational facilities until they become adolescents, and before the tenth grade, they like Levittown better than the boys. Dislikes revolve around "nothing to do." The sixth- and eighth-grade boys say there are not enough gyms, playing fields, or hills, and no transportation for getting to existing facilities. Both sexes complain about the lack of neighborhood stores and that the houses are too small, lack privacy, and are poorly built. By the twelfth grade, disenchantment with the existing facilities has set in; those who like Levittown stress the newness and friendliness of the community, but references to the pool, the shopping center, and the bowling alley are nega-

26 The students were asked what they liked and disliked about living in Levittown, and what they missed from their former residence. Since they were not asked to sign their names, and the questions were general, I believe the essays were honest responses. I purposely included no questions about the schools, and teachers were instructed not to give any guidance about how the questions should be answered. (One teacher did tell the children what to write, and these essays were not analyzed.) The data presented here are based on a sample of one sixth- and one eighth-grade class from each of the three elementary schools, and of all tenth- and twelfth-grade classes.

27 The data are not strictly comparable, for the adults were asked outright whether they liked or disliked living in Levittown, whereas the teenagers' attitudes were inferred from the tone of the essays.

tive.[28] As one twelfth-grader pointed out, "Either you have to pay a lot of money to go to the movies or the bowling alley, or you go to too many parties and that gets boring." Lack of facilities is reported most often by the older girls, for the boys at least have athletic programs put on by civic groups.[29]

But the commonest gripe is the shortage of ready transportation, which makes not only facilities but, more important, other teenagers inaccessible. One girl complained, "After school hours, you walk into an entirely different world. Everyone goes his own separate way, to start his homework, take a nap, or watch TV. That is the life of a vegetable, not a human being." A car, then, becomes in a way as essential to teenagers as to adults. Moreover, many small-town teenagers like to meet outside the community, for it is easier to "have fun" where one's parents and other known adults cannot disapprove. A high school senior who took a job to buy a car put it dramatically:

> I had no choice, it was either going to work or cracking up. I have another week of boring habits, then (when I get the car) I'll start living. I can get out of Levittown and go to other towns where I have many friends. . . . In plain words, a boy shouldn't live here if he is between the ages of 14–17. At this age he is using his adult mind, and that doesn't mean riding a bike or smoking his first cigarette. He wants to be big and popular and go out and live it up. I am just starting the life I want. I couldn't ask for more than being a senior in a brand new high school, with the best of students and teachers, and my car on its way.

Girls are less likely to have access to a car, and one explained, "We have to walk, and the streets wind, and cause you to walk two miles instead of one as the crow flies."

The adults have provided some facilities for teenage activities, but not always successfully. One problem is that "teenage" is an adult tag; adolescents grade themselves by age. Older ones refused to attend dances with the younger set, considering forced association with their juniors insulting.[30] Some adolescents also found the adult chaperones oppressive. At

---

[28] Twenty-eight per cent of the boys liked the community's newness; 18 per cent, the friendly people. Among the girls, 34 per cent liked the people; 20 per cent, Levittown's newness.

[29] Twenty-five per cent of the tenth-graders and 50 per cent of the twelfth-graders say there is nothing to do, and 25 per cent and 46 per cent, respectively, mention the lack of recreational facilities. Among the twelfth-grade girls, 56 per cent mention it.

[30] Similarly in the elementary schools, seventh- and eighth-graders complained about having to go to school with "immature" and "childish" students; when they were moved to the high school, the older students objected to their presence in the same terms.

first, the chaperones interfered openly by urging strangers to dance with each other in order to get everyone on the floor and to discourage intimate dancing among couples. When the teenagers protested, they stopped, but hovered uneasily in the background.[31]

Specifically, adolescent malcontent stems from two sources: Levittown was not designed for them, and adults are reluctant to provide the recreational facilities and gathering places they want. Like most suburban communities, Levittown was planned for families with young children. The bedrooms are too small to permit an adolescent to do anything but study or sleep; they lack the privacy and soundproofing to allow him to invite his friends over. Unfortunately, the community is equally inhospitable. Shopping centers are intended for car-owning adults, and in accord with the desire of property owners, are kept away from residential areas. Being new, Levittown lacks low-rent shopping areas which can afford to subsist on the marginal purchases made by adolescents. In 1961, a few luncheonettes in neighborhood shopping centers and a candy store and a bowling alley in the big center were the only places for adolescents to congregate.[32] Coming in droves, they overwhelmed those places and upset the merchants. Not only do teenagers occupy space without making significant purchases, but they also discourage adult customers. Merchants faced with high rent cannot subsist on teenage spending and complain to the police if teenagers "hang out" at their places. Street corners are off limits, too, for a clump of adolescents soon becomes noisy enough to provoke a call to the police. Eventually they feel hounded and even defined as juvenile delinquents. Said one twelfth-grade girl, "I feel like a hood to be getting chased by the police for absolutely nothing."

The schools were not designed for after-hours use, except for adults and for student activities which entertain adults, such as varsity athletics. The auditoriums were made available for dances, although when these began, the school administration promptly complained about scuffed floors and damaged fixtures. Only at the swimming pool are teenagers not in the way of adult priorities, and during the day, when adults are not using it, it is their major gathering place. But even here, smoking and noisy activities are prohibited.

The design deficiencies cannot be altered, and should not be if they are a problem only for teenagers, but there is no inherent reason why teenage facilities cannot be provided. However, adults disagree on what is needed and, indeed, on the desirability of facilities, for reasons partly

31 There was also a dispute over programming: the adults wanted slow music and the traditional dances they knew best; the teenagers wanted the latest best-selling records and the newest dances. They signed petitions for the ouster of the man who chose the records, but the adults refused to accept the petitions, arguing that they would be followed by petitions to oust the school superintendent.

32 Indeed, the existing teenage hangouts in little luncheonettes resulted from the lucky accident that the builder and the township planner were unable to regulate and limit the number of small shopping centers which sprang up on the edge of the community.

political, but fundamentally social and psychological. For one thing, adults are uncertain about how to treat teenagers; for another, they harbor a deep hostility toward them which is cultural and, at bottom, sexual in nature.

There are two adult views of the teenager, one permissive, the other restrictive. The former argues that a teenager is a responsible individual who should be allowed to run his own affairs with some adult help. The latter, subscribed to by the majority, considers him still a child who needs adult supervision and whose activities ought to be conducted by adult rules to integrate him into adult society. For example, when one of the community organizations set up teenage dances, there was some discussion about whether teenagers should run them. Not only was this idea rejected, but the adults then ran the dances on the basis of the "highest" standards.[33] Boys were required to wear ties and jackets, girls, dresses, on the assumption that this would encourage good behavior, whereas blue jeans, tee shirts, and sweaters somehow would not. The adults could not resist imposing their own norms of dress in exchange for providing dances.

The advocates of restriction also rejected the permissive point of view because they felt it wrong to give teenagers what they wanted. Believing that teenagers had it "too easy," they argued that "if you make them work for programs, they appreciate them more." Logically, they should, therefore, have let the teenagers set up their own activities, but their arguments were not guided by logic; they were, rather, rationalizations for their fear of teenagers. Although the "permissives" pointed out that teenagers might well set up stricter rules than adults, the "restrictives" feared catastrophes: fights, the "wrong crowd" taking over, pregnancies, and contraceptives found in or near the teenage facility. These fears accounted for the rules governing dances and inhibited the establishment of an adult-run teenage center, for the voluntary associations and the politicians were afraid that if violence or sexual activity occurred, they would be blamed for it.

The problem is twofold: restrictive adults want adolescents to be children preparing for adulthood, and are threatened by the teenage or youth culture they see around them. By now, adolescents are a cultural minority like any other, but whereas no Levittowners expect Italians to behave like Jews, most still expect teenagers to behave like children. They are supposed to participate in the family more than they do and, legally still under age, to subsume their own wishes to the adults'. The failure of teenagers to go along is blamed on the parents as well. If parents would only take more interest in their adolescent children, spend more time with them, be "pals" with them, and so on, then misbehavior—and even youth culture—would not develop. This argument is supported by the claim that delinquency is caused by broken homes or by both parents' holding full-time jobs.

Such views are espoused particularly by Catholics, who share tradi-

---

[33] At one point adult-run dances failed to attract teenagers, and a group of teenage leaders were delegated to run the dances themselves. This foundered because other teenagers disagreed with the rules and program set up by these leaders, and since only one opportunity for dancing was provided, they could express their disagreement only by nonattendance.

tional working class attitudes; the parochial school, with its emphasis on discipline to keep children out of trouble, is their embodiment. Even adult-devised programs are considered undesirable, for, as one Catholic working class father put it, "In summer, children should either work or be at home. Summer arts and crafts programs are a waste of time. My kid brought home dozens of pictures. What's he going to do with so many pictures?" The adolescents' social choices are also restricted. Adults active in youth programs frequently try to break up their groups, damning them as cliques or gangs, and even separating friends when athletic teams are chosen. Some teenagers react by minimizing contact with adults, pursuing their activities privately and becoming remarkably uncommunicative. In essence, they lead a separate life which frees them from undue parental control and gives an air of mystery to the teenager and his culture.

Among restrictive adults, the image of the teenager is of an irresponsible, parasitic individual, who attends school without studying, hangs out with his peers looking for fun and adventure, and gets into trouble—above all, over sex. There were rumors of teenage orgies in Levittown's school playgrounds, in shopping center parking lots, and on the remaining rural roads of the township. The most fantastic rumor had 44 girls in the senior class pregnant, with one boy singlehandedly responsible for six of them. Some inquiry on my part turned up the facts: two senior girls were pregnant and one of them was about to be married.

If the essays the students wrote for me have any validity, the gap between adult fantasy and adolescent reality is astonishing. Most teenagers do not even date; their social life takes place in groups. Judging by their comments about the friendliness of adult neighbors, they are quiet youngsters who get along well with adults and spend most of their time preparing themselves for adulthood. Needless to say, these essays would not have revealed delinquent activities of sex play. However, I doubt that more than 5 per cent of the older teenagers live up to anything like the adult image of them.

What, then, accounts for the discrepancy? For one thing, adults take little interest in their children's education; they want to be assured that their children are getting along in school, but not much more. The bond that might exist here is thus absent. Changes in education during the last two decades have been so great that even interested parents can do little to help their children with their school work. Consequently, adults focus on teenagers in their nonstudent roles, noting their absence from home, the intensity of their tie to friends and cliques, and their rebelliousness.

Second, there is the normal gap between the generations, enlarged by the recent flowering of youth culture, much of which is incomprehensible or unesthetic to adults. Despite the parents' belief that they should be responsible for their adolescents' behavior, they cannot participate in many joint activities or talk meaningfully with them about the experiences and problems of teenage life. This gap is exacerbated by a strange parental amnesia about their own—not so distant—adolescence. I recall a letter written by a twenty-one-year-old mother who wanted to help the Township Committee set up a delinquency prevention council because she was concerned about teenage misbehavior.

Third, there is enough teenage vandalism and delinquency to provide raw material for the adult image, although not enough to justify it. According to the police and the school superintendent, serious delinquency in Levittown was minimal; in 1961, about 50 adolescents accounted for most of it. Many were children from working class backgrounds who did poorly in school, or from disturbed middle class families. From 1959 to 1961, only 12 cases were serious enough to go to the county juvenile court, and some were repeaters. Vandalism is more prevalent. The first victim was the old Willingboro YMCA, which was wrecked twice before it was torn down. Schools have been defaced, windows broken, garbage thrown into the pools, flowerbeds destroyed, and bicycles "borrowed." The perpetrators are rarely caught, but those who are caught are teenagers, thus making it possible for adults to suspect all adolescents and maintain their image.

Finally, some adults seem to project their own desires for excitement and adventures onto the youngsters. For them, teenagers function locally as movie stars and beatniks do on the national scene—as exotic creatures reputed to live for sex and adventure. Manifestly, teenagers act as more prosaic entertainers: in varsity athletics, high school dramatic societies, and bands, but the girls are also expected to provide glamor. One of the first activities of the Junior Chamber of Commerce was a Miss Levittown contest, in which teenage girls competed for honors in evening gown, bathing suit, and talent contests—the "talent" usually involving love songs or covertly erotic dances. At such contests unattainable maidens show off their sexuality—often unconsciously—in order to win the nomination. Men in the audience comment *sotto voce* about the girls' attractiveness, wishing to sleep with them and speculating whether that privilege is available to the contest judges and boyfriends. From here, it is only a short step to the conviction that girls are promiscuous with their teenage friends, which heightens adult envy, fear, and the justification for restrictive measures. The sexual function of the teenager became apparent when the popularity of the Miss Levittown contest led to plans for a Mrs. Levittown contest. This plan was quickly dropped, however, for the idea of married women parading in bathing suits was thought to be in bad taste, especially by the women. Presumably, young mothers are potential sexual objects, whereas the teenagers are, like movie stars, unattainable, and can therefore serve as voyeuristic objects.

Although suburbia is often described as a hotbed of adultery in popular fiction, this is an urban fantasy. Levittown is quite monogamous, and I am convinced that most suburbs are more so than most cities.[34] The desire for sexual relations with attractive neighbors may be ever present, but when life is lived in a goldfish bowl, adultery is impossible to hide from the neighbors—even if there were motels in Levittown and baby-sitters could be found for both parties. Occasionally such episodes do take place,

[34] A comparison of urban and suburban marriages indicated that extramarital affairs occur principally in older and well-educated populations, and that place of residence is irrelevant. Ubell. For another observer's skepticism about suburban adultery, see Whyte (1956), pp. 355–357.

after which the people involved often run off together or leave the community. There are also periodic stories of more bizarre sexual escapades, usually about community leaders. In one such story, a local politician was driving down the dark roads of the township in a sports car with a naked young woman while his wife thought he was at a political meeting. If there was any roadside adultery, however, it remained unreported, for no cases ever appeared on the police blotters during the two years I saw them.[35] Similar stories made the rounds in Park Forest, the new town I studied in 1949, and one of them, which began after a party where some extramarital necking had taken place, soon reported the gathering as a wife-swapping orgy.

"The Juvenile Problem" and Its Solutions

The cultural differences between adults and adolescents have precipitated an undeclared and subconscious war between them, as pervasive as the class struggle, which prevents the adults from solving what they call "the juvenile problem." Indeed, putting it that way is part of the trouble, for much of the adult effort has been aimed at discouraging delinquency, providing recreational activities in the irrational belief that these could prevent it. Sports programs were supposed to exhaust the teenagers so that they would be too tired to get into trouble (harking back to the Victorian myth that a regimen of cold showers and sports would dampen sexual urges, although ironically, varsity athletes were also suspected of being stellar sexual performers); dances were to keep them off the street. When delinquency did not abate, a Youth Guidance Commission to deal with "the problem," and a Teenage Panel to punish delinquencies too minor for court actions, were set up. The police chief asked for a curfew to keep youngsters off the street at night, hoping to put pressure on parents to act as enforcing agents and to get his department out of the cross fire between teenagers, merchants, and home owners. Chasing the teenagers from shopping centers and street corners was useless, for having no other place to go they always returned the next night, particularly since they knew people would not swear out complaints against their neighbors' (or customers') children. The police chief also did not want "the kids to feel they are being bugged," for they would come to hate his men and create more trouble for them.[36] If he cracked down on them, they would retaliate; if he did not, the adults would accuse him of laxity. Although the curfew was strongly supported by parents who could not control their children, it was rejected as unenforceable.

Adult solutions to the juvenile problem were generally shaped by

---

[35] Since the blotter listed adolescent promiscuity, adult suicide attempts, and even drunkenness and family quarrels among community leaders, I assume it was not censored to exclude adultery.

[36] Actually, since the police usually sided with the merchants against the teenagers, the latter did feel "bugged."

other institutional goals which took priority over adolescent needs. The organizations which scheduled dances wanted to advertise themselves and their community service inclinations, even competing for the right to hold them, and the churches set up youth groups to bring the teenagers into the church. Indeed, those who decide on adolescent programs either have vested interests in keeping teenagers in a childlike status (parents and educators, for example) or are charged with the protection of adult interests (police and politicians). The primacy of adult priorities was brought out by a 1961 PTA panel on "How Is Our Community Meeting the Needs of the Adolescents?" With one exception the panelists (chosen to represent the various adults responsible for teenagers) ignored these needs, talking only about what teenagers should do for *them*. For example, the parent on the panel said, "The needs of adolescents should first be met in the home and young energies should be guided into the proper normal channels." The teacher suggested that "parents should never undermine the authority of the teacher. Parents should help maintain the authority of the school over the child, and the school will in turn help maintain the authority of the parent over the child." The minister urged parents to "encourage youth leadership responsibilities within the church," and the police chief explained "the importance of teaching adolescents their proper relationship to the law and officers of the law." [37]

Political incentives for a municipal or even a semipublic recreation program were also absent. Not only were prospective sponsors afraid they would be held responsible for teenage misbehavior occurring under their auspices, but in 1961 not many Levittowners had adolescent children and not all of them favored a public program. Middle class parents either had no problems with their youngsters or objected to the working class advocacy of municipal recreation, and some working class parents felt that once children had reached adolescence they were on their own. The eventual clients of the program, the adolescents, had no political influence whatsoever. They were too young to vote, and although they might have persuaded their parents to demand facilities for them, they probably suspected that what their parents wanted for them was more of what had already been provided.

In the end, then, the adults got used to the little delinquency and vandalism that took place, and the teenagers became sullen and unhappy, complaining, "This place is Endsville," and wishing their parents would move back to communities which had facilities for them or pressuring them for cars to go to neighboring towns.

The best summary of what is wrong—and what should be done—was stated concisely by a twelfth-grade essayist: "I think the adults should spend less time watching for us to do something wrong and help us raise money for a community center. We're not asking for it, we only want their help." If one begins with the assumption that adolescents are rational and responsible human beings whose major "problem" is that they have become a distinctive minority subculture, it is not too difficult to suggest

[37] "Panel Features Junior High P.T.A. Meeting," *Levittown Herald*, January 26, 1961.

programs. What else the teenagers want in the way of recreation can be readily inferred from their essays: besides the center, a range of inexpensive coffeehouses and soda shops and other meeting places, bowling alleys, amusement arcades, places for dancing, ice and roller skating rinks, garages for mechanically inclined car owners (all within walking or bicycling distance or accessible by public transportation), and enough of each so that the various age groups and separate cliques have facilities they can call their own. Since adolescents are well supplied with spending money, many of these facilities can be set up commercially. Others may need public support. It would, for example, be possible to provide some municipal subsidies to luncheonette operators who are willing to make their businesses into teenage social centers.[38]

Recreational and social facilities are not enough, however. Part of the adolescents' dissatisfaction with the community—as with adult society in general—is their functionlessness outside of school. American society really has no use for them other than as students, and condemns them to spend most of their spare time in recreational pursuits. They are trying to learn to be adults, but since the community and the larger society want them to be children, they learn adulthood only at school—and there imperfectly. Yet many tasks in the community now go unfilled because of lack of public funds, for example, clerical, data-gathering, and other functions at city hall; and tutoring children, coaching their sports, and leading their recreational programs. These are meaningful duties, and I suspect many adolescents could fill them, either on a voluntary or a nominal wage basis. Finally, teenagers want to learn to be themselves and do for themselves. It should be possible to give them facilities of their own—or even land on which they could build—and let them organize, construct, and run their own centers and work places.

Needless to say, such autonomy would come up against the very real political difficulties that faced the more modest programs suggested in Levittown, and would surely be rejected by the community.[39] The ideal solution, therefore, is to plan for teenage needs outside the local adult decision-making structure, and perhaps even outside the community. It might be possible to establish Teenage Authorities that would play the same interstitial role in the governmental structure as other authorities set up in connection with intercommunity and regional planning functions. Perhaps the most feasible approach is to develop commercially profitable facilities, to be set up either by teenagers or by a private entrepreneur who would need to be less sensitive to political considerations than a public agency. If and when the "juvenile problem" becomes more serious in the suburbs, federal funds may become available for facilities and for programs to create jobs, like those now being developed for urban teenagers. Most likely, this will only happen when "trouble" begins to mount.

---

38 A combination neighborhood store and social center has been proposed in the plan for the new town of Columbia, Maryland.

39 In 1966, no teenage centers had yet been established in Levittown, and campaigning politicians were still arguing about the wisdom of doing so.

REFERENCES

Anderson, Judith, and Settani, Nicholas. "Resales in Levittown, Pennsylvania, 1952–1960." Unpublished paper, Department of City Planning, University of Pennsylvania, 1961.

Fried, Marc. "Grieving for a Lost Home," in Leonard J. Duhl, ed., *The Urban Condition*. New York: Basic Books, 1963, pp. 151–171.

Fromm, Erich. *The Sane Society*. New York: Holt, Rinehart and Winston, 1955.

Gabower, Genevieve. *Behavior Problems of Children in Navy Officers' Families as Related to Social Conditions of Navy Life*. Washington: Catholic University of America Press, 1959.

Gans, Herbert J. *The Urban Villagers: Group and Class in the Life of Italian-Americans*. New York: Free Press of Glencoe, 1962(a).

Gordon, R., Gordon, K., and Gunther, M. *The Split Level Trap*. New York: Geis, 1961.

Gutman, Robert. "Population Mobility in the American Middle Class," in Leonard J. Duhl, ed., *The Urban Condition*. New York: Basic Books, 1963, pp. 172–183.

Keats, John. *The Crack in the Picture Window*. Boston: Houghton-Mifflin, 1956 (Ballantine Books paperback, 1957).

Kornhauser, William. *Politics of Mass Society*. New York: Free Press of Glencoe, 1959.

Lipset, S. M. *Political Man*. Garden City: Doubleday, 1960.

Orzack, Louis H., and Sanders, Irwin T. *A Social Profile of Levittown, New York*. Ann Arbor: University Microfilms, O. P. 13438, 1961.

Pederson, Frank A., and Sullivan, Eugene. "Effects of Geographical Mobility and Parent Personality Factors on Emotional Disorders in Children." Washington: Walter Reed General Hospital, 1963, mimeographed.

Riesman, David (with N. Glazer and R. Denney). *The Lonely Crowd*. New Haven: Yale University Press, 1950.

Stein, Maurice. *The Eclipse of Community*. Princeton: Princeton University Press, 1960.

Ubell, Earl. "Marriage in the Suburbs." *New York Herald-Tribune*, January 4–8, 1959.

Vidich, Arthur J., and Bensman, Joseph. *Small Town in Mass Society*. Princeton: Princeton University Press, 1958.

Webber, Melvin M. "Order in Diversity: Community Without Propinquity," in Lowdon Wingo, Jr., ed., *Cities and Space: The Future Use of Urban Land*. Baltimore: Johns Hopkins University Press, 1963, pp. 23–54.

Whyte, William H., Jr. *The Organization Man*. New York: Simon & Schuster, 1956.

Wilensky, Harold L. "Life Cycle, Work Situation and Participation in Formal Associations," in Robert W. Kleemeier, ed., *Aging and Leisure*. New York: Oxford University Press, 1961, pp. 213–242.

Willmott, Peter. *The Evolution of a Community*. London: Routledge & Kegan Paul, 1963.

The Counter-Culture

WILLIAM L. O'NEILL

If we use the term "culture" to refer to the way of life of a people, then American society from its very beginning has been made up of a variety of cultures. However, throughout our history a more or less prevailing culture has dominated or attempted to dominate competing or conflicting cultures. Over the years, attempts have been made to describe this dominant culture, and many studies have pointed out aspects of the culture that have had a tremendous success in creating certain attitudes, if not always in controlling behavior.

The idea of culture contains both attitudes and behavior, and the secret of successful studies of any culture derives from the ability of the scholar to ferret out the patterns of behavior that may, in fact, run counter to the overt attitudes of a group.

What interests us in the following selection, however, is not the conflict between attitude and behavior, but the conflict between the dominant culture and a deviant culture that has as its goal a deliberate attack on the dominant culture and an elimination of the gap between attitude and behavior—what the participants in this counter-culture call hypocrisy.

Ever since the founding of the Massachusetts Bay Colony, the body of New World society has contained deviant cultural elements. This description refers, not to such entirely foreign cultures as the American Indian or the African, but to those deviations from the dominant culture that were exhibited by the settlers themselves. The English settlers who danced with Indians around a Maypole at Merry Mount in the 1630s presented a challenge to the prevailing culture; such challenges persist to the present day. The dominant culture has usually had the power of public opinion or, when necessary, the power of police authority to subdue deviants in its midst. This power, however, is not always invoked. In the twentieth century, there has developed a tradition often referred to as "bohemian" culture, restricted almost entirely to a small number of artists, writers, and composers. These creative bohemians have not sought to foster their way of life —composed as it is of a freedom from what they call bourgeois morality—on the rest of America. They merely want to be left alone. And they usually are unless they become too flagrant in their violations of community norms.

In the 1960s, an extremely powerful challenge to the dominant culture came into being. The term counter-culture, rather than subculture, can correctly be applied to this movement because it saw itself as a frontal attack on what it called "straight" culture. It had a visionary purpose—to "turn on" the world. At the heart of the counter-culture was a contempt for all traditional forms of authority and, theoretically, an intent to replace them with the authority of in-

ner experience and interpersonal relationships. Since these new authorities were difficult to isolate and identify, much less obey, the
counter-culture's adherents turned to all sorts of gurus (spiritual leaders) in an attempt to find their way into the brave new world they
forecast.

In the chapter from his book on the 1960s reprinted below,
William O'Neill, of Rutgers University, describes many facets of the
counter-culture movement of the decade. He notes the critical importance of the mass media, which proved so influential in spreading the
new gospel as well as in denigrating it. O'Neill rightly points out that
the movement was not limited to the young but increasingly began to
attract older people to certain aspects of the freedom it espoused. In
his concluding paragraphs, the author, perhaps, renders too harsh a
judgment on the movement. A longer perspective will allow future
historians to evaluate more accurately the impact of this flashy and
furious attempt to find a more meaningful and more human life-style
in the midst of what many saw as an inhuman and materialistic
middle-class morality.

Counter-culture as a term appeared rather late in the decade. It largely
replaced the term "youth culture," which finally proved too limited.
When the sixties began, youth culture meant the way adolescents lived.
Its central institutions were the high school and the mass media. Its principal activities were consuming goods and enacting courtship rituals. Critics
and students of the youth culture were chiefly interested in the status and
value systems associated with it. As time went on, college enrollments increased to the point where colleges were nearly as influential as high
schools in shaping the young. The molders of youthful opinion got more
ambitious. Where once entertainers were content to amuse for profit,
many began seeing themselves as moral philosophers. Music especially became a medium of propaganda, identifying the young as a distinct force in
society with unique values and aspirations. This helped produce a kind of
ideological struggle between the young and their elders called the "generation gap." It was the first time in American history that social conflict was
understood to be a function of age. Yet the young were not all rebellious.
Most in fact retained confidence in the "system" and its norms. Many
older people joined the rebellion, whose progenitors were as often over
thirty (where the generation gap was supposed to begin) as under it. The
attack on accepted views and styles broadened so confusingly that "youth
culture" no longer described it adequately. Counter-culture was a sufficiently vague and elastic substitute. It meant all things to all men and em-

braced everything new from clothing to politics. Some viewed the counter-
culture as mankind's best, maybe only, hope; others saw it as a portent of
civilization's imminent ruin. Few recalled the modest roots from which it
sprang.

Even in the 1950's and very early sixties, when people still worried
about conformity and the silent generation, there were different drummers
to whose beat millions would one day march. The bohemians of that era
(called "beatniks" or "beats") were only a handful, but they practiced
free love, took drugs, repudiated the straight world, and generally showed
which way the wind was blowing. They were highly publicized, so when
the bohemian impulse strengthened, dropouts knew what was expected of
them. While the beats showed their contempt for social norms mostly in
physical ways, others did so intellectually. Norman Mailer, in "The White
Negro," held up the sensual, lawless hipster as a model of behavior under
oppressive capitalism. He believed, according to "The Time of Her Time,"
that sexual orgasm was the pinnacle of human experience, perhaps also an
approach to ultimate truth. Norman O. Brown's *Life Against Death*, a
psychoanalytic interpretation of history, was an underground classic which
argued that cognition subverted intuition. Brown called for a return to
"polymorphous perversity," man's natural estate. The popularity of Zen
Buddhism demonstrated that others wished to slip the bonds of Western
rationalism; so, from a different angle, did the vogue for black humor.
    The most prophetic black humorist was Joseph Heller, whose novel
Catch-22 came out in 1960. Though set in World War II the book was
even more appropriate to the Indochinese war. Later Heller said, "That
was the war I had in mind; a war fought without military provocation,
a war in which the real enemy is no longer the other side, but someone
allegedly on your side. The ridiculous war I felt lurking in the future
when I wrote the book." *Catch-22* was actually written during the Cold
War, and sold well in the early sixties because it attacked the perceptions
on which that war, like the Indochinese war that it fathered, grew. At the
time reviewers didn't know what to make of *Catch 22*. World War II had
been, as everyone knew, an absolutely straightforward case of good versus
evil. Yet to Heller there was little moral difference between combatants.
In fact all his characters are insane, or carry normal attributes to insane
lengths. They belong to a bomber squadron in the Mediterranean. Terrified of combat, most hope for ground duty and are free to request it, but:
"There was only one catch and that was Catch-22, which specified that a
concern for one's own safety in the face of dangers that were real and
immediate was the process of a rational mind. Orr was crazy and could be
grounded. All he had to do was ask; and as soon as he did, he would no
longer be crazy and would have to fly more missions. Orr would be crazy
to fly more missions and sane if he didn't, but if he was sane he had to fly
them. If he flew them he was crazy and didn't have to; but if he didn't
want to he was sane and had to."
    The squadron's success depends more on having a perfect bomb pat-

tern than hitting the target. Milo Minderbinder is the key man in the
Theater, though only a lieutenant, because he embodies the profit motive.
He puts the entire war on a paying basis and hires the squadron out impartially to both sides. At the end Yossarian, the novel's hero, resolves his
dilemma by setting out for neutral Sweden in a rubber raft. This was what
hundreds of real deserters and draft evaders would be doing soon. It was
also a perfect symbol for the masses of dropouts who sought utopian
alternatives to the straight world. One day there would be hundreds of
thousands of Yossarians, paddling away from the crazed society in frail
crafts of their own devising. *Catch-22* was not just black comedy, nor even
chiefly an anti-war novel, but a metaphor that helped shape the moral
vision of an era.[1]

Although children and adolescents watched a great deal of television
in the sixties, it seemed at first to have little effect. Surveys were always
showing that youngsters spent fifty-four hours a week or whatever in front
of the tube, yet what they saw was so bland or predictable as to make
little difference. The exceptions were news programs, documentaries, and
dramatic specials. Few watched them. What did influence the young was
popular music, folk music first and then rock. Large-scale enthusiasm for
folk music began in 1958 when the Kingston Trio recorded a song, "Tom
Dooley," that sold two million records. This opened the way for less
slickly commercial performers. Some, like Pete Seeger, who had been singing since the depression, were veteran performers. Others, like Joan Baez,
were newcomers. It was conventional for folk songs to tell a story. Hence
the idiom had always lent itself to propaganda. Seeger possessed an enormous repertoire of message songs that had gotten him blacklisted by the
mass media years before. Joan Baez cared more for the message than the
music, and after a few years devoted herself mainly to peace work. The
folk-music vogue was an early stage in the politicalization of youth, a fore-
runner of the counter-culture. This was hardly apparent at the time. Folk
music was not seen as morally reprehensible in the manner of rock and roll.
It was a familiar genre. Folk was gentle music for the most part, and even
when sung in protest did not offend many. Malvina Reynolds' "What
Have They Done to the Rain?" complained of radioactive fallout which
all detested. Pete Seeger's anti-war song "Where Have All the Flowers
Gone?" was a favorite with both pacifists and the troops in Vietnam.

Bob Dylan was different. Where most folk singers were either clean-
cut or homey looking, Dylan had wild long hair. He resembled a poor
white dropout of questionable morals. His songs were hard-driving, powerful, intense. It was hard to be neutral about them. "The Times They Are
a-Changing" was perhaps the first song to exploit the generation gap.
Dylan's life was as controversial as his ideology. Later he dropped politics

[1] Lenny Bruce was a more tragic harbinger of change. He was a successful night club
comedian who created an obscene form of black comedy that involved more social
criticism than humor. Bruce was first arrested for saying "motherfucker" on stage
in 1962. Later he was busted for talking dirty about the Pope and many lesser
offenses. He may have been insane. He died early from persecution and drug abuse,
and then became an honored martyr in the anti-Establishment pantheon. He was
one of the spiritual fathers of the yippies.

and got interested in rock music. At the Newport Jazz Festival in 1965 he was booed when he introduced a fusion of his own called "folk-rock." He went his own way after that, disowned by the politically minded but admired by a great cult following attracted as much, perhaps, by his independent life as by his music. He advanced the counter-culture in both ways and made money too. This also was an inspiration to those who came after him.

Another early expression, which coexisted with folk music, though quite unlike it, was the twist. Dance crazes were nothing new, but the twist was remarkable because it came to dominate social dancing. It used to be that dance fads were here today and gone tomorrow, while the two-step went on forever. Inexpert, that is to say most, social dancers had been loyal to it for generations. It played a key role in the traditional youth culture. Who could imagine a high school athletic event that did not end with couples clinging to one another on the dimly lit gym floor, while an amateur dance band plodded gamely on? When in 1961 the twist became popular, moralists were alarmed. It called for vigorous, exhibitionistic movements. Prurient men were reminded of the stripper's bumps and grinds. They felt the twist incited lust. Ministers denounced it. Yet in the twist (and its numerous descendants), bodies were not rubbed together as in the two-step, which had embarrassed millions of schoolboys. Millions more had suffered when through awkwardness they bumped or trod on others. The twist, by comparison, was easy and safe. No partner was bothered by the other's maladroitness. It aroused few passions. That was the practical reason for its success. But there was an ideological impulse behind it also. Amidst the noise and tumult each person danced alone, "doing his own thing," as would soon be said. But though alone, the dancer was surrounded by others doing their own thing in much the same manner. The twist celebrated both individuality and communality. This was to become a hallmark of the counter-culture, the right of everyone to be different in much the same way. The twist also foretold the dominance of rock, to which it was so well suited.

No group contributed more to the counter-culture than the Beatles, though, like folk music and the twist, their future significance was not at first apparent. Beatlemania began on October 13, 1963, when the quartet played at the London Palladium. The police, caught unawares, were hardly able to control the maddened throngs. On February 9, 1964, they appeared on U.S. television. The show received fifty thousand ticket requests for a theater that seated eight hundred. They were mobbed at the airport, besieged in their hotel, and adored everywhere. Even their soiled bed linen found a market. Their next recording, "Can't Buy Me Love," sold three million copies in advance of release, a new world's record. Their first movie, *A Hard Day's Night* (1964), was both a critical and a popular success. Some reviewers compared them with the Marx brothers. They became millionaires overnight. The Queen decorated them for helping ease the balance-of-payments deficit. By 1966 they were so rich that they could afford to give up live performances.

For a time the Beatles seemed just another pop phenomenon, Elvis Presley multiplied by four. Few thought their music very distinguished.

The reasons for its wide acceptance were hard to fathom. Most felt their showmanship was the key factor. They wore their hair longer than was fashionable, moved about a lot on stage, and avoided the class and racial identifications associated with earlier rock stars. Elvis had cultivated a proletarian image. Other rock stars had been black, or exploited the Negro rhythm-and-blues tradition. The Beatles were mostly working class in origin but sang with an American accent (like other English rock stars) and dressed in an elegant style, then popular in Britain, called "mod." The result was a deracinated, classless image of broad appeal.

The Beatles did not fade away as they were supposed to. Beatlemania continued for three years. Then the group went through several transformations that narrowed its audience to a smaller but intensely loyal cult following in the Dylan manner. The group became more self-consciously artistic. Their first long-playing record took one day to make and cost £400. "Sergeant Pepper's Lonely Hearts Club Band" took four months and cost £25,000. They were among the first to take advantage of new recording techniques that enabled multiple sound tracks to be played simultaneously. The Beatles learned new instruments and idioms too. The result was a complex music that attracted serious inquiry. Critics debated their contributions to musicology and argued over whether they were pathfinders or merely gifted entrepreneurs. In either case, they had come a long way aesthetically from their humble beginnings. Their music had a great effect on the young, so did their styles of life. They led the march of fashion away from mod and into the hairy, mustached, bearded, beaded, fringed, and embroidered costumes of the late sixties. For a time they followed the Maharishi, an Indian guru of some note. They married and divorced in progressively more striking ways. Some were arrested for smoking marijuana. In this too they were faithful to their clientele.

John Lennon went the farthest. He married Yoko Ono, best known as an author of happenings, and with her launched a bizarre campaign for world peace and goodness. Lennon returned his decoration to the Queen in protest against the human condition. Lennon and Ono hoped to visit America but were denied entry, which, to the bureaucratic mind, seemed a stroke for public order and morality. They staged a bed-in for peace all the same. They also formed a musical group of their own, the Plastic Ono Band, and circulated nude photographs and erotic drawings of themselves. This seemed an odd way to stop the war in Indochina, even to other Beatles. The group later broke up. By then they had made their mark, and, while strange, it was not a bad mark. Whatever lasting value their music may have, they set a good example to the young in most ways. Lennon's pacifism was nonviolent, even if wildly unorthodox. At a time when so many pacifists were imitating what they protested against, that was most desirable. They also worked hard at their respective arts and crafts, though others were dropping out and holding up laziness as a socially desirable trait. The Beatles showed that work was not merely an Establishment trick to keep the masses in subjection and the young out of trouble.

*   *   *

Beatlemania coincided with a more ominous development in the emerging counter-culture—the rise of the drug prophet Timothy Leary. He and Richard Alpert were scientific researchers at Harvard University who studied the effects of hallucinogenic drugs, notably a compound called LSD. As early as 1960 it was known that the two were propagandists as well as scientists. In 1961 the University Health Service made them promise not to use undergraduates in their experiments. Their violation of this pledge was the technical ground for firing them. A better one was that they had founded a drug cult. Earlier studies of LSD had failed, they said, because the researchers had not themselves taken the drug. In order to end this "authoritarian" practice, they "turned on" themselves. Their work was conducted in quarters designed to look like a bohemian residence instead of a laboratory. This was defended as a reconstruction of the natural environment in which social "acid-dropping" took place. They and many of their subjects became habitual users, not only of LSD but of marijuana and other drugs. They constructed an ideology of sorts around this practice. After they were fired the *Harvard Review* published an article of theirs praising the drug life: "Remember, man, a natural state is ecstatic wonder, ecstatic intuition, ecstatic accurate movement. Don't settle for less."

With some friends Leary and Alpert created the International Foundation for Internal Freedom (IF-IF) which published the *Psychedelic Review*. To advertise it a flyer was circulated that began, "Mescaline! Experimental Mysticism! Mushrooms! Ecstasy! LSD-25! Expansion of Consciousness! Phantastica! Transcendence! Hashish! Visionary Botany! Ololiuqui! Physiology of Religion! Internal Freedom! Morning Glory! Politics of the Nervous System!" Later the drug culture would generate a vast literature, but this was its essential message. The truth that made Western man free was only obtainable through hallucinogenic drugs. Truth was in the man, not the drug, yet the drug was necessary to uncover it. The natural state of man thus revealed was visionary, mystical, ecstatic. The heightened awareness stimulated by "consciousness-expanding" drugs brought undreamed-of sensual pleasures, according to Leary. Even better, drugs promoted peace, wisdom, and unity with the universe.

Alpert soon dropped from view. Leary went on to found his own sect, partly because once LSD was banned religious usage was the only ground left on which it could be defended, mostly because the drug cult *was* a religion. He wore long white robes and long blond hair. And he traveled about the country giving his liberating message (tune in, turn on, drop out) and having bizarre adventures. His personal following was never large, but drug use became commonplace among the young anyway. At advanced universities social smoking of marijuana was as acceptable as social drinking. More so, in a way, for it was better suited to the new ethic. One did not clutch one's solitary glass but shared one's "joint" with others. "Grass" made one gentle and pacific, not surly and hostile. As a forbidden pleasure it was all the more attractive to the thrill-seeking and the rebellious. And it helped further distinguish between the old world of grasping, combative, alcoholic adults and the turned-on, cooperative culture of the young. Leary was a bad prophet. Drug-based mystical religion was not the wave of the future. What the drug cult led to was a lot of dope-smoking and some hard drug-taking. When research suggested that LSD caused genetic damage, its use declined. But the effects of grass were hard to determine, so its consumption increased.

Sometimes "pot" smokers went on to other drugs—a deadly compound called "speed," and even heroin. These ruined many lives (though it was never clear that the lives were not already ruined to begin with). The popularity of drugs among the young induced panic in the old. States passed harsher and harsher laws that accomplished little. Campaigns against the drug traffic were launched periodically with similar results. When the flow of grass was interrupted, people turned to other drugs. Drug use seemed to go up either way. The generation gap widened. Young people thought marijuana less dangerous than alcohol, perhaps rightly. To proscribe the one and permit the other made no sense to them, except as still another example of adult hypocrisy and the hatred of youth. Leary had not meant all this to happen, but he was to blame for some of it all the same. No one did more to build the ideology that made pot-smoking a morally constructive act. But though a malign influence, no one deserved such legal persecution as he experienced before escaping to Algeria from a prison farm.

In Aldous Huxley's prophetic novel *Brave New World,* drug use was promoted by the state as a means of social control. During the sixties it remained a deviant practice and a source of great tension between the generations. Yet drugs did encourage conformity among the young. To "turn on and drop out" did not weaken the state. Quite the contrary, it drained off potentially subversive energies. The need for drugs gave society a lever should it ever decide to manipulate rather than repress users. Pharmacology and nervous strain had already combined to make many adult Americans dependent on drugs like alcohol and tranquilizers. Now the young were doing the same thing, if for different reasons. In a free country this meant only that individual problems increased. But should democracy fail, drug abuse among both the young and old was an instrument for control such as no dictator ever enjoyed. The young drug-takers thought to show contempt for a grasping, unfeeling society. In doing so they opened the door to a worse one. They scorned their elders for drinking and pill-taking, yet to outsiders their habits seemed little different, though ethically more pretentious. In both cases users were vulnerable and ineffective to the extent of their addiction. Of such ironies was the counter-culture built. . . .

The rebellion against traditional fashion went in two directions, though both were inspired by the young. The line of development just described emphasized brilliant or peculiar fabrics and designs. Here the emphasis was on costuming in a theatrical sense. People wore outfits that made them look like Mongols or cavaliers or whatever. These costumes, never cheap, were often very costly, though not more so than earlier styles. They were worn by others besides the young. What they owed to the emerging counter-culture was a certain freedom from constraint, and a degree of sensuality. Though the mini-skirt became a symbol of rebellious youth, it was so popular that wearing it was not an ideological statement, even if Middle Americans often thought so.

The other direction clothing took was more directly related to counter-cultural patterns. This mode had two seemingly incompatible elements—surplus military garments and handcrafted ones. Army and navy surplus clothing was the first style to be adopted by young people looking for a separate identity. Socially conscious youths began wearing army and navy jackets, shirts, and bell-bottom trousers in the early sixties. This was not meant to show contempt for the military, for anti-war sentiment was then at a low ebb, but as a mark of ostentatious frugality in the high-consumption society. As these garments became more in demand, the price went up and more expensive commercial imitations appeared. Wearing them accordingly meant less, but a certain flavor of austere nonconformity stuck to them all the same. They remained favorites of dissenting youths thereafter, even though worn by the merely fashionable too.

The hippies made handcrafted items popular. The implication here was that the wearer had made them, thus showing his independence and creativity. In the beginning this may often have been so. Soon, however, the market was so large and the people with skill and patience so limited that handcrafted items were commercially made and distributed, frequently by entrepreneurs among the young, sometimes through ordinary apparel channels. Bead shops and hippie boutiques became commonplace. Though their products were often quite costly, the vogue persisted among deviant youths anyway, partly because it was clear that whatever they wore would soon be imitated, partly because the message involved was too dear to abandon. Wearing beads, bangles, leather goods, fringes, colorful vests, and what all showed sympathy for American Indians, who inspired the most common designs, and fitted in with the popular back-to-nature ethic. When combined with military surplus garments they enabled the wearer to touch all the counter-cultural bases at once. Thus these fashions transmitted, however faintly, signals meaning peace, love, brotherhood, noble savagery, community, folk artistry, anti-capitalism and anti-militarism, and, later, revolutionary zeal.

This hippie *cum* military surplus mode also had a functional effect. It was a great leveler: when everyone wore the same bizarre costumes, everyone looked alike. Even better, it gave the ugly parity with the beautiful for the first time in modern history. Most of these costumes were pretty ghastly. A string of beads or an Indian headband did not redeem faded blue jeans and an army shirt. Long stringy hair or an untrimmed beard only aggravated the effect. Yet the young called such outfits beautiful. In effect, aesthetics were exchanged for ethics. Beauty was no longer related to appearance but to morality. To have the proper spirit, though homely, was to be beautiful. This was a great relief for the poorly endowed and a point in the counter-culture's favor. Yet it enraged adults. Once the association between beads, beards, and military surplus goods on the one hand, and radicalism and dope on the other, was established, Middle America declared war on the counter-culture's physical trappings. School systems everywhere waged a relentless struggle against long hair. To dress this way in many places was a hostile act which invited reprisals. The style became a chief symbol of the generation gap, clung to fanatically by youngsters the more they were persecuted for it, as fiercely resisted by their elders. The progress of the generational struggle could almost be measured by the spread of these fashions.

No doubt older people would have resented the new styles in any case, but the way they emerged made them doubly offensive. They were introduced by young bohemians, mainly in New York and San Francisco, whose deviant attributes were highly publicized. New York hippies were concentrated in a section called the East Village. (Greenwich Village, the traditional bohemian refuge, had gotten too commercial and expensive.) By the mid-sixties a sizable community of radicals, dropouts, youthful vagrants, unrecognized avant-garde artists, and others were assembling there and a variety of cults beginning to flourish. One of the odder was called Kerista. It was a religio-sexual movement that planned to establish a colony in the Caribbean. "Utopia Tomorrow for Swingers," its publication, the *Kerista Speeler*, proclaimed. Kerista invoked a murky, perfectionist theology revolving around sexual love. Sometimes the members engaged in bisexual gropes to advance the pleasure principle. This sounded like more fun than it actually was, according to visitors.

The mainstream of East Village cultural life was more formally political and artistic. The many activities of Ed Sanders suggest the range of enterprises generated there. He was editor and publisher of *Fuck You: A Magazine of the Arts*. A typical editorial in it begins: "Time is NOW for TOTAL ASSAULT ON THE MARIJUANA LAWS. It is CLEAR to us that the cockroach theory of grass smoking has to be abandoned. IN THE OPEN! ALL THOSE WHO SUCK UP THE BENEVOLENT NARCOTIC CANNABIS, TEENSHUN!! FORWARD, WITH MIND DIALS POINTED: ASSAULT! We have the facts! Cannabis is a nonaddictive gentle peace drug! The marijuana legislations were pushed through in the 1930's by the agents and goonsquads of the jansensisto-manichean fuckhaters' conspiracy. Certainly after 30 years of the blight, it is time to rise up for a bleep blop bleep assault on the social screen. . . . But we can't wait forever you grass cadets to pull the takeover: grass-freak senators, labor leaders, presidents, etc.! The Goon Squads are few and we are many. We must spray our message into the million lobed American brain IMMEDIATELY!"

Sanders was also head of the East Village's most prominent rock group, The Fugs. They sang obscene songs of their own composition, and created equally obscene instruments for accompaniment (such as the erectophone, which appeared to be a long stick with bells on it). Among their better efforts were "What Are You Doing After the Orgy?" and the memorable "Kill for Peace." *The Fugs Song Book* described their music thusly:

The Fug-songs seem to spurt into five areas of concentration:
a) nouveau folk-freak
b) sex rock and roll
c) dope thrill chants
d) horny cunt-hunger blues
e) Total Assault on the Culture
    (anti-war/anti-creep/anti-repression)
. . . The meaning of the Fugs lies in the term BODY POETRY, to get
    at the frenzy of the thing, the grope-thing, The Body Poetry
    Formula is this:
The Head by the way of the Big Beat to the genitals
The Genitals by way of Operation Brain Thrill to the Body
    Poetry.

In his spare time Sanders made pornographic movies. His most epic work, *Mongolian Cluster Fuck!*, was described in *Fuck You* as a "short but searing non-socially redeeming porn flick featuring 100 of the lower east side's finest, with musical background by Algernon Charles Swinburne & THE FUGS." Though more versatile and creative than most, Sanders was typical of the East Village's alienated young artists. Tiny papers like *Fuck You* were springing up everywhere. All tried to be obscene, provocative, and, it was thought, liberating. They despised form, caring only for the higher morality and aesthetics it was their duty to advance. Some were more political (porno-political usually) than others. Collectively they were soon to be known as the "underground press."

Several cuts above the underground press were the flourishing little magazines. They were avant garde in the traditional sense and aimed, in their way, for greatness. By 1966 there were at least 250 of these (as against sixty or so in the 1920's). The better financed *(Outsider, Steppenwolf)* were tastefully composed and printed; others were crudely photo-offset *(Kayak, Eventorium Muse)*. The *Insect Trust Gazette,* an annual experiment, once published an issue in which the original manuscripts were simply photographed and printed without reduction. About a third of the "littles" were mimeographed. There was even a little magazine for scientists, the *Worm-Runners' Digest,* edited by a droll researcher at the University of Michigan for people of like taste.

Older cultural rebels contributed to the ferment. George Brecht's musical composition "Ladder" went as follows: "Paint a single straight ladder white/Paint the bottom rung black/Distribute spectral colors on the rungs between." Even more to the point was "Laugh Piece" by John Lennon's future wife, Yoko Ono. It went "Keep laughing for a week." Nam June Paik composed a work known as "Young Penis Symphony." He was also an underground film producer and put on elaborate performances resembling the late happenings. One such was given at the Film-Makers Cinematheque using film, live music, and the cellist Charlotte Moorman. The audience saw short segments of a film by Robert Breer, alternating with views of Miss Moorman, silhouetted by backlighting behind the projection screen, playing short phrases of a Bach cello sonata. On completing each phrase she removed a garment. Another film clip would then be shown. This continued until she was lying on the floor, completely nude, playing her cello which was now atop her. Miss Moorman, "the Jeanne d'Arc of New Music," as she was called, appeared in other Paik compositions. She had been trained at the Juilliard School and was a member of Leopold Stokowski's American Symphony Orchestra.

As these few examples suggest, the East Village gained from its proximity to the New York avant garde. The mature counter-culture owed a lot to this relationship, but even in its early stages the East Village suffered from the influx of teenie-boppers and runaways who were to spoil both it and the Haight-Ashbury for serious cultural radicals. The people who were soon to be called hippies meant to build alternatives to the straight world. Against the hostile competitive, capitalistic values of bourgeois America they posed their own faith in nonviolence, love, and community. Drugs were important both as means to truth and advancers of the pleasure principle. The early hippies created institutions of sorts. Rock bands like the Jefferson Airplane, the Grateful Dead, Country Joe and the Fish flourished, as did communal societies, notably the Diggers. They were inspired by the seventeenth-century communists whose name they took. In practice they were a hip version of the Salvation Army.

Hippies lived together, in "tribes" or "families." Their golden rule was "Be nice to others, even when provoked, and they will be nice to you." In San Francisco their reservation was the Haight-Ashbury district near Golden Gate Park. They were much resented in the East Village by the natives, poor ethnics for the most part. In the Hashbury, on the other hand, they were welcome at first. Though peculiar, they were an improvement over the petty criminals they displaced. Even when freaked-out in public from drugs, a certain tolerance prevailed. After all, stepping over a drooling flower child on the street was better than getting mugged. Civic authorities were less open-minded. The drug traffic bothered them especially, and the Hashbury was loaded with "narks" (narcotics agents). Hunter S. Thompson wrote that "love is the password in the Haight-Ashbury, but paranoia is the style. Nobody wants to go to jail."

The fun-and-games era did not last long, perhaps only from 1965 to 1966. The hippie ethic was too fragile to withstand the combination of police surveillance and media exposure that soon afflicted it. The first hippies had a certain earnestness. But they were joined by masses of teen-age runaways. Nicholas von Hoffman observed that the Hashbury economy that began as a fraternal barter system quickly succumbed to the cash nexus. It became the first community in the world to revolve entirely around the buying and selling and taking of drugs. Marijuana and LSD were universal; less popular, but also commonplace, were LSD's more powerful relative STP, and amphetamines. "Speed kills" said the buttons and posters; speed freaks multiplied anyhow. To support themselves some hippies worked at casual labor or devised elaborate, usually unsuccessful schemes to make money out of hippie enterprises. Panhandling was popular, so was theft, disguised usually as communism.

Bohemians invariably deplore monogamy, and the hippies were no exception. As one member of the Jefferson Airplane put it "The stage is our bed and the audience is our broad. We're not entertaining, we're making love." Though committed to sexual freedom on principle, and often promiscuous in fact, the hippies were not really very sexy. Timothy Leary notwithstanding, drugs seemed to dampen the sexual urge. And the hippies were too passive in any case for strenuous sex play. Conversely, the most ardent free lovers, like those in the Sexual Freedom League, had little interest in drugs. Among hippies the combination of bad diets, dope, communal living, and the struggle to survive made for a restricted sex life. Of course the hippies were always glad of chances to shock the bourgeoisie, which made them seem more depraved than they were. Then too, people expected them to be sexually perverse, and the more public-spirited hippies tried to oblige. Like good troupers they hated to let the public down, though willing to put it on.

Hippie relations with black people were worse than might have been supposed. Hippies owed blacks a lot. Their jargon was derived from the ghetto. They admired blacks, as certain whites always have, for being more emotional, sensual, and uninhibited. But there were very few black hippies. Superspade, a beloved Negro drug pusher, was an exception. Most hippies were frightened of blacks. "Spades are programmed for hate" was the way many put it. The Hashbury was periodically swept by rumors of impending black attacks. Some hippies looked to the motorcycle outlaws to protect them from black rage. This was not without a certain logic. Outlaws hated blacks and loved to fight. But they played their role as hippie militiamen uneasily. In truth they were more likely to destroy a hippie than defend him.

In the end it was neither the bikers nor the blacks but the media that destroyed hippiedom. The publicity given the summer of love attracted countless thousands of disturbed youngsters to the Hashbury and the East Village in 1967. San Francisco was not burdened with the vast numbers originally expected. But many did come, bringing in their train psychotics, drug peddlers, and all sorts of criminals. Drug poisoning, hepatitis (from infected needles), and various diseases resulting from malnutrition and exposure thinned their ranks. Rapes, muggings, and assaults became commonplace. Hippies had little money, but they were irresistibly easy marks. Hippie girls were safe to assault. They reacted passively, and as many were drug users and runaways they could not go to the police.

So the violence mounted. On the West Coast one drug peddler was stabbed to death and his right forearm removed. Superspade's body was found hanging from a cliff top. He had been stabbed, shot, and trussed in a sleeping bag. On October 8 the nude bodies of Linda Rea Fitzpatrick, eighteen, and James Leroy "Groovy" Hutchinson, twenty-one, were discovered in an East Village boiler room. They had been murdered while high on LSD. Though pregnant, Miss Fitzpatrick had also been raped. That was how the summer of love ended. Two days earlier the death and funeral of hippie had been ritually observed in San Francisco's Buena Vista Park. But the killing of Linda and Groovy marked its real end. The Hashbury deteriorated rapidly thereafter. Bad publicity drove the tourists away, and the hippie boutiques that serviced them closed. Some local rock groups dissolved; others, like the Jefferson Airplane and even the Grateful

Dead, went commercial. The hippies and their institutions faded quietly away. The Hashbury regained something of its old character. The East Village, owing to its more diverse population and strategic location, changed less.

At its peak the hippie movement was the subject of much moralizing. Most often hippies were seen as degenerate and representative of all things godless and un-American. A minority accepted them as embodying a higher morality. The media viewed them as harmless, even amusing, freaks —which was probably closest to the truth. But before long it was clear that while the hippie movement was easily slain, the hippie style of life was not. Their habit of dressing up in costumes rather than outfits was widely imitated. So was their slang and their talk of peace, love, and beauty. The great popularity of ex-hippie rock groups was one sign of the cultural diffusion taking place, marijuana another. Weekend tripping spread to the suburbs. While the attempt to build parallel cultures on a large scale in places like the Hashbury failed, the hippies survived in many locales. Isolated farms, especially in New England and the Southwest, were particularly favored. And they thrived also on the fringes of colleges and universities, where the line between avant-garde student and alienated dropout was hard to draw. In tribes, families, and communes, the hippies lived on, despite considerable local harassment wherever they went.

Though few in number, hippies had a great effect on middle-class youth. Besides their sartorial influence, hippies made religion socially acceptable. Their interest in the supernatural was contagious. Some of the communes which sprang up in the late sixties were actually religious fellowships practicing a contemporary monasticism. One in western Massachusetts was called the Cathedral of the Spirit. Its forty members were led by a nineteen-year-old mystic who helped them prepare for the Second Coming and the new Aquarian Age when all men would be brothers. The Cathedral had rigid rules against alcohol, "sex without love," and, less typically, drugs. Members helped out neighboring farmers without pay, but the commune was essentially contemplative. Its sacred book was a fifty-seven-page typewritten manuscript composed by a middle-aged bus driver from Northfield, Massachusetts, which was thought to be divinely inspired. Another commune in Boston, called the Fort Hill Community, was more outward looking. Its sixty members hoped to spread their holy word through the mass media.

Some of the communes or brotherhoods sprang from traditional roots. In New York City a band of young Jews formed a Havurah (fellowship) to blend Jewish traditions with contemporary inspirations. They wanted to study subjects like "the prophetic mind; new forms of spirituality in the contemporary world; and readings from the Jewish mystical tradition." At the University of Massachusetts a hundred students celebrated Rosh Hashanah not in a synagogue but in a field where they danced and sang all night. Courses in religion multiplied. At Smith College the number of students taking them grew from 692 in 1954 to nearly 1,400 in 1969, though the student body remained constant at about 2,000. Columbia University had two hundred applicants for a graduate program in religion with only twenty openings.

Students saw traditional religion as a point of departure rather than a place for answers. Comparatively few joined the new fellowships, but large numbers were attracted to the concepts they embodied. Oriental theologies and the like grew more attractive, so did magic. At one Catholic university a coven of warlocks was discovered. They were given psychiatric attention (thereby missing a great chance. If only they had been exorcised instead, the Establishment would have shown its relevance). When a Canadian university gave the studentry a chance to recommend new courses they overwhelmingly asked for subjects like Zen, sorcery, and witchcraft. A work of classic Oriental magic, *I Ching*, or the *Book of Changes*, became popular. The best edition, a scholarly product of the Princeton University Press, used to sell a thousand copies a year. In 1968 fifty thousand copies were snapped up. Sometimes magic and mysticism were exploited more in fun than not. The Women's Liberation Movement had guerrilla theater troupes calling themselves WITCH (Women's International Terrorist Conspiracy from Hell). During the SDS sit-in at the University of Chicago they cursed the sociology department and put a hex on its chairman.

But there was a serious element to the vogue for magic. Teachers of philosophy and religion were struck by the anti-positivist, anti-science feelings of many students. Science was discredited as an agent of the military-industrial complex. It had failed to make life more attractive. Whole classes protested the epistemology of science as well as its intellectual dominion. Students believed the Establishment claimed to be rational, but showed that it was not. This supported one of the central truths of all religion, that man is more than a creature who reasons. Nor was it only the young who felt this way. Norman Mailer was something of a mystic, so was Timothy Leary. And the most ambitious academic effort to deal with these things, Theodore Roszak's *The Making of a Counter Culture*, ended with a strong appeal to faith. Like the alienated young, Roszak too rejected science and reason—"the myth of objective consciousness" as he called it. Instead of empiricism or the scientific method he wanted "the beauty of the fully illuminated personality" to be "our standard of truth." He liked magic as "a matter of communion with the forces of nature as if they were mindful, intentional presences." What he admired most in the New Left was its attempt, as he thought, to revive shamanism, to get back to the sanity and participatory democracy of prehistoric society. But he urged the left to give up its notion that violence and confrontation would change the world. What the left must do to influence the silent majority "was not simply to muster power against the misdeeds of society, but to transform the very sense men have of reality."

The anti-war movement was strongly affected by this new supernaturalism. On Moratorium Day in 1969 a University of Massachusetts student gave an emotional speech that brought the audience to its feet shouting, "The war is over." "He went into a dance, waving his arms," a campus minister said. "It was the essence of a revival meeting, where the audience makes a commitment to Christ at the end." The great peace demonstrations in 1969 were full of religious symbolism. In Boston 100,000 people gathered before a gigantic cross on the Common. In New York lighted candles were carried to the steps of St. Patrick's Cathedral. Candles were placed on the White House wall during the November mobilization. At other demonstrations the shofar, the ram's horn sounded by Jews at the beginning of each new year, was blown. Rock, the liturgical music of the young, was often played. So was folk music, which continued as a medium of moral expression after its popular decline.

. . . On its deepest level the counter-culture was the radical critique of Herbert Marcuse, Norman O. Brown, and even Paul Goodman. It also meant the New Left, communes and hippie farms, magic, hedonism, eroticism, and public nudity. And it included rock music, long hair, and miniskirts (or, alternatively, fatigue uniforms, used clothes, and the intentionally ugly or grotesque). Most attacks on the counter-culture were directed at its trivial aspects, pot and dress especially. Pot busts (police raids), often involving famous people or their children, became commonplace. The laws against pot were so punitive in some areas as to be almost unenforceable. Even President Nixon, spokesman for Middle American morality that he was, finally questioned them. Local fights against long hair, beards, and short skirts were beyond number. The American Civil Liberties Union began taking school systems to court for disciplining students on that account. New York City gave up trying to enforce dress codes. It was all the more difficult there as even the teachers were mod. At one school the principal ordered women teachers to wear smocks over their minis. They responded by buying mini-smocks.

Nor were athletics—the last bastion of orthodoxy, one might think— exempt, though coaches struggled to enforce yesterday's fashions. At Oregon State University one football player, the son of an Air Force officer, went hippie and dropped the sport. His coach said, "I recruited that boy thinking he was Jack Armstrong. I was wrong. He turned out to be a free-thinker." At the University of Pennsylvania a star defensive back showed up for summer practice with shoulder-length hair, sideburns down to the neck, beads, bells, thonged sandals, and a cloth sash round his waist. He was the only man on the team to bring a pet dog and a stereo set to the six-day camp. After a war of nerves culminating in an ultimatum from the coach, he grudgingly hacked a few inches off his mane. And so it went all over America.

Both sides in this struggle took fashion and style to be deadly serious matters, so political conflicts tended to become cultural wars. In the fall of 1969 the most important radical student group at New York University was called Transcendental Students. At a time when SDS could barely muster twenty-five members, five hundred or more belonged to TS. It began the previous semester when a group protesting overcrowding in the classroom staged a series of freak-outs in classrooms. This proved so attractive a custom that it was institutionalized. Rock, pot, and wine parties had obvious advantages over political action. The administration shrewdly made a former restaurant available to TS for a counter-cultural center. The students welcomed it as a haven for "guerrilla intellect" where the human spirit could breathe free. The administration saw it as just another recreational facility, which, of course, it was. And what dean would not rather have the kids singing out in a restaurant than locking him in his office? Sometimes culture and politics were united. When the $12 million center for the performing arts opened in Milwaukee, Wisconsin, on September 18, 1969, six hundred students disrupted the inaugural concert. They rubbed balloons, blew bubble pipes, threw rolls of toilet paper, and demanded that 20 per cent of the seats be given free to welfare recipients.

The greatest event in counter-cultural history was the Woodstock Festival in Bethel, New York. It was organized on the pattern of other large rock festivals. Big-name groups were invited for several days of continuous entertaining in the open. A large crowd was expected, but nothing like the 300,000 or 400,000 youngsters who actually showed up on August 15, 1969. Everything fell apart in consequence. Tickets could not be collected nor services provided. There wasn't enough food or water. The roads were blocked with abandoned autos, and no one could get in or out for hours at a time. Surprisingly, there were no riots or disasters. The promoters chartered a fleet of helicopters to evacuate casualties (mostly from bad drug trips) and bring in essential supplies. Despite the rain and congestion, a good time was had by all (except the boy killed when a tractor accidentally drove over his sleeping bag). No one had ever seen so large and ruly a gathering before. People stripped down, smoked pot, and turned on with nary a discouraging word, so legend has it. Afterward the young generally agreed that it was a beautiful experience proving their superior morality. People were nicer to each other than ever before. Even the police were impressed by the public's order (a result of their wisely deciding not to enforce the drug laws).

But the counter-culture had its bad moments in 1969 also. Haight-Ashbury continued to decay. It was now mainly a slum where criminals preyed on helpless drug freaks. Worse still was the Battle of Berkeley, which put both the straight culture and the counter-culture in the worst possible light, especially the former. The University of California owned a number of vacant lots south of the campus. The land had been cleared in anticipation of buildings it was unable to construct. One block lay vacant for so long that the street people—hippies, students, dropouts, and others—transformed it into a People's Park. Pressure was brought on the University by the local power structure to block its use, which was done. On May 15 some six thousand students and street people held a rally on campus, then advanced on the park. County sheriffs, highway patrolmen, and the Berkeley police met them with a hail of gunfire. One person died of buckshot wounds, another was blinded. Many more were shot though few arrested. Those who were arrested were handled so brutally that the circuit court enjoined the sheriff to have his men stop beating and abusing them. Disorders continued. Governor Reagan declared a state of emergency and brought in the National Guard. Five days later one of its helicopters sprayed gas over the campus, thus making the educational process at Berkeley even more trying than usual.

Of course the Establishment was most to blame for Vietnamizing the cultural war. But the meretricious aspects of the counter-culture were evident too. If the police were really "fascist pigs," as the street people said, why goad and defy them? And especially why harass the National Guardsmen who didn't want to be in Berkeley anyhow? This was hardly on the same order as murdering people with shotguns. Yet such behavior was stupid, pointless, and self-defeating, like so much else in the counter-culture. The silent majority was not won over. Nor was the People's Park saved. A year later the area was still fenced in. (Though vacant. The University, having pretended to want it as a recreational area, tried to make it one. But as the students thought it stained with innocent blood, they avoided it.)

The rock festival at Altamont that winter was another disaster. It was a free concert that climaxed the Rolling Stones' whirlwind tour of the U.S. They called it their gift to the fans. Actually it was a clever promotion. The Stones had been impressed with the moneymaking potential of Woodstock. While Woodstock cost the promoters a fortune, they stood to recoup their losses with a film of the event. This inspired the Stones to do a Woodstock themselves. At the last minute they obtained the use of Dick Carter's Altamont Raceway. It had been doing poorly and the owner thought the publicity would help business. Little was done to prepare the site. The police didn't have enough notice to bring in reserves, so the Stones hired a band of Hell's Angels as security guards (for $500 worth of beer). The Stones did their thing and the Angels did theirs.

The result was best captured by a *Rolling Stone* magazine photograph showing Mick Jagger looking properly aghast while Angels beat a young Negro to death on stage. A musician who tried to stop them was knocked unconscious, and he was lucky at that. Before the day was over many more were beaten, though no others fatally. Sometimes the beatings were for aesthetic reasons. One very fat man took off his clothes in the approved rock festival manner. This offended the Angels who set on him with pool cues. No one knows how many were clubbed that day. The death count came to four. Apart from Meredith Hunter, who was stabbed and kicked to death, they mostly died by accident. A car drove off the road into a clump of people and killed two. A man, apparently high on drugs, slid into an irrigation canal and drowned. The drug freak-outs were more numerous than at Woodstock. The medical care was less adequate. Not that the physicians on hand didn't try; they just lacked the support provided at Woodstock, whose promoters had spared no expense to avert disaster. Oddly enough the press, normally so eager to exploit the counter-culture, missed the point of Altamont. Early accounts followed the customary rock festival line, acclaiming it as yet another triumph of youth. In the East it received little attention of any kind.

It remained for *Rolling Stone*, the rock world's most authoritative journal, to tell the whole story of what it called the Altamont Death Festival. The violence was quite bad enough, but what especially bothered *Rolling Stone* was the commercial cynicism behind it. That huge gathering was assembled by the Stones to make a lucrative film on the cheap. They could have hired legitimate security guards, but it cost less to use the Angels. (At Woodstock unarmed civilians trained by the Hog Farm commune kept order.) They were too rushed for the careful planning that went into Woodstock, too callous (and greedy) to pour in the emergency resources that had saved the day there. And, appropriately, they faked the moviemaking too so as to have a documentary of the event they intended, not the one they got. *Rolling Stone* said that a cameraman was recording a fat, naked girl freaking out backstage when the director stopped him. "Don't shoot that. That's ugly. We only want beautiful things." The cameraman made the obvious response. "How can you possibly say that? Everything here is so ugly."

Rolling Stone thought the star system at fault. Once a band got as big as the Stones they experienced delusions of grandeur, "ego trips" in the argot. And with so much money to be made by high-pressure promotions, "the hype" became inevitable. Others agreed. The *Los Angeles Free Press*, biggest of the underground papers, ran a full-page caricature of Mick Jagger with an Adolf Hitler mustache, arm draped around a Hell's Angel, while long-haired kids gave them the Nazi salute. Ralph Gleason of the *San Francisco Chronicle* explained Altamont this way: "The name of the game is money, power, and ego, and money is first as it brings power. The Stones didn't do it for free, they did it for money, only the tab was paid in a different way. Whoever goes to the movie paid for the Altamont religious assembly." [2] Quite so. But why did so many others go along with the Stones? The Jefferson Airplane, and especially the Grateful Dead, reputedly the most socially conscious rock bands, participated. So did counter-culture folk heroes like Emmet Grogan of the Diggers. Here the gullibility—innocence, perhaps—of the deviant young was responsible. Because the rock bandits smoked pot and talked a revolutionary game, they were supposed to be different from other entertainers. Even though they made fortunes and spent them ostentatiously, their virtue was always presumed. What Altamont showed was that the difference between a rock king and a robber baron was about six inches of hair. [3]

If Altamont exposed one face of the counter-culture, the Manson family revealed another. Late in 1969 Sharon Tate, a pregnant movie actress, and four of her jet-set friends were ritually murdered in the expensive Bel-Air district of Los Angeles. Though apparently senseless, their deaths were thought related to the rootless, thrill-oriented life style of the Beautiful People. But on December 1 policemen began arresting obscure hippies. Their leader, Charles Manson, was an ex-convict and seemingly deranged. Susan Atkins, a member of his "family," gave several cloudy versions of

[2] Gleason was the best writer on popular music and the youth culture associated with it, which he once admired greatly. For an earlier assessment see his "Like a Rolling Stone," *American Scholar* (Autumn 1967).

[3] This is to criticize the singer, not the song. Whatever one might think of some performers, there is no doubt that rock itself was an exciting musical form. Adults rarely heard it because rock seldom was played on television, or even radio in most parts of the country. Rock artists appeared mainly in concerts and clubs, to which few over thirty went. Not knowing the music, there was little reason for them to buy the records that showed rock at its most complex and interesting. Like jazz, rock became more sophisticated with time and made greater demands on the artist's talent. Even more than jazz, rock produced an army of amateur and semi-professional players around the country. Though often making up in volume what they lacked in skill, their numbers alone guaranteed that rock would survive its exploiters.

what had happened. On the strength of them Manson was indicted for murder. Though his guilt remained unproven, the basic facts about his past seemed clear. He was a neglected child who became a juvenile delinquent. In 1960 he was convicted of forgery and spent seven years in the penitentiary. On his release he went to the Hashbury and acquired a harem of young girls. After floating through the hippie underground for a time, he left the Hashbury with his family of nine girls and five boys early in 1968. They ended up at Spahn's Ranch in the Santa Susana Mountains, north of the San Fernando Valley. The owner was old and blind. Manson terrified him. But the girls took care of him so he let the family stay on. They spent a year at the ranch before the police suspected them of stealing cars. Then they camped out in the desert until arrested.

Life with the Manson family was a combination of hippieism and paranoia. Manson subscribed to the usual counter-cultural values. Inhibitions, the Establishment, regular employment, and other straight virtues were bad. Free love, nature, dope, rock, and mysticism were good. He believed a race war was coming (predicted in Beatle songs) and armed his family in anticipation of it. Some of the cars they stole were modified for use in the desert, where he meant to make his last stand. And, naturally, he tried to break into the rock music business. One reason why he allegedly murdered Miss Tate and her friends was that they were in a house previously occupied by a man who had broken a promise to advance Manson's career. The Manson family was thought to have killed other people even more capriciously. Yet after his arrest most of the girls remained loyal to Manson. Young, largely middle class, they were still "hypnotized" or "enslaved" by him. Those not arrested continued to hope for a family reunion. Of course hippies were not murderers usually. But the repressed hostility, authoritarianism, perversity, and mindless paranoia that underlay much of the hippie ethic were never displayed more clearly. The folkways of the flower children tended toward extremes. At one end they were natural victims; at the other, natural victimizers. The Manson family were both at once.

Taken together the varieties of life among deviant youths showed the counter-culture to be disintegrating. What was disturbing about it was not so much the surface expression as its tendency to mirror the culture it supposedly rejected. The young condemned adult hypocrisy while matching its contradictions with their own. The old were materialistic, hung up on big cars and ranch houses. The young were equally devoted to motorcycles, stereo sets, and electric guitars. The old sought power and wealth. So did the young as rock musicians, political leaders, and frequently as salesmen of counter-cultural goods and services. What distinguished reactionary capitalists from their avant-garde opposite numbers was often no more than a lack of moral pretense. While condemning the adult world's addiction to violence, the young admired third-world revolutionaries, Black Panthers, and even motorcycle outlaws. The rhetoric of the young got progressively meaner and more hostile. This was not so bad as butchering Vietnamese, but it was not very encouraging either. And where hate led, violence followed.

Adults pointed these inconsistencies out often enough, with few good results. Usable perceptions are always self-perceptions, which made the *Rolling Stone* exposé of Altamont so valuable. This was a small but hopeful sign that the capacity for self-analysis was not totally submerged, despite the flood of self-congratulatory pieties with which the deviant young described themselves. The decline of the New Left was another. Once a buoyant and promising thing, it became poisoned by hate, failure, and romantic millennialism. Its diminished appeal offered hope of sobriety's return. So did the surge of student interest in environmental issues at the decade's end. These were not fake problems, like so many youthful obsessions, but real ones. They would take the best efforts of many generations to overcome. No doubt the young would lose interest in them after a while as usual. Still, it was better to save a forest or clean a river than to vandalize a campus. No amount of youthful nagging was likely to make adults give up their sinful ways. It was possible that the young and old together might salvage enough of the threatened environment to leave posterity something of lasting value. The generations yet unborn were not likely to care much whether ROTC was conducted on campus or off. But they will remember this age, for better or worse, with every breath they take.

One aspect of the counter-culture deserves special mention: its assumption that hedonism was inevitably anti-capitalist. As James Hitchcock pointed out, the New Left identified capitalism with puritanism and deferred gratifications. But this was true of capitalism only with respect to work. Where consumption was concerned, it urged people to gratify their slightest wish. It exploited sex shamelessly to that end, limited only by law and custom. When the taboos against nudity were removed, merchants soon took advantage of their new freedom. Naked models, actors, even waitresses were one result, pornographic flicks another. Who doubted that if marijuana became legal the tobacco companies would soon put Mexican gold in every vending machine? It was, after all, part of Aldous Huxley's genius that he saw how sensual gratification could enslave men more effectively than Hitler ever could. Victorian inhibitions, the Protestant Ethic itself were, though weakened, among the few remaining defenses against the market economy that Americans possessed. To destroy them for freedom's sake would only make people more vulnerable to consumerism than they already were. Which was not to say that sexual and other freedoms were not good things in their own right. But there was no assurance that behavioral liberty would not grow at the expense of political freedom. It was one thing to say that sex promoted mental health, another to say it advanced social justice. In confusing the two young deviants laid themselves open to what Herbert Marcuse called "repressive de-sublimation," the means by which the socio-economic order was made more attractive, and hence more durable. Sex was no threat to the Establishment. Panicky moralists found this hard to believe, so they kept trying to suppress it. But the shrewder guardians of established relationships saw hedonism for what it partially was, a valuable means of social control. What made this hard to get across was that left and right agreed that sex was subversive. That was why the Filthy Speech Movement arose, and why the John Birch Society and its front groups divided a host of communities in the late sixties. They insisted that sex education was a communist plot to fray the country's moral fiber. They could hardly have been more wrong. As practiced in most schools, sex education was anything but erotic. In fact, more students were probably turned off sex than on to it by such courses. The Kremlin was hardly less orthodox than the Birch Society on sexual matters, sexual denial being thought a trait of all serious revolutionaries. But the sexual propaganda of the young confirmed John Birchers in their delusions. As elsewhere, the misconceptions of each side reinforced one another.

Still, the counter-culture's decline ought not to be celebrated prematurely. It outlasted the sixties. It had risen in the first place because of the larger culture's defects. War, poverty, social and racial injustice were widespread. The universities were less human than they might have been. The regulation of sexual conduct led to endless persecutions of the innocent or the pathetic to no one's advantage. Young people had much to complain of. Rebellious youth had thought to make things better. It was hardly their fault that things got worse. They were, after all, products of the society they meant to change, and marked by it as everyone was. Vanity and ignorance made them think themselves free of the weaknesses they saw so clearly in others. But adults were vain and ignorant too, and, what's more, they had power as the young did not. When they erred, as in Vietnam, millions suffered. The young hated being powerless, but thanks to it they were spared the awful burden of guilt that adults bore. They would have power soon enough, and no doubt use it just as badly. In the meantime, though, people did well to keep them in perspective.

The dreary propaganda about youth's insurgent idealism continued into the seventies. So did attempts to make them look clean-cut. American society went on being obsessed with the young. But all popular manias are seasonal. Each era has its own preoccupations. The young and their counter-culture were a special feature of the 1960's and would probably not be regarded in the old way for very long afterward. And, demographically speaking, youth itself was on the wane. The median age of Americans had risen steadily in modern times, reaching a peak of thirty years of age in 1952. The baby boom reversed this trend, like so many others. In 1968 the median age was only 27.7 years. But as the birthrate fell the median age began to rise. By 1975 it would be over twenty-eight. By 1990 it should be back up to thirty again, putting half the population beyond the age of trust. Their disproportionate numbers was one reason why youth was so prominent in the sixties. It was reasonable to suppose they would become less so as their numbers declined in relation to older people.

Common sense suggested that work and the pleasure principle would both continue. Once life and work were thought to be guided by the same principles. In the twentieth century they had started to divide, with one set of rules for working and another for living. The complexities of a post-industrial economy would probably maintain that distinction. The discipline of work would prevail on the job. The tendency to "swing" off it would increase, and the dropout community too. The economy was already rich enough to support a substantial leisure class, as the hippies demonstrated. The movement toward guaranteed incomes would make idleness even more feasible. A large dependent population, in economic terms, was entirely practical—perhaps, given automation, even desirable. How utopian to have a society in which the decision to work was voluntary! Yet if economic growth continued and an effective welfare state was established, such a thing was not unimaginable, however repugnant to the Protestant Ethic. Perhaps that was what the unpleasant features of life in the sixties pointed toward. Later historians might think them merely the growing pains of this new order. A Brave New World indeed!

A further reason for taking this view was the rise of an adult counter-culture. Americans have always been attracted to cults and such. No enthusiasm, however bizarre, fails to gain some notice in so vast and restless a country. Crank scientists and religious eccentrics are especially welcomed. In the 1960's this was more true than ever, and there seemed to be more uniformity of belief among the cults than before. Perhaps also they were more respectable. The Esalen Institute in northern California was one of the most successful. It offered three-day seminars conducted by Dr. Frederick S. Perls, the founder of Gestalt therapy. When his book by that title was published in 1950 it won, as might have been expected, little attention. But in the sixties it flourished to the point where perhaps a hundred Gestalt therapists were in practice. As employed at Esalen, Gestalt therapy involved a series of individual encounters within a group context. Perls tried to cultivate moments of sudden insights that produced a strong awareness of the present moment. Unlike psychoanalysis, Gestalt therapy was directive. The therapist diagnosed the ailment and organized its cure in short bursts of intensive treatment. People were encouraged to act out dreams so as to discover their hidden message. The emphasis was on sensuality, spontaneity, and the reduction of language which was seen as more a barrier to understanding than a means of communication. There was much role-playing, aggression-releasing exercises, and "unstructured interaction." Esalen itself, with its hot sulphur baths where mixed nude bathing was encouraged, combined the features of a hip spa, a mental clinic, and a religious center. It brought social scientists and mystics together in common enterprises. By 1967 Esalen grossed a million dollars a year. Four thousand people attended its seminars. Twelve thousand used its branch in San Francisco.

Though Esalen was the most celebrated center of "Third Force Psychiatry," it was hardly alone. Encounter groups, T-groups, sensitivity groups all practiced variations of the same theme. So, in a more intense way, did Synanon. Synanon was founded in 1958 by an ex-alcoholic named Charles E. Dederich. It began as a way of reclaiming alcoholics, and especially drug addicts, through communal living and group therapy. It aimed to peel away the defenses that supported addiction. The cure was a drastic one and the Synanon ethic extremely authoritarian, as a treatment based not on clinical experience but actual street life would naturally be. Synanon's most popular feature was the Synanon game, a kind of encounter group open to outsiders. From its modest beginning Synanon expanded rapidly into a network of clinics and small businesses operated by members to support the therapeutic program. Already a corporation by the decade's end, Dederich expected it to become a mass movement in time. Others thought so too. Abraham Maslow of Brandeis University declared that "Synanon is now in the process of torpedoing the entire world of psychiatry and within ten years will completely replace psychiatry."

Esalen and Synanon got much publicity, but, though substantial efforts, they were only the tip of the iceberg. Beneath them were literally thousands of groups dedicated to better mental health through de-sublimation, often sponsored by businesses and universities. In a sense what they did was rationalize the counter-cultural ethic and bend it to fit the needs of middle-class adults. For some, expanding their consciousness meant little more than weekend tripping, with, or more commonly without, drugs. If most didn't give up work in the hippie manner, they became more relaxed about it. Some thought less about success and more about fun. Some found new satisfaction in their work, or else more satisfying work. The range of individual response was great, but the overall effect was to promote sensuality, and to diminish the Protestant Ethic. As with the counter-culture, an inflated propaganda accompanied these efforts. Ultimate truth, complete harmony with self, undreamed-of pleasures, and the like were supposed to result from conversion. De-sublimation did not mean license, of course. As the Haight-Ashbury showed, without self-denial there is self-destruction. The cults tried to develop more agreeable mechanisms to replace the fears and guilts undergirding the old morality. They wanted people to live more rich and immediate social lives, but they didn't propose to do away with restraint entirely. Mystic cults promoted self-discipline through various austere regimes. Psychiatric cults used the group as a control. One learned from his fellows what was appropriate to the liberated spirit.

The sensuality common to most of these groups was what the sexual revolution was all about. Properly speaking, of course, there was no sexual revolution. Easy divorce, relatively free access to contraceptives, and tolerated promiscuity were all well established by the 1920's. Insofar as the Kinsey and other reports are historically reliable, there had been little change since then in the rate of sexual deviance. What had changed was the attitude of many people toward it. In the 1960's deviance was not so much tolerated as applauded in many quarters. Before, college students having an affair used discretion. Later they were more likely to live together in well-advertised nonmarital bliss. Similarly, adults were not much more promiscuous in the sixties than in the forties or fifties, but they were more disposed to proclaim the merits of extra-marital sexuality. The sexualization of everyday life moved on. This was often desirable, or at least harmless, except for the frightening rise in the incidence of VD after the Pill made condoms seemingly obsolete.

Fornication, though illegal in most places, was not usually regarded as actionable. But there remained many laws against sexual behavior that were enforced, if erratically. Contraceptives were difficult to get in some places, especially for single women. Legal abortions were severely limited. Homosexuals were persecuted everywhere. Attempts to change these laws were part of the new moral permissiveness. Few legal reforms were actually secured in the sixties. Liberalized abortion laws were passed in Colorado and elsewhere to little effect. Abortions remained scarce and expensive. The overwhelming majority continued to be illegal. Contraceptive laws did not change much either, though in practice contraceptives became easier to get. Nor were the laws prohibiting homosexuality altered much. Here too, though, changes in practice eased conditions. The deliberate entrapment of homosexuals declined in some cities. Some police forces, as in San Francisco, made more of an effort to distinguish between harmless (as between consenting adults) and anti-social perversions.

More striking still was the willingness of sexual minorities to identify themselves. Male homosexuals were among the first to do so. In the Mattachine Society and later organizations they campaigned openly for an end to discriminatory laws and customs. The Daughters of Bilitis did the same for lesbians. Even the most exotic minorities, like the transvestites and transsexuals (men, usually, who wanted to change their sex surgically), became organized. Most of the groups were, their sexual customs excepted, quite straight. The creation of homosexual churches, like the Metropolitan Community Church of Los Angeles, testified to that. They hoped mainly to be treated the same as heterosexuals. But in the Gay Liberation Front the sexual underground produced its own New Left organization. Its birth apparently dated from the night of June 28, 1969, when police raided a gay bar in Greenwich Village called the Stonewall Inn. Homosexuals usually accepted arrest passively. But for some reason that night it was different. They fought back, and for a week afterward continued to agitate, ending with a public march of some one thousand people.

More sober homosexuals greeted this event with mixed emotions. They were astonished to find such spirit among the so-called street queens, the poorest and most trouble-prone homosexuals of all. But they didn't really dig the violence. As one leader of the Mattachine Society (a sort of gay NAACP) put it: "I mean, people did try to set fire to the bar, and one drag queen, much to the amazement of the mob, just pounded the hell out of a Tactical Patrol Force cop! I don't know if battering TPF men is really the answer to our problem." In any event, the Gay Liberation Front followed these events. Rather like a Homosexuals for a Democratic Society, the GLF participated in the next Hiroshima Day march that summer. It was the first time homosexuals ever participated in a peace action under their own colors. The "Pink Panthers" were mostly young, of course. But whether their movement flourished or, most probably, withered away, the mere fact of its existence said a lot about changing mores in America.

While it was difficult in 1969 to tell where the counter-culture would go, it was easy to see where it came from. Artists and bohemians had been demanding more freedom from social and artistic conventions for a long time. The romantic faith in nature, intuition, and spontaneity was equally old. What was striking about the sixties was that the revolt against discipline, even self-discipline, and authority spread so widely. Resistance to these tendencies largely collapsed in the arts. Soon the universities gave ground also. The rise of hedonism and the decline of work were obviously functions of increased prosperity, and also of effective merchandising. The consumer economy depended on advertising, which in turn leaned heavily on the pleasure principle. This had been true for fifty years at least, but not until television did it really work well. The generation that made the counter-culture was the first to be propagandized from infancy on behalf of the pleasure principle.

But though all of them were exposed to hucksterism, not all were convinced. Working-class youngsters especially soon learned that life was different from television. Limited incomes and uncertain futures put them in touch with reality earlier on. Middle-class children did not learn the facts of life until much later. Cushioned by higher family incomes, indulged in the same way as their peers on the screen, they were shocked to discover that the world was not what they had been taught it was. The pleasure orientation survived this discovery, the ideological packaging it came in often did not. All this had happened before, but in earlier years there was no large, institutionalized subculture for the alienated to turn to. In the sixties hippiedom provided one such, the universities another. The media publicized these alternatives and made famous the ideological leaders who promoted them. So the deviant young knew where to go for the answers they wanted, and how to behave when they got them. The media thus completed the cycle begun when they first turned youngsters to pleasure. That was done to encourage consumption. The message was still effective when young consumers rejected the products TV offered and discovered others more congenial to them.

Though much in the counter-culture was attractive and valuable, it was dangerous in three ways. First, self-indulgence led frequently to self-destruction. Second, the counter-culture increased social hostility. The generation gap was one example, but the class gap another. Working-class youngsters resented the counter-culture. They accepted adult values for the most part. They had to work whether they liked it or not. Beating up the long-haired and voting for George Wallace were only two ways they expressed these feelings. The counter-culture was geographical too. It flourished in cities and on campuses. Elsewhere, in Middle America especially, it was hated and feared. The result was a national division between the counter-culture and those adults who admired or tolerated it—upper-middle-class professionals and intellectuals in the Northeast particularly—and the silent majority of workers and Middle Americans who didn't. The tensions between these groups made solving social and political problems all the more difficult, and were, indeed, part of the problem.

Finally, the counter-culture was hell on standards. A handful of bohemians were no great threat to art and intellect. The problem was that a generation of students, the artists and intellectuals of the future, was infected with romanticism. Truth and beauty were in the eye of the beholder. They were discovered or created by the pure of heart. Formal education and training were not, therefore, merely redundant but dangerous for obstructing channels through which the spirit flowed. It was one thing for hippies to say this, romanticism being the natural religion of bohemia. It was quite another to hear it from graduate students. Those who did anguished over the future of scholarship, like the critics who worried that pop art meant the end of art. These fears were doubtlessly overdrawn, but the pace of cultural change was so fast in the sixties that they were hardly absurd.

Logic seemed everywhere to be giving way to intuition, and self-discipline to impulse. Romanticism had never worked well in the past. It seemed to be doing as badly in the present. The hippies went from flower power to death-tripping in a few years. The New Left took only a little longer to move from participatory democracy to demolition. The counter-cultural ethic remained as beguiling as ever in theory. In practice, like most utopian dreams, human nature tended to defeat it. At the decade's end, young believers looked forward to the Age of Aquarius. Sensible men knew there would be no Aquarian age. What they didn't know was the sort of legacy the counter-culture would leave behind. Some feared that the straight world would go on as before, others that it wouldn't.

The Meaning of "Soul"

ULF HANNERZ

There seems to be no end to the study of Afro-Americans. Both the focus and substance of these studies shift with changes in scholarly ideologies and alterations in the relationship between the races. At least three major areas of black life in American history are undergoing revision at this time. All three are concerned with the concept of culture, or the way of life, of black people.

First, and perhaps most significant, are the studies of the culture of slavery. Rather than viewing slavery as simply a dehumanizing process aimed at emasculating the slaves, scholars are now investigating the positive aspects of slave culture—not the positive aspects of slavery as an institution, but the adaptation made to that institution by the Africans and their descendants. As a result, scholars are presenting studies that are concerned with family life, religious belief and practice, education, and work experiences other than simple field labor. Such studies enable us to see, then, that even in a system as oppressive to mind and body as slavery was, men, women, and children do go on living and making the best of their lives under difficult circumstances.

The second area being reconsidered is the life of black people in urban communities after emancipation and before the modern era. The primary focus here is on family life and work experience. One purpose of these studies is to counteract the notion that after freedom, black people were reduced to poverty and ended up completely demoralized because of segregation and discrimination. The research leads to the conclusion that there was a relatively high level of working-class family stability, a level that compares favorably with other, nonblack families in the same economic circumstances.

The third area undergoing special scrutiny today is represented by the selection reprinted below. While studies of the urban black are not new (W. E. B. DuBois' **The Philadelphia Negro** was published in 1899), the contemporary examinations of urban black ghetto culture are informed by a different perspective. Deriving their methodology from urban anthropology, these studies seek to identify and evaluate the adaptive qualities of the ghetto blacks, much as the new historical studies have done with blacks in the slave culture. This has resulted in publication of community studies of black ghettos that describe the way of life, or culture, of the people dwelling there.

Perhaps the most thorough study of this type is **Soulside,** an examination of part of Washington, D.C.'s black ghetto, by Ulf Hannerz, a Swedish anthropologist. The article reprinted below is adapted from one chapter of this book. In his attempt to identify commonalities of black ghetto life, Hannerz analyzes the concept of "soul," a term widely used by urban blacks.

It is important to point out in this connection that an outsider like Hannerz may be able to identify and define cultural characteristics that would not be recognized as such by those within the culture. Ghetto dwellers readily and confidently use the term "soul" to describe qualities that are familiar to them and with which they empathize. Rarely, however, would they attempt to define the concept, for reasons elucidated in the article below.

A serious danger exists in conducting such ghetto-community studies—the temptation to romanticize ghetto life, which some scholars find difficult to resist. Ghetto life is hard, very hard, and this must also be reflected. The physical conditions of ghetto life and the lack of life chances for ghetto residents lead to psychological pain and frustration, in addition to simple physical brutality and hunger. The best studies carefully avoid glossing over the difficulties of ghetto life. Nevertheless, contemporary examination of the ghetto culture does perform a valuable function in portraying yet again the resiliency of the human spirit.

In the black ghettos of the large cities of the northern United States, the last few years have witnessed the emergence of the concept of "soul." For instance, in every riot from Watts to Washington, hastily printed signs were rushed to doors and windows of Negro-owned businesses, all carrying the same message: Soul Brother. These businesses were usually spared. Perhaps this is why the term cropped up in a cartoon during the Washington riots—the cartoon showed a "Soul Brother" sign on the iron fence surrounding the White House.

Recently, while doing field work in a lower-class Negro area in Washington, D.C., I considered soul from the standpoint of its typical meanings in Negro slums in Northern American cities. The neighborhood's inhabitants share the characteristics of America's lower-class urban poor: a high rate of unemployment; a considerable amount of crime (including juvenile delinquency); and households headed, more often than not, by adult women, while the men are either absent or only temporarily attached to the family.

Of the people at the field site, a minority were born in Washington, D.C. The majority are emigrants from the South, particularly from Virginia, North Carolina, and South Carolina. Apart from conducting field work in this area by means of traditional participant observation, I also paid attention to those impersonal media that are specifically intended for a lower-class Negro audience: radio stations (three in Washington were clearly aimed at Negroes); the recording industry; and stage

"What Negroes Mean by 'Soul'" by Ulf Hannerz (Editor's title: "The Meaning of 'Soul'"). Published by permission of Transaction, Inc. from *Transaction*, 5, no. 8 (July–August, 1968), pp. 57–61. Copyright © 1968 by Transaction, Inc.

shows featuring Negro rock and roll artists and comedians. (The phrase "rhythm and blues" used by whites to denote Negro rock and roll is now widely used by the Negroes themselves.) These media have played a prominent part in promoting the vocabulary of soul. On the other hand, both the local Negro press, such as the Washington *Afro-American,* and the national Negro publications, like the monthly *Ebony,* are largely middle-class-oriented and thus of limited value for understanding life in the ghetto.

THE NATURE OF SOUL

What, then, is soul? As the concept has come to be used in urban ghettos, it stands for "the essence of Negroness." And, it should be added, this "Negroness" refers to the kind of Negro with which the urban slum-dweller is most familiar—people like himself. The question whether a middle-class, white-collar, suburban Negro also has soul is often met with consternation. In fact, soul seems to be a folk conception of the lower-class urban Negro's own "national character." Modes of action, personal attributes, and certain artifacts are given the soul label. In conversations one typically hears statements such as "Man, he got a lot of soul." This appreciative opinion may be given concerning anybody in the ghetto, but more often by younger adults or adolescents about their peers. Soul talk is particularly common among younger men. This sex differentiation in the use of soul may be quite important in understanding the basis of the soul concept.

The choice of the term "soul" for this "Negroness" is in itself note-worthy. First of all, it shows the influence of religion on lower-class Negroes, even those who are not themselves active church members. Expressions of religious derivation—such as "God, have mercy!"—are frequent in everyday speech among all lower-class Negroes, in all contexts. A very great number of people, of course, have been regular church-goers at some point, at least at the time they attended Sunday school, and many are involved in church activities—perhaps in one of the large Baptist churches, but more often in small spiritualist storefront churches. Although the people who use the soul vocabulary are seldom regular churchgoers themselves, they have certainly been fully (although sometimes indirectly) exposed to the religious idiom of "soul-stirring" revival meetings.

Further, the choice of soul (a term that in church usage means "the essentially human") to refer to "the essentially Negro," as the new concept of soul does, certainly has strong implications of race pride. If soul is Negro, the non-Negro is non-soul, and, in a unique turnabout, somewhat less human. Although I have never heard such a point of view spelled out, it seems to be implicitly accepted as part of soul ideology. What is soul is not only different from what is not soul (particularly what is mainstream, middle-class American); it is also superior. The term "soul" appraises as well as describes. If one asks a young man what a soul brother is, the answer is usually something like "Someone who's hip, someone who

knows what he's doing." It may be added here that although both soul
brother and soul sister are used for soul personified, the former is more
common. Like soul, soul brother and soul sister are terms used particularly
by younger men.

SOUL MUSIC—SOUL FOOD

Let us now note a few fields that are particularly soulful. One is music
(where the concept may have originated), especially progressive jazz and
rock and roll. James Brown, a leading rock and roll singer, is often referred to as "Soul Brother Number One"; two of the largest record stores
in Washington, with almost exclusively Negro customers, are the "Soul
Shack" and the "Soul City." Recently a new magazine named *Soul* appeared; its main outlet seems to be these de facto segregated record stores.
It contains stories on rock and roll artists, disc jockeys, and so on. Excellence in musical expression is indeed a part of the lower-class Negro's
self-conception, and white rock and roll is often viewed with scorn as
a poor imitation of the Negro genius. Resentment is often aimed at the
Beatles, who stand as typical of white intrusion into a Negro field. (Occasionally a Beatles melody has become a hit in the Negro ghetto as well,
but only when performed in a local version by a Negro group, such as
the recording of "Day Tripper" by the Vontastics. In such a case, there
is little or no mention of the melody's Beatles origin.)

The commercial side of Negro entertainment is, of course, directly
tied to soul music. The Howard Theater in Washington, with counter-
parts in other large Negro ghettos in the United States, stages shows of
touring rock and roll groups and individual performers. Each show usually runs a week, with four or five performances every day. Larger shows
also make one-night appearances at the Washington Coliseum. Occasionally, a comedian takes part; Moms Mabley, Pigmeat Markham, and Redd
Foxx are among those who draw large, predominantly Negro audiences.

The emcees of these shows are often celebrities in their own right.
Some, such as "King" Coleman and "Gorgeous" George, tour regularly
with the shows, and others are local disc jockeys from the white-owned
Negro radio stations. In Washington, such disc jockeys as "The Nighthawk," Bob Terry of the WOL "Soul Brothers," and "Soulfinger," Fred
Correy of the WOOK "Soul Men," make highly appreciated appearances
at the Howard. It is clear that the commercial establishments with a
vested interest in a separate Negro audience have latched onto the soul
vocabulary, using it to further their own interests as well as to support its
use among the audience. Thus there is also, for instance, a WWRL "soul
brother radio" in New York. But the soul vocabulary is not just a commercial creation. It existed before it was commercialized, and the fact that
it seems so profitable for commercial establishments to fly the banner of
soul indicates that, whatever part these establishments have had in promoting soul, it has fallen into already fertile ground.

A second area of widespread soul symbolism is food. The dishes that

Negroes now call soul food they once called "Southern cooking" and still do to some extent; but in the Northern ghettos these foods increasingly come to stand for race rather than region. In the center of the Washington Negro area, for instance, the Little Harlem Restaurant advertises "soul food." There are a number of such foods: chitlins, hog maw, black-eyed peas, collard greens, corn bread, and grits. Typically, they were the poor man's food in the rural South. In the urban North, they may still be so to some degree, but in the face of the diversity of the urban environment they also come to stand as signs of ethnicity. References to soul food occur frequently in soul music—two of the hits of the winter 1966–67 were "Grits and Cornbread" by the Soul Runners and the Joe Cuba Sextet's "Bang! Bang!," with the refrain "corn bread, hog maw, and chitlin." Sometimes the names of soul foods may themselves be used as more or less synonymous with soul—Negro entertainers on stage, talking of their experiences while journeying between ghetto shows around the country, sometimes refer to it as "the chitlin circuit," and this figure of speech usually draws much favorable audience reaction.

THE NEGRO WAY OF LIFE

What, then, is "soul" about soul music and soul food? It may be wise to be cautious here, since there is little intellectualizing and analyzing on the part of the ghetto's inhabitants on this subject. I believe that this comparative absence of defining may itself be significant, and I will return to this later. Here, I will only point to a few basic characteristics of soul that I feel make it "essentially Negro"—referring again, of course, to urban lower-class Negroes.

There is, of course, the Southern origin. The "Down Home" connotations are particularly attached to soul food; but while Negro music has changed more, and commercial rock and roll is an urban phenomenon, this music is certainly seen as the latest stage of an unfolding heritage. Thus the things that are soul, while taking on new significance in the urban environment, provide some common historical tradition for ghetto inhabitants. One might also speculate that the early and, from then on, constant and intimate exposure to these foods and to this music—radios and record players seem to belong to practically every ghetto home—may make them appear particularly basic to a "Negro way of life."

When it comes to soul music, there are a couple of themes in style and content that I would suggest are pervasive in ghetto life, and are probably very close to the everyday experience of ghetto inhabitants.

One of these is lack of control over the environment. There is a very frequent attitude among soul brothers that one's environment is somewhat like a jungle, where tough, smart people may survive and where a lot happens to make it worthwhile and enjoyable just to "watch the scene"—if one does not have too high hopes of controlling it. Many of the reactions to listening to progressive jazz seem connected with this view: "Oooh, man, there just ain't nothing you can do about it but sit there and feel it goin' all the way into you." Without being able to do much about proving it, I feel that experiences—desirable or undesirable —in which one can only passively perceive what is happening are an essential fact of ghetto life, for better or for worse: thus it is soul.

Related to this theme are unstable personal relationships, in particular between the sexes. It is well known that among lower-class urban Negroes there are many "broken" families (households without a husband and father), many temporary common-law unions, and in general relatively little consensus on sex roles. It is not much of an exaggeration, then, to speak of a constant battle of the sexes. Indeed, success with the opposite sex is a focal concern in lower-class Negro life. From this area come most of the lyrics of contemporary rock and roll music. (It may be objected that this is true of white rock and roll as well; but this is very much to the point. For white rock and roll is predominantly adolescent music, and reaches people who also have unstable personal relationships. In the case of lower-class urban Negroes, such relationships are characteristic of a much wider age-range, and music on this theme also reaches this wider range.) Some titles of recent rock and roll hits may show this theme: "I'm Losing You" (Temptations), "Are You Lonely" (Freddy Scott), "Yours Until Tomorrow" (Dee Dee Warwick), "Keep Me Hangin' On" (Supremes). Thus soul may also stand for a bittersweet experience that arises from contacts with the other sex (although there are certainly other sources). This bittersweetness, of course, was already typical of the blues.

Turning to style, a common element in everyday social interaction —as well as among storefront-church preachers, Negro comedians, and rock and roll singers—is an alternation between aggressive, somewhat boastful behavior and plaintive behavior from an implicit underdog position. This style occurs in many situations and may itself be related to the unstable personal relationships mentioned above. In any case, it seems that this style is seen as having soul; without describing its elements, soul brothers tend to describe its occurrences in varying contexts as "soulful."

I have hesitated to try to analyze and define soul, because what seems to be important in the emergence of the present soul concept is the fact that there is *something* that is felt to be soul; *what* that something is isn't so important. There is, of course, some logic to this. If soul is what is "essentially Negro," it should not be necessary for soul brothers to spend much time analyzing it. Asking about soul, one often receives answers such as, "You know, we don't talk much about it, but we've all been through it, so we know what it is anyway." Probably this is to some extent true. What the lack of a clear definition points to is that soul vocabulary is predominantly for the in-crowd. It is a symbol of solidarity among the people of the ghetto—but not in more than a weak and implicit sense of solidarity *against* anybody else. Soul is turned inward; and so everybody who is touched by it is supposed to know what it means.

The few interpreters of soul to the outside world are, in fact, outsiders. LeRoi Jones, the author, is a convert to ghetto life who, like so many converts, seems to have become more militantly partisan than the authentic ghetto inhabitants. Originally he rather impartially noted the ethnocentric bias of soul:

> . . . the soul brother means to recast the social order in his own image. White is then not "right," as the old blues had it, but a liability, since the culture of white precludes the possession of the Negro "soul."

Now he preaches the complete destruction of American society, an activist program that I am sure is far out of step with the immediate concerns of the average soul brother. Lerone Bennett, an editor of the middle-class *Ebony* magazine, is not particularly interested in what he calls "the folk myth of soul," yet he explains what he feels soul really is:

> . . . the American counterpart of the African concept of Negritude, a distinct quality of Negroness growing out of the Negro's experience and not his genes. . . . Soul is the Negro's antithesis to America's thesis (white), a confrontation of spirits that could and should lead to a higher synthesis of the two.

I am not convinced that Bennett's conception is entirely correct; it is certainly not expressed in the idiom of the ghetto. Charles Keil, an ethnomusicologist, probably comes closer to the folk conception than anyone else—by giving what amounts to a catalogue of those ghetto values and experiences that the inhabitants recognize as their own:

> "The breath of life"; "It don't mean a thing if you ain't got that swing"; "Grits and greens"; and so on.

In doing so, of course, one does not get a short and comprehensive definition of soul that is acceptable to all and in every situation—one merely lists the fields in which a vocabulary of soul is particularly likely to be expressed.

The vocabulary of soul, then, is a relatively recent phenomenon, and it is used among younger Negro ghetto dwellers, particularly young men, to designate in a highly approving manner the experiences and characteristics that are "essentially Negro." As such, it is employed within the group, although it is clear that by discussing what is "typically Negro" one makes an implicit reference to non-Negro society. Now, why has such a vocabulary emerged in this group at just this point of Negro history?

For a long time, the social boundaries that barred Negro Americans from educational and economic achievements have been highly impermeable. Although lower-class Negroes largely accepted the values of mainstream American culture, the obvious impermeability of social boundaries has probably prevented a more complete commitment on their part to the achievement of those goals that have been out of reach. Instead, there has been an adjustment to the lower-class situation, in which goals and values more appropriate to the ascribed social position of the group have been added to, and to some extent substituted for, the mainstream norms. The style of life of the lower class, in this case the Negro lower class, is different from that of the upper classes, and the impermeability of group boundaries and the unequal distribution of resources have long kept the behavioral characteristics of the groups relatively stable and distinct from each other. However, to a great extent, one of the groups—the lower-class Negroes—would have preferred the style of life of the other group—the middle-class whites—had it been available to them.

Lower-class Negroes have only been able to do the best they could with what they have had. They have had two cultures—the mainstream culture they are relatively familiar with, which is in many ways apparently superior and preferable and which has been closed to them, and the ghetto culture, which is a second choice and is based on the circumstances of the ascribed social position.

This, of course, sounds to some extent like the position of what has often been described as that of "the marginal man." Such a position may cause psychological problems. But when the position is very clearly defined and where the same situation is shared by many, it is perhaps reasonably acceptable. There is a perfectly understandable reason for one's failure to reach one's goal. Nobody of one's own kind is allowed to reach that goal, and the basis of the condition is a social rule rather than a personal failure. There are indications that marginality is more severely felt if the barrier is not absolute—if crossing a boundary, although uncertain, is possible. According to Alan C. Kerckhoff and Thomas C. McCormick,

> . . . an absolute barrier between the two groups is less conducive to personality problems than "grudging, uncertain, and unpredictable acceptance." The impact of the rejection on an individual's personality organization will depend to some extent upon the usual treatment accorded members of his group by the dominant group. If his group as a whole faces a rather permeable barrier and he meets with more serious rejection, the effect on him is likely to be more severe than the same treatment received by a more thoroughly rejected group (one facing an impermeable barrier).

Recent changes in race relations in the United States have indeed made the social barriers to achievement seem less impermeable to the ghetto population. One often hears people in the ghetto expressing opinions such as, "Yeah, there are so many programs, job-training and things, going on, man, so if you got anything on the ball you can make it." On the other hand, there are also assertions about the impossibility of getting anywhere. Obviously, a clear-cut exclusion from mainstream American culture is gradually being replaced by ambivalence about one's actual chances. This ambivalence, of course, seems to represent an accurate estimate of the situation: The lower-class Negro continues to be disadvantaged, but his chances of moving up and out of the ghetto are probably improving. People do indeed trickle out of the ghetto.

It is in this situation that the vocabulary of soul has emerged. It is a response, I feel, to the uncertainty of the ghetto dweller's situation. This uncertainty is particularly strong for the younger male, the soul brother. While women have always been able to live closer to mainstream culture norms, as homemakers and possibly with a job keeping them in touch with the middle-class world, men have had less chance to practice and become competent in mainstream culture. Older men tend to feel that current social changes come too late for them, but they have higher expectations for the following generation. Therefore, the present generation of young men in the Negro ghettos of the United States is placed in a new situation, to which they are making new responses, and much of the unrest in the ghettos today is perhaps the result of these emerging pressures.

This new situation must be taken into account if we are to understand the emergence of the soul vocabulary. The increasing ambivalence about one's opportunities in the changing social structure may be accompanied by doubts about one's own worth. Earlier, the gap between mainstream culture norms and the lower-class Negro's achievements could be explained easily, by referring to social barriers. Today, the suspicion arises that under-achievement is due to one's own failure, and self-doubt may result.

THE RHETORIC OF ESTEEM

Such self-doubt can be reduced in different ways. Some young men, of course, are able to live up to mainstream norms of achievement, thereby reducing the strain on themselves (but at the same time increasing the strain on the others). Higher self-esteem can also be obtained by affirming that the boundaries are still impermeable. A third possibility is to set new standards for achievement, proclaiming one's own achievements to be the ideals. It is not necessary, of course, that the same way of reducing self-doubt always be applied. In the case of soul, the method is that of idealizing one's own achievements, proclaiming one's own way of life to be superior. Yet the same soul brother may argue at other times that he is what he is because he is not allowed to become anything else.

In any case, soul is by native public definition superior, and the motive of the soul vocabulary, I believe, is above all to reduce self-doubt by persuading soul brothers that they are successful. Being a soul brother is belonging to a select group instead of to a residual category of people who have not succeeded. Thus, the soul vocabulary is a device of rhetoric. By talking about people who have soul, about soul music and about soul food, the soul brother attempts to establish himself in the role of an expert and connoisseur; by talking to others of his group in these terms, he identifies with them and confers the same role on them. Using soul rhetoric is a way of convincing others of one's own worth and of their worth. As Kenneth Burke expresses it,

A man can be his own audience, insofar as he, even in his secret thoughts, cultivates certain ideas or images for the effect he hopes they may have upon him; he is here what Mead would call "an 'I' addressing its 'me' "; and in this respect he is being rhetorical quite as though he were using pleasant imagery to influence an outside audience rather than one within.

The soul vocabulary has thus emerged from the social basis of a number of individuals, in effective interaction with one another, with similar problems of adjustment to a new situation. The use of soul rhetoric is a way of meeting their needs as long as it occurs in situations where they can mutually support each other. Here, of course, is a clue to the confinement of the rhetoric to in-group situations. If soul talk were directed toward outsiders, they might not accept the claims of its excellence—it is not *their* "folk myth." Viewing soul as such a device of rhetoric, it is also easier to understand why the soul brothers do not want it made the topic of too much intellectualizing. As Clifford Geertz has made clear, by analyzing and defining an activity one achieves maximum intellectual clarity at the expense of emotional commitment. It is doubtful that soul rhetoric would thrive on too much intellectual clarity; rather, by expressing soul ideals in a circumspect manner—in terms of emotionally charged symbols such as soul food and soul music—one can avoid the rather sordid realities underlying these emotions. As I pointed out already, the shared lower-class Negro experiences that seem to be the bases of soul are hardly such as to bring out a surge of ethnic pride. That is the psychological reason for keeping the soul concept diffuse.

There is also, I believe, a sociological basis for the diffuseness. The more exactly a soul brother would define soul, the fewer others would probably agree upon the "essential Negroness" of his definition; and, as we have seen, a basic idea of the rhetoric of soul is to cast others into roles that satisfy them and at the same time support one's own position. If people are cast into a role of soul brother and then find that there has been a definition established for that role that they cannot accept, the result may be overt disagreement and denial of solidarity, rather than mutual deference. As it is, soul can be an umbrella concept for a rather wide variety of definitions of one's situation, and the soul brothers who are most in need of the race-centered conception can occasionally get at least fleeting allegiance to soul from others with whom, in reality, they share relatively little—for instance, individuals who are clearly upwardly mobile. Once I listened to a long conversation about soul music in a rather heterogeneous group of young Negro men, who all agreed on the soulfulness of the singers whose records they were playing. Afterwards I asked one of the men, who was clearly upwardly mobile, about his conception of soul. He answered that soul is earthy, that "There is nothing specifically Negro about it." Yet the very individuals with whom he had just agreed on matters of soul had earlier given me the opposite answer—only Negroes have soul. Thus, by avoiding definitions, they had found together an area of agreement and satisfaction in soul by merely assuming that there was a shared basis of opinion.

THE FUTURE OF SOUL

To sum up: Soul has arisen at this point because of the Negro's increasingly ambivalent conceptions about the opportunity structure. Earlier, lack of achievement according to American mainstream ideals could easily be explained in terms of impermeable social barriers. Now the impression is gaining ground that there are ways out of the situation. The young men who come under particularly great strain if such a belief is accepted must either achieve (which many of them are obviously still unable to do); explain that achievement is impossible (which is probably no longer true); or explain that achievement according to mainstream ideals is not necessarily achievement according to their *own* ideals. The emergence of soul goes some way toward meeting the need of stating alternative ideals, and also provides solidarity among those with such a need. And it is advantageous to maintain a diffuse conception of soul, for if an intellectually clear definition were established, soul would probably be both less convincing and less uniting.

The view of soul taken here is, in short, one of a piecemeal rhetorical attempt to establish a satisfactory self-image. I am sure that, for the great majority of soul brothers, this is the major basis of soul. It may be added that LeRoi Jones and Charles Keil take a more social-activist view of soul, although Keil tends to make it a prophecy rather than an interpretation. At present, I think that there is little basis for their connecting the majority of soul brothers with militant black nationalism. But organized black nationalism may be able to recruit followers by using some kind of transformed soul vocabulary, and I think there are obviously political attempts now under way to make more of soul. Thus, if at present it is not possible to speak of more than a "rhetoric of soul," it may well be that in the future we will have a "soul movement."

Inside the New York Telephone Company

ELINOR LANGER

Labor historians have been primarily concerned with men and industry. The long struggle of the worker in heavy industry to organize was finally ended during the mobilization for the Second World War. Although there continues to be conflict between unions and management over wages, conditions of work, and fringe benefits, both big labor and big business have come to realize that cooperation is a better tool than conflict in most labor disputes. Thus, if the economy does not deteriorate completely, continued improvement in wages and working conditions for organized labor seems assured.

What is often not recognized, however, is the limited extent of union membership. The long-established and conservative craft unions, the newly arrived industrial unions, and the increasingly active white-collar and service unions still cover less than half of the American labor force. Women make up a disproportionate number of these unorganized workers, and most of these women are in the increasingly important service sector of the economy.

Recent legislation by the federal government that prohibits discrimination by sex in the labor market and the movement to amend the United States Constitution to grant equal rights to women have focused national attention on the working woman. The history of women as a factor in the labor force began in the nineteenth century. Women had always worked, of course, in home, farm, and mill. But urbanization in the nineteenth century forced many women into the workplace so that their families could have a survival income. Three nineteenth-century technological developments—the invention of the typewriter, the telephone, and the sewing machine—permitted women to enter the work force in unusually large numbers. It would be impossible to determine how many women willingly exchanged drudgery in the home for drudgery in the office or telephone exchange. As a matter of fact, it is well known that most of these working women had two full-time jobs—the office and the home.

Today half of all women between the ages of eighteen and sixty-four are in the labor force. Nine million of these (almost one-third of the total) are secretaries. Women are overrepresented in several service areas—key punch operation, telephone company employment, and clerical work. Four out of ten working women are mothers and 36 percent of these have children under the age of six. In many cases, these women have been discriminated against in wages, hiring policy, and promotion. As a result of lawsuits brought by women against their employers, millions of dollars have been won in settlements for back wages that had been denied them because of systematic discrimination. The American Telephone and Telegraph Company alone has had to pay over $75 million in back pay and compensation, most of it to women, because of discriminatory practices.

Telephone companies have served as particularly visible examples of the way in which industry discriminates against women by sex-typing certain jobs and then using the result of the sex-typing—the employee's inability to gain experience and knowledge of company procedures—as a reason for refusing to promote women equally with men. And, although the American Telephone and Telegraph Company has had to pay a considerable price for this practice, still years will elapse before a situation of real equality exists. In the meantime, women now are being hired as linemen and men as operators, perhaps the most sex-typed job in the American economy.

Elinor Langer, a journalist, went to work for the telephone company is order to write the articles reprinted below. She was not employed as an operator, a job for which she was suspiciously overqualified, but as a customer's service representative, a low-level job that consists largely of answering complaints and selling services. Her analysis of the conditions of work, the demands for company loyalty, and the policies of surveillance can be applied to many of the white-collar office jobs in which women find themselves. Of course, men in the same positions work under the same system. But traditional discrimination has ensured that women fill these jobs and, in the past, has prevented their promotion beyond a set level—supervising the very kind of job they just left. As "affirmative action" programs of all kinds attack the previous policy, we shall have to wait and see to what extent the society will give up one of its most cherished traditions—male dominance in the marketplace.

From October to December 1969 I worked for the New York Telephone Company as a Customer's Service Representative in the Commercial Department. My office was one of several in the Broadway–City Hall area of lower Manhattan, a flattened, blue-windowed commercial building in which the telephone company occupies three floors. The room was big and brightly lit—like the city room of a large newspaper—with perhaps one hundred desks arranged in groups of five or six around the desk of a Supervisor. The job consists of taking orders for new equipment and services and pacifying customers who complain, on the eleven exchanges (although not the more complex business accounts) in the area between the Lower East Side and 23rd Street on the North and bounded by Sixth Avenue on the West.

"Inside the New York Telephone Company" by Elinor Langer. From *New York Review of Books*, 14 (March 12, 1970), pp. 16–24; (March 26, 1970), pp. 14–18, 21–22. Reprinted by permission of Elinor Langer c/o International Famous Agency. Copyright © 1970 by Elinor Langer.

My Supervisor is the supervisor of five women. She reports to a Manager who manages four supervisors (about twenty women) and he reports to the District Supervisor along with two other managers. The offices of the managers are on the outer edge of the main room separated from the floor by glass partitions. The District Supervisor is down the hall in an executive suite. A job identical in rank to that of the district supervisor is held by four other men in Southern Manhattan alone. They report to the Chief of the Southern Division, himself a soldier in an army of division chiefs whose territories are the five boroughs, Long Island, Westchester, and the vast hinterlands vaguely referred to as "Upstate." The executives at ———— Street were only dozens among the thousands in New York Tel alone.

Authority in their hierarchy is parceled out in bits. A Representative, for example, may issue credit to customers up to, say, $10.00; her supervisor, $25.00; her manager, $100.00; his supervisor, $300.00; and so forth. These employees are in the same relation to the centers of power in AT&T and the communications industry as the White House guard to Richard Nixon. They all believe that "The business of the telephone company is Service" and if they have ever heard of the ABM or AT&T's relation to it, I believe they think it is the Associated Business Machines, a particularly troublesome customer on the Gramercy-7 exchange.

I brought to the job certain radical interests. I knew I would see "bureaucratization," "alienation," and "exploitation." I knew that it was "false consciousness" of their true role in the imperialist economy that led the "workers" to embrace their oppressors. I believed those things and I believe them still. I know why, by my logic, the workers should rise up. But my understanding was making reality an increasing puzzle: Why didn't people move? What things, invisible to me, were holding them back? What I hoped to learn, in short, was something about the texture of the industrial system: what life within it meant to its participants.

I deliberately decided to take a job which was women's work, white collar, highly industrialized and bureaucratic. I knew that New York Tel was in a management crisis notorious both among businessmen and among the public and I wondered what effect the well-publicized breakdown of service was having on employees. Securing the position was not without hurdles. I was "overqualified," having confessed to college; I performed better on personnel tests than I intended to do; and I was inspected for symptoms of militance by a shrewd but friendly interviewer who noticed the several years' gap in my record of employment. "What have you been doing lately?" she asked me. "Protesting?" I said: "Oh, no, I've been married," as if that condition itself explained one's neglect of social problems. She seemed to agree that it did.

My problem was to talk myself out of a management traineeship at a higher salary while maintaining access to the job I wanted. This, by fabrications, I was able to do. I said: "Well, you see, I'm going through a divorce right now and I'm a little upset emotionally, and I don't know if I want a career with managerial responsibility." She said: "If anyone else said that to me, I'm afraid I wouldn't be able to hire them," but in the end she accepted me. I had the feeling it would have been harder for her to explain to her bosses why she had let me slip away, given my qualifications, than to justify to them her suspicions.

I nonetheless found as I began the job that I was viewed as "management material" and given special treatment. I was welcomed at length by both the District Supervisor and the man who was to be my Manager, and given a set of fluffy feminist speeches about "opportunities for women" at New York Tel. I was told in a variety of ways that I would be smarter than the other people in my class; "management" would be keeping an eye on me. Then the Manager led me personally to the back classroom where my training program was scheduled to begin.

The class consisted of five students and an instructor. Angela and Katherine were two heavy-set Italian women in their late forties. They had been promoted to Commercial after years of employment as clerks in the Repair Department where, as Angela said, "they were expected to be robots." They were unable to make the transition to the heavier demands of the Representative's job and returned to Repair in defeat after about a week.

Billy was a high-school boy of seventeen who had somehow been referred by company recruiters into this strange women's world. His lack of adult experience made even simple situations difficult for him to deal with: he could not tell a customer that she had to be in the apartment when an installer was coming without giggling uncontrollably about some imaginary tryst. He best liked "drinking with the boys," a pack of Brooklyn high schoolers whose alcoholism was at the Singapore Sling stage; he must have belonged to one of the last crowds in Brooklyn that had never smoked dope.

Betty was a pretty, overweight, intelligent woman in her mid-twenties who had been a Representative handling "Billing" and was now being "cross-trained" (as they say in the Green Berets) in Orders. She was poised, disciplined, patient, ladylike, competent in class and, to me, somewhat enigmatic outside it: liberal about Blacks, in spite of a segregated high-school education, but a virtual Minuteman about Reds, a matter wholly outside her experience. By the end of the class Betty and I had overcome our mutual skepticism enough to be almost friends and if there is anyone at the phone company to whom I feel slightly apologetic—for having listened always with a third ear and for masquerading as what I was not—it is Betty.

Sally, the instructor, was a pleasant, stocky woman in her early thirties with a frosted haircut and eyes made up like a raccoon. She had a number of wigs, including one with strange dangling curls. Sally's official role was to persuade us of the rationality of company policies and practices, which she did skillfully and faithfully. In her private life, however, she was a believer in magic, an aficionado rather than a practitioner only because she felt that while she understood how to conjure up the devil, she did not also know how to make him go away. To Sally a disagreeable female customer was not oppressed, wretched, impoverished in her own life, or merely bitchy: she was—literally—a witch. Sally ex-

plained to herself by demonology the existence of evils of which she was
far too smart to be unaware.

The Representative's course is "programmed." It is apparent that
the phone company has spent millions of dollars for high-class management consultation on the best way to train new employees. The two
principal criteria are easily deduced. First, the course should be made so
routine that any employee can teach it. The teacher's material—the remarks she makes, the examples she uses—are all printed in a loose-leaf
notebook that she follows. Anyone can start where anyone else leaves
off. I felt that I could teach the course myself, simply by following the
program. The second criterion is to assure the reproducibility of results,
to guarantee that every part turned out by the system will be interchangeable with every other part. The system is to bureaucracy what Taylor
was to the factory: it consists in breaking down every operation into dis-
crete parts, then making verbal the discretions that are made.

At first we worked chiefly from programmed booklets organized
around the principle of supplying the answer, then rephrasing the question. For instance:

> It is annoying to have the other party to a conversation leave the
> line without an explanation.

> Before leaving, you should excuse yourself and _____ what you
> are going to do.

Performing skillfully was a matter of reading, and not actual compre-
hension. Katherine and Angela were in constant difficulty. They "never
read," they said. That's why it was hard for them.

Soon acting out the right way to deal with customers became more
important than self-instruction. The days were organized into Lesson
Plans, a typical early one being: How to Respond to a Customer If You
Haven't Already Been Trained to Answer His Question, or a slightly
more bureaucratic rendering of that notion. Sally explained the idea,
which is that you are supposed to refer the call to a more experienced
Representative or to the Supervisor. But somehow they manage to com-
plicate this situation to the point where it becomes confusing even for
an intelligent person to handle it. You mustn't say: "Gosh, that's tough.
I don't know anything about that, let me give the phone to someone
who does," though that in effect is what you do. Instead when the phone
rings, you say: "Hello. This is Miss Langer. May I help you?" (The Rule
is, get immediate "control of the contact" and hold it lest anything un-
expected happen, like, for instance, a human transaction between you
and the customer.)

He says: "This is Mr. Smith and I'd like to have an additional wall
telephone installed in my kitchen."

You say: "I'll be very glad to help you, Mr. Smith (Rule the Second: Always express interest in the Case and indicate willingness to help),
but I'll need more information. What is your telephone number?"

He tells you, then you confess: "Well, Mr. Smith, I'm afraid I haven't been trained in new installations yet because I'm a new representative, but let me give you someone else who can help you." (Rule the Third: You must get his consent to this arrangement. That is, you must say: *May* I get someone else who can help you? *May* I put you on hold for a moment?)

The details are absurd but they are all prescribed. What you would do naturally becomes unnatural when it is codified, and the rigidity of the rules makes the Representatives in training feel they are stupid when they make mistakes. Another lesson, for example, was What to Do If a Customer Calls and Asks for a Specific Person, such as Miss Smith, another Representative, or the Manager. Whatever the facts, you are to say "Oh, Miss Smith is busy but I have access to your records, may I help you?" A customer is never allowed to identify his interests with any particular employee. During one lesson, however, Sally said to Angela: "Hello, I'd like immediately to speak to Mrs. Brown," and Angela said, naturally, "Hold the line a minute, please. I'll put her on." A cardinal sin, for which she was immediately rebuked. Angela felt terrible.

Company rhetoric asserts that this rigidity does not exist, that Representatives are supposed to use "initiative" and "judgment," to develop their own language. What that means is that instead of using the precise words "Of course I'll be glad to help you but I'll need more information," you are allowed to "create" some individual variant. But you must always (1) express willingness to help and (2) indicate the need for further investigation. In addition, while you are doing this, you must always write down the information taken from the customer, coded, on a yellow form called a CF-1, in such a way as to make it possible for a Representative in Florida to read and translate it. "That's the point," Sally told us. "You are doing it the same way a rep in Illinois or Alaska does it. We're one big monopoly."

The logic of training is to transform the trainees from humans into machines. The basic method is to handle any customer request by extracting "bits" of information: by translating the human problem he might have into bureaucratic language so that it can be processed by the right department. For instance, if a customer calls and says: "My wife is dying and she's coming home from the hospital today and I'd like to have a phone installed in her bedroom right away," you *say*, "Oh, I'm very sorry to hear that sir, I'm sure I can help you, would you be interested in our Princess model? It has a dial that lights up at night," meanwhile *writing* on your ever-present CF-1: "Csr wnts Prn inst bdrm immed," issuing the order, and placing it in the right-hand side of your work-file where it gets picked up every fifteen minutes by a little clerk.

The knowledge that one is under constant observation (of which more later) I think helps to ensure that contacts are handled in this uniform and wooden manner. If you varied it, and said something spontaneous, you might well be overheard; moreover, it is probably not possible to be especially human when you are concentrating so hard on extracting the bits, and when you have to deal with so many bits in one day.

Sometimes the bits can be extraordinarily complicated. A customer (that is, a CSR) calls and says rapidly, "This is Mrs. Smith and I'm moving from 23rd Street to 68th Street, and I'd like to keep my green Princess phone and add two white Trimlines and get another phone in a metallic finish and my husband wants a new desk phone in his study." You are supposed to have taken that all down as she says it. Naturally you have no time to listen to how she says it, to strike up a conversation, or be friendly. You are desperate to get straight the details.

The dehumanization and the surprising degree of complication are closely related: the number of variables is large, each variable has a code which must be learned and manipulated, and each situation has one—and only one—correct answer. The kind of problem we were taught to handle, in its own language, looks like this:

A CSR has: IMRCV EX CV GRN BCHM IV
He wants: IMRCV WHT EX CV WHT BCHM IV

This case, very simplified, means only that the customer has regular residential phone service with a black phone, a green one, and an ivory bell chime, and that he wants new service with two white phones and a bell chime. Nonetheless, all these items are charged at differing monthly rates which the Representative must learn where to find and how to calculate; each has a separate installation charge which varies in a number of ways; and, most important, they represent only a few of the dozens of items or services a customer could possibly want (each of which, naturally, has its own rates and variables, its own codes).

He could want a long cord or a short one, a green one or a white one, a new party listed on his line, a special headset for a problem with deafness, a Touchtone phone, and on and on and on. For each of the things he could possibly want there would be one and only one correct charge to quote to him, one and only one right way to handle the situation.

It is largely since World War II that the Bell System abandoned being a comparatively simple service organization and began producing such an array of consumer products as to rival Procter and Gamble. It is important to realize what contribution this proliferation makes both to creating the work and to making it unbearable. If the company restricted itself to essential functions and services—standard telephones and standard types of service—whole layers of its bureaucracy would not need to exist at all, and what did need to exist could be both more simple and more humane. The pattern of proliferation is also crucial, for, among other things, it is largely responsible for the creation of the "new"— white collar—"working class" whose job is to process the bureaucratic desiderata of consumption.

In our classroom, the profit motivation behind the telephone cornucopia is not concealed and we are programmed to repeat its justifications: that the goods were developed to account for different "tastes" and the "need of variation." Why Touchtone Dialing? We learn to say that "it's the latest thing," "it dials faster," "it is easier to read the letters and numbers," and "its musical notes as you depress the buttons are pleasant to hear." We learn that a Trimline is a "space-saver," that it has an "entirely new feature, a recall button that allows you to hang up without replacing the receiver," and that it is "featured in the Museum of Modern Art's collection on industrial design." Why a night-light? we were asked. I considered saying, "It would be nice to make love by a small sexy light," but instead helped to contribute the expected answers: "It gives you security in the bedroom," "it doesn't interfere with the TV."

One day a woman named Carol Nichols, whose job it is to supervise instruction, came to watch our class. Carol is a typical telephone company employee: an aging, single woman who has worked her way up to a position of modest authority. In idle conversation I inquired into the origins of our programmed instruction. Carol said it was all prepared under centralized auspices but had recently benefited from the consultation of two Columbia professors. One, she believed, was the chairman of the English department; another, an English professor. Their principal innovation, I gathered, was to suggest formal quizzes in addition to role-playing.

Carol took the content of the work very seriously. She was concerned to impress on us the now familiar Customer's Service Ideology that We Do Help the Customer no matter what his problem. She said: "If the customer tells you to drop dead, you say 'I'll be very glad to help you, sir.' " I couldn't resist raising the obvious question, wondering what is the Rule covering obscene propositions, but saying innocently, "Gee, I can think of things a customer might say that you wouldn't want to help him with." Carol looked very tough and said: "Oh. We don't get *those* kind of calls in the Commercial Department."

Carol threw herself into role-playing tests with gusto. In one of the tests she pretended to be a Mrs. Van Der Pool from Gramercy Park South, whose problem was that she had four dirty white phones that needed cleaning and one gold phone that was tarnishing. Carol enjoyed playing the snotty Mrs. VDP to the hilt, and what sense of identity, projection, or simple resentment went into her characterization it is hard to say. On the other hand, despite her caricatured and bossy airs, Carol was very nice to the women in the class. At the end, when Angela and Katherine were complaining that they were doing so poorly, Carol gave them a little pep talk in which she said that she had been miserable on her first day as a Rep, had cried, but had just made up her mind to get through it, and had been able to do so.

"Many have passed this way and they all felt the way you do," she told them. "Just keep at it. You can do it." Angela and Katherine were very grateful to Carol for this. Later in the week when, frustrated and miserable, Katherine broke down and cried, Sally too was unobtrusive, sympathetic, encouraging.

Selling is an important part of the Representative's job. Sally introduced the subject with a little speech (from her program book) about the concept of the "well-telephoned home," how that was an advance from the old days when people thought of telephone equipment in a merely functional way. Now, she said, we stress "a variety of items of beauty and convenience." Millions of dollars have been spent by the

Bell System, she told us, to find out what a customer wants and to sell it to him. She honestly believed that good selling is as important to the customer as it is to the company: to the company because "it makes additional and worthwhile revenue," to the customer because it provides services that are truly useful. We are warned not to attempt to sell when it is clearly inappropriate to do so, but basically to use every opportunity to unload profitable items. This means that if a girl calls up and asks for a new listing for a roommate, your job is to say: "Oh. Wouldn't your roommate prefer to have her own extension?"

The official method is to avoid giving the customer a choice but to offer him a total package which he can either accept or reject. For instance, a customer calls for new service. You find out that he has a wife, a teen-age daughter, and a six-room apartment. The prescription calls for you to get off the line, make all the calculations, then come back on and say all at once: "Mr. Smith, suppose we installed for you a wall telephone in your kitchen, a Princess extension in your daughter's room and one in your bedroom, and our new Trimline model in your living room. This will cost you only X dollars for the installation and only Y dollars a month."

Mr. Smith will say, naturally, "That's too many telephones for a six-room apartment," and you are supposed to "overcome his objections" by pointing out the "security" and "convenience" that comes from having telephones all over the place.

Every Representative is assigned a selling quota—so many extensions, so many Princesses—deduced and derived in some way from the quota of the next largest unit. In other words, quotas are assigned to the individual because they are first assigned to the five-girl unit; they are assigned to the unit because they are assigned to the twenty-girl section; and they are assigned to the section because they are assigned to the district: to the manager and the district supervisor. The fact that everyone is in the same situation—expected to contribute to the same total— is one of the factors that increase management-worker solidarity.

The women enact the sales ritual as if it were in fact in their own interest and originated with them. Every month there is a sales contest. Management provides the money—$25.00 a month to one or another five-girl unit—but the women do the work: organizing skits, buying presents, or providing coffee and doughnuts to reward the high sellers. At Thanksgiving the company raffled away turkeys: the number of chances one had depended on the number of sales one had completed.

As the weeks passed our training grew more and more rigid. For each new subject we followed an identical Army-like ritual beginning with "Understanding the Objectives" and ending with "Learning the Negotiation." The Objectives of the "Lesson on Termination of Service," for instance, were:

1. To recognize situations where it is appropriate to encourage users to retain service.
2. To be able to apply "Save effort" successfully.
3. To negotiate orders for Termination.

4. To offer "Easy Move."
5. To write Termination orders.

Or, for example, Cords. It is hard to believe such a subject could be complicated but in fact it is: cords come in different sizes, standard and special, and have different costs, different colors, and different installation intervals. There is also the weighty matter of the distinction between the handset cord (connecting the receiver to the base) and the mounting cord (connecting the base to the wall or floor). The ritual we were taught to follow when on the telephone with a customer goes like this, and set up on our drawing board it looked like this as well:

> *Fact-finding:*
> 1. Business or residence.
> 2. New or existing service.
> 3. Reason for request
>   a. handset or mounting cord
>   b. approximate length
> 4. Type of set or location.
> 5. Other instruments in the household and where located.
> 6. Customer's phone number.

Then you get:

> *Off the line,* where you
> 1. Get Customer's records.
> 2. Think and plan what to do.
> 3. Check reference materials.
> 4. Check with supervisor if necessary.

Then you return to the line with a:

> *Recommendation:*
> 1. Set stage for recommendation.
> 2. Suggest alternative where appropriate or
> 3. Accept order for cord.
> 4. Suggest appropriate length.
>   a. Verify handset or mounting.
> 5. Present recommendation for suitable equipment that "goes with" request including monthly rental (for instance, an extension bell).
> 6. Determine type of instrument and color.
> 7. Quote total non-recurring charges.
> 8. Arrange appointment date, access to the apartment, and whom to see.

On the floor, substantial departure from this ritual is an Error (more later). This pattern of learning became so intolerable that, one day, while waiting for Sally to return from lunch, the class invented a lesson of its own. We called it Erroneous Disconnections. The Objectives were:

1. To identify situations in which it is appropriate to disconnect Customer.
2. To apply the necessary techniques so that disconnects can be accomplished with minimum irritation to the Representative.
3. To accomplish these ends without being observed.

We then identified a variety of situations in which our natural response would be to disconnect. I was surprised by how deeply Billy and Betty were caught up in our parody, and I thought it represented an ability to dissociate from the company, which most of the time was very little in evidence; it seemed to me somehow healthy and promising.

As the weeks wore on our classes became in some ways more bizarre. On several afternoons we were simultaneously possessed by the feeling that we simply couldn't bear it and subtly at first but with increasing aggression as time passed—we would simply stop work: refuse to learn any more. At these times all kinds of random discussions would take place. On one occasion we spent an entire afternoon discussing the Seven Wonders of the Ancient World and calling up information services of newspapers to find out what they were; on another afternoon Sally explained at great length her views on magic.

At first I believed that these little work stoppages were spontaneous but later, as we completed our class work close to schedule, I came to believe that this was not so: that they were a part of our program and were meant to serve as an opportunity for the instructor to discover any random things about our views and attitudes the company might find it useful to know. In any event, partly because of these chats and partly because of the intensity of our training experience, by the end of the class we were a fairly solid little unit. We celebrated our graduation with perfume for Sally, a slightly alcoholic and costly lunch, and great good feeling all around.

Observers at the phone company. They are everywhere. I became aware of a new layer of Observation every day. The system works like this. For every five or six women there is, as I have said, a Supervisor who can at any moment listen in from the phone set on her desk to any of her Representatives' contacts with a customer. For an hour every day, the Supervisor goes to a private room off the main floor where she can listen (herself unobserved) to the conversations of any of her "girls" she chooses. The women know, naturally, *when* she is doing this but not *whose* contact she is observing.

Further off the main floor is a still more secret Observing Room staffed by women whose title and function is, specifically, Observer. These women "jack in" at random to any contact between any Representative and a customer: their job is basically to make sure that the Representatives are giving out correct information. Furthermore, these Observers are themselves observed from a central telephone company location elsewhere in the city to make sure that they are not reporting as incorrect information which is actually correct. In addition the Observers make "access calls" by which they check to see that the telephone lines are open for the customers to make their connections. This entire structure of observation is, of course, apart from the formal representative–supervisor–manager–district supervisor–division head chain of managerial command. They are, in effect, parallel hierarchical structures.

One result of the constant observation (the technology being unbounded) is that one can never be certain where the observation stops. It is company policy to stress its finite character, but no one ever knows for sure. Officials of the Communications Workers of America have testified, for instance, that the company over-indulged in the wired-Martini stage of technology, bugging the pen sets of many of its top personnel. At ——— Street there were TV cameras in the lobby and on the elevators. This system coexists with the most righteous official attitude toward wire-tapping. Only supervisors and managers can deal with wiretap complaints; Federal regulations about the sanctity of communications are posted; and the overt position toward taps, in the lower managerial echelons, is that they are simply illegal and, if they exist, must be the result of private entrepreneurship (businesses bugging one another) rather than Government policy.

"If someone complains about a tap," Sally said, "I just ask them: Why would anyone be tapping your phone?" Consciousness of the Government's "internal security" net is simply blacked out. Nonetheless, the constant awareness of the company's ability to observe creates unease: Are the lounge phones wired into the Observing structure? Does the company tap the phones of new or suspicious personnel? Is union activity monitored? No one can say with confidence.

Sally had two voices, one human, one machine, and in her machine voice on the very first day she explained the justification for Observation. "The thing about the phone company," she said, "is that it has No Product except the Service it Gives. If this were General Motors we would know how to see if we were doing a good job: we could take the car apart and inspect the parts and see that they were all right and that it was well put together. But at the phone company we can't do that. All we can do is check ourselves to see that we are doing a good job."

She took the same attitude toward "access calls," explaining that a completed access call is desirable because it indicates to the manager and everyone up the line that the wires are open and the system is working as it should. The position toward Observers she attempted to inculcate was one of gratitude: Observers are good for you. They help you measure your job and see if you are doing well.

The system of Observers is linked with the telephone company's ultimate weapon, the Service Index by which Errors are charted and separate units of the company rated against each other. Through training—in class and in our days on the floor—hints of the monumental importance of the Index in the psychic life of the employees continually emerged. "Do you know how many Errors you're allowed?" Sally would ask us. "No Errors"—proud that the standard was so high. Or: "I can't afford an

Error"—from my supervisor, Laura, on the floor, explaining why she was keeping me roped in on my first days on the job. But the system was not revealed in all its parts until the very end of training when as a *pièce de résistance* the manager, Y, came in to give a little talk billed as a discussion of "Service" but in fact an attempt to persuade the class of the logic of observation.

Y was a brooding, reserved man in his mid-twenties, a kind of Ivy League leftover who looked as if he'd accidentally got caught in the wrong decade. His talk was very much like Sally's. "We need some way to measure Service. If a customer doesn't like Thom McAn shoes he can go out and buy Buster Brown. Thom McAn will know something is wrong. But the phone company is a monopoly, people can't escape it, they have no other choice. How can we tell if our product, Service, is good?" He said that observation was begun in 1924 and that, although the company had tried other methods of measuring service, none had proved equally satisfactory. Specifically, he said, other methods failed to provide an accurate measure of the work performance of one unit as opposed to another.

Y's was a particularly subtle little speech. He used the Socratic method, always asking us to give the answers or formulate the rationales, always asking, Is it right? Is it fair? (I'm certain that if we did not agree it was right and fair, he wanted to know.) He stressed the limited character of observation. His units (twenty "girls"), he said, took about 10,000 calls per month; of these only about 100 were observed, or about five observations per woman per month. He emphasized that these checks were random and anonymous. He explained that the Index has four components which govern what the observers look for:

Contact Performance Defects (CPD)
Customer Waiting Interval (CWI)
Contacts Not Closed (CNC)
Business Office Accessibility (BOA)

The CPD is worth 70 per cent of the Index, the other factors 10 per cent each. The elements of CPD are, for example, incomplete or incorrect information, making inadequate arrangements, or mistreating a customer; the elements of BOA are the amount of time it takes a customer to reach the central switchboard, and the promptness of the Representative in answering the phone after the connection has been made. Points are assigned on a scientific basis, based on the number of errors caught by the observers. Charts are issued monthly, rating identical units of the company against each other. Y's unit (mine) was the top unit in Manhattan, having run for the preceding three months or so at about 97 or 98 per cent. While I was there, there was a little celebration, attended by high company officials, in which Y was awarded a plaque and the women on the floor given free "coffee and danish."

Now, a number of things about this system are obvious. First, demeaning and demanding as it is, it clearly provides management with information it believes it has a desperate need to know. For instance, there was a unit on the East Side of Manhattan running at about an 85 per cent level. The mathematics of it are complicated but it basically means that about 12,000 people every month were getting screwed by the department in one form or another: they asked for a green phone and the Representative ordered a black one; they arranged to be home on the 24th and the woman told the installer to come on the 25th; they were told their service would cost $10.00 and it actually cost $25.00, and so forth. Management has to know which of its aspirants, scrambling up the ladder, to reward and which to punish.

On the other hand, their official justifications for observation are a lie for two reasons. First, the Index does not measure actual service: our unit could run at 98 per cent while half the phones in our area were out of service because the Index does not deal with the service departments of the company which are, in fact, where its troubles are. The angriest customer in Manhattan would not show up as an error on the Index if he were treated politely and his call transferred: the Commercial Index is a chimera capable of measuring only its internal functioning, and that functioning, being simply bureaucratic, is cut off from the real world of telephone service and servicing. Secondly, it is a lie because it does not spring from the root that management claims—that is, the absence of a tangible physical product (observation is in fact commonplace in industry where the non-existence of a product is not an issue) but from another root: the need to control behavior. That is, if the system is technically linked to measurement of service it is functionally linked to control.

Furthermore, it works: it absolutely controls behavior. On December 24, the one day of the year when there is no observation (and no contribution to the Index) the concept of service utterly disappeared. The women mistreated the customers and told them whatever came into their minds. Wall lights whose flickering on a normal day indicates that customers are receiving busy signals were flashing wildly; no one cared about the BOA.

But on a normal day, the Index is King. It is a rule, for instance, that if one Representative takes over a call for another, the first must introduce the second to the customer, saying "Sir, I'm going to put Miss Laramie on the line. She'll be able to help you." "Don't forget to introduce me," said Miss L. anxiously to me one day. "An observer might be listening." Or: we were repeatedly told *never* to check the box labeled "Missed on Regular Delivery" on the form authorizing delivery of directories. "It will look as if Commercial made an Error," Sally told us, "when the Error is really Directory's." This awareness of observers and Errors is constant not because of fear of individual reprisal—there is none—but because of block loyalty: first to the immediate unit of five women, then to the twenty-women unit, then to the still larger office.

The constant weighing, checking, competition also binds the managers to the women and is another source of the overwhelmingly paternalistic atmosphere: the managers are only as good as their staffs and they are rated by the same machine. The women make, or don't make, the Errors; the managers get, or don't get, the plaques and the promotions.

What the system adds up to is this: if we count both supervisors and

observers, at least three people are responsible for the correct performance of any job, and that is because the system is based on hiring at the
lowest level, keeping intelligence suppressed, and channeling it into
idiotic paths. The process is circular: hire women who are not too
talented (for reasons of social class, limited educational opportunities,
etc.); suppress them even further by the "scientific" division of the job
into banal components which defy initiative or the exercise of intelligence; then keep them down by the institutionalization of pressures and
spies.

Surely it would be better if the jobs' horizons were broadened—a
reformist goal—if women were encouraged to take initiative and responsibility, and then left on their own. And it would be better yet if
those aspects of the work directly tied to the company's profit-oriented
and "capitalistic" functions—the Princess and Trimline phones and all the
bureaucratic complications that stem from their existence—were eliminated altogether and a socialized company concentrated on providing all
the people with uniform and decent service. But . . .

Daily life on the job at the New York Telephone Company consists
largely of pressure. To a casual observer it might appear that much of the
activity on the floor is random, but in fact it is not. The women moving
from desk to desk are on missions of retrieving and refiling customers' records: the tête-à-têtes that look sociable are anxious conferences with a
Supervisor in which a Representative is Thinking and Planning What to
Do Next. Of course the more experienced women know how to use the
empty moments that do occur for social purposes. But the basic working
unit is one girl–one telephone, and the basic requirement of the job is to
answer it, perhaps more than fifty times a day.

For every contact with a customer, the amount of paperwork is huge:
a single contact can require the completion of three, four, or even five
separate forms. No problems can be dispensed with handily. Even if, for
example, you merely transfer a customer to Traffic or Repair you must
still fill out and file a CF-1. At the end of the day you must tally up and
categorize all the services you have performed on a little slip of paper and
hand it in to the Supervisor, who completes a tally for the unit: it is part
of the process of "taking credit" for services rendered by one unit vis-à-vis
the others.

A Representative's time is divided into "open" and "closed" portions,
according to a recent scientific innovation called FADS (for Force Administration Data System), of which the company is particularly proud;
the innovation consists in establishing how many Representatives have to
be available at any one moment to handle the volume of business antici-
pated for that month, that day, and that hour. Under this arrangement the
contact with the customer and the processing of his request are carried
out simultaneously: that is, the Representative does the paperwork needed
to take care of a request while she is still on the line. For more complex
cases, however, this is not possible and the processing is left for "closed"
time: a time when no further calls are coming in.

This arrangement tends to create a constant low-level panic. There is a kind of act which it is natural to carry to its logical conclusion: brushing one's teeth, washing a dish, or filling out a form are things one does not leave half done. But the company's system stifles this natural urge to completion. Instead, during "open" time, the phone keeps ringing and the work piles up. You look at the schedule and know that you have only one hour of "closed" time to complete the work, and twenty minutes of that hour is a break.

The situation produces desperation: How am I to get it done? How can I call back all those customers, finish all that mail, write all those complicated orders, within forty minutes? Occasionally, during my brief time at the job, I would accidentally press the wrong button on my phone and it would become "open" again. Once, when I was feeling particularly desperate about time, I did that twice in a row and both times the callers were ordering new telephone service—a process which takes between eight and ten minutes to complete.

My feeling that time was slipping away, that I would never be able to "complete my commitments" on time was intense and hateful. Of course it was worse for me than for the experienced women—but not much worse. Another situation in which the pressure of time is universally felt is in the minutes before lunch and before five o'clock. At those times, if your phone is open, you sit hoping that a complex call will not arrive. A "new line" order at five minutes to five is a source of both resentment and frustration.

Given the pressure, it becomes natural to welcome the boring and routine—the simple suspensions or disconnections of service—and dread the unusual or complex. The women deal with the pressure by quietly getting rid of as many calls as they can, transferring them to another department although the proper jurisdiction may be a borderline matter. This transferring, the lightening of the load, is the bureaucratic equivalent of the "soldiering" that Taylor and the early scientific managers were striving to defeat. It is a subtle kind of slowdown, never discussed, but quickly transmitted to the new Representative as legitimate. Unfortunately, it does not slow things down very much.

As Daniel Bell points out in his extraordinary essay, "Work and Its Discontents," the rhythm of the job controls the time spent off the job as well: the breaks, the lunches, the holidays; even the weekends are scarcely long enough to reestablish a more congenial or natural path. The work rhythm controls human relationships and attitudes as well. For instance: there was a Puerto Rican worker in the Schrafft's downstairs whose job was to sell coffee-to-go to the customers: he spent his day doing nothing but filling paper cups with coffee, fitting on the lids, and writing out the checks. He was very surly and very slow and it looked to me as if the thoughts swirling in his head were those of an incipient murderer, not an incipient revolutionary. His slowness was very inconvenient to the thousands of workers in the building who had to get their coffee, take it upstairs, and drink it according to a precise timetable. We never had more than fifteen minutes to get there and back, and buying coffee generally took longer. The women resented him and called him "Speedy Gonzales," in tones of snobbery and hate. I know he hated us.

The women of the phone company are middle class or lower middle class, come from a variety of ethnic backgrounds (Polish, Jewish, Italian, Irish, black, Puerto Rican), mainly high-school graduates or with a limited college education. They live just about everywhere except in Manhattan: the Bronx, Brooklyn, Staten Island, or Queens. Their leisure time is filled, first of all, with the discussion of objects. Talk of shopping is endless, as is the pursuit of it in lunch hours, after work, and on days off. The women have a fixation on brand names, and describe every object that way: it is always a London Fog, a Buxton, a White Stag. This fixation does not preclude bargain-hunting: but the purpose of hunting a bargain is to get the brand name at a lower price. Packaging is also important: the women will describe not only the thing but also the box or wrapper it comes in. They are especially fascinated by wigs. Most women have several wigs and are in some cases unrecognizable from day to day, creating the effect of a continually changing work force. The essence of wiggery is escapism: the kaleidoscopic transformation of oneself while everything else remains the same. Anyone who has ever worn a wig knows the embarrassing truth: it *is* transforming.

Consumerism is one of the major reasons why these women work. Their salaries are low in relation to the costs of necessities in American life, ranging from $95.00 to $132.50 *before* taxes: barely enough, if one is self-supporting, to pay for essentials. In fact, however, many of the women are not self-supporting, but live with their families or with husbands who also work, sometimes at more than one job. Many of the women work overtime more than five hours a week (only for more than five extra hours do they get paid time and a half) and it seems from their visible spending that it is simply to pay for their clothes, which are expensive, their wigs, their color TV's, their dishes, silver, and so forth.

What the pressures of food, shelter, education, or medical costs contribute to their need to work I cannot tell, but it seems to me the women are largely trapped by their love of objects. What they think they need in order to survive and what they endure in order to attain it is astonishing. Why this is so is another matter. I think that the household appliances play a real role in the women's family lives: helping them to run their homes smoothly and in keeping with a (to them) necessary image of efficiency and elegance. As for the clothes and the wigs, I think they are a kind of tax, a tribute exacted by the social pressures of the work-place. For the preservation of their own egos against each other and against the system, they had to feel confident of their appearance on each and every day. Outside work they needed it too: to keep up, to keep their men, not to fall behind.

The atmosphere of passionate consuming was immeasurably heightened by Christmas, which also had the dismal effect of increasing the amount of stealing from the locker room. For a period of about three weeks nothing was safe: hats, boots, gloves. The women told me that the same thing happens every year: an overwhelming craving, a need for material goods that has to find an outlet, even in thievery from one another.

The women define themselves by their consumerism far more than by their work, as if they were compensating for their exploitation as workers by a desperate attempt to express their individuality as consumers. Much of the consuming pressure is generated by the women themselves: not only in shopping but in constant raffles, contests, and so forth in which the prize is always a commodity—usually liquor. The women are asked to participate in these raffles at least two or three times a week.

But the atmosphere is also deliberately fostered by the company itself. The company gave every woman a Christmas present: a little wooden doll, about four inches tall, with the sick-humor look that was popular a few years ago and still appears on greeting cards. On the outside the doll says "Joy is . . ." and when you press down the springs a little stick pops up that says "Extensions in Color" (referring to the telephone extensions we were trying to sell). Under that label is another sticker, the original one, which says "Knowing I wuv you." The doll is typical of the presents the company distributes periodically: a plastic shopping bag inscribed with the motto "Colorful Extensions Lighten the Load"; a keychain with a plastic Princess telephone saying "It's Little, It's Lovely, It Lights"; plastic rain bonnets with the telephone company emblem, and so forth.

There were also free chocolates at Thanksgiving and, when the vending machine companies were on strike, free coffee for a while in the cafeteria. The women are disgusted by the company's gift-giving policies. Last year, I was told, the Christmas present was a little gold-plated basket filled with velour fruit and adorned with a flag containing a company motto of the "Extensions in Color" type. They think it is a cheap trick—better not done at all—and cite instances of other companies which give money bonuses at Christmas.

It is obvious that the gifts are all programmed, down to the last cherry-filled chocolate, in some manual of Personnel Administration that is the source of all wisdom and policy; it is clear from their frequency that a whole agency of the company is devoted to devising these gimmicks and passing them out. In fact, apart from a standard assortment of insurance and pension plans, the only company policy I could discover which offers genuine advantage to the employees and which is not an attempt at manipulation is a tuition support program in which the company pays $1,000 out of $1,400 of the costs of continuing education.

Going still further, the company, for example, sponsors a recruiting game among employees, a campaign entitled "People Make the Difference." Employees who recruit other employees are rewarded with points: 200 for a recommendation, an additional thousand if the candidate is hired. Employees are stimulated to participate by the circulation of an S&H-type catalogue, a kind of encyclopedia of the post-scarcity society. There you can see pictured a GE Portable Color Television with a walnut-grained polystyrene cabinet (46,000 points), a Silver-Plated Hors d'Oeuvres Dish by Wallace (3,900 points), a staggering assortment of mass-produced candelabra, linens, china, fountain pens, watches, clothing, luggage, and —for the hardy—pup tents, power tools, air mattresses.

Similarly, though perhaps less crudely, the company has institution-alized its practice of rewarding employees for longevity. After every two years with the company, the women receive a small gold charm, the men a "tie-tac." These grow larger with the years and after a certain period jewels begin to be added: rubies, emeralds, sapphires, and even-tually diamonds and bigger diamonds. The tie-tac evolves over the years into a tie-clasp. After twenty-five years you may have either a ceremonial luncheon or an inscribed watch: the watches are pre-fixed, pre-selected, and pictured in a catalogue.

The company has "scientifically structured" its rewards just as it has "scientifically structured" its work. But the real point is that the sys-tem gets the women as consumers in two ways. If consumption were less central to them, they would be less likely to be there in the first place. Then, the company attempts to ensnare them still further in the mesh by offering as incentives goods and images of goods which are only further way stations of the same endless quest.

Another characteristic of the telephone company is a kind of pro-grammed "niceness" which starts from the top down but which the women internalize and mimic. For management the strategy is clear (the Hawthorne experiments, after all, were carried out at Western Electric): it is, simply, make the employees feel important. For trainees this was ac-complished by a generous induction ceremony complete with flowers, films, a fancy buffet, and addresses by top division representatives, all of which stressed the theme: the company cares about you.

The ceremonies had another purpose and effect: to instill in the minds of new employees the image the company would like the public to have of it, that it is a goodhearted service organization with modest and regulated profits. A deliberate effort was made to fend off any free-floating negative ideas by explaining carefully, for instance, why AT&T's monopolistic relationship with Western Electric was a good thing. The ideology of Service, embraced without much cynicism by the low-level managers who are so abundant, is in that way—and others—passed along.

The paternalism, the "niceness," filters down and is real. Employees are on a first-name basis, even the women with the managers. The women are very close to one another, sharing endless gossip, going on excursions together, and continually engaging in ceremonial celebration of one an-other's births, engagements, promotions. The generosity even extends to difficult situations on the job. I have, for example, seen women voluntarily sharing their precious closed time when one of them was overcommitted and the other slightly more free. Their attitude toward new employees was uniformly friendly and helpful. When I first went out on the floor my presence was a constant harassment to the other women in my unit: I didn't know what to do, had to ask a lot of questions, filed incorrectly. As a newcomer, I made their already tense lives far more difficult. None-theless I was made to feel welcome, encouraged. "Don't feel bad," one or another would say at a particularly stupid error. "We were all new once. We've all been through it. Don't worry. You'll catch on." In the same way I found them invariably trying to be helpful in modest personal crises: solicitous about my health when I faked a few days of illness, comforting in my depression when a pair of gloves was stolen, always friendly, cheering me (and each other) on.

This "niceness" is carefully preserved by the women as a protection against the stress of the work and the hostility of customers. "We have to be nice to each other," Sally told me once. "If we yelled at each other the way the customers yell at us, we'd go crazy." At the same time it is a triumph of their spirit as well. There is some level on which they are too proud to let the dehumanization overtake them; too decent to let the rat race get them down.

On the job, at least, the women's sense of identification with the company is absolute. On several occasions I tried to bring up issues on which their interests—and the public's—diverged from that of the company, and always I failed to make my point. It happened, for example, on the issue of selling, where I told my class frankly that I couldn't oversell, thought it was wrong, and that people needed far fewer telephones than we were giving them. Instead of noticing that I was advocating a position of principle, my class thought that, because I was so poor myself (as measured by having only one black telephone), I just somehow couldn't grasp the concept of the "well-telephoned home," but that I would catch on when I became convinced that the goods and services in question were truly valuable and desirable.

It happened again during a discussion of credit ratings when, because welfare women are always put in the lowest category, I said I thought credit rested on racist assumptions. The class explained to me that "if you worked in Billing and knew how hard it is to collect from those people" I wouldn't feel that way. And it happened another time during a particularly macabre discussion over coffee when the women were trading horror stories about tragic cases where telephone service had to be cut off because people weren't paying their bills: they were grotesque tales about armless veterans and blind old ladies of eighty-five.

I kept saying that terminating those services was intolerable, that some way should be found for people to have services free. Instead of thinking that was an odd position, the women reported that "every new representative feels that way," that they used to feel that way themselves, but they'd gotten over it. In other words they began their jobs with all the feelings any decent (never mind radical) person would have, and gradually learned to overcome them, because of the creeping identification with the company produced by their having to act out daily a company-defined role. Their basic belief in the legitimacy of the "make a buck" system established in their minds a link between company revenue and their own paychecks. "That's where your money comes from" was a common conclusion to these discussions.

The women have a strangely dissociated attitude toward company operations that aren't working well. What company *policy* is—that is, the way they learn things are supposed to be—gets pressed into their heads so much that they get a little confused by their simultaneous understanding that it isn't really working that way at all. I pointed that out a lot, to see what would happen. For instance our lesson books say: "Customers always get Manhattan directories delivered with their regular installations." I said, in class: "Gee, that's funny, Sally, I had a telephone installed recently and I didn't get any phone books at all." Sally would make sure not to lose control and merely repeat: "Phone books are delivered with the regular installations."

It was the same with installation dates, which, in the company's time of troubles, are lagging behind. Company *policy* is that installations are made two days from the date they are requested. In reality we were making appointments for two, three, or even four weeks in advance. There are explanations for these lapses—everyone knows that things go wrong all the time—but there are no reasonable explanations which do not undermine the basic assumption that the company has everything "scientifically" under control. Thus the "policy" is that they are not happening at all.

The effect of the pressure of work and the ethos of niceness is to defuse political controversy. There is a kind of compact about tolerance, a governing attitude which says, "Let's not talk about religion or politics." During the time I was there I heard virtually no discussion of Vietnam, the city elections, or race. There was a single exception—an argument between Betty and myself over Song My—after which I had the feeling that something had been breached, that she would take particular care not to let it happen again.

This is not characteristic of the men's departments of the company where political discussion is commonplace, and I believe the women think that such heavy topics are properly the domain of men: they are not about to let foolish "politics" interfere with the commonsensical and harmonious adjustments they have made to their working lives. Race relations were governed by the same kind of neutrality and "common sense." The black women of the Commercial Department were of the same type as the whites: lower middle class and upwardly mobile. Among the Representatives, not an Afro was in sight. There were good and close relationships between the blacks and the whites—close enough for jokes about hair and the word "nigger"—and, as far as I could tell, the undercurrents of strain that existed were no greater (though certainly no less intense) than are characteristic of such relations in the more educated and "liberal" middle classes.

.   .   .   .

Perhaps the best way to think about the women of the telephone company is to ask the question: what reinforces company-minded behavior and what works against it? It is a difficult question. The reinforcement comes not from the work but from the externals of the job: the warmth of friendships, the mutual support, the opportunities for sharing and for gossip, the general atmosphere of company benevolence and paternalism; not to mention the need for money and the very human desire to do a good job.

I never heard any of the women mouth the company rhetoric about "service to the customer" but it was obvious to me that a well-handled contact could be satisfying in some way. You are the only person who has access to what the customer needs—namely, telephones—and if you can provide him with what he wants, on time and efficiently, you might reasonably feel satisfied about it. The mutual support—the sharing of closed time, helping one another out on commitments—is also very real. The continual raffles, sales contests, gimmicks, and parties are part of it, too. They simply make you feel part of a natural stream.

Working in that job one does not see oneself as a victim of "Capitalism." One is simply part of a busy little world which has its own pleasures and satisfactions as well as its own frustrations but, most important, it is a world, with a shape and an integrity all its own. The pattern of co-optation, in other words, rests on details: hundreds of trivial, but human, details.

What is on the other side? Everyone's consciousness of the iron fist, though what they usually see is the velvet glove; the deadening nature of the work; the low pay; what is going on in the outside world (to the extent that they are aware of it); the malfunctioning of the company; the pressure of supervision and observation. There was a sign that sat on the desk of one of the women while I was there, a Coney Island joke-machine sign: "Due to Lack of Interest, Tomorrow Will be Postponed." For a time I took it as an emblem and believed that was how the woman really felt. But now I am not sure.

I think that for these women to move they would have to have a sense of the possibility of change—not even to mention the desirability of change—which I am certain they do not feel. They are more satisfied with their lives than not, and to the extent that they are not, they cannot see even the dimmest possibility of remedial action through collective political effort. The reason they do not have "class-consciousness"—the magic ingredient—is that in fact they are middle class. If they feel oppressed by their situation, and I think many of them do, they certainly see it only as an individual problem, not as something which it is their human right to avoid or overcome.

How one would begin to change that, to free them to live more human lives, is very hard to know. Clearly it would require a total transformation of the way they think about the world and about themselves. What is impossible to know is whether the seeds of that transformation lie close beneath the surface and are accessible, or whether they are impossibly buried beyond rescue short of general social convulsion. It is hard to believe that the women are as untouched as they seem by the social pressures which seem so tangible to radicals. Yet I saw little evidence that would make any other conclusion possible.

I have a strong feeling of bad faith to have written this at all. I know the women will not recognize themselves in my account, but will nonetheless be hurt by it. They were, after all, warm and friendly: sympathetic about my troubles, my frustrations; helpful in the work; cheerful in a businesslike way. Betty, at least, was a friend. It is almost as if a breach of the paternalism of the company is involved. I fear a phone call asking "Was that a nice thing to do?" and I would say, perhaps not, perhaps the intellectual and political values of my life by which I was judging yours make equally little sense. Perhaps the skills which give me leverage to do it allow me only to express alienation and not to overcome it; perhaps I should merely be thankful that I was raised as an alpha and not a beta. Sometimes I am not sure. But I know that however it will seem to them, this piece is meant to be for the women of the telephone company, and that it is written for them with both love and hope.

Suggestions for Further Reading

The history of suburban development is found in Kenneth T. Jackson, "The Crabgrass Frontier: 150 Years of Suburban Growth in America," in *The Urban Experience: Themes in American History,** edited by Raymond A. Mohl and James F. Richardson (Belmont, Cal., 1973). For works by critics of suburban life, see John Keats, *The Crack in the Picture Window* (Boston, 1956); William H. Whyte, Jr., *The Organization Man** (New York, 1956); and R. Gordon, K. Gordon, and M. Gunther, *The Split-Level Trap* (New York, 1961). The suburban myth developed by the critics was challenged by Herbert J. Gans, *The Levittowners** (New York, 1967), and Bennett M. Berger, *Working Class Suburb** (Berkeley, Cal., 1960). See also J. Seeley, R. Sim, and E. Loosley, *Crestwood Heights** (New York, 1956), a study of a Canadian suburb. An interesting study illustrating the suburbanization of small towns is found in Arthur J. Vidich and Joseph Bensman, *Small Town in Mass Society** (Princeton, N.J., 1958).

Lower-middle-class family life is explored by Mirra Komarovsky, *Blue Collar Marriage** (New York, 1964). The problems of adolescents in the 1950s and early 1960s are critically explored in Paul Goodman, *Growing Up Absurd** (New York, 1960), and in two works by educational sociologist Edgar Z. Friedenberg, *The Vanishing Adolescent** (Boston, 1959) and *Coming of Age in America** (New York, 1965). For an interesting contrast, compare James S. Coleman's two works on young people, *The Adolescent Society** (Glencoe, Ill., 1961) and *Youth: Transition to Adulthood** (Chicago, 1974).

A good place to begin studying the youth of the counter-culture years is in two works by Kenneth Keniston that deal with nonhippie youth, *The Uncommitted: Alienated Youth in American Society** (New York, 1965) and *Young Radicals** (New York, 1968). A historian, Theodore Roszak, has written a sympathetic exploration of the reasons for the growth of the counter-culture in *The Making of a Counter-Culture** (New York, 1969). Many of the books that describe the cultural developments of the late 1960s also advocate change. See, for example, Tom Wolfe, *The Electric Kool-Aid Acid Test** (New York, 1968); Charles Reich, *The Greening of America** (New York, 1960); and William Braden, *The Private Sea: LSD and the Search for God* (Chicago, 1967). Nicholas von Hoffman, a journalist, has explored the hippie phenomenon in *We Are the People Our Parents Warned Us Against** (Chicago, 1968). The adult counter-culture is described in Rasa Gustaitis, *Turning On** (New York, 1969). For events leading to

* Available in paperback edition.

372

the music explosion among the counter-culture, see the work of art historian Carl Belz, *The Story of Rock* (New York, 1968). The impact of Eastern religions on the United States can be seen in Robert Ellwood, Jr., *Religious and Spiritual Groups in Modern America** (Englewood Cliffs, N.J., 1973), and Jacob Needleman, *The New Religions** (New York, 1970). Two science fiction works that had a great influence on the counter-culture are Robert Heinlein, *Stranger in a Strange Land** (New York, 1961), and Frank Herbert, *Dune** (Philadelphia, 1965).

For a comparison with Elinor Langer's article, see Dorothy Richardson, *The Long Day: The Story of a New York Working Girl*, first published in 1905 and printed, along with the Langer piece, in *Women at Work,** edited by William O'Neill (Chicago, 1973). General works on women in the twentieth century include Lois Banner, *Women in Modern America: A Brief History** (New York, 1974), and William H. Chafe, *The American Woman: Her Changing Social, Economic, and Political Roles, 1920–1970** (New York, 1972). The modern women's movement can be dated from the publication of Betty Friedan, *The Feminine Mystique** (New York, 1963), and its progress and literature are well represented in two collections of essays: Robin Morgan, ed., *Sisterhood Is Powerful: An Anthology of Writings from the Women's Liberation Movement** (New York, 1970), and Vivian Gornick and Barbara K. Moran, eds., *Women in Sexist Society, Studies in Power and Powerlessness** (New York, 1971). On working women, see Robert W. Smuts, *Women and Work in America** (New York, 1959), and Elizabeth Faulkner Baker, *Technology and Woman's Work* (New York, 1964). The conditions of work are explored in an unusual government report: *Work in America: Report of a Special Task Force to the Secretary of Health, Education, and Welfare** (Cambridge, Mass., 1973). For personal insights into the world of work, see Studs Terkel, ed., *Working: People Talk About What They Do All Day and How They Feel About What They Do* (New York, 1974). Two excellent recent books about the working class are Patricia and Brendan Sexton, *Blue Collar and Hard Hats** (New York, 1972), and Jonathan Cobb and Richard Sennett, *The Hidden Injuries of Class** (New York, 1972).

The revisionist works on slave culture include John Blassingame, *The Slave Community: Plantation Life in the Ante-Bellum South** (New York, 1972); Gerald Mullin, *Flight and Rebellion: Slave Resistance in Eighteenth Century Virginia** (New York, 1972); and Eugene Genovese, *Roll, Jordan, Roll* (New York, 1974). See also the controversial Robert W. Fogel and Stanley L. Engerman, *Time on the Cross: The Economics of American Negro Slavery** (Boston, 1974). On the post-bellum black family, see Elizabeth H. Pleck, "The Two-Parent Household: Black Family Structure in Late Nineteenth Century Boston," *Journal of Social History* 6 (Fall 1972): 1–31, and the forthcoming work on this subject by Herbert Gutman. The recent controversy on the black family is explored in Lee Rainwater and William Yancey, eds., *The Moyni-han Report and the Politics of Controversy** (Cambridge, Mass., 1967), and Andrew Billingsley, *Black Families in White America** (Englewood Cliffs, N.J., 1968). Studies of urban black life in the modern period begin with St. Clair Drake and Horace R. Cayton, *Black Metropolis: A Study of Negro Life in a Northern City** (New York, 1945). The two best recent anthropological treatments are both studies of Washington, D.C.: Ulf Hannerz, *Soulside** (New York, 1969), and Elliot Liebow, *Tally's Corner: A Study of Negro Streetcorner Men** (Boston, 1967). Kenneth Clark has studied Harlem in *Dark Ghetto: Dilemmas of Social Power** (New York, 1965). One aspect of the culture of urban blacks is examined in Charles Keil, *Urban Blues** (Chicago, 1966). A group of essays from *Trans-action* (now called *Society*) are edited by Lee Rain-water under the title *Soul** (New Brunswick, N.J., 1970). Two black autobiographies that compellingly portray the difficulties of urban life are *The Autobiography of Malcolm X** (New York, 1965), and Claude Brown, *Manchild in the Promised Land** (New York, 1965).